ᏍᎪ ᏦᎢ ᎢᏳᏟᎶᏛ, ᎯᏍᎦᏍᎪ ᎯᏍᎩ ᏑᏓᎳᏍᎪᏃ
ᎤᏓᏕᏒᏛ, ᏗᎴᏅᎲ ᎢᏯᏍᏗ; ᎯᎠ ᎢᎦᎢ ᎢᎦᎵᏍᏗᏍᎩ

ᎨᏒᎢ, ᏦᎦᏚ ᎢᏳᏆᏁᏅᏛ, ᎯᏍᎩᏧᏈ ᎦᎵᏆᏍᎪ ᏅᎩ ᎢᏯᎦᏴᎵ, ᎠᏍᎪᎯᏧᏈ ᏦᎠᏍ
ᎯᏍᎩ ᎢᏳᏟᎶᏛ ᏂᎦᏚᏃ ᎢᏯᏍᎪᎯᏧᏈᏁ ᎢᏳᏟᏉᏛ ᎢᎦᏛᎯ ᎦᏓ ᎨᏒᎢ. ᎠᎴ ᎬᏂ
ᏳᏉ, ᎤᎾᏚᏓᏕᎾᏛ ᏗᎦᏚᏏᎢ ᎾᏍᏉ ᎢᎤᏅᏂᏌᏅ ᎧᏁᎢᏍᏔᏅᎯ ᏟᎶᏛ ᎦᏓ Ꭰ
ᏧᏁᎵᏧᏈ ᎢᏯᎦᏴᎵ ᎢᏳᏟᎶᏛ ᎢᎩᏛ ᎦᏓ ᎠᎲ ᎠᏟᎶᏛ ᎢᎬᏁᏄᎯ, ᎠᎴ ᎯᎠ ᏄᏍᏛ
ᎠᏟᎶᎢᏙᏄ ᏄᏍᏛ ᎪᎵᏍᏗᎼ ᎯᎠ ᎠᏂ ᏥᎸᏩᏧᏗ ᏣᏎᎯᏍᏏ ᎢᎬᏂ:

ᎠᏓᎴᏂᏍᎩ ᎤᎦᎾᏮ ᎤᏕᎵᎬ ᎾᏚᏳᎪᏛ ᎢᏗᏢ ᎤᏅᏏᏴ ᏩᏌᏏ ᎤᎾᏤᎵᎪᎯ Ꭸ
ᎠᏎᎯᎯ ᏥᎩ ᎾᏏ ᎨᏒ ᏅᏯ ᎠᎲᎢ, ᏨᏁᏉᎦ ᎠᏓᏯ ᏔᎳᏍᎪ ᎢᏯᏏᏔᏗᏍᏗ ᎢᎩᏛ
ᏗᎬᏩᎶᏒᎯ ᎤᎦᎾᏮ ᎾᏚᏳᎪᏛ ᏔᎳᏍᎪ ᎦᎵᏉᎩᏁ ᎾᏍᏓᏅᏅ ᏗᎧᏄᎬ ᎢᏗᏢ ᎨᏒ
ᎦᎵᏆᏍᎪ ᏑᏓᎵ ᎢᏯᏍᎪᎯᏧᏈᏁ ᎢᎦᏛ ᎦᏅᏅᎯ ᎤᏓᏕᏒᏛ ᎢᏴᏛ, ᎠᎴ ᎾᏍᏉ Ꮷ
ᏧᎾᏔᏅ ᎠᏓ ᏥᏉᎦ ᏦᎠᏍᎪ ᎢᏯᏏᏔᏗᏍᏗ ᎢᎩᏛ ᏗᎬᏩᎶᏒᎯ, ᎤᎦᎾᏮ ᎾᏚᏳᎪᏛ
ᎯᏍᎦᏍᎪ ᏐᏁᎵᏁ ᎾᏍᏓᏅᏅ ᎤᏕᎵᎬ ᎢᏗᏢ ᎨᏒ ᏌᏉ ᎢᎦᏅᏅ ᎤᏓᏕᏒᏛ ᎢᏴᏛ
ᎠᎴ ᎾᏍᏉ ᏐᎢ ᏅᏩᏓᎴ ᏧᎴ ᏧᎾᏔᏅ ᎠᏓ ᏥᏉᎦ, ᏦᎠᏍᎪ ᎢᏯᏏᏔᏗᏍᏗ ᎢᎩᏛ
ᏗᎬᏩᎶᏒᎯ, ᎤᏴᏢ ᎾᏚᏳᎪᏛ ᏧᏁᎵᏁ ᎾᏍᏓᏅᏅ ᎤᏕᎵᎬ ᎢᏗᏢ ᎨᏒ ᏌᏉ ᎠᎴ ᏦᎠ
ᏍᏁ ᎦᎵᏉᎩ ᎢᏯᏍᎪᎯᏧᏈᏁ ᎢᎦᎢ ᎢᎦᏅᏅᎯ ᎤᏓᏕᏒᏛ; ᎠᎴ ᎾᏍᏉ ᏅᏩᏓᎴ ᏐᎢ
Ꮣ ᏧᎾᏔᏅ ᎠᏓ ᏥᏉᎦ ᏅᎦᏍᎪᎯ ᎢᏯᏏᏔᏗᏍᏗ ᎢᎩᏛ ᏗᎬᏩᎶᏒᎯ ᎨᏒ ᎤᏴᏢ ᎾᏚ
ᏳᎪᏛ ᏦᎠᏍᎪᎯᏁ ᎾᏍᏓᏅᏅ ᎤᏕᎵᎬ ᎢᏗᏢ ᎨᏒ ᏌᏉ ᏁᎳᏍᎪᏃ ᏌᏉ ᎢᏯᏍᎪᎯ
ᏧᏈᏁ ᎢᎦᎢ ᎦᏅᏅᎯ ᏅᏓᏕᏒᏛ ᏗᎧᏄᎬᏃ ᎾᏚᏳᎪᏛ ᎦᎶᏍᎩ ᎯᏍᎩᏦᏁ ᎢᏳᏟᎶᏛ
ᎢᏴᏛ ᎢᏯᏍᏗ ᏅᏯ ᏗᎲ ᎤᏕᎵᎬ ᎢᏗᏢ ᏟᎶᏛ ᎬᏧᏛ ᏨᏧᎵ ᏍᎦᏚᎩ ᎨᏒᎢ, ᏨᏁᏉ
ᎦᏃ ᏧᏍᎦ ᎠᏓ ᎠᏍᎪᎯ ᎢᏯᏏᏔᏗᏍᏗ ᎢᎩᏛ ᏗᎬᏩᎶᏒᎯ ᎤᏴᏢ ᎾᏚᏳᎪᏛ ᏅᎦᏍᎪ

ᏣᎳᎩ ᎠᏰᎵ

ᏥᏚᎶᏒᏃᎴᎡ ᎤᏂᏍᏗᏍᎡ, ᎤᏛᎥ ᏧᎧᎥᎵ,
ᎠᏐ ᎤᏬᏯᏛᏙ ᎨᎱᎡ

CHEROKEE NATION

A History of Survival, Self Determination, and Identity

Written by
Bob Blackburn
Duane King
Neil Morton

Principal Chief William C. Rogers, the last elected chief prior to Oklahoma statehood, addresses the Cherokee Nation in front of the capitol building, c. 1903. Image courtesy of the Cherokee National Historical Society.

Cherokee Nation
P.O. Box 948
Tahlequah, OK 74465
918-453-5000
www.cherokee.org

ISBN: 978-0-692-08766-4
©2018 All Rights Reserved

All rights reserved. No parts of this publication may be reproduced or utilized in any form or by any means, electronically or mechanical, including photocopying, recording, or by any information storage system or retrieval system, without written permission from the publisher.

Printed in Canada

ᏣᎳᎩ ᎠᏰᎵ

ᎯᏓᏍᏙᎯᎸᎢ ᎤᏂᏍᏗᎶᎯ, ᎤᎾᎯ ᏧᎦᏗᎢ, ᎠᏓ ᎤᎾᏝᏙᏃ ᎨᏎᎢ

CHEROKEE NATION
A History of Survival, Self Determination, and Identity

Written by
Bob Blackburn
Duane King
Neil Morton

Design, Graphics, & Layout by
Roy Boney, Jr.

Published by Cherokee Nation

Dust jacket cover artwork: Going Snake's Trail by Daniel HorseChief. Image courtesy of Cherokee Nation Businesses.

Opposite Page: Cherokee Number System, 1839 (detail). Ink on paper. 8 3/4" x 5 5/8" (22.2. x 19.4 cm). GM 4026.312. Gilcrease Museum, Tulsa, Oklahoma.

ᏔᎪᏄᏗ ᎠᏫᏯᎢ

Table of Contents

ᎤᎬᏫᏳ ᏗᏯᎳ ᎤᏪᏯᏫᎣᏩ **Chief's Foreword**	x
ᎠᏫᏞ ᎠᏫᎵᏯ ᎤᏃᏤᏆᎦ **Authors' Preface**	xiii
ᎠᏍᏆᎢ 1: ᎤᏩᏃ ᏧᏣᎳᎣ ᏗᏓᎲᏍᎬ ᏧᏣᏆᏍᏬᎢ **Chapter 1: Since the Beginning of Time**	1
ᎠᏍᏆᎢ 2: ᎾᎢᏔ ᎢᏧᏞ ᏗᏥᎯᏍᏗ ᎠᏓ ᏧᏍᏗᏳ 1765 - 1794 **Chapter 2: Frontier Contact and Conflict**	17
ᎠᏍᏆᎢ 3: ᎤᏩᏃ ᏣᏫ ᏯᎦᎦᏓ ᎤᏢᎲᏎᎢ 1794 - 1828 **Chapter 3: Rise of the Cherokee State**	35
ᎠᏍᏆᎢ 4: ᎤᏍᏛᏍᏏ ᏚᎨᏴ ᎨᎳᎦᏞᎢ 1828 - 1839 **Chapter 4: Blunt Force of Removal**	51
ᎠᏍᏆᎢ 5: ᎤᏯᏣᏎᏍᎬ ᎾᏯ ᎢᏞ ᏞᎯᎤᏞᏗᎣᎢ 1839 - 1861 **Chapter 5: Dawn of New Opportunities**	71
ᎠᏍᏆᎢ 6: ᎠᎶᎵ ᎤᏅᎢᏞ ᏞᏞᏗᏃᏞᎢ 1861 - 1865 **Chapter 6: A Nation Divided**	87
ᎠᏍᏆᎢ 7: ᏞᏯᏍᏯᏎ ᎤᏃᏞᏥᏯ ᎠᏎᏍᏔ 1865 - 1887 **Chapter 7: Reconstructing from Ashes**	111
ᎠᏍᏆᎢ 8: ᎤᎾᎦ ᎬᏧ ᏧᏍᏆᎦᏬ ᎤᎣᏔ ᎠᎶᎵ ᎤᎾᎥᎵ ᎤᏪᏳᎣ 1876 - 1907 **Chapter 8: Assault on Nationhood**	137
ᎠᏍᏆᎢ 9: ᎤᏣᎺᏬᏎᏍᏬ ᎾᎻᎢ ᎠᏬᏟᎢ ᎾᏯ ᎤᎻᏍᏈᎡ 1907 - 1935 **Chapter 9: Adrift in a Sea of Survival**	165
ᎠᏍᏆᎢ 10: ᎤᏍᎩ ᎤᏎᎠᎦᏚ ᎦᏎᎶᎩ ᎾᏯᎾ ᎠᏃᏆᏎᎢᎢ 1936 - 1997 **Chapter 10: A Glimmer of Hope for Rebuilding**	197
ᎠᏍᏆᎢ 11: ᎤᎤᎬ ᏧᎦᎠᏫᎭᏞᎢ - ᎾᏯᏃ ᏣᏫ ᎤᏦᎭᏞᎢ **Chapter 11: Self Determination - The Cherokee Way**	227
ᎩᏣᎯᏯᎡ ᏚᎠᏫᏆᎢ **Endnotes**	236
ᎠᏉᏔ ᏗᎠᏫᎵ ᏗᏃᏮᏯ ᏎᏃᏫᏬᎢ **Selected Bibliography**	266
ᎠᏫᏯᎢ ᎠᏞᏃᎢᎦᎢ **Index**	275

Opposite Page: Cherokee National Male Seminary after burning, c. 1910. Image courtesy of the Cherokee National Historical Society.

List of Maps, Tables, and Illustrations

Maps

1. Homeland of the Five Civilized Tribes   1
2. Cherokee Settlement Areas at the Time of European Contact   2
3. Historic Towns of the Cherokees in the Southeast   5
4. Cherokee Lower Towns in South Carolina   8
5. The Continued Loss of Cherokee Territory   9
6. Places in London Visited by the Cherokee Delegation in 1762   11
7. The Transylvania Purchase   17
8. Map of the Overhill Country   19
9. Cherokee Invasion of Washington District, Pendetlon District, and Carter's Valley   24
10. Boundaries of the 1777 Treaty at the Long Island of Holston   30
11. Battle of Horeshoe Bend   40
12. Cherokee Nation in 1820   45
13. Removal Routes of the Cherokees   51
14. Louisiana Purchase With Modern-Day State Name and Boundaries   55
15. Texas Cherokees Territory   82
16. Battles in the Civil War that Included Indian Troops   87
17. Cherokee Strip and the Neutral Lands   119
18. Map of Railroads and Towns in the Cherokee Nation   134
19. Map of Cherokee Nation c. 1890   145
20. Land Cessions as a Result of the Treaty of 1866   155
21. Proposed State of Sequoyah   163
22. Combined Map of Indian and Oklahoma Territories   173

Tables

1. Executive Committe Members Named at the July 30, 1948 Convention   211
2. Results of the Cherokee Nation Election for Principal Chief   223

Illustrations

Front Matter, Foreword, Authors' Preface

1. Principal Chief Rogers Addressing a Crowd In Front of the Capitol Building, c. 1903   i-ii
2. Detail from Sequoyah's Original Numeral System   iii
3. Cherokee National Male Seminary After Burning, c. 1912   v
4. Cherokee Nation Capitol Building   viii
5. Principal Chief Bill John Baker   x
6. *Osiyo Chooch* by Brooks Henson   xi
7. Cherokee Nation Land Patent   xv

Chapter 1

1. *Dreams of the Ancestors* by Dewayne Fishinghawk Matthew   6

2. *Night Dancer* by Sam Watts-Scott — 10
3. *Cunne Shote* by Francis Parsons — 12
4. *Scyagust Ukah* by Sir Joshua Reynolds — 13
5. The Cherokee Delegation 1762 — 14

Chapter 2

1. *Cherokee Fishermen* by Gebon Barnoski — 21
2. Cherokee Flute Player by Daniel HorseChief — 23
3. Detail From One of the Drafts of the Declaration of Indepedence — 25
4. *Stickballer* by Gebon Barnoski — 33

Chapter 3

1. Springplace, the Home of James Vann — 35
2. First Ever Printing of Cherokee Syllabary — 38
3. *Gathering Pokeberries* by Virginia Stroud — 39
4. Portrait of Creek Leader Menawa — 41
5. Elias Boudinot — 43
6. *Sequoyah* by Daniel HorseChief — 43
7. Detail of Sequoyah's Handwritten Cursive Syllabary — 44
8. Modern Day Cherokee Syllabary Chart — 44
9. John Ross — 46
10. Andrew Jackson — 47
11. Chief Justice John Marshall — 48

Chapter 4

1. Heirloom White Eagle Cherokee Corn — 53
2. Woods on the Cherokee Reservation in Cherokee, North Carolina — 54
3. George Washington — 56
4. Cherokee Syllabary Typeset Block — 58
5. *I Rise in Opposition* by Virginia Stroud — 59
6. Removal Petition Scroll — 61
7. John Ridge — 61
8. Major Ridge — 62
9. *Many Died But They All Cried* by Bill Rabbit — 64

Chapter 5

1. *Grand Council, 1843* by Andy Thomas — 71
2. *Ama, Atsila, Elohi (Water, Fire, Earth)* by Dorothy Sullivan — 72
3. William Potter Ross — 74
4. George Lowery — 77
5. Cherokee Male Seminary, c. 1902 — 80
6. The Murrell Home/Hunter's Home — 81
7. Sam Houston's Bandolier Bag — 83

Chapter 6

1. Stand Watie — 88
2. Albert Pike — 89
3. *First Cherokee Mounted Rifles Fording the Illinois River* by Jim Wilson — 92
4. William Penn Adair — 94
5. *Third Indian Home Guard Crossing the Illinois River* by Jim Wilson — 95
6. Flag of the Cherokee Braves — 96
7. Rose Cottage, Home of John Ross — 98
8. General Douglas Cooper — 102
9. General James Blunt — 102
10. The Battle of Honey Springs — 103

11. Elias Boudinot As a Young Man 105
12. Daughters of the Confederate Honored Dead Dedicating a Memorial 108

Chapter 7

1. Cherokee Orphan Asylum Faculty 111
2. 1866 Cherokee Nation Delegation to Washington, DC 115
3. Chief William Potter Ross 116
4. Lewis Downing 117
5. Log Cabin 120
6. Golda's Mill 123
7. Elias C. Boudinot 125
8. *Paying the Indians for the Cherokee Strip–Scenes Around the Government Paymaster's Quarters* by Frederic Remington 127
9. Light Horsemen Guarding the Cherokee Outlet Payment 128
10. Cherokee Male Seminary Postcard 129
11. Cherokee Female Seminary Postcard 130
12. Cherokee Orphan Asylum Kindergarten Students 131
13. Cherokee Capitol Building Postcard 132
14. Cherokee Nation Jail 133
15. Zeke Proctor 135

Chapter 8

1. Construction on the Ozark and Cherokee Railroad 137
2. Homestead with Log Cabin 138
3. Elks Day in Vinita, Indian Territory 139
4. Colonel William Penn Adair 143
5. Dwight Mission 144
6. US Senator Robert L. Owen 145
7. Christy School with Cherokee Students 146
8. Charles Thompson 147
9. Cherokee Senators at Tahlequah 148
10. Stilwell Hotel 149
11. *Cherokee Advocate* Printing Office 151
12. Exterior of the Cherokee Advocate Printing Office 152
13. Joel B. Mayes 156
14. The Dawes Commission 157
15. Redbird Smith 158
16. Keetoowah Nighthawks 159
17. Full-blood Cherokees Who Came to Enroll at the Dawes Commission 160
18. Henry Meigs 162

Chapter 9

1. Cherokee Male Seminary Prior to Burning With Students Out Front 165
2. Northeastern Normal School 166
3. Cherokee Land Office Allotment Slip 167
4. Senator Robert L. Owen 168
5. W. C. Rogers 174
6. Wauhila Home Guards 175
7. Hickory Ridge School 176
8. Spring House on the Site of the Cherokee Orphan Asylum in Salina, Oklahoma 177
9. Cherokee Council 1890 178
10. Cherokee Female Seminary Students

Shearing Sheep 179
11. Cherokee Male and Female Students Gathered Together 180
12. Notice of Cherokee Land Allotment 183
13. Interior of the Tahlequah Land Office 184
14. Keetoowah Nighthawks 185
15. *Cherokee Code Talker* by Roy Boney, Jr. 188
16. Cherokees in Uniform, WWI 190
17. Brown's Business College 191
18. Tom Buffington 192
19. Will Rogers 194
20. Go Back Christie and His Son 195

Chapter 10

1. Cherokee Family Butchering a Hog 197
2. Cherokee Woman Using a Spinning Wheel 198
3. Grand River Dam 201
4. Cherokee Students Participating in a Social Dance 202
5. Cherokee Loom Weaving 204
6. Cecil Dick 205
7. Jack C. Montgomery 206
8. Joseph J. Clark 207
9. Keetoowh Nighthawk Society Displaying Wampum Belts 209
10. J. B. Milam 213
11. W. W. Keeler 215
12. *History of the Inter Tribal Council of the Five Civilized Tribes* 218
13. Ray's Grocery Story 219
14. Ancient Village at the Cherokee Heritage Center 220
15. Ross O. Swimmer 224
16. Wilma Mankiller 225

Chapter 11

1. Cherokee Nation W. W. Keeler Complex 227
2. Detail from the Signature Page of the Cherokee Nation Constitution 228
3. Cherokee Nation Casino 230
4. Redbird Smith Health Center 231
5. The Place Where They Play 233
6. Cherokee Language Keyboard 234
7. Sequoyah Cabin Museum 235

ᎤᎬᏩᎵ ᏣᎳᎩ ᎤᏩᏒᏉᎢ

Chief's Foreword

Cherokee Nation Capitol Building. Image courtesy of the Cherokee Nation.

Cherokee Nation will always tell our story. Telling our history ensures it is preserved, told accurately and that there is a way to pass it down for future generations of Cherokees. From our great success as society-builders to the darkest chapters of forced removal, Cherokee

Chief's Foreword

Nation's history is intertwined with the history of the United States.

Many people have a broad sense of the Cherokee narrative, but historians Dr. Duane King, Dr. Neil Morton and Dr. Bob Blackburn have created a history book that is as unique as it is authoritative. This single-volume Cherokee history book has the full support of the Cherokee Nation. The authors, immensely knowledgeable and skilled as researchers and writers, have devoted their professional and personal lives to education, to the Cherokee Nation and to northeast Oklahoma. They are Cherokee history experts and will forever be respected as friends of the Cherokee Nation. Sadly, just before the publication of this book, Dr. Duane King walked on. He will always be remembered as a consummate academic scholar, devoted to the preservation of Cherokee Nation's unique and critical role in American history.

This history book details the epic travails of our Cherokee leaders to ensure our people survived. Those brave men and women preserved our government, our clans and our way of life. Where we came from is an important part of who we are as Cherokee people, and this book, detailing the plight of the Cherokee Nation, will be equally at home in public education and university settings as well as private libraries. This will be something that stands the test of time and will be used in many beneficial ways.

Telling the real and accurate history of the Cherokee Nation benefits our people and creates an unprecedented opportunity to educate. Today, we are using our success to build stronger and healthier families, provide a quality education to our children, make health care accessible, ensure our citizens have adequate housing and employment, and protect our core Cherokee cultural values.

Cherokees have created sophisticated societies numerous times in our ancient and modern history. Our original and ancestral homelands are in the southeastern United States. The lands across modern-day states like Georgia, Tennessee and North Carolina are where our tribal systems of government and education were born, where our ancestors are buried, and where our ceremonial dances and songs were developed and shared. When we were forcibly removed from our homelands, our ancestors traveled to Indian Territory in the darkest chapter of American and Cherokee history – the Trail of Tears. We endured unfathomable hardships and tragedy. We estimate a quarter of the 16,000 Cherokees who started out on the Trail of Tears perished.

However, our ancestors never gave up. They never relinquished the fortitude to survive. Day after day, step after step, our people arrived in Indian Territory, which is now modern-day Oklahoma. After removal, the Cherokee people reestablished our government. Tribal school systems were recreated and courts were reestablished. Periodicals and other publications, printed in both English and Cherokee, informed and educated our citizens and our neighbors.

ᎤᎬᏫᏳᎯ ᎠᏥᎳ ᎤᏬᏂᎯᏍᏗ

Principal Chief of the Cherokee Nation Bill John Baker. Image courtesy of the Cherokee Nation.

During the Allotment and Termination eras, the federal government tried to break apart our way of life, as non-Cherokees again wanted our land and our homes. The annihilation of our government was accomplished, and the breakup of our society was attempted. We struggled and we persevered to remember and rebuild everything we have today. Our Cherokee values – family, community, spirituality, and responsibility— have enabled us to withstand every dark chapter and celebrate every positive milestone.

Like the proverbial Phoenix, we have risen from the ashes and are once again soaring. We are thriving today in northeastern Oklahoma as a sovereign government with a living culture because every adversity throughout history has made us stronger today than ever before. As the largest federally recognized tribe in America, it is critically important we represent ourselves and our ancestors.

We are Cherokee, the Principal People, with one eye toward a brighter future and one eye on our historic past, reminding us of where we have been and where we are going. I hope you appreciate this book as much as I do, as every Cherokee Nation citizen does. It is our story, and it is told correctly and in its entirety.

ᎭᏌ Wado,

Bill John Baker

Chief Bill John Baker

ᎠᏌᎵ ᎠᏫᎵᏍᏯ ᎤᏃᏢᏛᎠ

Authors' Preface

Osiyo Chooch by Brooks Henson. Image courtesy of Cherokee Nation Businesses.

Seven is a sacred number to the Cherokee people. There are seven clans, the Bird, Deer, Wolf, Longhair, Wild Potato, Blue, and Paint Clans, from which all Cherokees descend through their mother's lineage. There are seven directions, north, south, east, west, up, down, and center, the latter being where you are at any given moment. Out of respect for those ancient traditions, the authors adopted seven goals when we started researching and writing this book.

First, we agreed with Principal Chief Bill John Baker and Chief of Staff Chuck Hoskin, Sr., that the book should serve first and foremost the Cherokee people, from students and new employees to elders and community leaders. The book hopefully will be read by non-citizens as well, but the primary audience is the Cherokee people.

Second, we wanted to encourage curiosity about Cherokee history that would lead to further study. In this slim volume, we knew we could not include all important people, places, and events that have shaped the Cherokee story, so we tried to include turning points and broad trends that can serve as portals to be followed now and in the future as more research and writing is completed.

Third, we wanted to create a tool for teachers in the classroom who understand the importance of Cherokee history but who have been limited by the over-abundance but disconnected bounty of previously published tribal histories. Instead of an encyclopedic approach to history with everything and anything, we knew we had to use a survey approach to history, trying to cover a lot of ground with select stories that can serve as guideposts for further exploration. Teachers will have other resources for that journey of discovery.

Fourth, we wanted to demonstrate that history is not predestined through the whims of fate but rather made by the decisions and actions of people who are faced with challenges and opportunities. Just as Dragging Canoe fought for the survival of Cherokee families and W. W. Keeler seized the opportunity to revive tribal government, Cherokees today and in the future need to understand that the decisions they make, the opportunities they embrace, and the challenges they overcome will shape the future for their children and grandchildren.

Fifth, we wanted to show respect to all authors, both Cherokee and non-citizens, who have plowed the fertile fields of tribal history for more than a century. A quick glance at the Library of Congress catalog shows that there have been more than 15,000 books written about the Cherokees. Our challenge was to select and summarize the best and most relevant stories that would help Cherokees connect the dots between their past and present to better prepare for the future.

Sixth, we wanted a book that would place the story of the Cherokees in the context of the outside world. Just as their ancestors needed to understand the complexities of European trade and the inner workings of Congress, modern Cherokees need to understand the relationships with outsiders today in order to manage compacts with the state, contracts with federal agencies, or partnerships with groups and individuals willing to embrace shared goals.

And seventh, we wanted a book that would foster a sense of community among all Cherokees regardless of their backgrounds or current conditions in life. There is much to divide us in modern society, from politics and religion to traditions and longstanding grudges.

Author's Preface

Through the pages of history, it should be clear that unity is strength, division is weakness.

As we set about accomplishing those seven goals, we developed a division of tasks among ourselves. First were primary assignments based on our previous specialties. Duane King, who had published many articles and books about early Cherokee history, took the lead in researching and writing the chapters up to the Civil War. Bob Blackburn, whose specialties have long included the general history of Oklahoma, took the lead in the chapters from the Civil War to statehood. Neil Morton, an educator who has served the Cherokee Nation since the administration of W.W. Keeler, used his first person experience to supplement his research on the revival of Cherokee government. For the past two years the authors have freely exchanged ideas, stories, and editorial comments to find a common narrative pace and voice.

The authors wish to thank a number of people who have made this book possible. Foremost are Principal Chief Bill John Baker and his Chief of Staff Chuck Hoskin, Sr., who approached the authors with the daunting challenge of condensing the vast scope of Cherokee history into one book. From the very beginning of our conversations, both of these tribal leaders let us know that they did not want this book to be seen as a politically motivated project. For that reason, we agreed that the resurrection of the Cherokee Nation's government would end with the modern Cherokee Constitution and the administrations of Ross Swimmer and Wilma Mankiller. A more comprehensive survey of the Cherokee government to date will await a future book.

On the production side, we want to thank Roy Boney for his unique design and map making skills. As a rising star among Cherokee artists, Roy brought to the team his deep understanding of tribal history as expressed through colors, iconography, and images. In many ways he served as an editor, making suggestions in his gentle way and adding value through each change along the way. We also want to thank Dr. Tim Zwink, who added an editorial consistency that helped bind the work of three scholars with their own distinctive styles into one narrative voice. We are sure that he went through several red pens as he used the most recent edition of the *Chicago Manual of Style* to grapple with introductory clauses, numbers, verb tense, commas, and all the nuances of sentence structure.

We also wish to acknowledge the following people for their contributions that make this book a much richer experience. John Ross, Jr., David Crawler, Dennis Sixkiller, Anna Sixkiller, and Phyllis Edwards from the Cherokee Nation translation office provided translations and proofreading of the Cherokee syllabary content, along with guidance on cultural and historical elements. It should be noted that when Cherokee names appear in syllabary these are the direct Cherokee spellings, so they might not match commonly known English phonetic spellings of these names. Special thanks goes to Mr. Ross who, in addition to providing translation and history on the Keetoowahs, also lent his expertise on Sequoyah's numbering system, which marks the beginning of each chapter. Jeff Edwards and Zachary Barnes, from the Cherokee Nation language technology program, served as research assistants and helped with graphic art, photography, and map making. Jennifer Pigeon and Neesie Blossom, from Cherokee Nation Education Services administration, provided much needed administrative support. Verlita Sugar, database specialist for Cherokee Nation, spent many hours transcribing handwritten notes and chapter drafts.

For their invaluable assistance with procuring of the images that illustrate this book, we wish to thank: Jerry Thompson, archivist for the Cherokee Heritage Center; Callie Chunestudy, curator for the Cherokee Heritage Center; Gina Olaya, director of cultural art and design for Cherokee Nation Businesses; Brenda Bradford, Ashley Stoddard, Blain McClain, and Kayla Hunt at Northeastern State University Archives and Special Collections; Diana Cox and Dr. Natalie Panther at the Gilcrease Museum; Jon May at the Oklahoma Historical Society; Tonya Bryant from Cherokee Nation's Johnson O'Malley Program; Pat Gwin with Cherokee Nation Natural Resources; Nancy Rackliff with Cherokee Nation GeoData Center; and Stephanie Remer and Jason McCarty from Cherokee Nation Communications.

Special acknowledgment is also due to Molly Jarvis, senior vice president of marketing, communications, and cultural tourism for Cherokee Nation Businesses, for her sponsorship of the project.

Finally, we want to thank the Cherokee people, past and present, who have clung to the core values of their culture. Although they might dress differently today and speak other languages, Cherokees share a common heritage that is emerging triumphant in the Twenty-first Century. Yes, there are still challenges to face and problems to solve, but if the past is prologue, the future of the Cherokee Nation is bright with promise.

ᎬᏩ Wado,

Bob Blackburn
Duane King
Neil Morton

Opposite Page. Cherokee Nation Land Patent signed by President Martin Van Buren. This document provided the title to the Cherokee Nation for its lands in Indian Territory. Image courtesy of the Cherokee National Historical Society.

Prominent Indian Men, Delegates to Consider Allotment of Indian Lands, 1894. *Image courtesy of the Oklahoma Historical Society.*

ᎠᏯᏙᎸᎢ 1
ᏃᏍᎩᏯᏃ ᏧᎦᏙᏩᏂ ᏋᏞᏍᎰᏋ ᏧᏓᎴᏏᏍᏬᏂᎢ

Chapter 1: Since the Beginning of Time

Figure 1. Homelands of the Five Civilized Tribes.

At the Treaty of Sycamore Shoals in 1775, the Cherokees were recognized as owners of the land since "the beginning of time." Today we know that the Cherokee territory in the South Appalachian area has been continuously occupied for at least the past ten thousand years. Traits associated with historic Cherokee culture such as check-stamped pottery, sub-structure temple mounds, a community building with adjacent plaza, paired summer-winter

Figure 2. Cherokee settlement areas at the time of European contact.

dwellings, and use of the bow and arrow as a primary hunting implement can all be traced back fifteen hundred to two thousand years, providing an excellent record of cultural continuity in the Cherokee heartland over the centuries.

At the time of European contact, the Cherokee people occupied both sides of the South Appalachian summit extending from the Piedmont of present South Carolina to the ridge and valley area of present East Tennessee. The towns were located on the headwaters of river systems flowing east, south, and west out of the mountains. The area was more diverse and richer in natural resources than most of the rest of the present Southeastern United States. The mountains, the fertile valleys, and the streams provided immediate access to multiple ecological niches that supported the Cherokees' diversified economy.

If local resources were of short supply, the Cherokees had only to venture farther into the expanse of wilderness that separated them from their neighbors. The entire range of hunting territory claimed by the Cherokees encompassed 140,000 square miles in portions of eight present states: the Carolinas, the Virginias, Kentucky, Tennessee, Georgia, and Alabama.[1] The actual land occupied was a much smaller area.

At the time of contact with Europeans, the Cherokees spoke three principal dialects; these corresponded roughly to the major geographical divisions of Cherokee settlements. The Lower or *Elati* dialect was spoken in the settlements along the Keowee River, the Tugaloo River, and the headwaters of the Savannah River in what is now northwestern South Carolina and northeastern Georgia. The Middle or *Kituhwa* dialect was spoken in the settlements on the Oconaluftee, Tuckaseegee, Nantahala, and Little Tennessee Rivers in present western North Carolina. The Western or *Otali* dialect, later called the Overhill dialect, was spoken in all the towns of East Tennessee and in the towns along the Hiwassee and Cheowa Rivers in present North Carolina.[2]

Although the archaeological record clearly demonstrates a long history of cultural development in the Cherokee homeland, the length of Cherokee occupation in the South Appalachian area has long been a subject of speculation. Some writers have proposed that the Cherokees were recent arrivals who had migrated to the area shortly before white contact.[3] These writers observed that the Cherokees spoke a language unrelated to those of their neighbors, had an array of migration legends, and were unable in the eighteenth century to explain the origins of the artificial mounds on which many of their townhouses were built. The oral traditions, the cumulative knowledge of plants used for food and medicine clearly reflect centuries if not millennia of experience in the same environment. Linguistic analysis, although not confirming the antiquity of the Cherokees in the mountains, does indicate that the group had been separate from its nearest linguistic relatives, the northern Iroquois, for at least thirty-five hundred years.[4]

The written history of the Cherokees presumably began with the DeSoto expedition in 1540. Sustained contact with Europeans, however, did not begin until the close of the seventeenth century. In 1673, two Virginia traders, Jems [James] Needham and Gabriel Arthur, made contact with Indians who may have been Cherokees living in what is now upper East Tennessee.

In 1684 the first Cherokee treaty with the whites was concluded by representatives from the Lower Towns of Toxawa and Keowa with officials in Charlestown, South Carolina.[5] In 1693 a delegation from the Lower Towns was again in Charlestown, this time asking for guns to use in its wars against the Esaws, Savannahs, and Congarees.[6]

By the early 1700s, the deerskin trade had developed into a full-blown enterprise with more than fifty thousand hides being exported annually from Charlestown.[7] In exchange for deerskins, the Cherokees received firearms, ammunition, metal knives, axes, garden implements, as well as an assortment of beads, baubles, vermilion for paint, clothing, and rum. Of the trade goods, firearms proved to be the most important. Firearms provided the means for national security and more efficient hunting, which was the basis for the economy.

In 1707 the Indian trade in Carolina came under government regulation. The Carolina Legislature quickly approved "the seizure of goods belonging to Virginia Indian traders." A bill was also passed for "the regulation of Virginia traders."[8] In 1711 officials in Virginia complained of the limitations placed on their traders by the Carolina government, which forced the Virginians to enter the Cherokee country by way of Carolina trade routes.[9] For decades the Cherokee trade was dominated by Carolina-based traders, while Virginians were considered to be interlopers.

The dependency on European manufactured goods resulted in overhunting the white tail deer population in the Southeast by the last quarter of the eighteenth century. Traditionally, young men gained status in Cherokee society by demonstrating courage and valor in relatively nondestructive warfare. In the early eighteenth century, the traditional enemies remained the same, but the introduction of firearms and, perhaps, the economic motivation of the fur trade brought changes in the previous balance of power.

Ready access to firearms and competition over prime hunting grounds led to conflicts between the Cherokees and most of their neighbors. In the second decade of the eighteenth century, the Cherokees engaged in wars that ended with the dispersion and removal of the Tuscarora from North Carolina and the Yuchi and Shawnee from Tennessee.[10] During this period, the Cherokees spoke of war as their "beloved profession." A rough census for the year 1715 indicated that the Overhills had nineteen towns, 900 men, 980 women, 400 boys, and 480 girls and that they were the most resourceful and vigorous part of the nation which had an estimated total population of eleven thousand.[11]

Sir Francis Nicholson, the first royal governor of South Carolina, in an effort to systematize Indian relations, created the title "Emperor of the Cherokee Nation." The thirty-seven chiefs who met with Nicholson at Charlestown in 1721 not only agreed to accept the radical idea of a single leader for all the Cherokees but also agreed to the first Cherokee land cession, yielding a strip between the Santee, Saluda, and Edisto Rivers.[12] The land cession occurred less than fifty years after the beginning of sustained contact with Europeans. At that time, the Cherokee homeland encompassed 125,000 square miles, or eighty million acres in parts of eight present states: the Carolinas, the Virginias, Kentucky, Tennessee, Georgia, and Alabama. A little more than a century and two dozen land cessions later, the once vast Cherokee territory was reduced to next to nothing.[13]

In 1725 when Col. George Chicken visited the Cherokee country, the capital or home of the emperor, or king, was the town of Tunnissee, from which the Tennessee River and the state derived their names.[14] On April 3, 1730, Sir Alexander Cuming in Nequassee Townhouse arranged for the election of a new emperor, Moytoy of Great Tellico.

When Moytoy was killed in battle in 1741, the Tellico-Hiwassee power structure sought to retain the advantages of the emperorship.[15] Using the European concept of a hereditary monarchy, the Tellico council gained British recognition of Ammonscossittee (Dreadful Water), the teenage son of Moytoy, as the new emperor.[16]

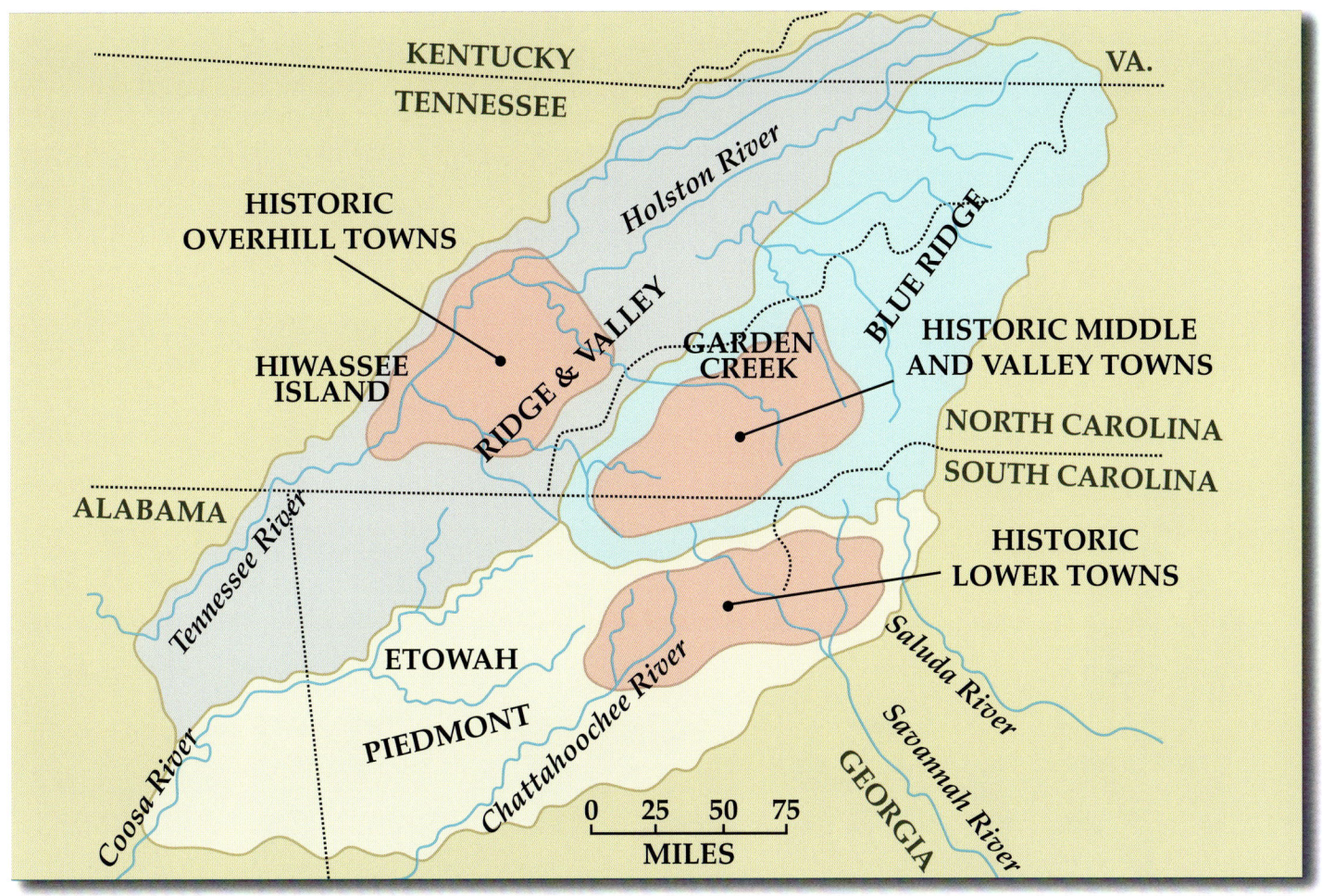

Figure 3. The historic towns of the Cherokees in the Southeast.

For more than a decade thereafter, the rising power base on the Little Tennessee River centered around the towns of Chota and Tunnissee, which competed with the Tellico-Hiwassee coalition for dominance.

In 1751 the colony of South Carolina placed an embargo on trade goods going to the Cherokees because of altercations with several traders and also because of the tribe's persisting war with the Creeks. Realizing the need for alternative supply sources, Ammonscossittee made an ill-fated trip to Virginia the following year. Returning in disgrace, preceded by rumors of his having betrayed the best interest of the Cherokee Nation, the young emperor lost support even in his own council.[17] With the increased political strife brought about by the faltering Tellico-Hiwassee coalition, South Carolina had no choice but to turn to Chota for leadership. In 1753 Old Hop, surrounded by a council of very capable leaders, became the emperor.

At the beginning of the French and Indian War in 1754, the British colonies invoked the Treaty of 1730 demanding that the Cherokees take up arms against the enemies of King George. The Cherokees, however, were reluctant to send warriors to the Virginia frontier unless the British assumed protection of the vulnerable Cherokee settlements. After both Virginia and South Carolina built forts in the Overhill coun-

Figure 4. Dreams of the Ancestors *by Dewayne Fishinghawk Matthew. Image Courtesy Cherokee Nation Businesses.*

try, the Cherokees sent several hundred warriors to fight on the frontier. The Cherokees distinguished themselves in service, and a number were killed in battle. Col. George Washington described the Cherokees as "twice as serviceable as white soldiers." However, when some returning Cherokee veterans were killed by Virginia frontiersmen, the alliance that Washington valued so highly was broken.[18]

When Cherokee veterans returning home from service with the Virginia militia were killed by frontiersmen, outraged clansmen of the dead were obligated by traditional law to seek justice. Maintaining the concept of corporate responsibility, they attacked the nearby Carolina frontier settlements rather than the offending and more distant settlements in Virginia. The South Carolina government in turn demanded satisfaction. A peace delegation led by Oconastota (ᏆᏐᎾ ᎠᏍᏓᏫ) traveled to Charlestown in fall 1759 to offer reassurances of goodwill and loyalty by the Cherokee leadership. The overture of peace was rejected by South Carolina officials, and the Cherokee delegation was marched back to the Cherokee country in chains escorted by thirteen hundred Carolina Provincials.

At Fort Prince George, near the town of Keowee in the Lower settlements, Governor William Lyttelton offered to exchange members of the peace delegation on an individual basis for the twenty-four warriors presumed guilty of murder in South Carolina since November 9, 1758.[19] It was an impossible situation for the Cherokees. They could not surrender Cherokee men for execution who had acted as agents of society under traditional law. On the other hand, they could not abandon innocent leaders who had sought only to reaffirm their allegiance to South Carolina. Finally, three alleged murderers were surrendered, and several of the captives, including Oconastota, were released.

Subsequently, Oconastota attempted to free by force the remaining members of the peace delegation held at Fort Prince George. In the attempt, after the fort's commander, Lt. Richard Coytmore, was mortally wounded, the soldiers murdered all twenty-two members of the Cherokee delegation. A few months later an army of 1,650 men comprised of the Seventy-seventh Highlanders and Carolina Provincials under Col. Archibald Montgomery invaded the Cherokee country. Montgomery destroyed five of the Lower Towns on June 1 and 2, 1760, but was later soundly defeated on June 27 as he attempted to lead his army into the Middle settlements.[20] The Cherokees, regarding their encounter with Montgomery's army as a moral victory, pressed their siege of Fort Loudoun on the Little Tennessee River. In August 1760, the garrison surrendered.

The following spring, another punitive expedition invaded the Cherokee Nation. Despite the Cherokee's desire for peace, the British were intent on destroying any adversarial military capability. The army of twenty-six hundred men, including the Seventheenth and Twenty-second Regiments, a battalion of Royal Scots, Carolina Provincials, and an Indian Corps comprised of Chickasaws, Catawbas, Stockbridges, and Munsees commanded by Lt. Col. James Grant, moved into the heart of the Cherokee Country without opposition. On June 10, 1761, they fought a major battle against the Cherokees under Oconastota at Cowee Pass near the same site where Montgomery was defeated a year earlier. In the end Grant's army burned fifteen towns, destroyed fifteen hundred acres of crops, and "sent 5,000 Cherokees into the mountains to starve."[21]

By fall 1761, the Overhill settlements in present-day east Tennessee were crowded with refugees from the Lower and Middle settlements destroyed by British armies. Another force of Virginia militia was moving toward the Overhills when a delegation of four hundred Cherokees met the army 140 miles away at the Long Island of the Holston in November that same year. There they signed a peace treaty ending the hostilities. Only the two soldiers, Ens. Henry Timberlake and Sgt. Thomas Sumter traveled to the Overhill towns as symbols of good faith. The three Cherokee leaders, Ostenaco (ᎤᏍᏕᏁᎦ), Cunne Shote (ᎬᏂ ᏍᎥᏍ), and Woyi (ᏬᏱ) returned with Timberlake and Sumter to Virginia and then on to England to meet with King George III

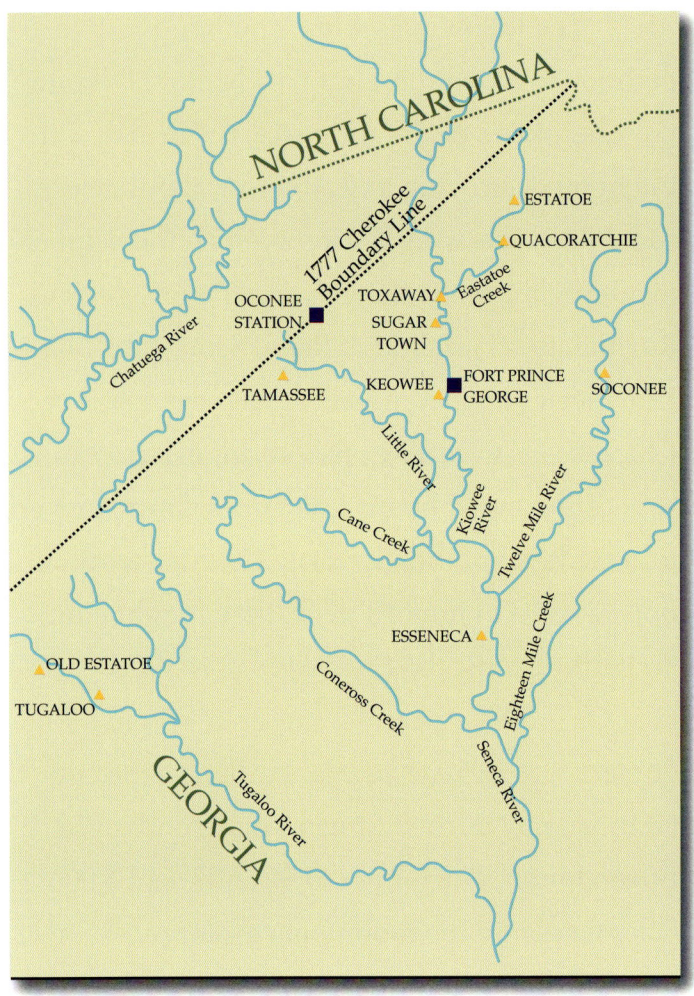

Figure 5. Cherokee Lower Towns in South Carolina.

to affirm the treaties that had been signed.²²

On July 8, 1762, the twenty-four-year-old monarch received three diplomats from the Cherokee Nation in the Drawing Room at Saint James Palace. The purpose of the visit was to reaffirm the peace established by treaties in 1761 ending a destructive three-year Anglo-Cherokee War in which hundreds of people were killed or wounded, dozens of settlements destroyed, and thousands of people on both sides left homeless. When the young monarch George III inherited the throne from his grandfather George II in October 1760, Great Britain was still suffering from the humiliating defeat a few months earlier of the Seventy-seventh Highlanders under Col. Archibald Montgomerie at the battle of Echowee Pass and the capitulation of the garrison of Fort Loudoun.²³

Treaties with the Carolinas and Virginia ended the hostilities, but the peace was fragile. As symbols of good faith, two British officers spent three months in the Overhill Country and later accompanied three Cherokee leaders to Williamsburg and on to London to meet with King George III. For the young monarch, it was his first face-to-face meeting with American Indians. He was mindful of the fact that they represented an indigenous nation that had held its own against the might of the British Empire by fighting two British armies inflicting significant casualties and dispersing thousands of settlers on the frontier.

The Cherokee delegation attracted considerable attention of the British press. "They spent more than an hour and a half with his Majesty… They were received by his Majesty and their Behavior was remarkably humble and meek… There seemed to be a Mixture of Majesty and Moroseness in their Countenances…The man who assisted as Interpreter was so much confused that he [the King] could ask but few Questions."²⁴

Another source noted, "Ostenaco dressed for the occasion in a mantle of rich blue covered with lace. On his breast he wore a silver gorget-engraved with His Majesty's arms. The other two Cherokees wore scarlet richly adorned with gold lace, and gorgets of plate on their breasts."²⁵

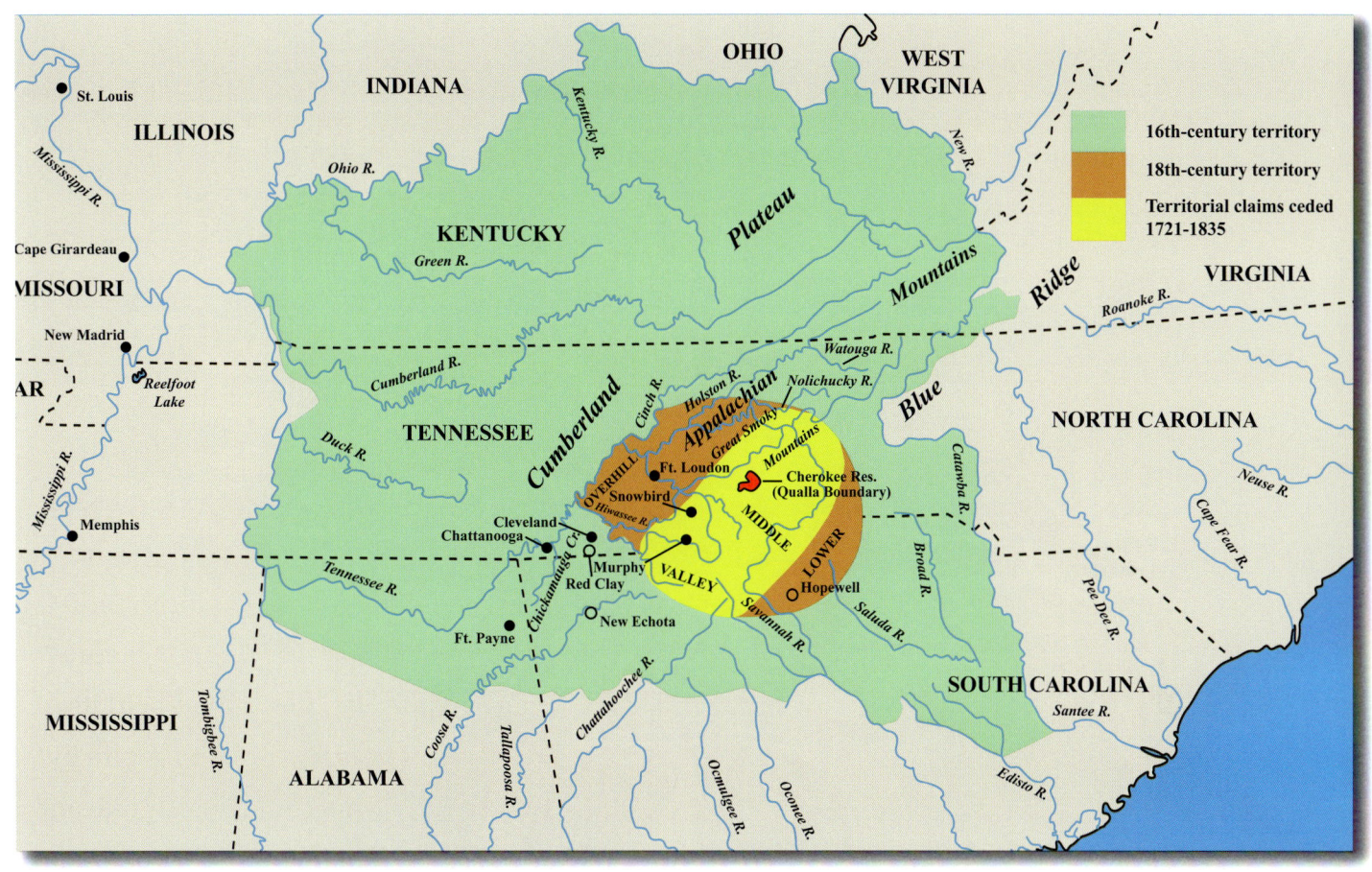

Figure 6. Map showing the continued loss of Cherokee territory.

Still another observer reported, "The Cherokees came from their audience of the King highly pleased with His Majesty's gracious manner of treating them, and talked earnest to each when they came out of the Presence Chamber; and the King seems proud of his Gorget or Breast Plate, which is very handsome."[26]

Although the press noted the military gorgets worn by the Cherokee leaders, there was no mention of medals presented to, or worn by, the Cherokees. Likewise, there is no mention of medals in the most detailed description of the physical appearance of the Cherokees. "The Chief [Ostenaco] had the Tail of a Comet revers'd painted Blue on his forehead, his Left Cheek black & His Left Eyelid Scarlet his Rt Eyelid Black and his Right Cheek Scarlet, all his teeth were cut through like Rings, He had a Blue Cloth Mantle laced with Gold & a silver Gorget. The second had nothing particular except his Eyelids which were painted Scarlet, the 3d had painted in Blue on his cheeks a large pair of wings which had a very odd Effect as he look'd directly as if his Nose & Eyes were flying away. The two last were in Scarlet and Silver with Silver Gorgets."[27]

Regal portraits of two of the diplomats painted in the days leading up to the audience with King George clearly show the Cherokees wearing British medals in addition to military gorgets. The portrait of Cunne Shote (Stalking Turkey) by Francis Parsons[28] and the portrait of

Figure 7. **Night Dancer** *by Sam Watts-Scott. This is an example of southeastern woodlands tribal iconography as portrayed by a contemporary Cherokee artist. Imagery similar to this would've possibly been incorporated in the Cherokee delegations' outfits on their trip to London. Image courtesy of Cherokee Nation Businesses.*

Scyagust Ukah by Sir Joshua Reynolds[29] are the earliest oil portraits of Cherokees.[30]

Shortly after their arrival in England on June 16, 1762, the first "cloaths" ordered for the Cherokee delegation were in the English fashion. Their companion, Ens. Henry Timberlake of the Virginia militia may have soon realized that dressing like Indians made them more conspicuous and more of a curiosity. By the end of June, the Cherokee leaders were sitting for two of London's leading portrait painters. Sir Joshua Reynolds, in his small pocket diary, recorded the names of his sitters for the month of June. He listed "The King of the Cherokees" with eight prominent Englishmen as sitters.[31]

Reynolds' appointment book indicated a single appointment with the King of the Cherokees on July 1, 1762 at 9 a.m. and one with "Miss(?) Cherocke on 5 July (at two)."[32] Two newspapers reported that "The Cherokee Chiefs

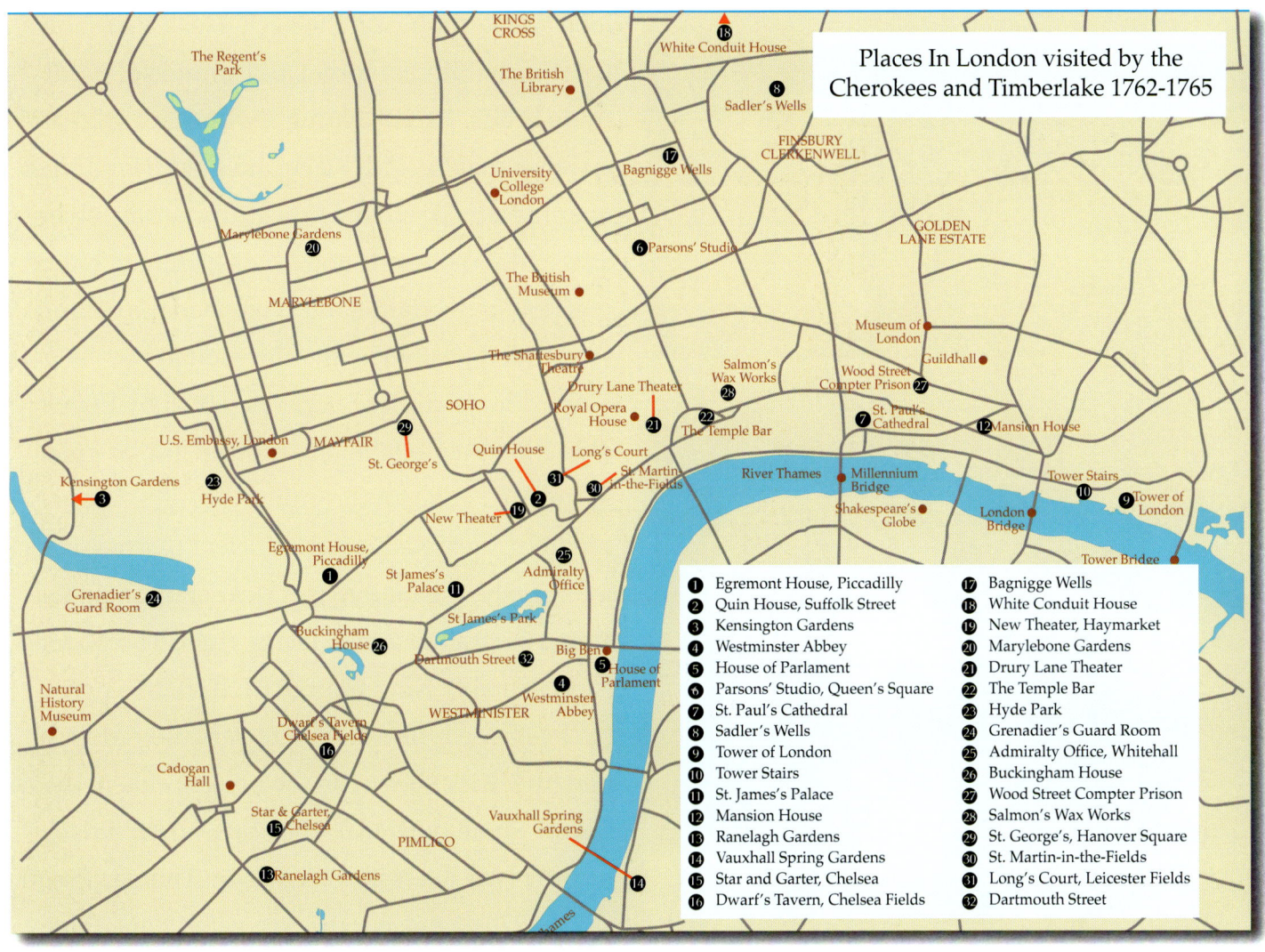

Figure 8. Places in London visited by the Cherokee delegation in 1762.

are sitting for their pictures to Mr. [afterward Sir Joshua] Reynolds."[33] A separate portrait was made of Ostenaco from which was made an illustration for a popular magazine in London.[34] From the newspaper reports it would appear that Reynolds may have painted portraits of all three Cherokees either separately or together. Only one oil portrait by Reynolds has survived, that of Scyacust Ukah. The engraved-copper prints of Austenaco attributed to Reynolds published in 1762 do not appear to be the same person who is in the Reynolds portrait entitled *Scyagust Ukah*. It is quite likely that Scyagust Ukah is not Austenaco as has long been assumed but rather the third member of the delegation, a man named Woyi (Pigeon) who also held the same military title Scyagust Ukah.[35]

In 1758 Reynolds raised his prices to twenty, forty, and eighty guineas for head, half length, and full-length portraits. In 1762 he was making six thousand pounds a year, perhaps the highest paid artist in England. The portrait of Scyagust Ukah should have cost forty guineas.[36] *The British Chronicle* reported that on June

Figure 9. Cunne Shote, Cherokee Chief, 1762 *by Francis Parsons. Oil on canvas. 35" x 27 1/2" (88.9 x 69.9 cm). GM 0176.1015. Gilcrease Museum, Tulsa, Oklahoma.*

29, "one of the Cherokee Chiefs (Cunne Shote) sat for his picture to Mr. (Francis) Parsons in Queens Square. He expressed much pleasure to the interpreter on the occasion, saying, "his friends would now have something to remember when he is gone to fight the French.'…a throng of ladies coming out of Mr. Parsons' room from seeing the pictures of the Cherokee Chief, one of them had the misfortune to fall down the Stairs and dislocate her knee; two surgeons were sent for, and she was carried home in a (sedan) Chair."[37]

The portrait of Stalking Turkey shows what appears to be a slit in a stretched left earlobe and tattooing on the neck. He is also shown wearing a military gorget and strands of black trade beads. He is wearing a white lace shirt and a scarlet mantle with black and gold trim draped over his left shoulder. He is also wearing silver arm and wrist bands and holds a knife in ready position in his right hand. Two medallions are suspended just below the shirt collar.

The portrait of Scyagust Ukah by Reynolds shows a medallion in bronze, gilt, or gold, suspended beneath the military gorget. Unfortunately, the detail is not sufficient to precisely identify the medallion. It is clear enough to discern a portrait of a man facing right. The portrait is presumably King George III. If so, this may be the obverse side of the Proclamation Medallion by J. Kirk shown on the reverse side in the Cunne Shote portrait.[38] The other possibilities include two Accession Medals by Thomas Pingo (1692-1776).[39] It is not the Accession Medallion by J. Colibert[40] or the official Coronation Medallion by L. Natter,[41] both of which face left.

Another medallion by Pingo, then assistant engraver at the Royal Mint, commemorated an event that occurred during the Cherokee delegation's visit. This was the birth of the Prince of Wales, later King George IV. The second and final meeting between the Cherokees and King George III took place at Saint James Palace on Friday, August 6, 1762.[42] At the time, Queen Charlotte, who was nine months pregnant, viewed the proceedings from a distance. "The Chiefs took leave of the King; the Queen, Princess Augusta [the King's eldest sister] and

Figure 10. Portrait of Scyagust Ukah *by Sir Joshua Reynolds. Oil on canvas. 47 1/4" x 35 3/8" (120 x 89.9 cm). GM 0176.1017. Gilcrease Museum, Tulsa, Oklahoma.*

the Prince of Mechlenburg stood at one of the windows fronting the courtyard to see them. The name of the head chief is Outacite, one of the Greatest warriors in the Cherokee Nation. His name signifies. 'Mankiller.'"[43] "[They] stood in one of the windows, with Sashes up, above Half an Hour, to take a View of them."[44]

A week later the Cherokees joined in the public celebration of the royal birth of the prince, who fifty-eight years later in 1820 would become King George IV. "The morning at half an hour past 7, the Queen was happily delivered of a Prince. His Royal Highness, the Princess Dowager of Wales, several Lords of his Majesty's Most Honorable Privy Council, and the Ladies of her Majesty's Bed Chamber, being present."[45] "This great and important news was immediately made known to the town, by the firing of the tower guns; and by the Privy Council, being assembled as soon as possible Thereupon; it was ordered that a form of Thanksgiving for the queen's safe delivery, etc. be prepared etc."[46] "On Thursday Night, [8/12/62] The Chief of the Cherokees visited the most public streets on this metropolis. He was no stranger to the cause of illuminations, bonfires, etc/ and testified a great approbation at their appearance, and heartily joined with those that cheerfully huzza'd for King George, Queen Charlotte, and the new born Prince."[47]

In 1763 Parsons displayed the portrait of Cunne Shote in an exhibition at the Spring Garden Rooms at Vauxhall, along with one of Miss Davis,[48] an opera singer, depicted in the character of Madge in *Love in a Village*. One critic said "these pictures, particularly the Chief, were as hard and unpleasant in the execution as the Indian himself was in his physiognomy."[49] Despite the criticism, the portrait of Cunne Shote became the source for several prints. One print by James McArdell was sold at the Golden Head in Queen's Square for two shillings, sixpence.[50] The portrait also inspired full-length depictions to illustrate dress by Thomas Jeffreys in 1772[51] and Pierre Duflos in the 1880s.[52]

At least nine engraved prints exist of Ostenaco derived from bust and full-length portraits by Reynolds.[53] They were printed

Figure 11. The Three Cherokees, came over from the head of the River Savanna to London, 1762 by George Bickham, the younger. Engraving on paper. 9" x 11 3/8" (22.9 x 28.9 cm) MG 3576.429. Gilcrease Museum, Tulsa, Oklahoma.

in various publications including three leading magazines.[54]

Two prints in the Gilcrease Museum collection depict all three members of the Cherokee delegation. On one print's masthead is "A new humorous song, on the Cherokee Chiefs Inscribed to the Ladies of Great Britain." By H. Howard, it is the only document printed during their time in England (June 16-August 24, 1762) that attempts to identify all three individuals by name.[55]

The second print, "The Three Cherokees, came over from the head of the River Savanna to London, 1762"[56] picks up on a fabricated story by the *St. James Chronicle* that William Shorey, who died at sea, was poisoned by his Cherokee wife who was upset because she was not invited to make the trip to England. The images are composite drawings based heavily on portraits entitled *Four Mohawk Chiefs* by Jan Verelst commissioned by Queen Anne in 1710. It does show one individual in the center wearing a medallion beneath a military-style gorget.

The portraits of the Cherokee diplomats in London in 1762 may be the earliest images of American Indians wearing British portrait medals. Although medals were given to Indians by the British as early as the Seventeenth century, the Anglo-American Peace Medal tradition symbolically important from the mid-1760s until the early 1870s had not yet taken hold. Indian leaders in the Great Lakes area, changing allegiances at the conclusion of the French and Indian War, began demanding replacements for the flags, certificates, and Louis XV medals given to them by the French. An army ensign sent from Fort Detroit to establish relations with Indians around Michilimakinac in 1762 reported that he was asked for medals but had none to give out.[57] Following Pontiac's Revolt in 1763, the English scrambled to meet Indian expectations. At the peace treaties signed in 1764 and 1766 Happy While United medals made in New York City were presented to Indian leaders, but Sir William Johnson privately complained about the quality noting that the prized French medals being exchanged were "finer and thicker."[58] General Thomas Gage promised to seek out "good Engravers at Phila."[59] The medals were being made in the colonies since none were sent from England.

In November 1761, while Ostenaco and four hundred Cherokees were treating with the British at Long Island of the Holston, the great warrior Oconastota was in New Orleans seeking support from the French. He returned to Chota with some gifts, possibly a medal but definitely a military commission signed by the governor of Louisiana, Louis de Kerelec, appointing him *Captaine grand chef medaille de la fond*.[60] No comparable medals were given to the Cherokee treaty signers by the British.

The medallions that were given to the Cherokees in 1762 in London were not the large silver peace medals proclaiming "Happy While United" that were distributed widely by William Johnson and others, but rather they were commemorative medallions produced in quantity for celebrants of royal events. They were not designed to be worn, but the Cherokees found a way to suspend them for public display. For the Cherokee diplomats and British authorities, the commemorative medallions served the same purpose as peace medals and military gorgets in that they were given to symbolize official recognition of Indian leadership, and they were worn as public professions of loyalty to specific monarchs and governments. This is perhaps best illustrated by the medallions in the portrait of Cunne Shote showing the cojoined portraits of King George III and Queen Charlotte and a Proclamation Medallion with a two-word message in exergu–a message that both King George III and Cunne Shote, because of their ancestries, wanted to re-enforce–that they were indeed "Entirely British."

The political instability and resulting warfare of the early 1760s considerably altered

ᎠᏍᏆᏗᎢ 1

Cherokee settlement patterns. Early in the century, Cherokee towns were compact, homogenous entities, with social and political life revolving around the townhouses. By the last quarter of the century, Cherokee towns had become sprawling communities of farmsteads extending for as much as two miles along the bottomlands. Locations of town sites also changed during this period. The Lower Towns, which suffered heavily both from the Creek War in the early 1750s and the Montgomery and Grant expeditions in 1760 and 1761, were almost depopulated by the end of the Revolutionary War.

New traditions were evolving as new challenges appeared on the horizon.

ᎠᏯᏙᎸᎢ 2
ᎾᎢᎧ ᏂᏗᏳᏞᎵ ᏗᏓᏂᏍᏛᎢ
ᎠᏎ ᏗᏞᏣᏙᎩ 1765-1794

Chapter 2: Frontier Contact and Conflict

Figure 1. The Transylvania Purchase, 1775.

By 1770 white settlements had reached the northeast corner of present-day Tennessee along the Watauga, Nolichucky, and Holston Rivers. At that time, expanses of uninhabited land still separated the white settlers from the Cherokees. At the treaty of Sycamore Shoals in March 1775, an aged war chief, reportedly Oconastota, delivered a passionate speech on the plight of the Cherokees.

He began with references to the

flourishing state of the Cherokees before the coming of the whites. He spoke of the continual encroachments by the whites and how nations of Indians had given up the territories of their forefathers so the intruders could have more land. Whole nations had melted away before the whites, he said, "like balls of snow before the sun." Many had left only their names behind, imperfectly recorded by their destroyers. He said the Indians had hoped the whites would not settle beyond the mountains so far from the ocean that connected them with their European homeland. But now that fallacious hope had vanished, and the settlers were encroaching on Cherokee lands. Believing that the whites' desire for land was insatiable, he expressed the fear that the Cherokee territory would be whittled away until nothing was left, and then the Cherokees would be forced to some distant wilderness.[1]

In spite of this ominous warning, the elderly chiefs signed away all the territory between the Cumberland and Kentucky Rivers on March 17, 1775, to the Transylvania Land Company. Two days later, the Watauga settlers purchased the land on which they resided. On March 25 Jacob Brown bought the land on both sides of the Nolichucky River as far west as Big Limestone Creek for a price of ten shillings.[2]

Not all Cherokee leaders favored the sale of tribal lands. Dragging Canoe, unable to prevent the transaction, told Richard Henderson, the head of the land company, "you have bought a fair land, but there is a cloud hanging over it. You will find its settlement dark and bloody."[3] He left the conference embittered and never again attended a land cession treaty with the whites. His cautionary words rang in the ears of frontiersmen for the following twenty years.

Dragging Canoe protested to John Stuart, British superintendent of Southern Indian Affairs. He expressed the fear that the settlers wanted to destroy the Cherokees as a people. He maintained that Chiefs Oconastota, Attakullakulla, and some others were too old to hunt and were forced to sell the land because of their poverty.[4] Since only the Crown had authority to purchase land from the Indians, arrest warrants were issued for the company officials. They, however, quickly retired to the security of their wilderness.[5]

Although both North Carolina and Virginia declared the purchase illegal, no arrests

"ᏕᏥᎦᎸ ᏍᏫ ᏣᎬᏔᎢ, ᎠᏎᏃ ᎤᎧᎠᏎᏗ ᎤᏐᎵᏍᎪᎢ. ᏞᏂᏣᎼᎠ ᏕᎦᎦᎣᎣᏣ ᏧᎵᏏ ᎠᏓ ᏴᏍᎪᎥᎢ." - ᏞᏂᏣ ᏧᎾᏍᎯ

"You have bought a fair land, but there is a cloud hanging over it. You will find its settlement dark and bloody."
- Dragging Canoe

Frontier Contact and Conflict 1765 - 1794

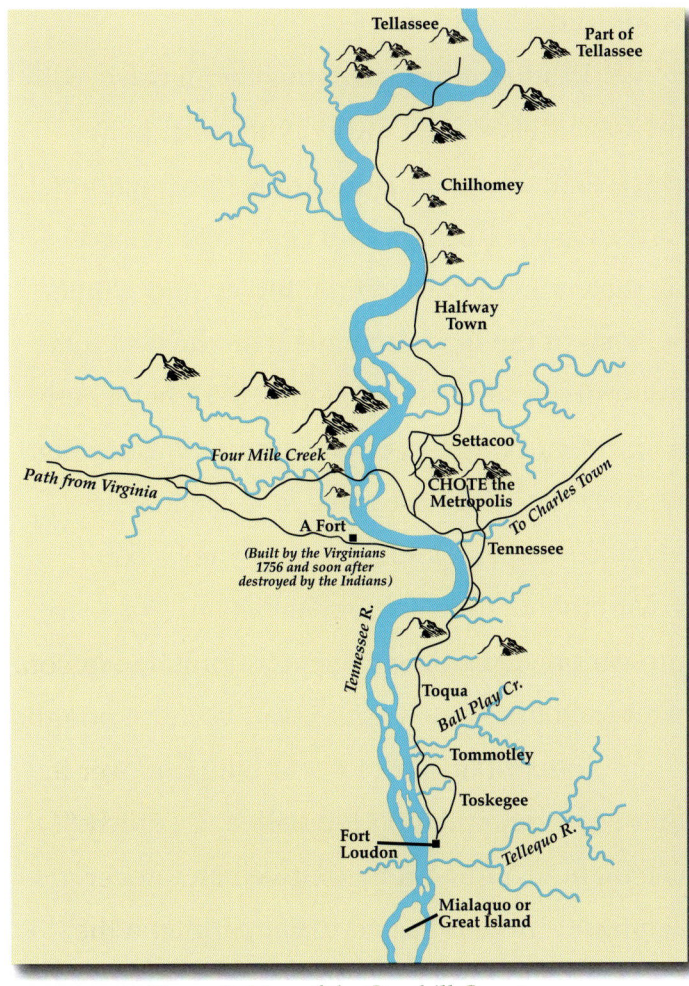

Figure 2. Map of the Overhill Country.

were made, and the agreement was considered binding on the Cherokees. In 1778 the land company was given two hundred thousand acres in each state, a small portion of the purchased land, as a reward for "peaceably extinguishing the Indian title."[6]

Immediately after the purchase, Daniel Boone and a party of workmen set to work cutting the Wilderness Road to "Caintucky." Dragging Canoe and his warriors, however, were determined to prevent the settlement of some of their best hunting grounds. Some of the first settlers were killed by roving war parties. Many others turned back because of the Indian threat. The colonial officials placed an embargo on trade goods destined for the Cherokees.

During this time, lines were being drawn that would lead to the American Revolution. War between whites who spoke the same language seemed incomprehensible to the Cherokees. Their loyalty, however, was with their trusted friend and benefactor John Stuart, now the British superintendent for the southern Indians. Stuart hoped that a war with Wataugans could be avoided and that Cherokee warriors could later supplement British regulars in the southern colonies.

When Henry Stuart, brother of the superintendent, arrived at Chota on April 24, 1776, the Cherokees had been without trade for almost nine months. The twenty-one horse loads of ammunition he brought were a welcome sight for the beleagured Cherokees.[7] They received him "with the greatest marks of Respect, Five Colours were displayed on the Town House, a party of naked and painted was detached from the Main Body with two Drums and Twelve Eagle Tails to meet him at the end of the Square where they danced and told of their War Exploits by Turns."[8]

Afterwards, Stuart and the other British agent present, Alexander Cameron, were escorted by the Beloved Men into the Chota Townhouse. After listening at length to complaints about the encroachment on tribal lands, the agents offered their help as representatives of the government to settle the dispute diplomatically. However, by this time, the lines had already been drawn for the

Dragging Canoe ᏃᎩ ᏣᴓᏜ
(1738 - 1792)

One of the greatest Cherokee warriors of all time was Dragging Canoe. He was raised in one of the Overhill towns on the Little Tennessee River in the 1730s and 1740s. A devastating small pox epidemic swept through the Cherokee Nation while he was a young, killing half of the population and leaving the youngster with deep scars.

He wanted to be a warrior from an early age. When his father told him he could not go on a war party, he hid in a canoe until discovered. His father told him he could go if he could carry the canoe. Although the craft was far too heavy for him to carry, he dragged it along the ground, convincing the warriors that he would be an asset on the war path. Thus, he earned his name, Dragging Canoe.

As the war leader of a town, he attacked scattered American settlements intruding on Cherokee land in 1776. Although defeated, he refused to give up and lead a group of tribal members to the far edge of Cherokee lands to establish towns on Chickamauga Creek, where he was joined by other dissidents who did not want to give up their war on white intruders. In 1788, when an American army attacked his towns, Dragging Canoe and his warriors won the decisive Battle of the Bluffs near Fort Nashborough. Three years later, after negotiating an alliance with the Creeks and Shawnees, his force defeated an American army led by the governor of the Northwest Territory.

Dragging Canoe died in 1792 in the town of Running Water.

American Revolution.

White frontiersmen in general sided with the rebels, especially those living west of the Appalachians in violation of the Proclamation Line of 1763. This boundary line established by the Crown separated the Indian and white subjects at the Appalachians with the hope of minimizing conflicts. Although the Cherokees had difficulty in conceptualizing a war between whites who spoke the same language, their loyalties nevertheless were with the British government, which offered some hope of protection against the ever-mounting tide of white settlers.[9]

John Stuart did not want the Cherokees fighting independently but instead planned to use them to augment regular British forces. The agents at Chota reflected the superintendent's wishes. Cameron wrote to Stuart on May 7, 1776: "I would not willingly have the Indians to commit any hostilities before some of the Kings Troops were actually in Arms in No Carolina So Carolina or Georgia."[10]

Henry Stuart also wrote reassuringly to his brother: "The young men I know will be ready at the first word but to employ them before something effectual can be done may be attended with bad consequences."[11] On May 7, 1776, Alexander Cameron and Henry Stuart wrote to the settlers in Watauga and Nolichucky. The letter contained the Cherokee demand that the whites remove within twenty days and the British offer of free land in present-day West Florida. The reply, which was received ten days

Frontier Contact and Conflict 1765 - 1794

Figure 3. Cherokee Fishermen by Gebon Barnoski. Cherokees were concerned about the encroachment of their rich homelands. Image courtesy of Cherokee Nation Businesses.

later according to Stuart, was "full of professions of Loyalty and promise to move back to their previous homes when times were better." The Cherokees knew the Wataugans were stalling for time. On May 23 Cherokee leaders sent another message to the settlers extending the time for removal by another twenty days.[12]

The young men expressed concern that an army might then be marching toward the Cherokee country. As apprehensions continued to build, a delegation of fourteen Indians from the northern tribes arrived with a Cherokee as interpreter. According to Stuart, they consisted of "some from the Confederate Nations and from the Mohawks, Ottawas, Nantucas, Shawnees, and Delawares." Entering the Chota Townhouse, they were all painted black. They reported that they had been seventy days on their journey. The Ohio Valley, where they formerly had seen nothing but deer and buffalo, was now thickly inhabited by people at arms. At Pittsburgh two thousand men were assembled. At a fort on Cedar River, a tributary of the Ohio, there were fifteen hundred men, and the smaller forts were numerous. The northern delegation told of taking a three hundred mile indirect route to avoid detection.[13]

The Mohawks said that in the spring the Americans invaded one of their towns by surprise, killed many of their people, and took Sir William Johnson's son prisoner. The patriots later killed Johnson by immersing him in boiling tar. The Mohawks said they had received assistance from the British and their old friends the French. They insisted that all Indians on the frontier were now united and prepared to go to war against the common enemy. They scheduled a grand talk to be held ten days after their arrival, and runners were sent to all parts of the Cherokee Nation. Stuart later reported, "After this day every young Fellow's face in the Overhill Towns appeared Blackened, and nothing was now talked of but War. The people of Tellico and the Island were busily employed in preparing spears, clubs, and scalping knives."[14]

Cameron and Stuart continued to try to dissuade the warriors. The older chiefs heeded their advice, but the younger men were growing increasingly impatient. Two days before the Grand Talk was scheduled, the standard of war was erected at Chota, and the flag staff and the support posts of the Townhouse were painted red and black. On the day of the talk, representatives from all parts of the Cherokee Nation assembled. All the warriors from Chilhowie, Settico, and Great Island with three or four exceptions were painted black. Some from all the other towns were blackened. The northern delegates were seated in places of honor in the Townhouse.

The principal Mohawk delegate spoke first. He produced a belt of white and purple wampum and explained the meaning of its design. He reiterated the plight of the Six Nations and the cruel death of the son of Sir William Johnson, their Great Beloved Man. His people, he said, were presently engaged in the fight, and all Indians should turn their eyes and their thoughts one way. Concluding his talk, he presented the war belt to Dragging Canoe.[15]

In turn, the Ottawa, Shawnee, and Delaware delegates spoke. Each produced a beaded war belt with meaningful designs, and the belts in turn were presented to Cherokee war chiefs. The Delaware representative was only a boy. His war belt was about nine feet long and six inches wide of purple wampum tinted with vermilion. He told of the treachery of the Virginians and their cruel treatment of his people. He declared that the Delaware, who only a few years before were a nation of great people, now were reduced to only a handful and that their once vast territory was now only enough land to stand on.

Silence gripped the audience after the speech. At last Ooskwa, or Abram, of Chilhowie, who had lived among the Mohawks and whose wife had lived in the home of Sir William

Frontier Contact and Conflict 1765 - 1794

Figure 4. Cherokee Flute Player *by Daniel HorseChief. Image Courtesy Cherokee Nation Businesses.*

Johnson, rose and took the belt from Dragging Canoe. According to Stuart, Abram "sung the war song and all the Northern Indians joined in the chorus."[16] His example was followed by most of the warriors from the various parts of the Cherokee Nation. The principal chiefs did not oppose the rashness of the spirited young warriors but rather sat dejected and silent, perhaps contemplating the destruction brought on by the vengeful white armies in the 1760 war. When the war belt was passed to Cameron and Stuart, they refused to touch it. This angered some younger warriors who made their feelings known at the war council held at Settico the following day.

As a token of the Cherokees' sincerity, Dragging Canoe gave the Shawnee deputy four scalps of whites recently taken on the Kentucky Road. Three Cherokees accompanied the Shawnees when they left the Overhill Town to carry the talks to the Creeks.[17] The next day, Dragging Canoe, painted black, entered the residence of the British agents at Toqua. He asked Stuart why all the traders were preparing to leave the Nation. Stuart replied that they could not be expected to stay when their lives were in danger.

Two days later, Dragging Canoe ordered all the traders to meet at Cameron's house at Toqua to confer with him and other headmen. According to Stuart, "The Dragging Canoe gave promises for their safety if they staid (sic) in the Nation…that they considered their White People to be the same as themselves; that if any of them inclined to join them in going to war they would be glad but they would not insist on their going but such that did not go to war should bring supplies and ammunition."[18]

The chiefs also asked Stuart to write a letter inquiring about the fate of Isaac Thomas. They would in turn send the letter by scouts to be affixed to some public place near the Watauga settlement. Stuart hesitated because of the criticism of some Cherokees that his earlier letters served only to put the settlers on their guard. Stuart, however, acquiesced on the condition that the letter be dictated to him. The letter informed the settlers that Thomas

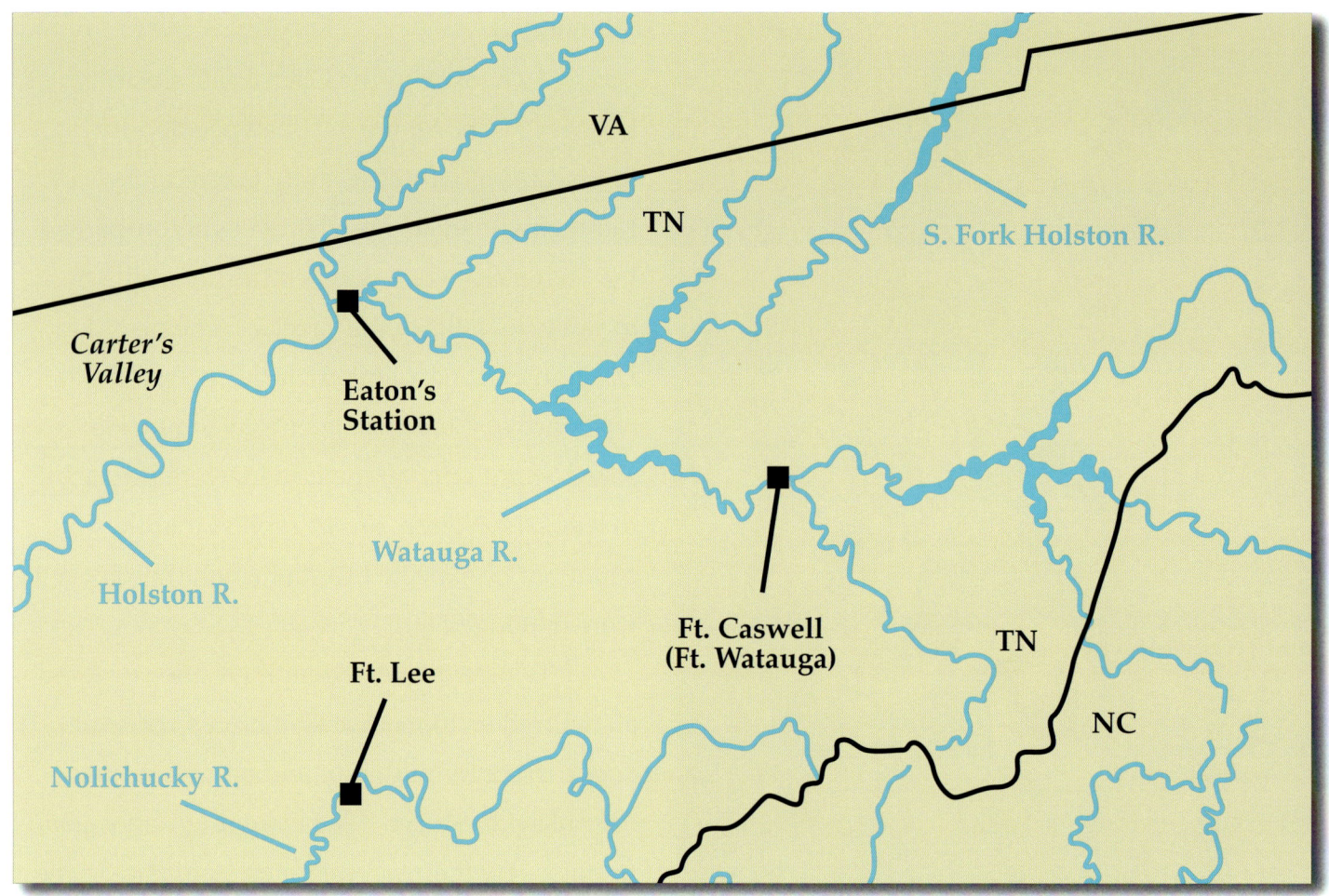

Figure 5. Map of the Cherokee invasion of the Washington District, Pendelton District, and Carter's Valley.

had been sent as courier for the Cherokees with a "very civil message" for them. Challenging the integrity of the Wataugans, the letter stated "that they (the Wataugans) had detained him contrary to what they understood had ever been done among the White People, and that among Indians such a thing was never done in time of War." If Isaac were still alive, they asked that he be sent back immediately, and if he did not return, they asked to be informed of the intentions of the Wataugans.[19]

The letter was reread and approved. The next morning scouts encountered the returning Thomas only a few miles from Toqua. Thomas carried a delayed reply from the Fincastle Committee of Safety to the forged Cameron letter circulated earlier. This letter accused the British agents of provoking a war from the "meanest motives of Interest and Revenge."[20] According to Stuart, the Fincastle talk "so exasperated the Indians that we had little hopes after this of being able to restrain them."[21] Thomas also reported that six thousand armed men were poised on the Virginia and North Carolina frontiers ready to invade the Cherokee country. He also said that a second letter was fabricated in Alexander Cameron's name by Jesse Benton at Watauga. The letter was supposedly left on the door of the Charles Robertson home by a man wrapped in a blanket

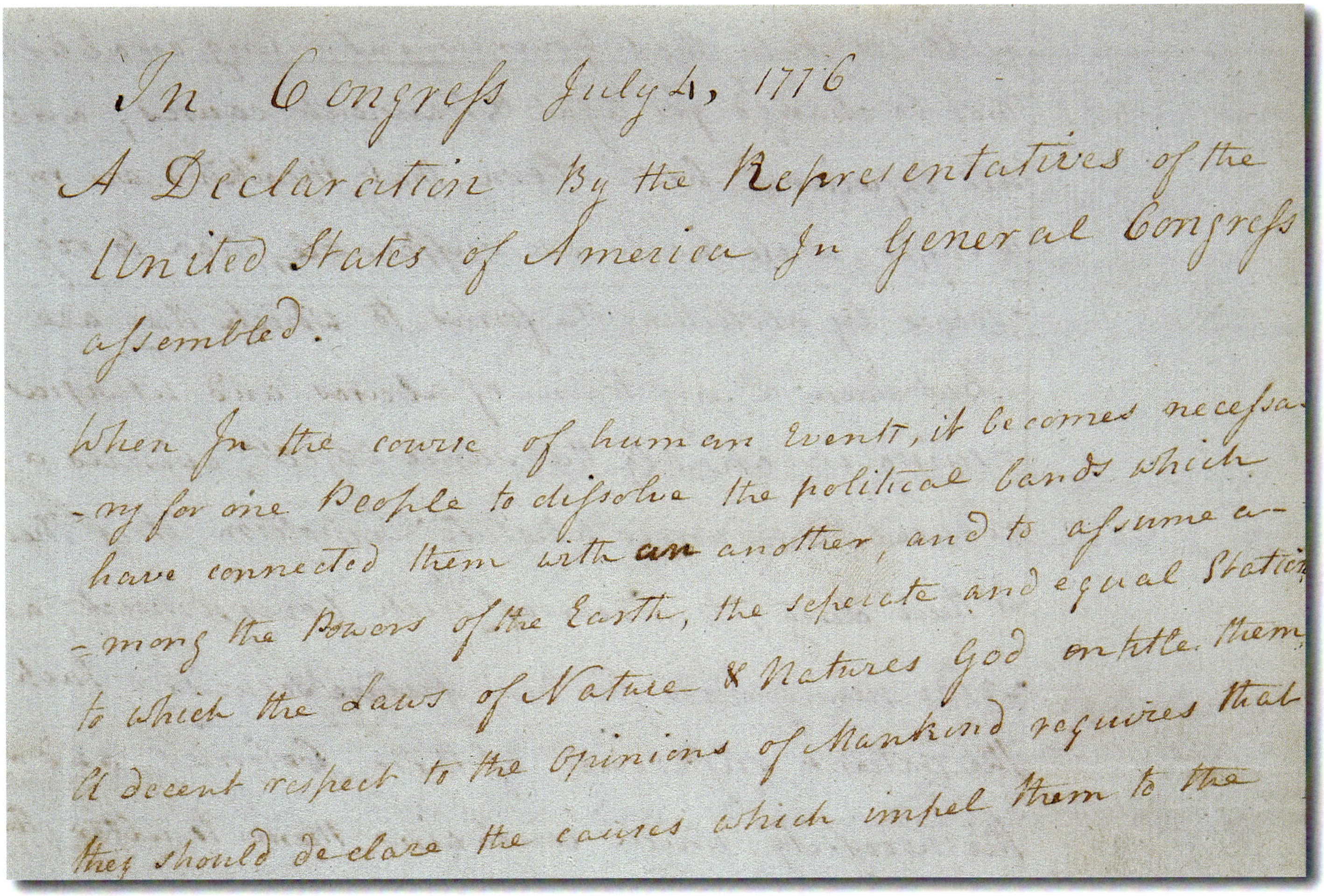

In Congress July 4, 1776
A Declaration By the Representatives of the United States of America In General Congress assembled.

When In the course of human events, it becomes necessa-
-ry for one People to dissolve the political bands which
have connected them with an another, and to assume a-
-mong the Powers of the Earth, the seperate and equal Station
to which the Laws of Nature & Natures God entitle them
A decent respect to the Opinions of Mankind requires that
they should declare the causes which impel them to the

Figure 6. Declaration of Independence 1777. Ink on paper. 9 1/8″ × 7 1/2″ (23.2 × 19.1 cm). GM 4026.901.a. Gilcrease Museum, Tulsa, Oklahoma.

who immediately rode off. The letter said that fifteen hundred Choctaws, Chickasaws, and Creeks along with British regulars from Pensacola and the entire Cherokee Nation were immediately preparing to invade the North Carolina and Virginia frontiers. The letter was forwarded to the governments of both colonies in order to get additional assistance for an invasion of the Cherokee country. When the forged letter was sent to South Carolina, the signature was changed from Cameron to Henry Stuart, who was better known in that area.[22]

A day was appointed for the Great Warrior to address the Nation. He had not yet given his opinion, but the warriors said they would be obliged to abide by his decision, war or peace. The hopes offered that war might yet be prevented were soon diminished. The night before they were to meet, Cherokee leaders received intelligence that the Lower Cherokee Towns had already taken up the hatchet. Inspired by the talks of the northern Indians, they had struck the first blow against the frontier settlements in South Carolina. War was now inevitable. The Chota Council members knew the whites would hold the Cherokee Nation corporately responsible for the actions of the Lower Towns.

On July 8, 1776, a general council of war was held at the Chota Townhouse. At the council, Dragging Canoe outlined the plan of attack, which was to be a three-prong assault against the settlers who had crossed the Proclamation Line of 1763. Abram of Chilhowie would lead three hundred warriors against the Nolichucky and Watauga settlements. Dragging Canoe himself would lead the center prong of 350 warriors against the settlements along the Holston River. And the Raven of Chota with a smaller party would strike Carter's Valley and the north Holston River Valley. They would all attack simultaneously on July 20, 1776.[23]

The Indians believed that there were a number of loyal British subjects in the Nolichucky settlement and wanted to send word to them to assemble themselves and put up a white flag. Nathanial Gist offered to deliver the message if he could get four white men who knew the woods and some Indians to go with him. Tish of Settico, whom Stuart described as a "very sensible Indian," offered himself and his nephew, who was bilingual. Four white men were chosen. The whites were all Virginians who chose to slip away the night before the scheduled departure. After this Stuart wrote: "All white people in the Nation thought the only security they could have was to go out with the Indians. Some went out with the Indians from the Overhills and Middle Settlements, and all the rest offered to accompany Mr. Cameron who was to set in a few days for the Lower Towns."[24]

The last parties of warriors departed from Chota and Toqua on July 12, the same day Stuart left for the Creek country. Isaac Thomas, Jarret Williams, William Faulin, and Isaac Williams, who had fled earlier, warned the frontier settlers that the Cherokees were pounding corn and preparing to march, and that the white men in the nation had shaven and would accompany them.[25]

Much to their surprise, Abram's warriors from Chilhowie, Tellassee, and Settico found the Nolichucky settlements abandoned. Not knowing which of the farmsteads belonged to loyalists and which to the rebels, they left all of the houses and crops intact and proceeded to the Watauga settlements. There they found the settlers assembled in Fort Caswell.[26]

The Holston settlers were also forewarned, and a large number assembled at Eaton's Station about six miles from Long Island. On the afternoon of July 19, a reconnaissance patrol from the fort sighted Dragging Canoe's war party. They quickly returned to the fort and in their excitement greatly exaggerated the number of Indians.

The news that the Cherokees were less than ten miles away created panic at the fort. The six militia captains present argued well into the night about what they should do. Some of the officers favored defending the fort; others wanted to meet with the Cherokees in open combat. Cpt. William Cocke argued that if they remained in the fort, the Cherokees would likely by-pass it and destroy their homes and crops that lay beyond. It was then decided that they would march out of the fort to meet the Cherokees in the morning.[27]

Frontier Contact and Conflict 1765 - 1794

Nancy Ward ᏇᎶᏏᎱ
(ca. 1738 - 1822)

Nancy was born in 1738 in the Cherokee town of Chota. Her mother, Tame Doe of the Wolf Clan, named her Nanye-hi.

When she was seventeen years old, already the mother of two children, Nanye-hi went into a battle beside her husband. When he was killed on the field of action, she picked up a rifle and charged the enemy. Others followed and the Cherokees won a great victory. Out of respect for her bravery and wisdom, the clans gave her the special title of "Beloved Woman."

Nanye-hi married a British trader named Ward, and thus her Angicized name became Nancy Ward, the Beloved Woman of the Cherokees. She chaired the Women's Council, had a seat at the Council of Chiefs, and was in charge of all captives. Occasionally she was called Agi-ga-u-e, or War Woman.

Nancy exerted considerable influence over both her fellow Cherokees and the white settlers who were pushing into the Cherokee domain from all directions. She advocated peace and actively participated in treaty negotiations. In her elderly years, she harbored Cherokee orphans and owned an inn on the Federal Road running through the Cherokee Nation. She died in 1822, the last Beloved Woman of the Cherokee Nation.

Unaware that their presence had been discovered, the Cherokees set up camp near the upper end of Long Island. At daybreak on July 20, 1776, the Cherokees broke camp and started for Eaton's Station. The militia men had left the fort two hours earlier and were coming to meet them. The advanced units of the two opposing forces met a short distance from the island. Shots were exchanged, and the Cherokee scouts withdrew to the main body.

As the militia men listened impatiently to a speech by one of the officers about his past accomplishments and future intentions, Dragging Canoe's warriors broke through the forests to hit the militia rear. The troops scattered on the first fire. At the height of the fighting, the battle line extended more than a quarter of a mile. When the battle was over, the militia men were the victors. Thirteen of Dragging Canoe's warriors lay dead on the field. Others, badly wounded, died later. Both Dragging Canoe and Little Owl, his brother, were wounded but lived to fight again. Some of the warriors, unwilling to return to the Nation in disgrace, headed for the more isolated Virginia settlements in search of scalps.[28]

In the meantime the western contigent under the Raven of Chota split into small parties and swept rapidly through Carter's Valley meeting little resistance. Warriors burned cabins and slaughtered livestock as they went. One of the bands surprised the Reverend Jonathan Mulkey and a friend as they attempted to cross the north fork of the Holston River. Mulkey's companion was knocked down and quickly scalped. Mulkey leaped into the river and was slightly wounded by a rifle shot. He was able, however, to swim to the other side and made his escape in the direction of Eaton's Station. While attention was diverted toward the minister, the scalped man leaped to his feet and bounded away with the speed of a deer. The Cherokees were so astonished that they did not attempt a pursuit. When Mulkey arrived at Eaton's Station, he found much to his surprise that his scalped companion, whom he had given up for dead, had arrived several hours earlier.[29]

After hearing of Dragging Canoe's defeat at Island Flats, Old Abram gave up his two-week seige of Fort Caswell. He returned to the Overhill Towns with only two prisoners, Lydia Bean and a youth named Samuel Moore. His warriors had lifted the scalps of fewer than half dozen stragglers near the Watauga settlement. Samuel Moore was taken to Tuskeegee Town and was burned at the stake. Mrs. Bean was taken to the top of Toqua mound to suffer the same fate; however, she was spared by Nancy Ward exercising her authority as the Beloved Woman.[30]

The Cherokee campaign against the frontier settlers in 1776 was a failure. The fears of the old chiefs that vengeful white armies would march into the Cherokee country were not long in being fulfilled. Within three months of Dragging Canoe's defeat at Island Flats, an army of eighteen hundred Virginians invaded the Overhill Towns, burning to the ground Great Island, Tuskeegee, Chilhowie, and other towns that had participated in the late war.[31]

In North Carolina, Col. Griffith Rutherford with twenty-six hundred militia destroyed the Middle and Out Towns.[32] Colonel Williamson destroyed the towns in South Carolina, and Cpt. Samuel Jack destroyed the Cherokee towns in Georgia.[33] By late fall 1776, the Cherokee Nation was in a state of devastation. The Cherokees sued for peace. At DeWitt's Corner in South Carolina on May 20, 1777, the Lower Cherokees ceded all of their remaining territory in that state except a narrow strip along the western boundary.[34]

The Overhill Cherokees were asked to meet at Long Island of the Holston to conclude a peace with North Carolina and Virginia. The meeting convened in late June with several hundred Cherokees and a large number of white spectators present. The negotiations were held at Fort Patrick Henry opposite the upper end of the island. The fort had been reconstructed from the remnants of Fort Robinson, originally built in 1761 by another Virginia militia preparing for the invasion of Cherokee country.

Both neighboring colonies appointed representatives to treat with the Cherokees. The commissioners for Virginia were Col. William Preston, Col. William Christian, and Col. Evan Shelby. Those for North Carolina were Waightstill Avery, William Sharpe, Robert Lanier, and Joseph Winston. Representing the Cherokees were Corn Tassel (ᎤᏩᏌ), the Raven of Chota (ᎠᏳᎦ), and the aged chiefs Oconastota and Attacullaculla (ᎠᏔᎫᎦᏩ). The interpreter was

Frontier Contact and Conflict 1765 - 1794

John McCormack, a fur trader who had lived among the Cherokees for many years and who had ably served Henry Timberlake as interpreter in 1761.

The last of the Cherokee dignitaries led by Oconastota arrived at the Long Island on June 30 in the company of Col. William Christian. Two days later as both parties were becoming well acquainted with each other with excellent prospects of an early tranquil settlement, a Cherokee youth named Big Bullet was mysteriously murdered. According to one story, he was shot while sitting on a small island between Fort Patrick Henry and the Cherokee camp on Long Island. This version relates that Big Bullet was mending his moccasins when the sound of a discharging musket was heard and that at the same time the young warrior slumped to the ground. Another version says that Big Bullet, at that time fifteen or sixteen years old, had climbed to the top of a tree to witness his father, John McCormack, in his important role as interpreter for the negotiations when he was shot. The Cherokees were so alarmed by the incident that they withdrew immediately suspecting treachery and a possible massacre.

Several days passed before the colonial commissioners could convince the Cherokees that they were not conspirators in the murder and that if the slayer could be found, he would be executed. As proof of their sincerity, they posted a $600 reward for the arrest of the murderer.[35] No arrest was ever made. Robert Young, a member of a notorious frontier family, was considered a prime suspect. His younger brother, Charles, had been killed several months earlier by one of Dragging Canoe's war parties that may have had a personal vendetta against Young for his participation in the death of Big Sawga at the Battle of Island Flats.[36]

On the Fourth of July, the Cherokees finally consented to the meeting. McCormack, who was overcome with grief, was replaced as interpreter by Joseph Vann. That day marked the first anniversary of the Declaration of Independence, and the event was celebrated by a parade and feast. There were many orations

"ᎾᏍᎩᏃ ᏦᎳᎬᎥ ᎠᎠ ᏦᏚᏚᎩ ᎾᎢ ᎠᏂᏂᏴ ᏗᏣᎵᏛ ᎤᏂᏃᏧᏆᏞᏍᏗ ᏦᏟᎦ, ᎠᎠ ᎤᎥᏚᎩ Ꭰᏸ ᏣᎶᎤᏓᏞᎢᎢ, ᎠᏊ ᏦᏦᎩᎩᎤᎢᏢ; ᎠᎢᏦᏗ ᏦᎩᎤᏐᏁᏦᏗ ᏦᎡᏣᎠᏁᏗ ᎯᎢᎡᎾ."

- ᎤᏂᎯᏣᏬ

"The giving up of this territory would spoil the hunting ground of my people, I hope you will consider this, and pity me; you require a thing I cannot do."
- Corn Tassel

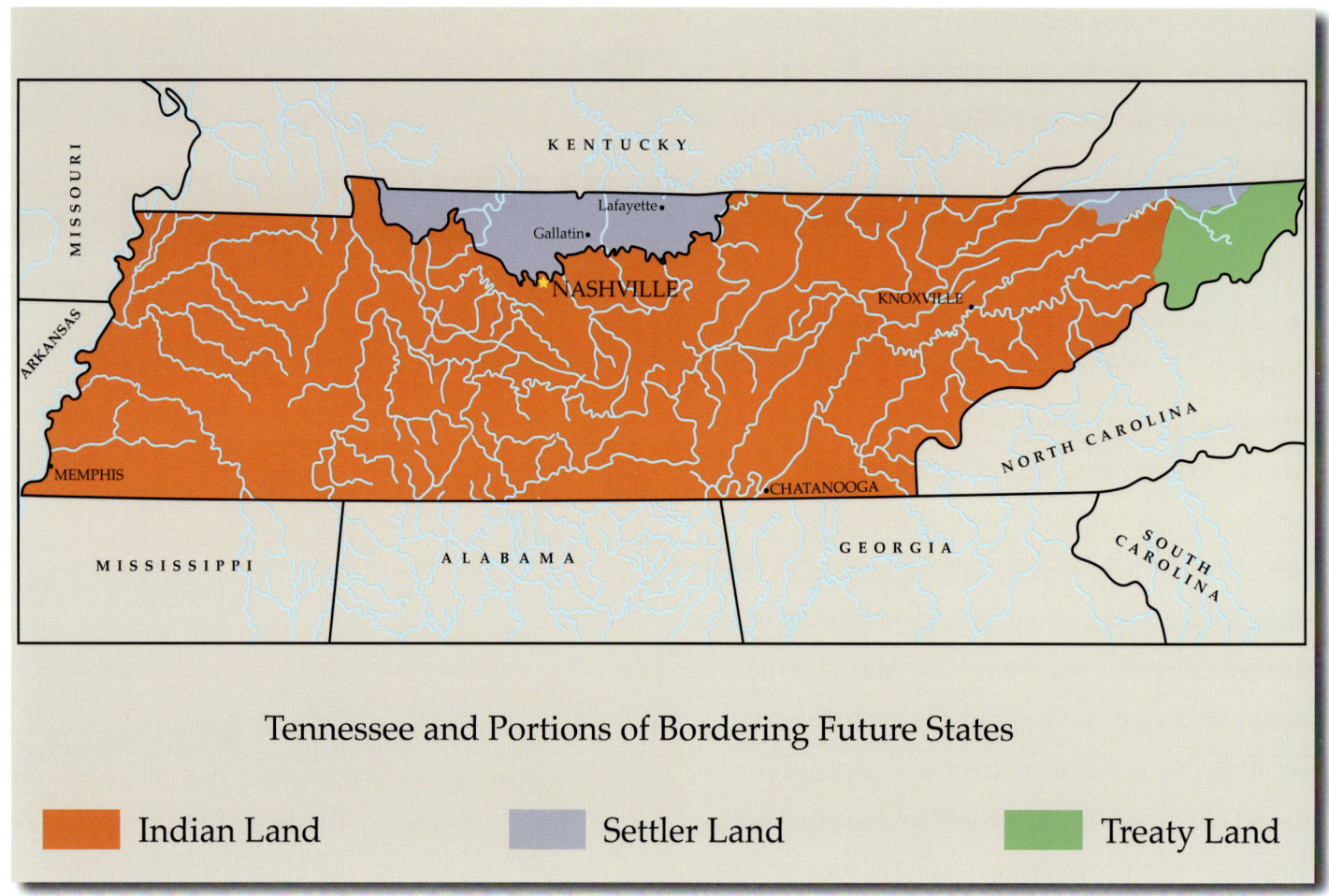

Figure 7. Boundaries of the 1777 Treaty at Long Island of the Holston.

about freedom and patriotism. The Cherokees listened quietly. When it was their turn to talk, they had a message of their own. They never completely trusted the whites and repeatedly made reference to the cowardly murder of Big Bullet. "Big talks" were presented by both sides. The commissioners were deliberate on all questions, allowing the chiefs as much time as they desired. They encouraged the Cherokee leaders to speak their sentiments without reservation, as they were not brought so far from their homes to be silent. The commissioners also expressed regret that Lying Fish and Dragging Canoe, who were considered to be the perpetrators of the most recent hostilities, were not present for the meeting.[37]

The Cherokees' main concern during the negotiations was the request by the colonies for more Cherokee land. On July 17, Corn Tassel expressed the sentiments of the Cherokee leaders indicating surprise at the proposed land cession saying that the Cherokees had not come for that purpose. They had come for peace. He maintained that "if this and another house were packed full of goods, they would not make satisfaction. The giving up of this territory would spoil the hunting ground of my people, I hope you will consider this, and pity me; you require a thing I cannot do."[38]

Giving the commissioners time to think

about this statement, he returned to his quarters to prepare a more eloquent rebuttal to the demands of the whites. William Tatum, who was present at the conference, recorded the English translation of Corn Tassel's speech. Corn Tassel challenged the authority of the whites to demand more land from the Cherokees. He admitted that, "The great God of Nature has placed us in different situations. It is true that he has given you many superior advantages; but he has not created us to be your slaves. We are a separate people! He has given each their lands, under distinct considerations and circumstances; he has stocked yours with cows, ours with buffalo; yours with hog, ours with bear; yours with sheep, ours with deer."[39] Corn Tassel contended that the whites had no right to impose their religion or culture on the Indians and that such a reformation by the Cherokees would not be practical.

When it became apparent that the whites were unyielding and would settle for nothing less than a major land cession, the Cherokees acquiesced from their previous position in the hopes of preserving peace. On July 20 separate treaties were signed with the colonies of Virginia and North Carolina. Article V of the Avery Treaty guaranteed the new line between the Cherokees and the colony of North Carolina as a permanent boundary. The Raven of Chota expressed the hope that the new boundary line would be "as a wall to the skies"[40] so that no one could pass it. His desire was to minimize conflicts between the whites and the Cherokees and to guarantee that no more of their land would be taken.

In spite of the large land cession, the one parcel of land that the Cherokees obstinately refused to yield was the Long Island of the Holston, because it was "their ancient treaty place and where since time out of mind, peace pacts had been made." Before the coming of the whites, the Cherokee had negotiated peace settlements at the Long Island with their northern enemies, the Iroquois and the Shawnee. Adjacent to the signature on both treaties, the following statement was written: "Memorandum before signing: That *The Tassel* yesterday objected against giving up the Great Island, opposite to Fort Henry, to any person or country whatsoever, except National Gist, for whom and themselves, it was reserved by the Cherokees. *The Raven* did the same this day on behalf of the Indians, and desired that Col. Gist might sit down upon it when he pleased, as it belonged to him and them to hold good talks on."[41]

Under the terms of the Long Island Treaty, both the colonies of North Carolina and Virginia appointed agents to the Overhill Cherokees. Joseph Martin was appointed for the colony of Virginia. He took up residence on the lower end of Long Island, and, according to his son, took a Cherokee wife at the same time. For several years, Colonel Martin lived on Long Island with Betsy Ward, the mixed-blood daughter of a South Carolina fur trader named Brian Ward and Nancy Ward, a native of Chota and a member of the Wolf Clan.

Nathaniel Gist, in the years following

the Long Island truce, engaged in military service for the new United States. His tour of duty took him permanently away from the Cherokee country. After the Treaty of Long Island, he believed that the Cherokees meant the land to be a personal gift to him. When he tried to sell it, he encountered other claimants including an old archrival Richard Pearis, who asserted ownership on the basis of a letter from Governor Robert Dinwiddie more than twenty years earlier approving the Long Island trading factory. Joseph Martin, who was living on the island with Betsy Ward at the time, brought the matter to the attention of the governor of Virginia. Patrick Henry wrote to Oconastota for clarification: "Captain Martin who is a good man and friend of your people, also tells me Col. Gist wants to take away this Island at Holston from you. I have desired him to write to me what you and your people say about it, as there is some misunderstanding about it; for Col. Gist says you gave him the ground to do what he would with it. Tell me if you did give it to him or not, & Justice shall be done to both sides.
yr. friend & Brother
P. Henry"[42]

Gist's claim to the Long Island was never recognized. During the war, he commanded Red Stone Fort in Pennsylvania for a while and was later captured by the British in Charleston, South Carolina. After the war, he resided in Virginia and in 1793 moved to Kentucky to develop the seven thousand acres of fine bluegrass land awarded him for services in the American Revolution. He died in 1796 in Kentucky. A quarter of a century later, his son George Gist, or Sequoyah as he would become known, was the first person in five thousand years of recorded history to devise a writing system without first being literate in some language.[43]

By fall 1776, virtually the entire Cherokee Nation was in a state of devastation.[44] Periodic military incursions into the Cherokee Nation continued throughout the war. During the last quarter of the eighteenth century, many Cherokee moved away from the frontier to avoid conflict with encroaching white settlers. New settlements were established along Chickamauga Creek near present-day Chattanooga. Eleven of those towns were destroyed by an expedition led by Col. Evan Shelby in April 1779.[45] The Chickamaugas, as they had become known, moved farther west and established the Lower Towns near the present Tennessee-Alabama state line. The five Lower Towns of Running Water, Nickajack, Long Island, Crow Town, and Lookout Mountain soon became the center of marauding activities against frontier settlements. By 1784 the Lower Towns had a population equal to that of the Upper Settlements on the Little Tennessee.[46] Gradual migrations continued to depopulate Cherokee settlements closest to the white frontier. Towns along the Little Tennessee River, the Cherokee political power base of the mid-eighteenth century, were virtually abandoned by the end of the century.

In 1785 the first treaty between the Cherokee and the US government was signed at

Frontier Contact and Conflict 1765 - 1794

Figure 8. Stickballer by Gebon Barnoski. Image Courtesy Cherokee Nation Businesses.

Hopewell, South Carolina. Shortly thereafter, a few families, dissatisfied with the terms of the treaty, became the first Cherokee emigrants to settle west of the Mississippi River. In dugout canoes, they descended the Tennessee, Ohio and Mississippi Rivers to the mouth of the Saint Francis River in present-day Arkansas. From there they traveled up the Saint Francis and selected homesites in the fertile fields along its banks. A few years later, they moved to a more satisfactory location on the White River.[47]

In the late 1780s and early 1790s, the Spanish received a number of Cherokee requests for permission to emigrate to Spanish Territory west of the Mississippi.[48] In May 1788, Toquo, also known as Turkey, petitioned Don Manuel Perez, governor of Spanish Illinois residing in Saint Louis, to grant him the favor of giving refuge to his whole nation in the territory of the Great King of Spain. Esteban Miro, commandant general of Louisiana, approved emigration of up to six villages.[49] Reports of Cherokee settlers in the vicinity of New Madrid were frequent during this period.[50]

With most of the older towns destroyed, Dragging Canoe and his followers withdrew to the Chattanooga area and continued their forays against the frontier settlements throughout the 1780s and early 1790s. Repeatedly, frontier armies were raised and sent against the Cherokees. By 1784 the Chickamaugas had a population "equal to that of the Upper settlements on the Little Tennessee."[51] Gradually, Cherokees moved away from the white frontier in easternTennessee. In 1788, after several peace chiefs including Old Tassel, Old Abram, and Abram's son were murdered under a flag truce, the Cherokees moved their capital from Chota to Ustanali, near the present-day Calhoun, Georgia.[52]

Cherokee politics of this period was dominated by the continual struggle with the settlers. Marauding war parties terrorized the frontier. War chiefs such as Bloody Fellow,

Doublehead, Bob Benge, and John Watts rose to prominence. The Cherokees, trying desperately to maintain their territorial boundaries, sought help from various Indian allies and European powers.

For nearly two decades from 1776 to 1794, the Chickamauga Cherokee sought to defend their territorial boundaries militarily while at the same time attempting to gain recognition of their remaining land base through treaties. The Spanish Territory provided a temporary respite for some of those engaged in the conflict. In April 1794, eighteen Cherokee families crossed the Mississippi River and pledged allegiance to Spanish authorities, offering scalps taken from settlements on the Cumberland River.[53] A short time later, *The Boston Gazette* published an article condemning the marauding Cherokees living at Cape Girardeau and the Spaniards who protected them.[54]

On June 11, 1794, a party of settlers, led by William Scott and his two nephews James and John Pettigrew, passing down the Tennessee River were overwhelmed near Muscle Shoals by 150 warriors. All aboard the two boats were killed except for twenty-two black slaves. According to later testimony of John W. Hunt, a trader living among the Chickamaugas, the leaders of the attack were Unacata (Unegadihi - White Killer), Connetoo, Leed, Terrapin, and Will Webber.

In response, an army consisting of 550 mounted infantry commanded by Maj. James Ore was raised from the Cumberland River and southern Kentucky region. On September 13, 1794, they destroyed Running Water and Nickajack towns, killing about seventy Cherokees.[55] A letter from the Spanish governor in Pensacola dated July 14, 1794, urging the Cherokee to make peace with the Americans was found in the coat pocket of Chief Breath, who was killed at Nickajack. On August 20, 1794, the Cherokee's northern allies were defeated at the Battle of Fallen Timbers by Gen. Anthony Wayne. With their most important towns destroyed and no assistance from their allies, the Cherokees had no choice except to sue for peace.[56]

The restoration of diplomatic relations brought increased pressure for the return of the slaves and cargo from Scott's and Pettigrew's boats and the punishment of those responsible. To avoid U.S. jurisdiction, eight or nine families led by Connetoo, Will Webber, Unacata, and a few young men who had participated in the Muscle Shoals attack fled to the Spanish Territory in 1796.[57] They first went to Arkansas Post and applied to the Quapaw Indians for permission to settle above them on the Arkansas River. The Quapaws denied the request. The Spanish governor of Louisiana informed the Cherokee that they could settle and hunt on the Saint Francis River.[58]

Defeated in battle and pressed from their ancestral homes, the Cherokee people were caught in the vortex of a rapidly changing frontier.

ᎠᏯᏙᎳᏗ 3
ᏃᎰᏴᏃ ᏣᎳᎩ ᏍᏓᏍᏯ ᎤᎵᎨᏫᏓᎸᎢ
1794-1828

Chapter 3: Rise of the Cherokee State

Figure 1. Springplace, the home of James Vann, who welcomed missionaries to teach school. Image from Wikipedia user Thomson200 under Creative Commons public domain dedication license.

The first quarter of the nineteenth century was a time of great social change for the Cherokees. The degree of acculturation was such that the lifestyle of the Cherokees closely paralleled that of southern whites. Clear-cut social classes began to emerge. Attitudes toward education and commerce became very progressive.

In the 1790s, the Cherokee political and societal structures began transformations to better facilitate external relations. In 1793 they established a central government formalizing the titles of principal chief and deputy chief. A national police force, called the Light Horse, was established in 1798. The first schools opened in the Cherokee Nation in 1801 at Springplace, and Christian missionaries were welcomed as long as their primary focus was academics instead of religion. Also in 1801 Black Fox (ᎤᏛᎵ) was named by the Council of Chiefs of the Lower and Upper Towns to succeed Little Turkey as principal chief of the original Cherokee Nation.[1] The majority of Cherokees at that time lived in the Lower Towns. They were more isolated from European-American contact and tended to be more conservative, maintaining traditional practices and language.

During his term in office, Black Fox was the leading negotiator for the Cherokee people with the US federal government. He is noted for relinquishing nearly seven thousand square miles (eighteen hundred square kilometers) of land in what is today Tennessee and Alabama (under the treaty of January 7, 1806), for which he was given a lifetime annuity of $100. A controversial leader, Black Fox was deposed for a period, only to later be reinstated as principal chief in a compromise between two regional factions of Cherokees.

The National Council abrogated the traditional law of blood revenge for all crimes except horse stealing in 1810. In 1817 it established a bicameral legislature patterned after the US Senate and House of Representatives. The Cherokee Nation was divided into eight judicial districts in 1819 and created the mechanisms to govern the districts. The Cherokee established a supreme court ten years before the State of Georgia had one. They adapted the southern concept of "states rights" to their own notions of tribal sovereignty.[2] When the Moravian missionary Albert Steiner returned to the Cherokee Nation in 1820 after his initial visit in 1801, he was surprised by the progress he witnessed. In a letter to John Calhoun, he deemed them "the most advanced in civilization of any of the Indian tribes without exception."[3]

The Cherokees established a constitutional government in 1827 and a national bilingual newspaper called the *Cherokee Phoenix* in 1828. An effort was also made to found a national museum at New Echota. However, the repressive laws passed by the state of Georgia in 1828 and 1829 greatly restricted public activities in the Cherokee Nation.

Despite the unifying institutions that mirrored those of neighboring white communities, the Cherokee people were being split both politically and geographically. Indian Agent Benjamin Hawkins reported in 1801 that the Cherokee settlement in Arkansas had one hundred gunmen.[4] In 1802 there were sixty Cherokee families living on the Saint Francis River. In a confidential message to Congress, dated January 18, 1803, President Thomas Jefferson suggested the desirability of removing tribes west of the Mississippi River.[5] The following year Congress appropriated $15,000 for that purpose.[6] In 1804 Meriwether Lewis, leading an expedition into the newly acquired territory for the United States, observed that the two large Cherokee towns on the Saint Francis could raise 250 warriors.[7] In November 1805, Chief Connetoo stated that the Cherokee population on the Saint Francis was then six hundred persons.

In the early months of 1806, more Cherokee arrived from the East and they brought with them between three hundred to four hundred horses and even more cattle. John Treat, appointed Indian agent at Arkansas Post in 1805, proclaimed the Cherokee to be the only people in Arkansas "who appear to have made or are desirous of making any great proficiency in civilization." On January 7, 1806, Doublehead, Tohluntuskee (ᎠᏊᎶᏍᎨᏯ), and others accepted private reservations in exchange for ceding ten million acres of tribal land to the United States. Doublehead was killed in June 1807 for his part in the treaty and other participants such as Tohluntuskee and Tuwali (ᏆᎬᏞ the Bowl) subsequently emigrated to Arkansas. In 1807 and 1808, large numbers of Cherokees emigrated as President Jefferson's resettlement policy was inaugurated.[8]

In January 1809, President Jefferson addressed a "talk" to the Lower Cherokee and authorized a delegation to visit Arkansas, promising that if a desirable location for their settlement might be found that the government would assign land and pay transportation costs. Agent Return J. Meigs later reported that large numbers, perhaps two thousand, signified their willingness to relocate. The United States was not prepared to defray the expenses of such a large migration at that time, and Meigs was instructed to discourage anything but the removal of individual families.[9]

By 1809 there were six Cherokee towns scattered along the Arkansas Post-Missouri road bordering Crowley's Ridge west of the Saint Francis River.[10] Connetoo, who emigrated to Arkansas with only ten Cherokee families in 1796, complained to Agent Meigs in June 1811 that he had been followed by so many other Cherokee that now "I am too much crowded."[11] Connetoo went on to say, "We do not intend to Get our Living intirely (sic) by hunting, but we still adhere to your advise, and follow farming, our Women Spin and Weave almost all the Clotheing (sic) We wear, Blankets excepted."[12] Kiamee, another Arkansas Cherokee chief, responding to Meigs's inquiries in 1811 reported, "We have good corn fields. We have plenty of Cattle and Hogs. We have plenty of Buffaloe (sic) and Deer."[13]

Between December 1811 and February 1812, the Saint Francis River valley, close to the epicenter of the New Madrid earthquake, was rocked by three massive earthquakes and hundreds of intermittent aftershocks. Although few people were killed, the landscape was vastly altered. Reelfoot Lake was created in northwest Tennessee. In the Saint Francis River valley, changes in elevation drained previously existing lakes and turned fertile farms into

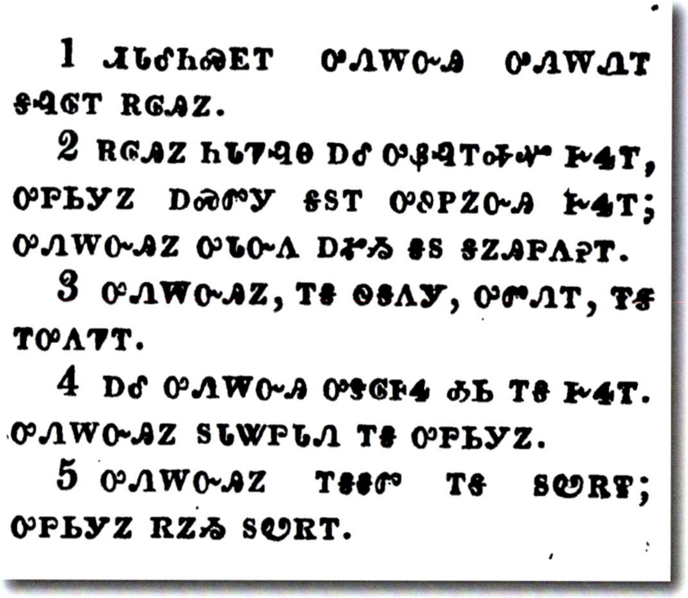

Figure 2. First Ever Printing of Cherokee Syllabary in December 1827 from the Book of Genesis. Verses 1–5 appeared in the American Board of Commisioners for Foreign Missions newsletter. Image Courtesy Cherokee Nation Language Program.

swamps. A newspaper report of an event in December 1811 stated that seven Cherokees had been "swallowed into the earth's bowels by a yawning crevasse." One Cherokee was lucky enough to escape having been spit out by rising water. He had to wade and swim four miles to reach dry land.[14]

Both the Cherokees and the whites in the area believed that the earthquakes reflected supernatural displeasure with human behavior. Many whites believed they were witnessing the apocalypse. The Cherokee believed the quakes were associated with Tecumseh, a Shawnee leader who before the quakes warned that harm would come to Indians who strayed from the true path and polluted traditional culture with white influences.[15] Tecumseh's attempt to create a confederacy of tribes from the Great Lakes to the Gulf of Mexico to halt the tide of white settlement was thwarted by the lack of Cherokee support.

In June 1812, Skaquaw (ᏍᎧᏆ the Swan), a Cherokee prophet at Crowtown, foretold of even greater destruction if the Cherokee should remain on the Saint Francis River. American naturalist Louis Bringier, present at the time, reported that "the result of these prophesies was the total evacuation of the St. Francis River. Within two or three months, all the Cherokees abandoned their farms, (some were very good ones) their cattle, and other property and removed, some to the White River, and the greatest part to the Arkansas."[16] Chief Connetoo may have been among the last to leave. In March 1813, Tahlonteskee wrote to Agent Meigs, "The Cherokees have now left the ponds and reachd (sic) the dry land and settled among the mountains. I now call on you hastily for a good place to build my houses. For two years I stood in water with patience. I remained in that situation until my feet got cold."[17]

The Cherokee Nation rejected Tecumseh's overtures to create an Indian confederacy. In autumn 1813, a hostile faction of Upper Muscogee-Creek Indians known as the "Red Sticks" joined Tecumseh's fight against white encroachment on Indian land. The Cherokees and Creeks loyal to the United States joined local and state militia to quell the rebellion. Able bodied men from across the Cherokee Nation enlisted. In October 1813, John Ross entered military service in Captain Sekekee's (ᏏᎨᎩ Katydid) company of mounted Cherokees with the rank of second Lieutenant under the

Rise of the Cherokee State 1794 - 1828

Figure 3. Gathering Pokeberries *by Virginia Stroud. Cherokees maintained many elements of their daily lives despite all the changes around them. Image Courtesy of Cherokee Nation Businesses.*

command of Col. Gideon Morgan.

In January 1814, the Cherokee regiment trained in military discipline, weapons firing, and hand-to-hand combat at Ross's Landing. At the beginning of the year, Gen. Andrew Jackson began assembling his forces at Fort Strother on the Coosa River below Turkeytown. At the same time, the Creeks had amassed a force of twelve hundred warriors at the Horseshoe, a bend in the Tallapoosa River fifty miles south of Fort Strother. By mid-March Jackson's forces had reached their maximum strength of nearly five thousand men, mostly Tennessee and Kentucky militia, but also the Thirty-Ninth U.S. Infantry, some friendly Creeks, and the Cherokee Regiment of 335 men.[18]

Menawa, the Creek commander, ordered the building of a massive stockade across the neck of the bend in the Tallapoosa River. Jackson's strategy was to launch a frontal assault on the barricade across the narrow part of the Horseshoe. When the battle was over, the Americans had lost twenty-six killed and 106 wounded. The Cherokees, who made up less than 10 percent of Jackson's forces, had eighteen killed and thirty-five wounded. For the Creeks, the battle was a crushing defeat with nearly eight hundred killed. Only a few Creek warriors including Menawa were able to escape the carnage.[19]

Two weeks after the battle, Ross ended his brief military career, perhaps contemplating the obvious lessons: no tribe could withstand the military power of the United States. The reward for armed resistance was annihilation. Perhaps a third lesson was to the victor goes the spoils.

By the Treaty of Fort Jackson, signed August 9, 1814, the defeated Creeks ceded twenty-three million acres of land and fixed

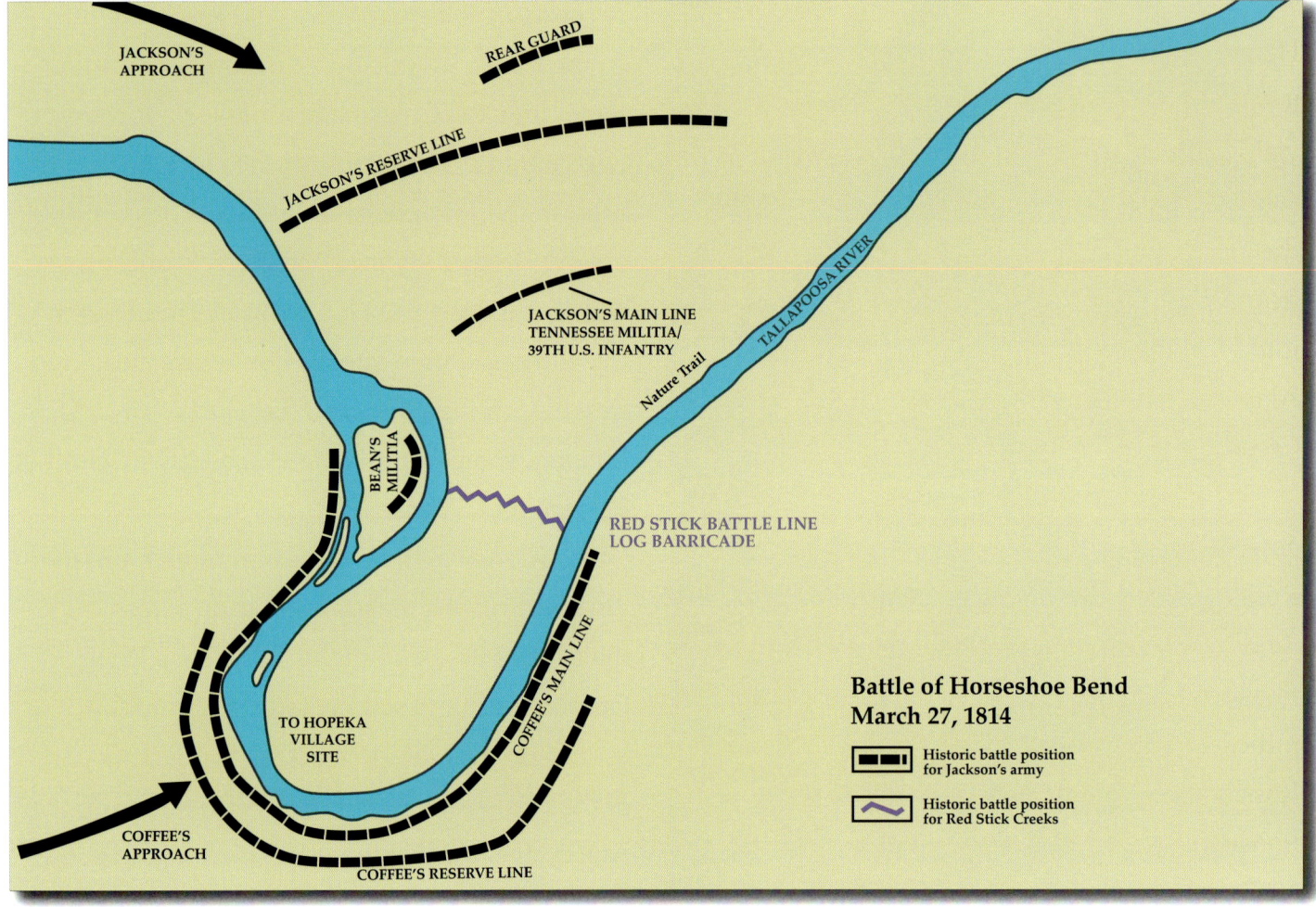

Figure 4. Battle of Horseshoe Bend.

the Creek-Cherokee boundary in favor of the Cherokees. The next nine documents written in 1815 and 1816 related to the reaffirmation of the new boundary between the Cherokees and Creeks.[20]

In 1816 the National Council named John Ross to his first delegation to Washington DC. The delegation of 1816 was directed to resolve the sensitive issues of national boundaries, land ownership, and white intrusions on Cherokee land. The instructions from Principal Chief Path Killer (ᎤᏔᎷᎻ) to the delegation included delivering claims against the East Tennessee settlers who plundered Cherokee farmsteads on their way home from the war. A letter from delegate John Lowry to President James Madison, dated February 19, 1816, also asked that Cherokees be treated the same as white soldiers.[21]

Of the delegates, only Ross was fluent in English, making him the central figure in the negotiations. This was a unique position for a young man in Cherokee society, which traditionally favored older leaders. Madison agreed with the Cherokee delegation that their veterans should be treated the same as white soldiers in regard to pensions for killed and wounded. Jackson protested, and he also did not want the Cherokee-Creek boundary redrawn. He was angry with the president for acceding to Cherokee wishes, proclaiming "I will not yield with a pen, what I have gained with a sword." In the meantime, Cherokees escaping the lawlessness of the Tennessee-Carolina frontier continued to move south and west into northwestern Georgia and northeastern Alabama onto lands formerly occupied by the Creeks.[22]

It has been widely reported and generally accepted that the only surviving home of John Ross in Georgia was built by his grandfather John McDonald in 1797 and occupied by John Ross as early as 1808. Recent evidence would indicate a much later date.[23] The writings of John Ross suggest that he moved to the Rossville house in 1817 or 1818. Ross's letters dated April 1817 are from Poplar Spring, Cherokee Nation.[24] In December 1818, Ross gives his return address as Rossville, Cherokee Nation.[25] From dendrochronology studies, most of the logs in the house were cut during winter 1816-17 and this corresponds to earliest historical records for the home.[26] This is significant because if the house was actually built a year after the logs cut in winter 1816-17 had time to season,[27] then it was probably built by John Ross, who lived there for nearly a decade until the spring or summer 1827.[28]

Farther to the west in Arkansas, Cherokee Agent Meigs reported that difficulties had arisen between the Cherokees and two groups that claimed the land where they had settled. In 1816

Figure 5. Menawa commanded the Creeks at Horseshoe Bend. Image Courtesy of the Oklahoma Historical Society.

the Osage claimed the land on the north side of the Arkansas River, and the Quapaw claimed the land on the south side. When the Arkansas Cherokees presented their complaints to federal authorities, they were told nothing could be done until the main body of Cherokees ceded land in the East equal to the area on which the emigrant party had located.[29] By 1817 between two thousand and three thousand Cherokees resided in Arkansas.[30]

The treaty of 1817 ceded two tracts of land in the East in exchange for a equal-sized but yet unsurveyed parcel of land between the Arkansas and White Rivers where most of the

Cherokee emigrants lived. The treaty was signed on July 18, 1817, and US officials, presuming ratification, immediately took measures to effect additional emigration. Within a month, Agent Meigs reported that more than seven hundred Cherokees had enrolled for emigration in the fall. A Cherokee delegation in Washington DC advised the secretary of war that the number of Cherokee emigrants in Arkansas was not higher than thirty-five hundred and they estimated the number remaining in the East adverse to removal to be about 12,544. Federal officials estimated the number of Cherokee in Arkansas by 1819 had increased to six thousand.[31]

The eastern boundary of the new Cherokee territory in Arkansas was surveyed by Gen. William Rector and certified by him on April 14, 1819, showing the length of the line from Point Remove Creek to the White River as seventy-one miles, fifty-five chains on the course north fifty-three degrees east.[32] The difficulty in determining the western boundary arose from the fact the western Cherokees were to receive an amount of land equal to that ceded in the East under the treaties of 1817 and 1819. The reports on surveys in North Carolina, Tennessee, and Georgia were not completed until early 1823. Government officials eventually determined that the Arkansas Cherokee were entitled to 4,282,216 acres. In January and February 1825, a provisional line parallel to the eastern boundary was run from the upper end of Table Rock Bluff on the Arkansas River northeast 132 miles to the White River where it struck a point opposite the mouth of the Little North Fork.[33]

In 1821 Sequoyah devised the syllabary that expedited the Cherokee Nation's rise as a political state. The acceptance of Sequoyah's syllabary facilitated effective communication on paper in the Cherokee language. Within a matter of months, the Cherokee Nation had a higher literacy rate than its white neighbors. Laws could be written in Cherokee. In 1827 the Cherokees adopted a constitutional form of government. On February 21, 1828, the *Cherokee Phoenix* made its debut as the first national bilingual newspaper in the United States.[34]

Rising in stature with the structure of Cherokee government was the political career of John Ross. His first political position came in November 1817 with the formation of the National Council. He was elected to the thirteen-

"Ꮈ ᏛᎵᏍᏞᎩᏏ ᎤᎠᏴ ᎷᎠᏯᎬᎢ ᎬᎳᎣᏱ, ᎢᏣᎯᎢ ᎠᏯᏂ-ᏉᎥᏊ ᎠᎦᎳᏯᎢ ᏍᏅᎯᏝ ᎬᎳᎣᏱ."

- ᏙᎩᏯᏏ

"I will not yield with a pen, what I have gained with a sword."
- Andrew Jackson

Rise of the Cherokee State 1794 - 1828

Figure 6. Elias Boudinot, first editor of the Cherokee Phoenix. *Image courtesy of the Oklahoma Historical Society.*

member body, where each man served two-year terms. The National Council was created to consolidate Cherokee political authority after General Jackson made two treaties with small cliques of Cherokees representing minority factions. Membership in the National Council placed Ross among the ruling elite of the Cherokee leadership. In November 1818, on the eve of the National Council meeting with Cherokee agent Joseph McMinn, Ross was elevated to the presidency of the National Committee. He held this position through 1827. The council selected Ross because they perceived him to have the diplomatic skill necessary to

Figure 7. Sequoyah *by Daniel HorseChief. Sequoyah was inventor of the Cherokee syllabary. Image courtesy of Cherokee Nation Businesses.*

rebuff US requests to cede Cherokee lands.

In May 1827, Ross was elected to the twenty-four-member constitutional committee, which drafted a constitution calling for a

The Cherokee Syllabary

Sequoyah developed the syllabary between 1809 and 1821. While it is often referred to as an alphabet, it is actually a syllabic writing system. This means that each symbol represents its own syllable sound, such as ka / Ꭷ, tsi / Ꮵ, or di / Ꮧ, for example. In addition to the syllables, Sequoyah also invented characters for the six different vowel sounds in the Cherokee language–D, R, T, Ꭳ, Ꭴ, and i sounds (a, e, i, o, u, and v respectively). Sequoyah originally designed over ninety different characters but as he refined the system, the number of them was reduced to eighty-six.

Sequoyah first developed a handwritten cursive version of the syllabary as seen in Figure 8. The writing evolved between 1821 and 1827 as the Cherokee Nation prepared to adapt the syllabary for the printing press. The cursive version did not become widely

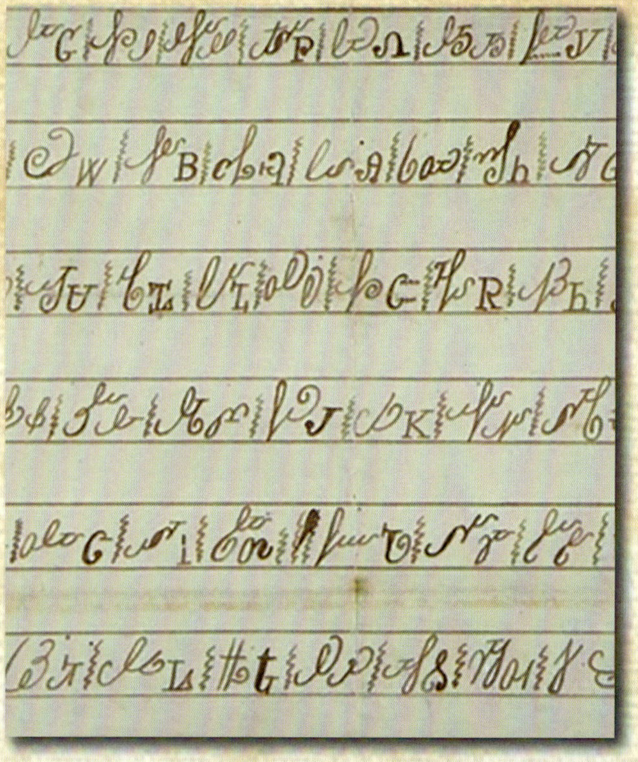

Figure 8. Sequoyah's Hand Syllabary (detail). Ink on paper. GM 4926.4488. Gilcrease Museum, Tulsa, Oklahoma.

Ꭰ a	Ꭱ e	Ꭲ i	Ꭳ o	Ꭴ u	Ꭵ v
Ꭶ ga Ꭷ ka	Ꭸ ge	Ꭹ gi	Ꭺ go	Ꭻ gu	Ꭼ gv
Ꭽ ha	Ꭾ he	Ꭿ hi	Ꮀ ho	Ꮁ hu	Ꮂ hv
Ꮃ la	Ꮄ le	Ꮅ li	Ꮆ lo	Ꮇ lu	Ꮈ lv
Ꮉ ma	Ꮊ me	Ꮋ mi	Ꮌ mo	Ꮍ mu	Ᏽ mv
Ꮎ na Ꮏ hna Ꮐ nah	Ꮑ ne	Ꮒ ni	Ꮓ no	Ꮔ nu	Ꮕ nv
Ꮖ qua	Ꮗ que	Ꮘ qui	Ꮙ quo	Ꮚ quu	Ꮛ quv
Ꮜ sa Ꮝ s	Ꮞ se	Ꮟ si	Ꮠ so	Ꮡ su	Ꮢ sv
Ꮣ da Ꮤ ta	Ꮥ de Ꮦ te	Ꮧ di Ꮨ ti	Ꮩ do	Ꮪ du	Ꮫ dv
Ꮬ dla Ꮭ tla	Ꮮ tle	Ꮯ tli	Ꮰ tlo	Ꮱ tlu	Ꮲ tlv
Ꮳ tsa	Ꮴ tse	Ꮵ tsi	Ꮶ tso	Ꮷ tsu	Ꮸ tsv
Ꮹ wa	Ꮺ we	Ꮻ wi	Ꮼ wo	Ꮽ wu	Ꮾ wv
Ꮿ ya	Ᏸ ye	Ᏹ yi	Ᏺ yo	Ᏻ yu	Ᏼ yv

Figure 9. Modern day chart of all 86 syllabary characters. Image courtesy of the Cherokee Nation Language Program.

adopted, but elements of the original designs would carryover into the syllabary typeset. Based on modifications to the characters as directed by Sequoyah, George Lowery, and Samuel Worcester, Cherokee Nation worked with the Baker and Greele Foundry in Boston to cast the Cherokee syllabary into typeset for printing. These shapes would be the basis for Cherokee writing that would be used for generations to come. The invention and use of the syllabary resulted in Cherokees having much higher rates of literacy in comparison to their non-Indian neighbors.

Over one million pages of Cherokee text were printed from the first printing of the *Cherokee Phoenix* in February 1828 up until Oklahoma statehood. Despite the shutting down of Cherokee Nation government print operations in 1907, Cherokees continued using the syllabary throughout the twentieth century for everyday correspondence, record keeping, and other literary pursuits. A new wave of language revitalization led to the syllabary being adapted to modern forms of digital media, and the tribe continues publishing in the langauge today online and in print.

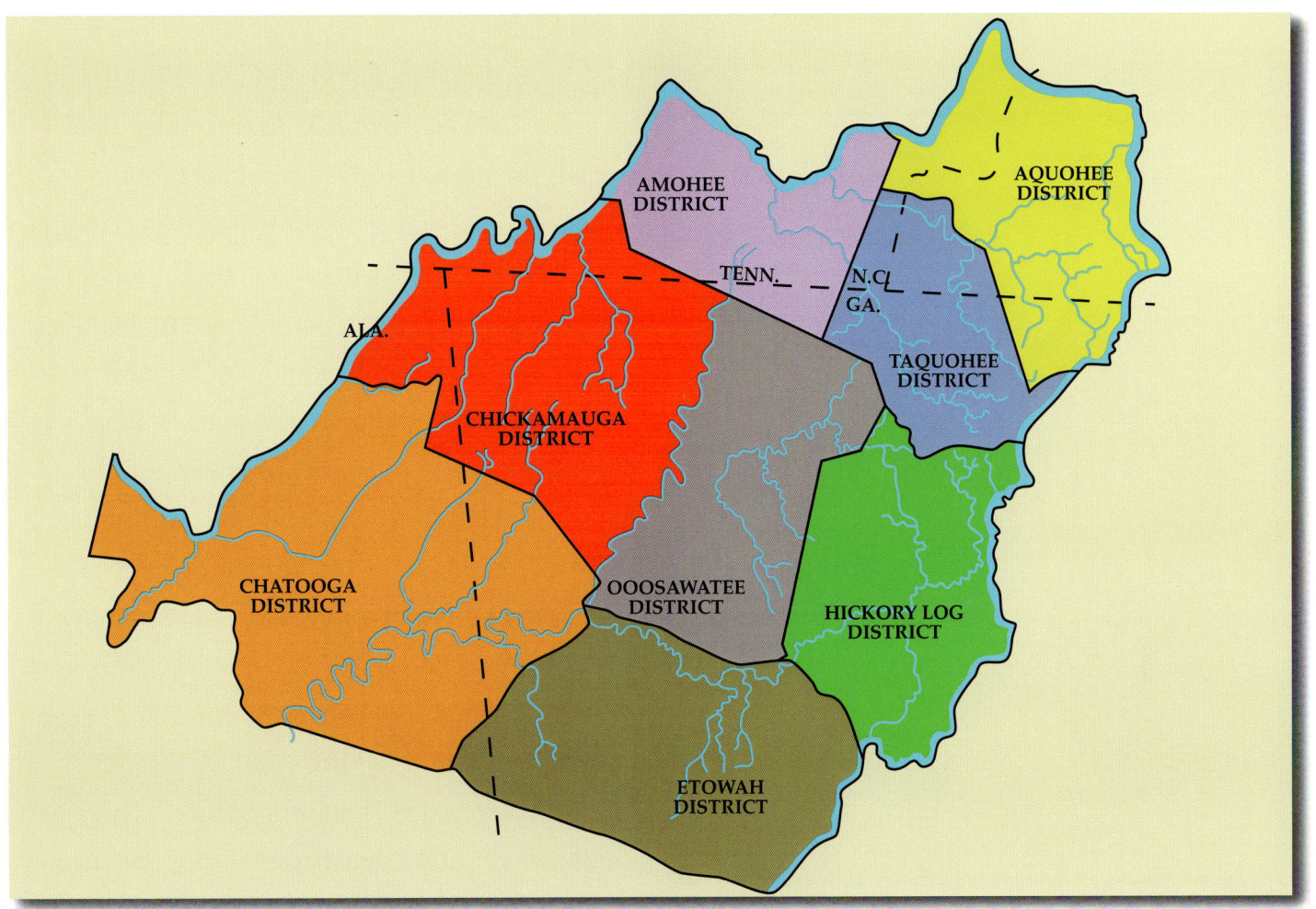

Figure 10. Cherokee Nation in 1820.

principal chief, a council of the principal chief, and a National Committee, which together would form the General Council of the Cherokee Nation. Although the constitution was ratified in October 1827, it did not take effect until October 1828, at which point Ross was elected principal chief. He was repeatedly reelected over the years and held this position until his death in 1866.

Born October 3, 1790, at Turkeytown, near present-day Center, Alabama, John Ross was the great-grandson of Ghigooie, a member of the Bird Clan, and William Shorey, Sr., a Virginia fur trader.[35] The Shoreys' oldest daughter, Annie, married John McDonald, who emigrated from Scotland to Charleston, South Carolina, in 1766.[36] A short time later, McDonald opened a supply store on Chickamauga Creek in present day Chattanooga, Tennessee. In 1776 after the Overhill Towns were destroyed by the Virginia militia, Cherokee war chief Dragging Canoe and the families that followed him established eleven new towns in the vicinity of McDonald's store. They became known as the Chickamauga Cherokees. They developed a reputation as marauders of the frontier because of their efforts to stem the tide of encroachment on prime hunting grounds after the American Revolution. In 1785 Daniel Ross, a native of Scotland, was

Figure 11. John Ross. Image courtesy of the Oklahoma Historical Society.

travelling down the Tennessee River on a trading mission to the Choctaws when he was captured by Chickamaugans. McDonald interceded, spared Ross's life, and gave him sanctuary in his home.[37]

Encouraged by Cherokee friends, Daniel Ross soon opened a trading post at Setico and within a year had married McDonald's daughter, Mollie. In 1788 Ross, his wife Mollie, and her parents, John and Annie McDonald, moved to Turkeytown on the Coosa River, near present-day Center, Alabama. There, two years later, their third child was born. Being the first son, he was named after his grandfather John McDonald. Thus, John Ross was seven-eighths Scottish by blood and was one hundred percent Cherokee by birth. In the matrilineal society, he inherited the clan of his mother, ᎠᏂᏥᏍᏆ (*Anitsiskwa*) or Bird Clan. His clan and family affiliations were unbroken throughout his lineage. During the period of removal, the federal government declared that anyone who had one-quarter Indian blood to be Indian. John Ross was one-eighth Cherokee and did not meet the federal criterion for being Indian. He considered himself to be Cherokee by birth. The federal government considered him to be Cherokee by choice, and as a result his property was confiscated and he was removed.[38]

By 1797 Daniel Ross and his family moved back to the Chattanooga area, where he established a store on Chattanooga Creek near the foot of Lookout Mountain and operated there until about 1816. Wanting a good education for his nine children, Daniel built a small school and employed John Barber Davis as the teacher. After attending Davis's school, John Ross went on to a school in Kingston, Tennessee, and later to the academy at Maryville, Tennessee.[39]

John Ross married Elizabeth Henley, a young widow, around 1813. Elizabeth, or Quatie, was previously married to Robert Henley, who was killed in the War of 1812. She had one child by Henley and six children by John Ross. Elizabeth was one-half Cherokee, and her children with John Ross were five-sixteenths Cherokee.[40]

By the time John Ross became principal

chief, more than three thousand Cherokees had already voluntarily immigrated to Arkansas to escape white encroachment. The Cherokee hope for permanent residency in Arkansas, however, was short-lived. On May 6, 1828, under intense pressure by federal officials in Washington DC, a western Cherokee delegation ceded the land in Arkansas in exchange for land in present-day Oklahoma and liberal promises of assistance from the federal government. After the treaty was signed, the delegation was so nervous about the reaction by their neighbors that the secretary of war felt compelled to write a letter to the Arkansas Cherokee praising the delegates for their integrity, good conduct, and earnest zeal for the welfare of their nation. In spite of the glowing testimonial, the delegation met with an angry reception on its return. The National Council proclaimed them to be guilty of deception and fraud, and declared the treaty to be null and void, having been made without any authority. Council members planned to send another delegation to Washington DC to correct the problem when Agent Duval was advised that the treaty had been ratified by the Senate on May 28, 1828, only three weeks after it had been signed.[41]

Among the problems with the 1828 treaty was that part of the land promised to the Cherokee had already been given the Creeks on January 24, 1826. The matter was resolved by the treaty concluded February 14, 1833, at Fort Gibson in which the Creeks were induced to accept other land farther south. In addition to the

Figure 12. Andrew Jackson *by Alonzo Chappel. Engraving on paper. 7 3/4" × 5 3/16" (19.7 × 13.2 cm). GM 15.1134. Gilcrease Museum, Tulsa, Oklahoma.*

seven million acres given to the Cherokees, they were also guaranteed "a perpetual outlet west, and a free and unmolested use of all the country lying west of the western boundary of said seven millions of acres, as far as the sovereignty of the United States and their right of soil extend."[42]

The Cherokee Nation was determined to maintain its remaining territory despite an 1802 promise by the United States to extinguish Indian title to land in the State of Georgia as soon as possible. Despite the adoption of a constitutional government, a written language, a bilingual newspaper, and other tangible evidence of rapid acculturation, the Cherokees were subjected to relentless demands for their land. The State of Georgia enacted repressive legislation in an effort to expedite Cherokee removal.

In 1828 Andrew Jackson was elected the seventh president of the United States, having campaigned largely on a platform of Indian removal. Inspired by his election, the State of Georgia passed a series of anti-Indian laws on December 20, 1828. By stripping the Cherokees of their rights, Georgia attempted to pressure Congress into expediting the removal.[43] In May 1830, Congress endorsed Jackson's policy of removal by passing the Indian Removal Act. It authorized the president to set aside lands west of the Mississippi to exchange for the lands of the Indian nations in the East.[44]

Ross found support in Congress from individuals in the National Republican Party, such as Senators Henry Clay, Theodore Frelinghuysen, and Daniel Webster and Representative Ambrose Spencer. Despite this support, in April 1829 Secretary of War John H. Eaton informed Ross that President Jackson would support the right of Georgia to extend her laws over the Cherokee Nation.

When Ross and the Cherokee delegation failed in their efforts to protect Cherokee lands through dealings with the executive branch and Congress, Ross took the radical step of defending Cherokee rights through the federal courts. In June of 1830, at the urging of Senators Webster

Figure 13. Chief Justice John Marshall by John Wesley Jarvis. Oil on canvas. 29" × 25" (73.7 × 63.5 cm). GM 0126.1011. Gilcrease Museum, Tulsa, Oklahoma.

and Frelinghuysen, the Cherokee delegation selected William Wirt, a US attorney general in the Monroe and Adams administrations, to defend Cherokee rights before the US Supreme Court.[45]

Wirt argued two cases on behalf of the Cherokee, *Cherokee Nation v. Georgia* and *Worcester v. Georgia*. In his decisions, Chief Justice John Marshall never acknowledged that the Cherokee were a sovereign nation. He did not compel President Jackson to take action that would defend the Cherokee from Georgia's laws. The Cherokee Nation claim was denied on the grounds that the Cherokees were a "domestic dependent sovereignty" and as such did not have the right as a nation state to sue Georgia. The court later expanded on this position in *Worcester v. Georgia*, ruling that Georgia could not extend its laws into Cherokee lands. It was not because they were fully sovereign, however, but because they were a domestic dependent sovereignty. As such the court ruled the Cherokee were dependent not on the state of Georgia but on the United States. According to the series of rulings, Georgia could not extend its laws because that was a power reserved to the federal government. The Cherokee were considered sovereign enough to legally resist the government of Georgia and were encouraged to do so.[46]

The court carefully maintained that the Cherokees were ultimately dependent on the federal government and were not a true nation state, or fully sovereign. Thus, the dispute was made moot when federal legislation in the form of the Indian Removal Act exercised the federal government's legal power to handle the whole affair. The series of decisions embarrassed Jackson politically, as Whigs attempted to use the issue in the 1832 election. They largely supported his earlier opinion that the "Indian Question" was best handled by the federal government and not local authorities.[47]

David Crockett was the only Tennessee congressman to vote against the Indian Removal Act. Crockett, a veteran of the Red Stick War, grew up in East Tennessee and developed friendship and respect for the Cherokees during the campaign. In 1830 Crockett was a freshman congressman from Tennessee. He argued vehemently against the Removal Act on the floor of the House. "Compelling the Indians to forsake their land" represented "oppression with a vengeance," he said. Crockett insisted than he would rather be "honestly and politically dead, than hypocritically immortalized, by supporting a wicked, unjust measure." He later recalled, "I gave a good honest vote, one that will not make me ashamed in the day of judgment."[48]

Ross wrote to Crockett on January 13, 1831, "To those gentlemen who have so honorably and ably vindicated the rights of the poor Indians in Congress, This nation owes a debt of gratitude, which the pages of history will bear record until time shall be no more."[49] Crockett's enemies rallied against him. He was defeated in his bid for reelection in 1831, won in 1833, and was defeated again in 1835. Ross appreciated Crockett's friendship and found inspiration in his words as indicated in a letter to William Underwood in 1834.[50]

Crockett's frustration with partisan politics in Washington DC compelled him to head for Texas, following in the footsteps of Sam Houston, another Tennessee politician and friend of the Cherokees. Both were caught up in the movement for Texas independence. Crockett died at the Alamo on March 6, 1836, and Houston went on to become president of the

ᎠᏧᏯᏗ 3

Republic of Texas and later governor of the State of Texas.

In the meantime, the Cherokees faced an uncertain future.

ᎠᏯᏙᎵ 4
ᏧᏂᎦᎶᏃ ᎦᎥᏅ ᏖᎳᏬᏍᎠᎢ
1828-1839

Chapter 4: Blunt Force of Removal

Figure 1. Map of the different removal routes of the Cherokee.

Unable to conclude an agreement with the duly authorized leaders of the Cherokee Nation, the US government signed a treaty with a minority faction willing to cede the last remaining portion of the original Cherokee homeland on December 29, 1835. Despite the protests of the overwhelming majority of Cherokee people, the fraudulent Treaty of New Echota was ratified by the US Senate on May 23, 1836. The Cherokees were given two years in which to voluntarily remove to the Indian Territory. When the time had expired, only two thousand of the nearly seventeen thousand Cherokees remaining in the East had departed their ancestral homeland.

To enforce the terms of the treaty, Gen. Winfield Scott and an army of seven thousand federal and state troops arrived in the Cherokee Nation in May 1838. Cherokee families were forced from comfortable homes into thirty-one stockades and open military stations scattered throughout the Cherokee Nation in southeastern Tennessee, western North Carolina, northwestern Georgia, and northeastern Alabama. From the stockades, the Cherokees were sent to the principal emigrating depots near Ross's Landing at Chattanooga, Tennessee; Fort Cass, near Calhoun, Tennessee; and a camp south of Fort Payne, Alabama.

In June 1838, the first three detachments of Cherokees captured by the Georgia Guard were forced to depart from Ross's Landing, Tennessee. Because of the high casualties of these first groups, Cherokee leaders petitioned General Scott to postpone the removal for a few months and to allow the Cherokees to superintend their own removal. Permission was granted.

The remainder of the Cherokees, in thirteen detachments, began their journey west in fall 1838. After enduring an extremely severe winter, all of the detachments had arrived in the West by the first days of spring 1839. The journey was arduous and was especially difficult for the very young and the very old. Hundreds of Cherokees were buried in unmarked graves at the concentration camps or along the route that has come to be known as the Trail of Tears. The true story of the forced removal for the Cherokee people is one of resiliency. In spite of the hardships, the Cherokees adapted and rebuilt their homes, government, and lives in the Indian Territory.

Although it is easy to point to certain nineteenth century politicians as the architects of removal, the fate of the Cherokees may have been sealed long before any white settlers encroached upon Cherokee lands. The European conquest of the Americas brought about major beneficial changes in Europe that, in turn, resulted in catastrophic changes for the Indian populations. The introduction of American foods and American cotton to Europe shortly after contact resulted in a population explosion. The population of Europe increased more than sevenfold in three and a half centuries, from 100 million in 1650 to more than 750 million in 2015. The increase in large part could be attributed to healthier, blight-resistant foods introduced from the Western Hemisphere. Similar increases could be seen in other parts of the world. Today, about sixty percent of the world cuisine is comprised of foods first cultivated by American Indians.[1]

The potato more than any other crop changed life in Europe. The potato spread in Europe from west to east from the end of the sixteenth to the early nineteenth centuries. With a shorter growing season, less care during cultivation, less susceptibility to pestilence, and more ease on the teeth than European grains, the

Figure 2. Heirloom Cherokee white eagle corn kernels. Image courtesy of Cherokee Nation Natural Resources.

potato quickly became the food staple in all areas it reached. Corn did for the animal population of Europe what potatoes did for the human population. Collectively, American foods did what centuries of prayer, work, and medicine had been unable to do. They cured Europe of episodic famines which had been the primary restraint on population growth.[2]

Corn and potatoes could be grown in Europe; American "Sea-Island" cotton, which replaced wool as the primary material for European clothing, could not. Not until American cotton arrived in England did the phrase "cotton cloth" appear in English. The earliest recorded use is in the 1552 *Oxford Dictionary*. Previously, Europeans wore wool supplemented by leather. The amount of clothing that could be produced was directly related to the number of sheep and the land available for sheep. The introduction of cotton gave rise to textile factories and a new industry in Europe.

The 1793 invention of the cotton gin by Eli Whitney allowed one worker to separate up to fifty pounds of cotton per day. Previously, slaves spent nearly three days picking out seeds for every day of picking cotton in the field. Cotton exports from the United States increased from 3,000 bales in 1790 to 4.5 million in 1860. The increased popularity of cotton, which as

Figure 3. Photo of the woods on the Cherokee reservation in Cherokee, North Carolina. Image courtesy of Roy Boney, Jr.

an agricultural crop rapidly depleted the soil, escalated the demand for suitable land and pushed southern planters from Georgia and the Carolinas all the way to Texas in the first decades of the nineteenth century. In the process, tremendous pressure was brought to bear on the Cherokees and other tribes in the Southeast–the Creeks, Choctaws, Chickasaws, and Seminoles, to yield all land with agricultural potential. Only in the rugged mountains of North Carolina, the swamps of Mississippi tributaries, and the Florida Everglades were Indians permitted to remain beyond the 1830s.[3]

By the early nineteenth century, the thin soils of the large coastal plantations, which grew rich through slavery and cotton production, were becoming rapidly depleted because of overplanting. The State of Georgia also had a large class of poor and landless whites, and the best unspoiled farmland was still under Indian control. The citizens of Georgia lived in a class-conscious and race-conscious society. The continued advancement of the white population was dependent on the subjugation and exploitation of minorities. The increasing prosperity of Cherokees and Creeks was perceived by some whites as a threat to the existing social order. Aspiring whites viewed the trappings of the aristocracy as a respected virtue when exhibited by other whites and decadent vice when displayed by nonwhites. By 1810 the Cherokee elite were competing economically with white aristocrats.

During the first decades of the nineteenth century, the political pressure for Indian removal intensified. Of all states with Indian populations, Georgia had developed the strongest case for Indian removal. Of all eastern tribes subjected to confiscation of lands, the Cherokees had developed the strongest case against forced removal.

Georgia's case was based heavily on an 1802 agreement with the United States whereby the federal government committed itself to extinguish Indian land titles within the remaining boundaries of the state. The Compact of 1802, as it was known, was the result of the most blatant political scandal in Georgia's

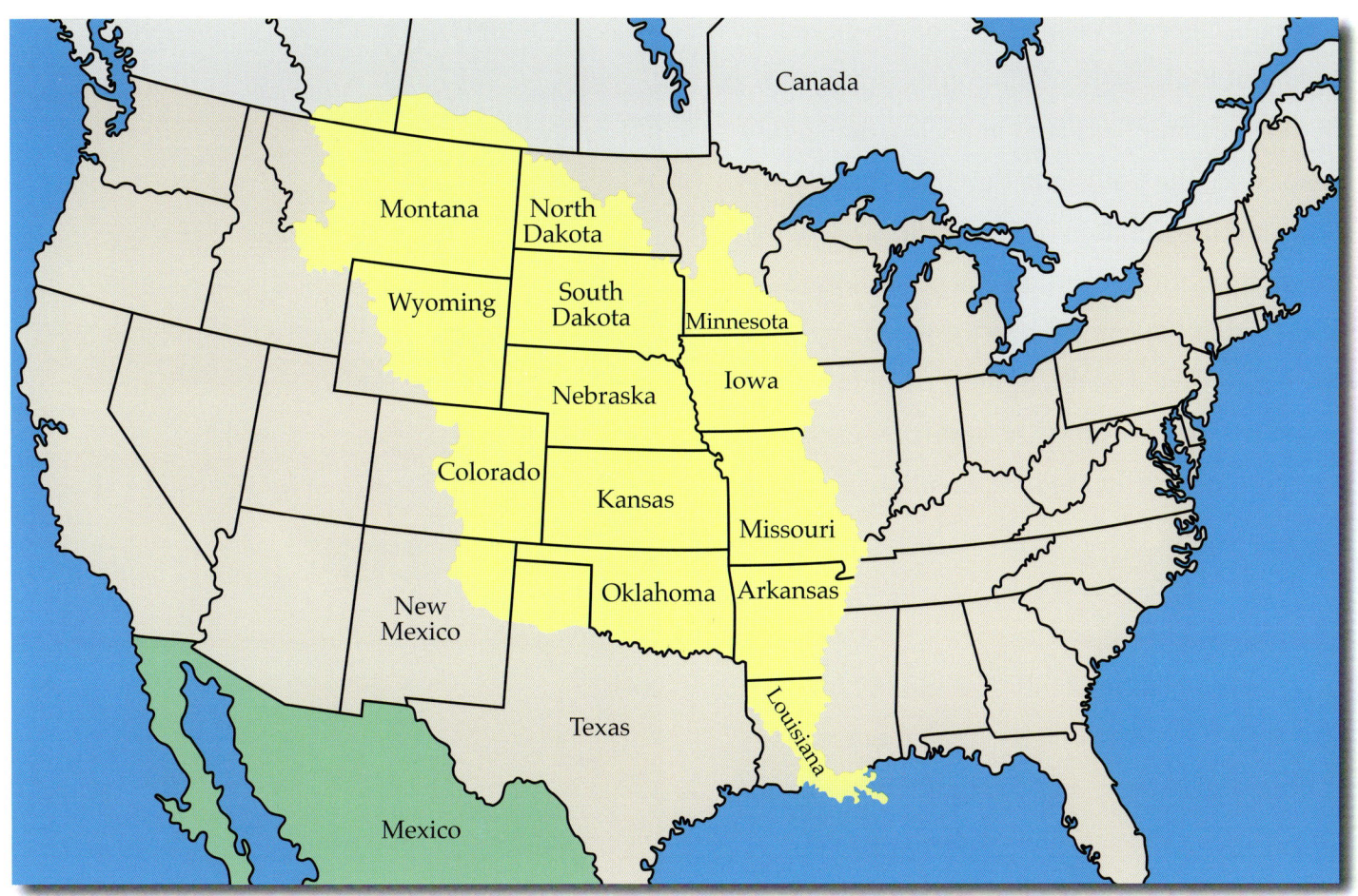

Figure 4. Map showing the Louisiana Purchase with modern-day state names and boundaries.

history. Throughout the eighteenth century, Georgia's boundaries extended westward to the Mississippi River and included most of the present states of Mississippi and Alabama. Georgia's corrupt legislature in 1795, under the influence of wholesale bribery, passed the infamous Yazoo Land Act which gave to land speculators thirty-five million acres of Georgia's western lands for about one and one half cents per acre. When a rescinding act passed the next year failed to undo the damage, the state decided to rid itself of the Yazoo problem by ceding its western lands to the federal government.[4]

The Articles of Agreement and Cession were concluded on April 24, 1802. In giving up the Alabama and Mississippi territories to the United States, Georgia received three commitments in exchange: (1) that the federal government would assume responsibility for settlement of the Yazoo land claims; (2) to pay to Georgia $1,250,000; and (3), that "the United States shall at their own expense extinguish for the use of Georgia, as early as the same can be peaceably obtained on reasonable terms, the Indian title to…all…lands within the State of Georgia."[5]

In 1802 extinguishing Indian title within the limits of Georgia probably was not envisioned as removal west of the Mississippi.

After all, George Washington had proposed in 1789 that Indians should become citizens as soon as they become "civilized and Christianized." Also, since the Louisiana Purchase did not occur until 1803, there was no land west of the Mississippi for the United States. Although approval of the compact by the Cherokees, who were recognized as the rightful owners to nearly one-third of the land in the state of Georgia, was not sought by either federal or state officials, the agreement would prove to be the single instrument most effectively employed to remove all Indians from the state.[6]

When Napoleon Bonaparte became strapped for cash while trying to finance his conquest of Europe, he sold to the United States for a meager sum of fifteen million dollars France's claim to all land west of the Mississippi River. The following year in 1804 President Thomas Jefferson suggested to a Cherokee delegation visiting Washington, DC, that if any or all Cherokees chose to remove west of the Mississippi, land would be given them in proportion to the number removing.[7] At that time, only a few hundred Cherokees were living west of the Mississippi.

The Indian policy developed during the Federal Period under George Washington and Henry Knox, secretary of war, sought an honorable role for the US Government. They were very cognizant of the history of Latin America and the wholesale genocide that had occurred in the Caribbean, Peru, and Mexico. They certainly wanted to avoid being relegated

Figure 5. Portrait of George Washington, 1770 by Charles Wilson Peale. Oil on canvas. 37 7/16" × 32 1/2" (95.1 × 82.6 × 8.9 cm). GM 0126.1013. Gilcrease Museum, Tulsa, Oklahoma.

to the same appellations as the conquerors of those areas. Knox, in particular, believed that Indian title could be extinguished gradually as white expansion moved west and as Indians became acculturated. He did not contemplate that the encroachment on Indian lands would be so rapid with such a blatant disregard of the rights of Indians by the frontier population, nor did he contemplate that Indians might not want to sell their land or become American. As a result of these factors, American Indian policy began to change from bringing Indians into the American system as proposed by Washington to excluding them from it as championed by Andrew Jackson. Even as the policy changed, the purported motivation remained the same–to save the Indians from destruction.

The policy of the Cherokees changed just as dramatically during the same period. From 1776 to 1794, the Cherokees sought to maintain their territorial imperative through military force. After successive military defeats and loss of Indian and Spanish allies, the Cherokees embraced Washington's concept of civilization with a passion, making tremendous progress in agriculture and commerce and developing a state-form of government within a few decades.

By the time of the 1824 presidential election, Indian removal was a major issue. The candidates for president of the United States in the 1824 election were Andrew Jackson, John Quincy Adams, William H. Crawford, and Henry Clay. The southern votes were divided among three regional candidates: Jackson of Tennessee, Clay of Kentucky, and Crawford of Georgia. In Georgia Crawford, who was the favorite son but in failing health, received two-thirds or ninety of the votes of the Electoral College. In spite of the fact that Jackson received the largest number of popular votes, the election was decided in the House of Representatives, and John Quincy Adams was selected president. Jackson immediately began campaigning for the 1828 election. Indian removal was a central theme in his campaign.

In 1825 the Georgia legislature created a Board of Public Works, whose responsibilities included surveying the state to determine how canals, railroads, and highways might improve the state's economy. The board had six members appointed by the legislature. One of these members was Wilson Lumpkin, who saw railroads as the way of the future. He examined the land between the then-state capital at Milledgeville and Chattanooga, Tennessee, and quickly concluded that a canal between the two was impractical but that a railroad could be built to great advantage. The only problem was that most of the land between those points was owned by the Cherokees.

Lumpkin became the architect of Cherokee removal in Georgia, luring the masses of whites to the cause with the promise of free land. He reserved for himself a grander vision of becoming a railroad magnate. At that time, the railroad industry was in the embryonic state. Only a few miles of railroad were then known to the world, and those were constructed of wood and propelled by animal force. The steam engine and iron rails were only a few years away. Lumpkin wrote that he "after full investigation of the subject, became fully satisfied that even wooden rail roads, with mule and horse power, should be preferred to any canal which could be constructed in middle and upper Georgia." He also took great pride in the fact that the routes that he and Fulton selected "in its whole distance have varied so slightly from the location of our present rail roads now in operation (1851). From that time to this I have looked to rail roads

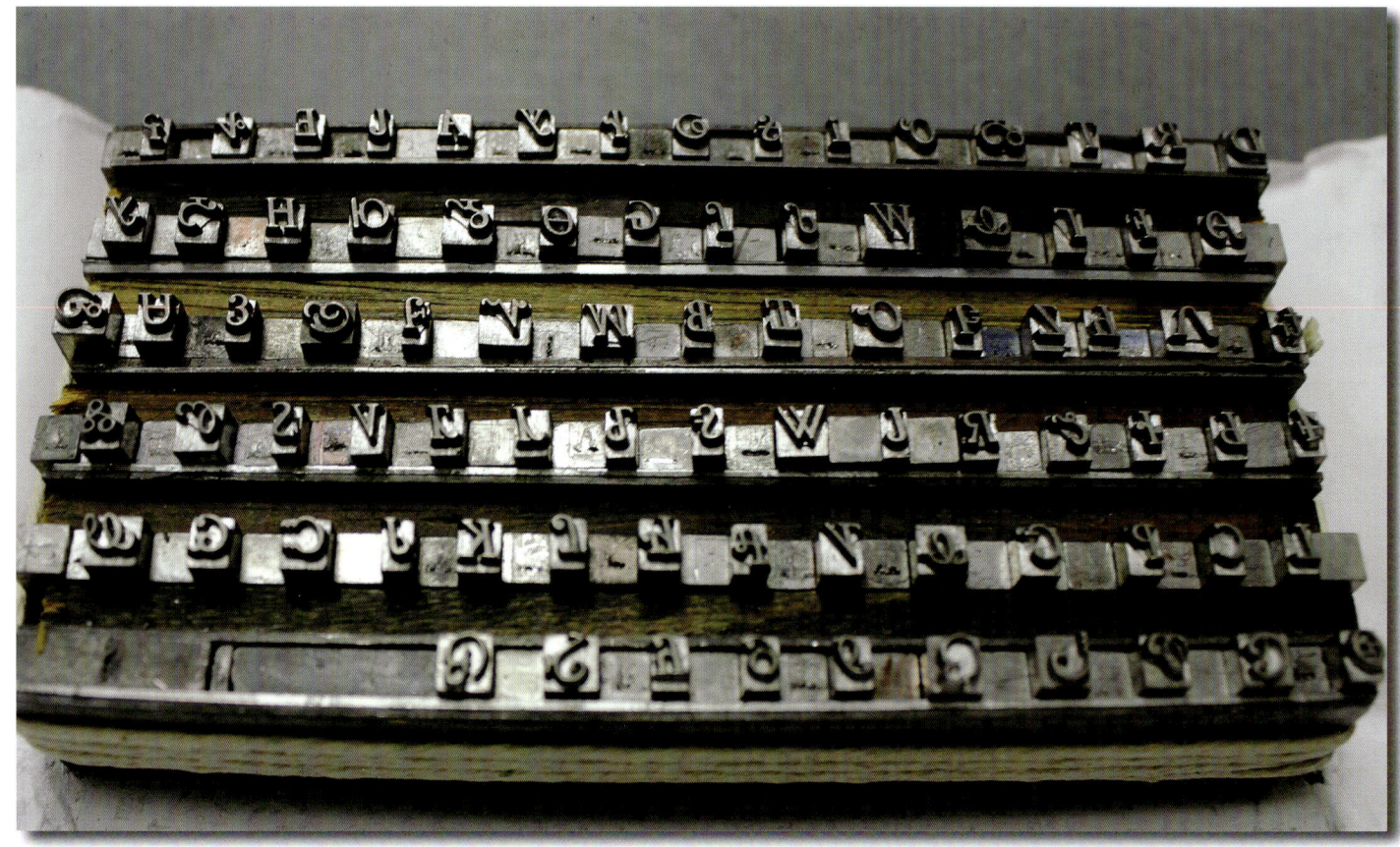

Figure 6. Cherokee Syllabary Typeset Block in the Cherokee Heritage Center Archives. Photo courtesy of Jeff Edwards.

as the great and leading work to promote the best interest of the country and have upon all fit occasions, whether in private or public life, contributed my best aid to the promotion of the rail road cause."[8]

In 1828 gold was discovered at Dalonega in the Cherokee Nation in Georgia. A horde of fortune seekers descended on the Cherokee Nation. Inspired by the election of Andrew Jackson that year, the State of Georgia quickly passed a series of anti-Indian acts. Cherokees were forbidden from mining gold on their own land. They could not assemble in groups of three or more for any purpose, including religious services. They could not testify in a court of law against a white person, and whites living in the Cherokee Nation were required to take an oath of allegiance to the State of Georgia. In extending the laws of the state over the annexed territory, Georgia abolished the Cherokee laws and authorized the use of the state militia to enforce the state laws and land claims.

The rest of the country had a different view of removal than did Georgia. Northern audiences were frequently impressed with the eloquent speeches of touring Cherokee scholars such as Elias Boudinot and John Ridge. They not only opened their hearts but also their pocketbooks in the fundraising efforts to buy a printing press for New Echota. Many Cherokees felt that their strongest fight against removal was public opinion. The *Cherokee Phoenix*, which

Blunt Force of Removal 1828 - 1839

Figure 7. I Rise in Opposition by Virginia Stroud. Cherokee removal was a contentious issue even among different Cherokee factions. Image courtesy of Cherokee Nation Businesses.

provided the main means of disseminating information, was short-lived. Six years after its debut in 1828, the state of Georgia confiscated the printing press, declaring the *Phoenix* to be a subversive newspaper.

In his inaugural address in 1829, President Jackson gave a great deal of attention to the situation in Georgia. Avowing that no independent government could be formed within the jurisdiction of an existing state, he countered the Cherokee's claim that the State of Georgia was infringing on their sovereign rights. President Jackson said that he had "advised them to emigrate beyond the Mississippi or submit to the laws of the states."

Wilson Lumpkin, the former surveyor, Indian commissioner, and Georgia Board of Public Works member, was elected to the House of Representatives from Georgia in 1826. A friend of Gov. George Troup and an ardent supporter of President Jackson, Lumpkin authored two versions of the Indian Removal Act, both of which were passed by Congress, the second in 1830. Not everyone supported Lumpkin's bills, however. He encountered strong resistance in the North, especially from Jeremiah Evarts of the American Board. Evarts, under the pseudonym of William Penn, wrote a series of letters that

"Ⅽh ᏗᏕhᎦᏫ ᏕᏗᏞ,
ᏃᏖᎸᏃ ᎤᏆᎻᏕ
ᎾᏚᏌᏙᏛ."

- ᏙᎩᏕᎩh

"John Marshall has made his decision, now let him enforce it."

- President Andrew Jackson

were widely published defending the Cherokee position.

The Cherokees also hired respected lawyers to help fight their legal battles. The most important was William Wirt, the former attorney general of the United States. On the state level in Georgia, they employed the firm of Underwood and Harris. In the early 1830s, two cases involving the Cherokees reached the US Supreme Court. The first, *Cherokee Nation vs. Georgia*, contended that the State of Georgia did not have the right to extend its laws over the Cherokee Nation, arguing that the tribe was a sovereign nation. The court concluded that the tribe was not a foreign nation but a dependent sovereign nation. Under the extension of Georgia law, a Cherokee man named Corn Tassel was tried for the murder of another Cherokee. He was brought to Gainesville before Judge Augustia Clayton, presiding as judge of the Hall County Superior Court. After being convicted, Corn Tassel was sentenced to hang. Wirt immediately appealed the case to the US Supreme Court on a writ of error, which was sanctioned by Chief Justice John Marshall. Governor Rockingham Gilmer was ordered to appear before the Supreme Court to defend the state's position, but he refused. Corn Tassel was hanged.

Wirt's second case was *Worcester v. Georgia*. Rather than considering the Cherokee Nation to be a foreign country after two missionaries were arrested on tribal land, Wirt based his position upon the constitutional provision that the establishment and regulation of intercourse with the Indians belonged exclusively to the government of the United States. By treaties and acts of Congress, he argued, federal jurisdiction applied to the case of the Cherokees. He argued that no state could interfere without a manifest violation of such treaties and laws. In conclusion, Wirt maintained that the indictment, conviction, and sentence being founded upon a statute of Georgia, which was unconstitutional and void, were themselves also void and of no effect and ought to be reversed.

Associate Supreme Court Justice Henry Baldwin ordered the state to present arguments before the court as to why the convictions of the missionaries should not be overturned. Wilson Lumpkin, who took office as governor on November 9, 1831, declined to appear or even

Blunt Force of Removal 1828 - 1839

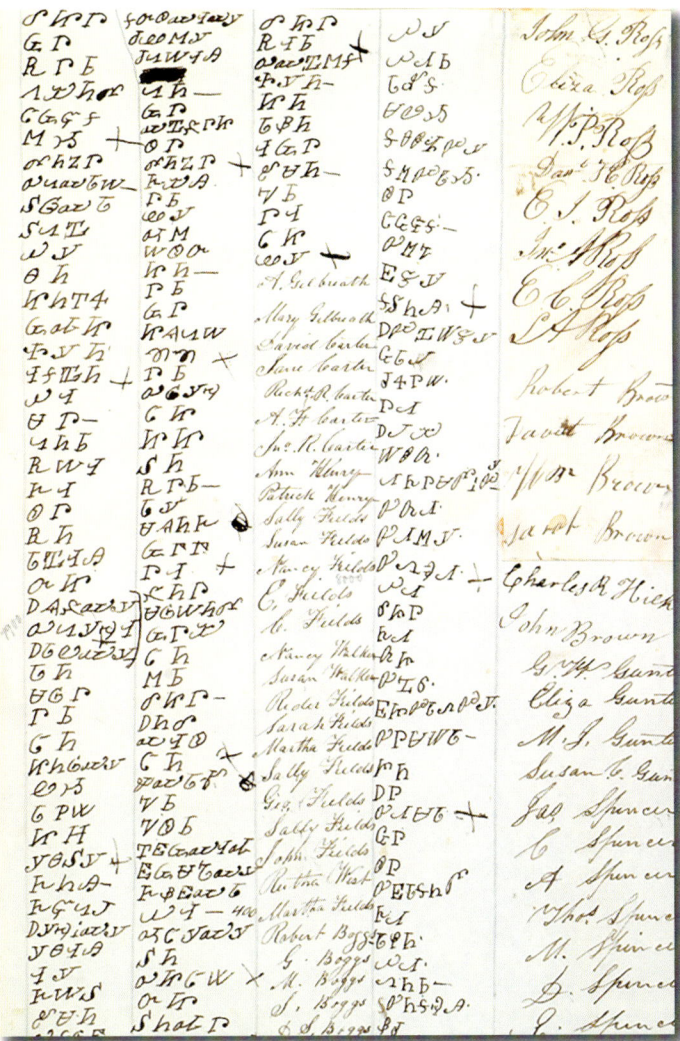

Figure 8. Portion of the petition scroll by Cherokees against the removal. Image courtesy of Cherokee Nation Businesses.

Figure 9. John Ridge, a member of the Treaty Party. Image courtesy of the Oklahoma Historical Society.

admit the Supreme Court had jurisdiction in the case. On March 3, 1832, Chief Justice Marshall delivered the court's majority opinion, declaring the state's laws unconstitutional and ordered the release of the missionaries.[9] Still, the state refused to acquiesce, and the president of the United States publicly denounced the court's decision, stating: "John Marshall has made his decision, now let him enforce it." Worcester and Butler remained in the state penitentiary. The Cherokees watched helplessly until the missionaries were released in January 1833 after accepting the ultimate humiliation and acknowledging the authority of the state. The verdict, however, was an enduring victory and became a case study in constitutional law. It is required reading for every aspiring law student, and along with an earlier decision, the *Cherokee Nation v. Georgia* (1831), it is still frequently cited in court cases involving Indian law.

In 1832 the State of Georgia held a land lottery parceling out to white citizens 160-acre tracts of land with whatever improvements made by the Cherokees. In 1833 Principal Chief

they signed on the entire population. The Treaty Party, as it became known, was led by Major Ridge (ᏄᏃᏟᎶᎦ), his son John Ridge (ᏬᏍᏯᏥᏍᎩ), and nephews Elias Boudinot (ᏕᏫᏴ ᏣᏗ), former editor of the *Cherokee Phoenix*, and Stand Watie (ᏕᏍᏙᏎ).

In fall 1835, John Howard Payne, one

Figure 10. Major Ridge, Portfolio 1844 by Thomas McKenney and James Hall. "History of Indian Tribes of North America." Lithograph. GM 2126.1814.43b. Gilcrease Museum, Tulsa, Oklahoma.

John Ross on a return trip from Washington, DC, found his ill wife living in the storeroom of their home and paying rent to the new owners.

The pressure to remove intensified. Offering larger and larger inducements to remove with only minimal results, the federal government despaired of reaching a treaty with the duly elected representatives of the Cherokee Nation. Unable to conclude a treaty with the legitmate Cherokee government, US officials sought to recognize a minority faction as the new leadership with the intent of imposing any treaty

"ᎾᏬᎾZ ᏤᏍᎦᎪᏫᎾ ᎾᏍᎩ ᏤᏗᏍ ᏏᏍᎾᎯᏯᏛ ᎠᏛ ᏗᏕᎥᏴᏬᏗ ᏏᎲᏕᎶᏬᏫᎾ. ᎾᏍᎩ ᎠᎾᏤᎵᏬᎥᏍᏬᏗ, ᎠᏍ ᏤᏓᎵᎭᏴᏗ. ᎲᏕᎥᏢ ᎲᏕᎶᏬᏫᎲᏤᎢᎢ, ᎠᏍ ᎠᏎ ᏤᏓᎶᏴᎧᏢ."

- ᎠᏍᎦᏰᎬᏍᎢ ᏣᎲ ᎤᎨᎲ

"...it will then be determined whether they will go peaceable or by force. If they hesitate, I will take them. Under any circumstances, I shall take hostages."

- General John E. Wool

of the best-known writers in America and the author of *Home Sweet Home,* was invited to write a history of the Cherokee people, which the National Council hoped to use to sway public opinion to the Cherokee cause. Informants, knowledgeable in Cherokee oral tradition, were employed to assist Payne in this work. Although Payne collected a great deal of information, his effort on behalf of the Cherokees was interrupted by his arrest by the Georgia Guard on December 5, 1838, at the home of John Ross near Cleveland, Tennessee. After a thirteen-day detainment at Camp Benton, Georgia, Payne and Ross were released without charge. Ross left immediately for Washington, DC. Less than two weeks later, the Treaty of New Echota was signed with the minority faction, sealing the fate of the Cherokee people. The papers confiscated from Payne by the Georgia Guard were used by government officials to discredit Payne, branding him as a French spy and an abolitionist. In spite of this, Payne sent a series of scathing anti-removal articles to various newspapers. Congressmen and senators were as little moved by Payne's writings as they were by the petitions presented by Ross, which contained 15,665 Cherokee signatures denouncing the Treaty of New Echota as a fraud. The Senate ratified the treaty on May 23, 1836, giving the Cherokees two years in which to remove.

Although Article 16 of the treaty gave the Cherokees two years from the date of ratification to peacefully and voluntarily remove from their homeland, Congress two days later authorized the deployment of a military force. Within a month on June 20, 1836, Bvt. Brig. Gen. John E. Wool, a distinguished soldier with more than twenty-four years service, was ordered to proceed immediately to the Cherokee country to determine the prospects of armed conflicts resulting from the government's action. In the event of Cherokee hostilities, Wool was instructed "to employ such force as…necessary to suppress them and subdue them to unconditional submission."[10] Although authorized to call the governors of the surrounding states for additional troops, his command upon arrival would consist of twenty-four soldiers from the regular army already at Fort Cass and recently activated Tennessee militia authorized by an act of Congress on May 25 and by a proclamation of Governor Newton Cannon on June 6.[11] To minimize the chances of Cherokee resistance, General Wool was ordered to "Take their weapons, using force if necessary."[12]

Five companies of Tennessee militia under command of Col. Nathanial Smith were sent to the mouth of Valley River, North Carolina, to establish a headquarters for General Wool. He believed that the large show of force in the Cherokee country would diminish the influence of Principal Chief John Ross. He cautioned against the advice of John Ross, who offered encouragement about the prospects for a rehearing and the chances for eventually setting aside the treaty. Wool insisted that they had no hope but that of removal according

Figure 11. Many Died But They All Cried *by Bill Rabbit. The loss of life during the removal was catastrophic for the Cherokee people. Image courtesy of Cherokee Nation Businesses.*

to the treaty. Any other course would lead to their destruction. He declared that it must be executed, and as soon as circumstances would permit. He found some listeners but no cooperation from either individual Cherokees or the National Council for his proposal to remove one-half of the Cherokees during fall 1836.[13]

Although Wool arrived amid rumors pending hostilities, he found the Cherokees seeking protection rather than confrontation with the military. He noted that the whites in Tennessee, Georgia, and North Carolina were engaged in "daily efforts to dispossess the Indians of their houses and lands." Wool attempted to establish his authority with the Cherokees. He believed it was his responsibility not only to prevent clashes between the whites and Indians but also to carry out the terms of the treaty by starting the Cherokees on their journey to the West.

In late July he moved his headquarters to the mountains of North Carolina near the mouth of Valley River in what Wool called "the midst of the most savage and troublesome part of the Cherokees, who are nearly or quite all opposed to the late treaty." Wool was either unaware or ignored the Declaration of Peace adopted by the Cherokee in North Carolina only a few weeks earlier. Delegates of the principal towns in the Aquohee and Taquohee Districts, which comprised that part of the Cherokee Nation within the chartered limits of North Carolina and Union County, Georgia, met at the Hiwassee Townhouse near Peach Tree Creek on Friday, July 1, 1836, to consider the appropriateness of making a public declaration on the subject of "Indian hostilities which has recently excited so much alarm." After some discussion and perhaps with the assistance of the Reverend Evan Jones in polishing the English version, it was unanimously adopted.

Although the Cherokees hoped to find a solution to their difficulties through diplomacy and negotiation, General Wool sought subjugation. Three days after his arrival at Valley Town, he reported that the "Indians are all together adverse to removal: I have had two meetings on the subject without any decision. On Wednesday next we are to have another, when I expect a large number to be present; it will then be determined whether they will go peaceable or by force. If they hesitate, I will take them. Under any circumstances, I shall take hostages."[14]

Roman Nose, chief of Cheloce, a conservative community located thirty miles northeast of Valley Town, and a signatory to the Declaration of Peace a month earlier, was one of those made a prisoner by Wool. To secure his release, his followers said they would submit to the treaty and give up their arms.[15] Wool defended his action, noting that it "commanded the confidence and respect of all the white men as well as the red men. Not a murmur was heard against it in this section of the country. All parties, including Governor Lumpkin, Ridge, Boudinot, Bell, and Currey, approbated it, and declared it was the true course, and the only one which would insure a peaceable and quiet execution of the treaty. It convinced a large proportion of the Cherokees that a treaty had been made with them, and that they had to go to the west."[16]

The secretary of war viewed the military action as risky and responded to the general with an admonishment: "I beg leave to observe that your instructions of the 20th June contemplated the application of military force only in the event of hostilities being commenced by the Cherokees. The treaty provides that they shall remove within two years, and that during that time they shall be protected in the peaceable possession of their country. Unwillingness to remove, or even resistance to a removal, will not authorize the employment of force; no intimidation or coercion must be used."[17]

Wool was later accused by Andrew Jackson of being too lax with the Cherokees by allowing them to conduct National Council meetings and forwarding communiques on their behalf to the War Department. Wool was also accused by the governor and legislature of Alabama of "having usurped the powers of the civil tribunals, disturbed the peace of the community, and trampled upon the rights of the citizens." A military board of inquiry headed by Winfield Scott cleared Wool of charges. Wool nevertheless left his position embittered and perplexed on July 1, 1837.

He was replaced by Col. William Lindsay. In the ten months during which Colonel Lindsay commanded the military in the Cherokee Nation, he built a force of thirty-one militia companies, established twenty-three posts for the troops, collected ordinance stores at Fort Cass, distributed subsistence stores at various strategic locations, and supplied hospitals at Fort Cass and Cantonment Wool near Missionary Ridge. Major General Winfield Scott replaced Col. Lindsay as military commander in the Cherokee Nation in May 1838.

Scott arrived in Athens, Tennessee, on May 8, 1838, and issued his first orders from there on May 10. Before leaving his command, Colonel Lindsay directed the assignments of the state troops. The federal troops under General Scott totaled about three thousand men and included elements of the First, Second, Third, and Fourth Artillery, Fourth Infantry and six companies of the Second Dragoons detailed to the Fourth Infantry and a battalion of US Marines. The combined units were officially called the Army of the Cherokee Nation. A battalion of Tennessee Militia was added to Scott's original call for state troops bringing the total of militia to about four thousand men. This included two regiments from Georgia, one each from North Carolina and Alabama, and one and one half regiments from Tennessee. In all, approximately seven thousand federal and state troops comprised the Army of the Cherokee Nation by early June 1838.

On May 17, 1838, Scott issued Order Number 25, which detailed the composition of his administrative staff, established three military districts to expedite the collection of the Indians, and instructed his troops in the nonviolent and merciful exercise of their duties. On May 23, 1838, the two years given the Cherokees for voluntary removal under the Treaty of New Echota expired. Only two thousand Cherokees had left for the West since the Treaty was ratified in May 1836. Maj. Gen. Scott, who had been assigned to the task of forcefully removing the remaining Cherokees, supplemented the twenty-two hundred federal troops with two regiments of Georgia militia and one regiment each of 740 men from North Carolina, Tennessee, and Alabama. Elizur Butler, a missionary and medical doctor who had spent fourteen months in the Georgia State Penitentiary for his support of the Cherokees,[18] reported on the number of military posts: "From the best information I can obtain there are four military establishments in Alabama, four in North Carolina, seven in Tennessee, and fifteen in Georgia. At the different posts, there are eight or nine thousands troops. Perhaps one soldier to two Cherokees counting men, women and children."[19]

The military roundup began in Georgia on May 26, 1838. Within a week, the two regiments of Georgia militia under Brig. Gen. Charles B. Floyd captured and confined in makeshift stockades most of the Cherokees in that state. Between May 30 and June 9, 1838, a total of 3,636 prisoners from the middle military district of the Cherokee Nation[20] were assembled near Ross's Landing,[21] one of the principal emigrating depots.

A. E. Blunt, a missionary for the American Board of Commissioners for Foreign Missions, wrote from the Candy's Creek Station on May 28, 1838: "The long looked for day (23rd of May) however it much was it desired by some and feared by others has arrived. Notwithstanding the prospects before us have looked appalling, it has been a matter of surprise to see the steady onward course of the Cherokees. I have heard it remembered by persons traveling in various parts of the Nation (Ga. excepted) that the people were never so forward in their crops & never appeared so industrious as at the present crisis. The movements in the whole country for several weeks past seemed to indicate war. The arrival of the military: Cannon, powder, lead, & boxes of arms has indeed looked like the shedding of blood. But…no enemy has been found to contend with, and while some of the volunteers have been most insulting, in some instances, the people have borne it patiently & have gone on, attending to their business.

"For some days previous to the 23rd, The military were riding through the country ordering the Cherokees to repair at certain points for emigration before the expiration of the time specified by the fraudulent treaty. All seems to have no effect. Onward, seems to be the motto of all the Cherokees. We have justice on our side let come what will, & some have told the officers that they should continue to attend to their own business until forced at the point of the bayonet…

"During all the storms which has clouded the nation there has been no sudden alarms or fright with the Cherokees, while on the other hand the whites in some instances have removed out of the Nation &, many have been ready to start at the rustling of a leaf."[22]

All except Alabama had provided troops by the date requested. In contrast to the federal troops who were professional soldiers, the state volunteers generally made up for poor training and discipline with enthusiasm for assigned tasks. For this reason, the state troops were frequently as much of a problem to friends as they were to foes. Scott reported to Poinsett: "I propose to hold the prisoners & voluntary emigrants, in convenient camps guarded by regular troops, around the two great emigrating depots. All the militia will be discharged as soon as the remaining Indians are brought in. I am in much want of additional paymasters as well as funds, to pay off the militia as fast as they are discharged."[23]

Stephen Foreman, a mixed-blood Cherokee in Tennessee, explained why he and

"Ꮜ ᎨᎠᏬᏓᎩ, ᎠᎴ ᎾᏍᎩᏃ ᎠᏂᏣᎳᎩ ᎤᎾᎵᏍᎪᎵ ᏔᎣᏂᏣᎯ ᏧᎦᎠᏬᏓᎩ, ᎾᏍᎩᏃ ᎠᏨᏆ ᎨᏗᎡᏘ, ᎠᏗ ᏕᏣᏆᏢᏋ ᎡᏉᏬᏓᎩ Ꮎ ᏒᏃᏞᏋ ᏚᎴᎦᏍᏬᏓᎢ Ꮃ ᎢᎦᎾᎬ ᏏᏫᏍᏗᏂᎲᏣ ᎠᏓᏃ Ꮃ ᏏᎶᎯᏣᎻᎦ ᎩᏬᏃ ᏱᏆᏫᏍᎴ ᎠᏍᎶᏥ ᎡᏬᏬᎩ ᏔᏍᎩᏨᎲᏉᏍᏬᏓᎩ."

- ᎤᎢᎬᏃᎮ

"My determination, and the determination of a large majority of the Cherokees, yet in the Nation, is, never to recognize this fraudulent instrument as a treaty nor remove under it until we are forced to do so at the point of the bayonet."

- Stephen Foreman

other Cherokees did not surrender: "How much longer we shall be permitted remain here among our lands, to enjoy our rights and privileges, I do not know. From the present aspect of affairs,

we shall very soon be without house & home. Indeed, ever since the 23rd of May, we have been looking almost daily for the soldiers to come, and turn us out of our houses. They have already warned us to make preparations, and come in to camps, before were forced to do so. But I have stated distinctly to some of the officers at Head quarters, what I thought of this so called treaty and what course I intended to persue [sic] in the event no new treaty was made; and see no reason yet why I should change my mind. My determination, and the determination of a large majority of the Cherokees, yet in the Nation is, never to recognize this fraudulent instrument as a treaty nor remove under it until we are forced to do so at the point of the bayonet. It may seem unwise and hazardous to the fraimers [sic] and friends of this instrument, that we should persue such a course; but I am fully satisfied it is the only one we can persue with clear consciences."[24]

Even after most of the Cherokees were prisoners, Principal Chief John Ross and a Cherokee delegation were still in Washington, DC, engaged in political maneuvering to attempt to avoid or at least postpone the removal. The pleas for more time, however, were to no avail.

Gen. Nathanial Smith, superintendent for the removal, ordered swift departures of the detachments of Georgia Cherokees. The *Niles Register* reported: "Then came the shipping off to the west. The agent endeavored to induce them to go into the boats voluntarily; but none would agree to go. The agent then struck a line through the camp;–the soldiers rushed in and drove the devoted victims into the boats, regardless of the cries and agonies of the poor helpless sufferers. In this cruel work, the most painful separations of families occurred.–Children were sent off and parents left, and so of other relations."[25]

On June 6, 1838, the first group consisting of 489 individuals departed on the steamboat *George Guess,* escorted by Lt. Edward Deas. This detachment made the trip in only fourteen days and had no deaths in route. The group equaled a speed record for the journey set by a detachment led by John S. Young in March 1837. On June 12 the second detachment under Lt. R. H. K. Whiteley also departed from Ross's landing by boat. Both of these groups traveled a portion of the distance by rail, sixty miles between Decatur and Tuscumbia, Alabama, to avoid the most treacherous shoals in the Tennessee River.[26]

The third detachment with 1,072 people, conducted by Cap. Gus Drane, left Ross's Landing on June 17. With no boats available, this group was forced to travel overland to Waterloo, Alabama, a distance of some two hundred miles. By the end of June, more than a dozen were dead, and 293 had escaped to make their way back to the concentration camps in East Tennessee. They began their journey again with other detachments later in the year. On the Arkansas River, the steamboats carrying the Whiteley and Drane detachments were both stranded by low water on sandbars downstream from Lewisburg (present-day Morrilton), Arkansas. From there they traveled overland through western Arkansas during the peak of the summer. In addition to hot, dry, and dusty conditions, both detachments suffered from excessive sickness along the way. Towards the end of the journey, Whiteley had to halt the detachment because more than half the members were sick. Whiteley reached the head of Lee's Creek in the Flint District on August 2, 1838, and reported seventy-two deaths on the 1,554 mile journey.[27] Drane left Ross's Landing on June 17 and arrived at Webber's Plantation in the Indian Territory on September 4 and turned over the detachment to an officer from Fort Gibson on September 7, 1838, reporting 146 deaths during the journey.[28]

Gen. Scott, military commander for the removal, had hoped to use the three detachments as an example of military efficiency and evenhandedness. Instead the military appeared as the instruments of oppression and invoked the ridicule and scorn even by the citizenry who were previously indifferent towards removal.

The reports of death and suffering on these detachments, brought back to concentration camps in East Tennessee by escapees pleading for help, had a profound effect on the strategy of the Cherokee leadership as well as the disposition of the military officials in charge of the removal. Almost immediately the adversarial groups began a dialogue that resulted in a postponement of the departure of the remaining detachments until after the summer season, arrangements for the Cherokees to superintend their own removal, and the choice by most of the remaining Cherokees of the overland route necessitated by water levels purported to be too low for steamboat passage. In spite of earlier predictions that the water route and overland route would cost approximately the same, the land route proved more expensive primarily because of the amount of time involved. The selection of the overland route was most fortunate for the agents and contractors appointed by John Ross, who had more to gain in profits from a lengthy trek, and for the credibility of the principal chief, who had repeatedly warned that the removal could be very costly for the government.[29]

On August 1, 1838, the Cherokee Council members, prisoners in the Aquohee Concentration Camp awaiting deportation, passed a resolution stating: "Whereas the title of the Cherokee People to their lands is the most ancient, pure and absolute known to man, its date is beyond the reach of human records, its validity confirmed and illustrated by possession and enjoyment antecedent to all pretense of claim by any other portion of the human race. The title can not, by Cherokee law, be alienated by the act of an illegal treaty, hence it follows that the original title and ownership of said lands rest in the Cherokee Nation unimpaired and absolute."[30]

Cherokee leaders had earlier petitioned General Scott to be allowed to superintend their own removal. When this was granted, Principal Chief John Ross organized his followers into twelve detachments of about one thousand each. These groups left the East between August 23 and October 23, 1838, and arrived in the Indian Territory between January 4 and March 24, 1839. Additionally, a group of Treaty Party members, not under Ross, left the agency on October 11 disbanding at Vinyard Post Office, Arkansas, on January 7, 1839. A group of several hundred sick and infirm among Ross's followers left by boat on December 5, 1838, and reached the Illinois Campground near Tahlequah on March 18, 1839. Within a few months of the Camp Aquohee Council Resolutions proclaiming the inherent right of the Cherokee to their ancestral homeland, the last detachment of emigrants had departed the camps in East Tennessee for the Indian Territory.

Of the nearly fifteen thousand immigrants subjected to the forced removal, nearly two thousand died as the result of arduous conditions of confinement or travel. Another one thousand managed to avoid removal by escaping to the Great Smoky Mountains or by claiming citizenship under previous treaties. The highest mortality rates were among the very old and the very young. No families were immune to the suffering. Quatie Ross, the wife of the principal chief, died on the steamboat *Victoria* at Little Rock, Arkansas, on February 1, 1839.

By Spring 1839, more than twenty thousand Cherokees had emigrated to the Indian Territory, either voluntarily or by force. They found themselves alienated from their ancestral homeland facing the challenge of adapting to a new land to which they had no historical ties.

ᏓᎾᏬᎯᎵ 5
ᎣᏍᏓᎴᏍᎨ ᎾᏍᎩ ᎢᏳ ᏓᏕᎶᏆᏍᏗᎡᏗ
1839-1861

Chapter 5: Dawn of New Opportunities

Figure 1. Grand Council, 1843 by Andy Thomas. Oil on canvas. DC7. Gilcrease Museum, Tulsa, Oklahoma.

The Cherokee Nation was highly factionalized at the conclusion of removal in 1839. Leaders of the three groups attempted to create a new government, but each had widely differing opinions about its form. The Old Settlers, about eight thousand Cherokees who had emigrated

Figure 2. Ama, Atsila, Elohi (Water, Fire, Earth) by Dorothy Sullivan. After the removal, Cherokees worked to overcome the challenge of reuniting the factionalized tribe. Image courtesy of Cherokee Nation Businesses.

before the Treaty of New Echota, already had a government in place and expected it to continue. They were joined by about two thousand Treaty Party members who for the most part, emigrated in the two years allowed for voluntary removal before May 23, 1838, and expected to be proportionately represented in any government. The Ross Party, opposed to the treaty with more than fourteen thousand tribal members, more than the other two parties combined, expected their government to be transplanted intact from the East.

The forced removal had taken its toll on the Cherokee Nation. Hundreds of people died in the camps while waiting for deportation or on the journey to the Indian Territory. The survivors blamed the collaborators with the US government for the property loss and suffering of those who resisted the removal. The hopes that many had for a peaceful transition of government were dashed when Major Ridge, his son John Ridge, and nephew Elias Boudinot, three leaders of the Treaty Party, were killed on June 22, 1839, allegedly by members of the Ross Party. A large number of Ross supporters had met at Double Springs, four miles northwest of Tahlequah, on June 20 to draw straws to determine who would act as agents of society to carry out the punishment for the violation of the law that Major Ridge, himself, had introduced ten years earlier in October 1829.[1] The law made it a capital offense for any Cherokee to cede land to the federal government without permission of the National Council or National Committee.

In spite of the factionalism that compounded the tragedy of the removal, the Cherokee people were able to make significant strides forward in the early years after the removal, rebuilding their progressive lifestyle by drawing from the remnants of society and culture they were forced to leave behind. Within months after the arrival of the last detachments, a constitutional convention was held, and a new constitution was adopted on September 6, 1839, in the first of three attempts to unify the Cherokee Nation in the first year after removal. The Cherokees also quickly transplanted their concepts of churches, schools, businesses, and literature. Tahlequah, founded in 1838, became the new capital and the center of business activity, and Park Hill, a residential suburb, emerged as a cultural oasis in the Indian Territory.

Principal Chief John Ross not only was challenged by bringing the Cherokee factions together but also by establishing peaceful relations with their new neighbors. During the 1830s, nearly all of the tribes east of the Mississippi River were forced from their traditional homelands and assigned new lands in the Indian Territory adjacent to groups who spoke different languages and historically had competed for lucrative hunting grounds. Removal to Indian Territory had brought the Five Civilized Tribes–the Cherokees, Choctaws, Chickasaws, Creeks, and Seminoles–closer together and had activated common problems that had been dormant in their old homes. Realizing the need for a general Indian convention, the Cherokee National Council during the 1842 session organized a meeting of the surrounding tribes. In addition to the eastern tribes that had lengthy contact with Anglo-Americans, there were also the Plains tribes that at this point had not yet faced the same pressures from the dominant society.

In 1841 the Creeks had attempted to organize a grand council with little result. In 1842 Principal Chief John Ross received permission from the National Council to invite representatives from all of the neighboring tribes to meet in Tahlequah. In January 1843, Chief Ross and John Looney, a member of the Cherokee Executive Council, met the chiefs of the Creek Nation, Rolly McIntosh and Ufalar Harjo, at Fort Gibson where Cherokee Agent Pierce Mason Butler helped to organize the proposed convention.

A pipe and tobacco along with an

Figure 3. William Potter Ross (center), c. 1880-90. Image Courtesy of the Cherokee National Historical Society.

invitation was sent to thirty-six tribes. The Creeks co-hosted the event and Cherokee Agent Butler, former governor of South Carolina who had been appointed to replace the aging Monfort Stokes in 1841, helped organize the council. At least nineteen groups sent representatives who arrived in Tahlequah in June 1843. The estimates of the number of people who attended the convention ranged from three thousand to ten thousand.

William Potter Ross, nephew of the principal chief, was in school at the time of removal but returned to the Cherokee Nation in 1842 after graduation from Princeton. He attended the Grand Council of Peace.[2] The artist John Mix Stanley was also in Tahlequah at the time. He painted portraits of some members of the Ross family including William Potter Ross. In his famous painting, *The 1843 Council at Tahlequah*, he depicts representatives of the Cherokee Nation meeting under the Council Shed with leaders of other tribes in the Indian Territory.[3]

A few months after the council meeting in October 1843, William P. Ross appeared for business at the capital under the Council Shed of Tahlequah. He was welcomed by the Chief, presented and introduced to the Senate and National Council. He was chosen clerk of the Senate, and during that session of the National Council was elected editor of the *Cherokee Advocate*. Its first edition appeared in September 1844 with the significant motto: "Our Country, Our Rights, Our Race."[4]

The deaths of Major Ridge, John Ridge, and Elias Boudinot in 1839 led to violence resulting from incriminations and reprisals among the factions during the post-removal period. The only survivor of the top leadership of the Treaty Party was Stand Watie, nephew of Major Ridge and brother of Elias Boudinot. In 1842 Watie encountered James Foreman, whom he recognized as one of his uncle's assassins. In the ensuing altercation, Foreman was killed, but Watie was acquitted by an Arkansas jury on the grounds of self–defense. Acts of violence continued, and by 1844 factionalism was so extreme that partition of the Cherokee Nation seemed inevitable. The following year was the most violent since the removal. During a ten month period in 1845 and 1846, thirty-four people were killed, including Stand Watie's brother Thomas Watie. Anarchy seemed to prevail.

On Saturday night, November 2, 1845, a number of men–purportedly Thomas Starr, Ellis Starr, Washington Starr, Suel or Ellis Rider and Ellis West–arrived at R. J. Meigs' house and demanded admittance. Meigs[5] escaped through the back door as they opened fire on him, and the next morning the bodies of two Cherokees were found less than a mile from his house.[6]

One week later on November 9, 1845, the father of the Starr brothers, James Starr, was murdered at his home east of present-day Stilwell.[7] According to his family, a group of armed men had ridden up to the family home at daybreak. Believing they were Light Horsemen, James told his family to say nothing, and let them search the house, then they would leave. There were about sixteen men in the group, most if not all were Cherokees. One was described as a mulatto, and most had painted their faces.[8]

The witnesses recognized some of the men and reported them as Anderson Benge, Talusky Tucquo, John Downing, Luis Tucquo, Bill Sour John, John Tato, Chico Canisky, and Big Stan. Tucquo fired the first shot and hit Starr in the left arm. A second shot penetrated his breast and may have been fired by Luis Nelm. Starr called for his son to make his escape and then died. The son, however, was shot three times and died six weeks later. Mary Starr,[9] the sixteen-year-old daughter, attempted to escape on horseback. Some in the company beat her horse with their guns and fretted him so that she was compelled to dismount. The three small sons in the house, ages ten, eight, and five, were protected by the women who put themselves between the party and the boys.

Had Mary been able to escape, she might have been able to warn Suel Rider and his mother, who lived one and a quarter-mile distant. The party, seemingly led by Tucquo, arrived there also in the early morning. John Tato walked into the kitchen and led Suel into the yard before the group opened fire. Shot seven times, Suel tried to escape but was chased down by a man named Big Stand and stabbed to death. Suel's mother, Mary Wood, or Rider, later stated that after the intruders shot Suel, a man shot at another of her sons who was only sixteen years of age, and he missed. Tucquo had ordered the boy not be killed because he believed him to be white. Her son belonged to the Old Settler and Treaty Party.

On the same day as the Starr and Rider murders, Bluford Rider and Washington Starr were sought by the same group. Both escaped but not without injury. Washington Starr identified members of the party he knew as Tucquo, Tallusca Tucquo, Lewis Nelm, Cho-Chucca, Cheu Conskee or Otter Lifter, John Downing (Sam's son), and Aaron Wilkinson. According to family oral tradition, Mary Rider was left with the task of burying Suel Rider by herself because all of the male relatives in the family had fled to Arkansas.[10] James Starr was buried in the Oak Grove Cemetery near present-day Stilwell.[11]

Gen. Matthew Arbuckle,[12] commanding the Second Military Department at Fort Smith, quickly sent Maj. B. L. E. Bonneville to investigate and ordered a company of First Dragoons stationed at Fort Gibson to Evansville, Arkansas, a camp between the warring factions.[13] Lt. Cave Johnson Couts was a member of this company.[14] On November 15, 1845, six days after the murders of Starr and Rider, General Arbuckle, from his headquarters in Fort Smith, wrote to Acting Chief George Lowery that he had sent Major Bonneville to investigate the commotion in the Flint District.[15]

From Bonneville's report, Arbuckle said that he learned that the "murder of Starr and Rider and the wounding of two of Starr's sons, and the consequence of disturbances in the Cherokee Nation have resulted, directly or indirectly, from Resolutions of the National Council or orders issued in pursuance thereof." The report also claimed that more than one hundred men had been driven from their homes by the reckless proceedings of the Light Horse. These men feared that by returning to their homes they may fall victim, no matter how innocent they might be, to the illegal and savage acts of an armed and irresponsible body…Arbuckle demanded that the Light Horse be disbanded at once and those persons concerned with the murder of James Starr and Rider arrested. Nothing short of this would be acceptable.

George Lowery,[16] acting chief in the absence of John Ross, refused to respond to Arbuckle directly but instead wrote to Col. James McKissick, the Cherokee agent. Lowery insisted that the information Arbuckle had received was incorrect. The assertion that the killing of Starr and Rider resulted from Resolutions of the National Council or order issued pursuant thereof was "entirely groundless." The charge against the Light Horse was "equally unfounded." The act was passed on November 8, and the captain and lieutenant were appointed on November 11. They hastily assembled some ten or twelve men and arrived in the Flint District on Wednesday, November 12, three days after the murders.[17]

Lowery appointed a committee to investigate the disturbances. The committee consisted of George Hicks, Stephen Foreman, John Thorn, and William Shorey Coody. The committee filed their report on November 25, 1845. The committee concluded that on the night of November 2, a number of men including Thomas Starr, Ellis Starr, Washington Starr, Suel or Ellis Rider, and Ellis West went to the house of R. J. Meigs and attempted to kill him. This same group was responsible for at least sixteen other murders and resulted in a group forming to go after them. The Treaty Party members who fled across the border assembled at the home of Samuel Downing near Evansville. The

Figure 4. George Lowery. Oil on canvas. 29 1/2" × 26 1/4" (74.9 × 66.7 × 4.1 cm). GM 0126.2180 Gilcrease Museum, Tulsa, Oklahoma.

committee went there and found about fifty men. At no time had the group ever been larger than sixty, far below the two hundred that had been reported.

On November 20, 1845, General Arbuckle again wrote to acting chief George Lowrey, "I have directed Captain Boone, with his company of dragoons, to remain near Evansville [Arkansas], and to notify all the refugees not to cross into the nation for the purpose of violence; that such a step on their part would forfeit for them the protection they now enjoy."[18]

In comparing the military and government reports with Couts's diary, it is apparent that his views put him at odds with all of his superiors including national celebrities in his own camp.[19]

President James K. Polk relied heavily on information and affidavits supplied by General Arbuckle from members of the Treaty Party. In a message to the Senate of the United States on April 13, 1846, President Polk called for prompt intervention by the US government into the internal feuds in the Cherokee Nation. He stated that: "Several unprovoked murders have been committed by the stronger party on the weaker party of the tribe which will probably remain unpunished by Indian authorities, and there is reason to apprehend that similar outrages will continue to be perpetrated, unless restrained by the authorities of the United States."

"Many of the weaker party," he reported, "have been compelled to seek refuge beyond the limits of the Indian country within the State of Arkansas and are destitute of the means for their daily subsistence. The military forces on the western frontier have been active in their exertions to suppress these outrages, and to execute the treaty of 1835, by which it is stipulated that the United States agree to protect the Cherokee Nation from domestic strife and foreign enemies."[20] The president asked Congress to make amendments to laws to allow for the trial and punishment of said offenders in the courts of the United States.

One week after the president's message to Congress calling for the punishment of the offenders including Tucquo, William Potter Ross wrote to Lieutenant Couts gifting him Tucquo's bandolier bag. Couts wrote in his diary, "Wm. Ross, Ed[i]t[or] of Adv[oca]t[e], I esteem very highly–through his hands, I recd, the most beautiful pouch &c. from Old Tucquo."[21] Although General Arbuckle wanted to defend the Treaty Party members who had willingly ceded their homelands to the US government a decade earlier, Couts and some of his men viewed the Treaty Party refugees as criminals and villains.[22] Arbuckle was obviously persuaded by the information from Treaty Party members who felt excluded and even oppressed by the dominant Ross Party group. Couts was likewise influenced by the people with whom he associated, many of whom were the socialites of the Cherokee aristocracy.[23]

Throughout winter and spring 1845-46, political violence continued in the Cherokee Nation. On December 27, 1845, Lt. John M. Brown of the Cherokee Light Horse was killed by Charles Smith at a frolic at William Boling's on the Caney River. Smith was an accomplice of Bean Starr, whom Lieutenant Brown had killed in a gun fight a year earlier when Bean was leaving the area with a herd of stolen horses. The next evening, Smith was dragged from bed at his mother's house near White Oak Springs in the Tahlequah District and shot to death in the front yard by a posse of five or six men, presumably Light Horsemen, led by the lieutenant's cousin, also named John Brown.

By mid-March 1846, President James Polk was leaning toward a division of the Cherokee Nation in accordance with the wishes of the Treaty Party. In April he reported to Congress his intent to divide the nation politically and geographically. On April 30, 1846, Wheeler Faught was hanged in the Going Snake District for the murder of Ta-ka-to-ka.[24] Before his execution, Faught implicated Tom, Ellis, Jim, Sam, William, and Washington Starr; John Rider; James Taylor; and a white man named Madison Gerring in the murder.

In May 1846, for the first time in eight years, Principal Chief John Ross presented Congress with a memorial. This petition argued that division of the nation was not desired by the mass of Cherokee people and that the Act of Union of 1840 was supported by the majority. In a final effort to mediate differences between the factions, the president appointed another commission to attempt to settle differences between feuding Cherokees. In July 1846, a compromise was reached, and President Polk presented the document to Congress on August 7. Representatives of the three Cherokee factions gathered in Polk's office on August 13, 1846, to sign the treaty promised by President John Tyler in 1841.

To keep the peace and the Cherokee Nation intact, John Ross and the National Party were forced to compromise with the Treaty Party and accept the fraudulent treaty of New Echota of a decade earlier.[25] In accepting the 1846 treaty, Ross called for a national meeting. Urging reconciliation between all three factions, he declared, "We are all of the household of the Cherokee family and of one blood…embracing each other as Countrymen, friends and relatives."[26] In closing Ross shook hands with Stand Watie, his bitter enemy and the defiant leader of the Treaty Party. The compromise was painful for both sides. The outnumbered Western Cherokee had to give up their autonomy and accede to Ross's leadership, while the Eastern Cherokee had to accept the finality of the Treaty of New Echota and all of its terms.[27]

On August 6, 1846, representatives of the three factions met in Washington, DC and signed a treaty to keep the Cherokee Nation intact.[28] Article 2 of the treaty of 1846 provided a general amnesty for all those guilty of political violence in the Cherokee Nation.[29] Afterwards, Principal Chief John Ross, who had spent much of his time in the 1840s in Washington, DC, away from the violence in the Cherokee Nation, returned to Rose Cottage, his home at Park Hill, with his bride Mary Stapler.[30] With the hostilities ended, the dragoons were recalled to Fort Gibson. After eleven months at the dragoon camp northwest of Evansville, Lieutenant Couts wrote, "the company left that delightfully villainous place on the 18th (of October, 1846) and arrived here (Fort Gibson) on October 19th."

With the treaty of 1846 came the release of federal funds due under the 1835 Treaty of New Echota. A sizable portion of the funds was set aside for education. The school system soon boasted of 144 elementary schools and a bilingual curricula. In 1847 the council appropriated funds to build two institutions of higher learning, the Cherokee Male Seminary in Tahlequah and the Cherokee Female Seminary in Park Hill. The female seminary was patterned after Mount Holyoke College in South Hadley, Massachusetts, and the male seminary was modeled after classical high schools such as Boston Latin School and Lawrenceville Academy near Princeton, New Jersey. The seminaries opened in 1851.[31] The emphasis on classical education and the publication of religious and secular materials in the Cherokee syllabary, introduced by Sequoyah in 1821, gave

Dawn of New Opportunities 1839 - 1861

"ᎾᏍᎩᏃ ᏂᎦᏓᏳ ᏣᎳᎩᏯ ᏓᎾᏓᏛᏐ ᎠᏓ ᎤᏌ ᎩᎡᎢ…ᎥᏙᏂᎲᎬ Ꮎ ᎠᏧᏣ ᎤᎾᎸᎦᎡ ᏓᎥᎾᎢ, ᎬᏓᎵ ᎠᏓ ᎠᎦᏍᎴ ᎬᏣᏓᎵ."

- ᎤᎬᏫᏳᎯ
ᏥᏂ ᏗᏂᏍᎩᏂ

"We are all of the household of the Cherokee family and of one blood… embracing each other as Countrymen, friends, and relatives."

- Chief John Ross

Figure 5. The Cherokee Seminary schools endured long after their initial formation. Cherokee Male Seminary with students c. 1902. Image Courtesy of the Cherokee National Historical Archives.

the Cherokees a broader scope for education and a higher literacy level than any of their neighboring tribes or states.

The 1850s were really a golden age for the Cherokee people. The open hostilities that followed the removal were set aside, and the Cherokee Nation showed signs of prosperity. The de-stabilization and animosities brought about by the forced removal might have remained buried forever had the Cherokees not been drawn into the larger regional issues that erupted in the American Civil War.

While the Cherokee people grappled with reunification of their country and reconstruction of their economy, other narratives were emerging on the stage of tribal history that would have long-term consequences. Although the issue of slavery would take center stage, a parallel story was being written by those who came to be called the Texas Cherokees.

The Texas Cherokees, under the leadership of Duwali, who was better known as "the Bowl," settled in Texas along the Sabine, Neches, and Angelina Rivers in winter 1819-20. They were welcomed by the Spanish as buffers against American encroachment. Earlier the Bowl and his people had immigrated to Arkansas from North Carolina after being issued a passport by R. J. Meigs on January 10, 1810. The passport was for passage of sixty-three Cherokees, including Sau-low-ee and the Bowl in twelve canoes and one flat-bottomed boat.

Dawn of New Opportunities 1839 - 1861

Figure 6. The Murrell Home. Image Courtesy Cherokee National Historical Archives.

The Murrell Home

The oldest home in Oklahoma is a two-story frame house in Park Hill, Cherokee Nation, long known as the George M. Murrell Home. Today, it is called Hunter's Home.

The original owners of the home were George and Minerva Murrell. George was a non-Indian native of Virginia who married Minerva Ross, the daughter of Lewis Ross, a prosperous Cherokee planter, and the niece of Principal Chief John Ross. According to Cherokee law and custom, George could not own land or improvements in the Cherokee Nation. Instead, in the matrilineal structure of Cherokee life, the home belonged to Minerva.

The home was built in 1845 and reflected the prosperity of the Murrell and Ross families. The Greek Revival home was two stories tall and surrounded by out-buildings such as slave quarters, a barn, a grist mill, blacksmith shop, corn crib, fence-enclosed fields, and a spring house covered with a rock building. In 1855 Minerva died and George married her sister, Amanda. They would have six children together.

The Murrells fled from the home and Park Hill during the Civil War. They would never return. Instead, members of the extended Ross family lived in the home until the twentieth century, when it was puchased by the State of Oklahoma and converted into a historic site. Today, the Hunter's Home is undergoing a transformation that will use the site and surrounding land to interpret Cherokee life and agriculture as it existed before the Civil War.

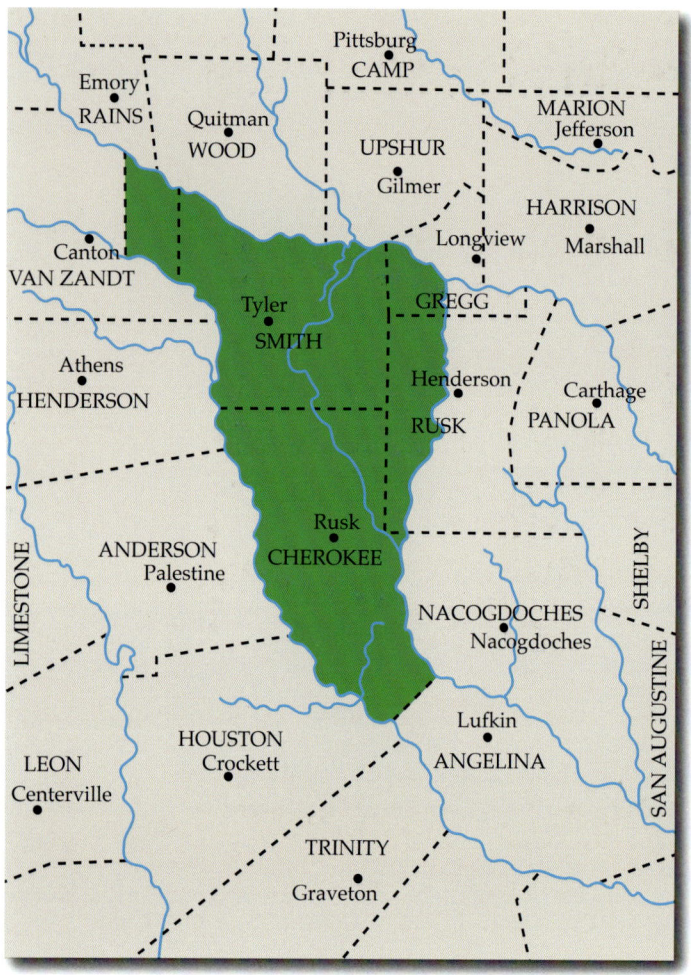

Figure 7. Map showing the Texas Cherokees Territory.

According to the passport, the Bowl was a man of good character who planned to settle on either the Arkansas or White Rivers. According to Meigs, the group was from a town 160 miles upstream from the Cherokee Agency on the Hiwassee River. The Bowl was not associated with the Muscle Shoal massacre as erroneously reported by Cephus Washburn and numerous other writers.[32]

Before emigrating to Texas, the Bowl reported that he and his followers lived on Petit Jean Creek in Arkansas. From there, they first moved to Lost Prairie and then to the Red River. In winter 1820-21, they relocated their village further westward to the Three Forks of the Trinity River. After another year and disputes over hunting rights with the Taovayas Indians, they moved into an uninhabited area north of Nacogdoches. They were soon followed by other Cherokee. By 1828 there were between eighty and one hundred Cherokee families in Texas with a total population of three hundred to four hundred living in three to seven towns. Most of the settlements were north of Nacogdoches on the Sabine River and its tributaries.[33]

In 1825 one village was on the Red River near the mouth of the Kiametia River. Tachee, its leader, moved the village north and south of the Red River as circumstances dictated. After the treaty of 1828 ceding the land in Arkansas, the population expanded to perhaps as many as eight hundred by 1833. They reportedly owned three thousand cattle, three thousand hogs, and more than five hundred horses. They were successful hunters and farmers and participated in the Nacogdoches marketplace. Empresario Frost Thorn, who lived near Nacogdoches, reported in 1828 that he had purchased $1,000 worth of corn and peas from the Cherokees for his colonists.[34]

Throughout the 1820s and 1830s, they sought legitimacy for their residency by frequently sending delegations to confer with government officials. They found themselves caught between the conflict between the Mexicans and Americans and between other Indians and non-Indians. They continued the war with the Osages until 1825, when the Osages were moved to a reservation in present-day

Dawn of New Opportunities 1839 - 1861

Kansas. They quickly took on new enemies in Texas including the Wacos, Tonkawas, Tawakonis, and Comanches. They were allied with other eastern tribes including the Shawnee, Delaware, Kickapoo, Creek, and Choctaw. The combined fighting strength of the eastern tribes in Texas in 1825 was estimated at five hundred warriors.

Cherokee life in Texas throughout its existence was unsettled. Villages frequently moved for reasons of political expediency, economic advantage, or defense. In 1828 the Bowl's village was on the Sabine River. By 1835 it was on Cherokee Creek nine miles north of present-day Henderson. In 1836 it had moved to Bowles Creek between Henderson and Tyler. In 1838 it was four miles west of present-day Alto near the Neches Saline. Gatunwali's (Hard Mush) Village moved from northwest present-day Rusk County to a location a few miles south of present-day Rusk. Richard Fields's village, which in 1823 was on the Sabine, moved by 1825 to Cypress Creek, a tributary of Sulphur Fork in present-day Cass County.[35]

On February 23, 1836, the Cherokees signed their one and only treaty with the provisional government of Texas. The treaty promised the Cherokees a permanent home in Texas. A few weeks later, Santa Anna's army captured the Alamo on March 6 and Goliad on March 27. The sudden flight of Texans in the face of the Mexican army no doubt alarmed the Cherokees. That summer several Indian tribes sent delegates to Matamoros to confer with

Figure 8. Cherokee Chief Tucquo's Bandolier Bag, *circa 1835. Wool and beads. GM 84.3409. Gilcrease Museum, Tulsa, Oklahoma.*

Mexican military officials. With the uncertainty of the outcome of the movement for Texas independence, the Cherokees were ambivalent and divided in their loyalties. In spite of the fact that some individual Cherokees fought for the Mexicans, the Texas Cherokees were protected by their old ally Sam Houston throughout his presidency.

On December 10, 1838, Houston was succeeded by Mirabeau Bounaparte Lamar, who had served as secretary to Governor George M.

Troup of Georgia between 1823 and 1826. Lamar indicated in his first policy statement that he intended to pursue the removal of the Cherokees from Texas. In May 1839, President Lamar sent the Cherokees a message which amounted to an ultimatum to leave the country. Diplomatic attempts to reconcile the differences failed. The Bowl's request to stay to harvest crops in the field were denied as were the requests to leave without military escort or to removing the locks from Cherokee guns.[36]

In the first battle a few miles north of the Bowl's village at dusk on July 15, 1839, eighteen Cherokees and two Texans were killed. The Cherokees and their allies the Shawnee, Delaware, and Kickapoo began moving north before daybreak on July 16. Despite the Bowl's assertion that they had little ammunition, they repulsed two attacks before being overrun. At the end of the battle, the Bowl sat alone on the battlefield wounded and unable to flee. The eighty-three-year-old chief was shot in the head at point blank range by a Texas militiaman. Around him were the bodies of Gatunwali and one hundred other Indians. The survivors dispersed into small groups and wandered for weeks without provisions. By spring 1840, most of the refugees had resettled with other groups. Some eighty Cherokee warriors were reported traveling with a Mexican agent. Some found homes among other tribes in Texas or present-day Oklahoma, and a large number reportedly moved to a location near Tachee's settlement at the confluence of Canadian and Arkansas Rivers in the Cherokee Nation.[37]

In 1854 Reverend Marcus Palmer observed that the Cherokee Nation "is fast tending towards a division into antagonistic parties (between) the mixed-bloods and the full Cherokees. The former constitute about one-third of the nation and the latter about two-thirds…(The) two classes are very naturally collecting into distinct and separate settlements." John Ross confided his own concerns about the divisiveness among the Cherokees to his trusted friend Rev. Evan Jones in May 1855. Ross knew that Jones supported his position on national unity as the best means to ensure Cherokee independence and survival. He also knew that Jones and his northern Baptist colleagues were staunchly antislavery. Ross shared with Jones news of a secret society being organized in the Delaware and Saline Districts to promote slavery and support political candidates with a pro-Southern agenda.[38]

To counter that proslavery faction, Evan Jones and his son, John Buttrick Jones, began to organize full-bloods in their churches into a well-informed and politically astute force to prevent proslavery forces from dominating the Cherokee political process. Before long the Keetoowah Society was formed as a response to the proslavery "Blue Lodges," later known as the Knights of the Golden Circle. The name Keetoowah came from an ancient town on the Tuckseigee River in present-day Swain County, North Carolina. The name was also used by an earlier society composed of the most wise and experienced elders charged with preserving the most esoteric knowledge of Cherokee rituals and oral traditions.[39]

The founders of the Keetoowah Society in 1855 were primarily full-blood northern Baptists. They were portrayed by their adversaries, the pro-Southern mixed-bloods and intermarried whites, as an abolitionist society under the influence of radical Northern missionaries, such as the Joneses. Abolition, however, was not a primary objective, and the Joneses were precluded from membership because of race. In the first few years, the Keetoowah Society met without any formal organization simply to work out their position on issues facing the nation. The meetings included ceremonies and dances, traditionalism inherent to the full-blood lifestyle.

Bud Gritts, a principal architect of the society, later reported that the formal organization began in 1858 when on April 15, the society decided to affiliate with the North on the issue of slavery and to seize the initiative from the mix-blood slaveholders in setting Cherokee policies. They, as the full-blood majority, would seek control of the Cherokee government and determine the destiny of their people. The Keetoowah constitution, membership lists, and society records were kept in the Sequoyan syllabary. Membership was limited to non-English-speaking Cherokee full-bloods. In addition to recruiting and supporting candidates for office, the Keetoowah Society developed into a mutual assistance organization to help those members in need, thus reviving the traditional concept of ᏍᏳ (*gadugi*). Prior to 1860, members began wearing crossed pins in their lapels as an emblem of their affiliation. Soon they were being referred to as the Pin Indians or Pins. By 1861 they numbered between fifteen hundred and two thousand members. They proved to be more than a match for the Knights of the Golden Circle. In the 1861 election, both houses of the Cherokee Legislature were dominated by Pins.[40]

The significance of slavery as a wedge issue was both political and economic. In 1809 the Cherokee population was 12,395. Only 125 of the 2,400 Cherokee families, less than 5 percent, owned slaves. At that time, there were 583 slaves and 75 free blacks living among the Cherokee. The 1835 census showed 1,592 slaves owned by 300 Cherokees, about 8 percent, of the 3,300 families or 16,395 Cherokee. After removal slave labor helped rebuild the Cherokee Nation. Those who had access to the ready supply of labor were able to clear land and construct homes and farm buildings sooner and engage in other economic enterprises more readily. The economic disparity between the Cherokee elite and the masses grew in tandem with slavery.[41]

Evan Jones reported that in 1848 only five of eleven hundred Cherokee Baptists owned slaves but noted they were almost entirely with full bloods who were too poor to own slaves. By 1860 approximately 10 percent, or four hundred out of forty-two hundred Cherokee families, owned slaves. At that time, the Cherokee population was twenty-one thousand and the slave population was thirty-five hundred to four thousand. Until 1854 the Ross Party's nationalistic policies had the greatest appeal to a majority of the four thousand Cherokee voters, whether slave holders or not. In the mid-1850s, slavery emerged as the most divisive issue in Cherokee politics.[42]

The hot winds of war were blowing both within and against the Cherokee Nation.

ᎠᏯᏙᎸᎢ 6
ᎠᏴᎵ ᎤᏊᎥᏢᎵ ᏓᏎᎵᏯᎵᎢ
1861-1865

Chapter 6: A Nation Divided

Figure 1. Map of battles in the Civil War that included Indian troops.

Unity had long been a goal of the Cherokee people. Whether it was defending their hunting grounds from neighboring tribes or pushing back against land-hungry Americans, the Cherokees knew that strength depended on unity. In 1861, as they watched the infant American nation descend into Civil War, the Cherokees were all too aware of the price they had paid when factionalism led to violence.

Unfortunately, the unity associated with the golden age of the Cherokee Nation from 1845 to 1861 was thin and fragile. At the most personal level was a lingering thirst for revenge. In 1849, more than a decade after members of the Ross faction had assassinated his father, John R. Ridge expressed the smoldering hatred that was shared by others when he suggested that his cousin Stand Watie should "raise some 25 to 30 white men to go and kill John Ross…I have a deep-seated principle of revenge which would never be satisfied…say the word and I am there." Watie, who had reached across the factional divide in a spirit of unity, declined the suggestion.[1]

More fundamental was the widening cultural and economic divide between the conservative full-bloods and the acculturated mixed-bloods. The former tenaciously clung to ancient traditions of hunting-gathering mixed with subsistence farming in isolated valleys nestled in the hills east of the Grand River. The latter adopted ways of southern farmers and merchants, complete with African American slaves, cotton culture, and free enterprise concentrated around communities with access to markets by river or proximity to border states.

The economic and social chasm between these two factions, although widening with each generation, was bridged somewhat by the art of compromise inherent in representative government. Skilled leaders, searching for the greatest good for the greatest number of people, could and did lead a dialog that often maintained a consensus when the issues were secular, such as education, commerce, and national defense–the pillars of the golden age

Figure 2. Stand Watie. Image courtesy of the Oklahoma Historical Society.

from 1845 to 1860. That willingness to accept compromise, however, did not extend to moral issues, and the great moral debate of the 1850s was a wedge issue like no other–slavery.

Once slavery became a moral rather than an economic issue, there was no gray area for compromise. By 1855 the Knights of the Golden Circle, organized to oppose abolitionists and protect the institution of African American slavery by force if necessary, had several chapters in the Cherokee Nation. On the other side of the moral divide was the Keetoowah Society, organized in the 1850s by full-bloods with the help of Evan Jones, an abolitionist Baptist minister who had lived among the Cherokees for more than forty years. The Keetoowahs marched against slavery with the Bible raised in one hand and devotion to traditional Cherokee values in the other. Both factions were sure God was on their side.[2]

If left to their own affairs, the Cherokees might have found solutions to these festering problems, but they were not. External forces were quickly changing the stage of history around the Cherokee Nation, stealing the time required to find consensus and pulling the factions to ever more radical positions. John Ross, the principal chief and a shrewd political leader, initially pushed back against the forces of division. In spring 1861, when Southern sympathizers from Arkansas demanded to know which side he would support if there were a war between the states, Ross held firm to his faith in unity and declared his devotion to neutrality.[3]

The descent into the American Civil War moved quickly after the election of Abraham Lincoln as president of the United States. It started when the state of South Carolina voted to secede from the Union, a right they said was embedded in the US Constitution. Other states followed, including Arkansas and Texas, and they banded together in what they called a new nation, the Confederate States of America. In April 1861, as the political rhetoric heated to a flash point, Confederate troops fired on Federal forces huddled behind the walls of Fort Sumter in Charleston Bay. The Civil War quickly escalated from words to guns.

Figure 3. Albert Pike. Image courtesy of the Oklahoma Historical Society.

While armies were organized, Confederate agents reached out to the Cherokee Nation. On June 5, 1861, Ross hosted a meeting at his home in Park Hill with Confederate Indian agent Albert Pike, an attorney, newspaperman, and poet from Fayetteville, Arkansas, and Confederate Gen. Ben McCulloch, a hero from the War for Texas Independence. They made generous promises of support, including the assumption of all US treaty stipulations, and asked that the Cherokees join them in resisting Union advances out of Kansas and Missouri. Ross, still hoping for neutrality as the safest course to tribal unity, declined the alliance but

"ᎠᏓᏲᎻᏗ ᎤᎾᏓᏡᎩ ᏔᎵᏃ ᎤᏂᏈᏴᏓ,
ᎤᏃᏍᏓᏅᎢ, ᎠᏲᎱᎯᏍᏗ, ᎤᏲᎢᏳ."

- ᎤᎬᏫᏳᎯ ᎤᏪᏥᎸᎢ ᏣᏂ ᏐᎦᎳᎾ

"Union is strength, dissension is weakness, misery, ruin."

- Chief John Ross

agreed to raise a regiment of home guards to protect the Cherokee borders.⁴

Pike continued on his mission by offering terms to the Creeks, Choctaws, Chickasaws, Seminoles, and Plains tribes to the west. Although the Creeks and Seminoles were divided, all of the tribal leaders signed treaties of alliance with the Confederate States of America. Meanwhile, early military action that spring and summer gave the impression that the South might be able to win its independence through force of arms. Federal troops abandoned every outpost in Indian Territory and retreated north into Kansas, while Confederate armies won decisive battles at Bull Run near Washington, DC and closer to the Cherokee Nation at Wilson's Creek near Springfield, Missouri.

While Principal Chief Ross watched the Confederacy secure allies on three sides of the Cherokee Nation, he anticipated that Pike would soon turn to Southern sympathizers in his own tribe to strike a deal. He had good reason to be suspicious. Two Southern Cherokees had already written Stand Watie and encouraged him to reach out to Pike. "Now is the time for us to strike," they said, "so that the power of the Ross Faction could be broken and our rights provided for and place us if possible at least on an honorable equity with this old Dominant party that has for years had its foot upon our neck… we must act quickly or all our work will have been in vain, our prospects destroyed, our rights disregarded, and we will be slaves to Ross's tyranny."⁵

Ross beat them to the punch. On August 21, 1861, he spoke to more than four thousand Cherokees gathered in a National Council at Park Hill. "The great object with me," he said, "has been to have the Cherokee people harmonious and united in the full and free exercise and enjoyment of all their rights of person and property. Union is strength, dissension is weakness, misery, ruin. The time has now come to adopt preliminary steps for an alliance with the Confederate States." After dinner the assembled tribal members accepted Ross's recommendation without dissent. Ross soon sent a letter to the Confederacy asking that Pike return to discuss a treaty.⁶

A Nation Divided 1861 - 1865

Speech by Principal Chief John Ross
August 21, 1861

"Our soil has not been invaded, our peace has not been molested, nor our rights interfered with by either Government (North or South). On the contrary, the people have remained at home, cultivated their farms in security, and are reaping fruitful returns for their labors. But for false fabrications, we should have pursued our ordinary vocations without any excitement at home, or misrepresentations and consequent misapprehensions abroad, as to the real sentiments and purposes of the Cherokee people.

"Alarming reports, however, have been pertinaciously circulated at home and unjust imputations among the people of the States. The object seems to have been to create strife and conflict, instead of harmony and good-will, among the people themselves, and to engender prejudice and distrust, instead of kindness and confidence, towards them by the officers and citizens of the Confederate states.

"The great object with me has been to have the Cherokee people harmonious and united in the full and free exercise and enjoyment of all their rights of person and property. Union is strength; dissension is weakness, misery, ruin. In time of peace, enjoy peace together; in time of war, if war must come, fight together. As brothers live, as brothers die. While ready and willing to defend our firesides from robber and murderer, let us not make war wantonly against the authority of the United or Confederate States, but avoid conflict with either, and remain strictly on our own soil. We have homes endeared to us by every consideration, laws adapted to our condition of our own choice, and rights and privileges of the highest character. Here they must be enjoyed or nowhere else. When these homes are lost, you will find no others like them.

"Then, my countrymen, as you regard your own rights, as you regard the welfare of your posterity, be prudent how you act. The permanent disruption of the United States is now probable. The State on our border and the Indian nations about us have severed their connection from the United States and joined the Confederate States. Our general interests are inseparable from theirs, and it is not desirable that we should stand alone. The preservation of our rights and of our existence are above every other consideration. And in view of all the circumstances of our situation I do say to you frankly that in my opinion the time has now come when you should signify your consent for the authorities of the nation to adopt preliminary steps for an alliance with the Confederate States upon terms honorable and advantageous to the Cherokee Nation."

From *War of the Rebellion: A Compilation of the Official Records of the Union and Confederate Armies*, Series 1, Vol. III, 673-675.

The terms included everything the Cherokees had been seeking from the federal government for decades. In addition to accepting all the financial obligations previously promised by the United States, the Confederacy recognized the following rights. The Cherokees were guaranteed the right of self government and jurisdiction over people and property within their nation. Agents to the tribe would be subject to approval by the Cherokee Nation. Cherokee lands could be dealt with only by the tribal government. The Cherokee Nation was entitled to a delegate in the Confederate House of Representatives. And the Confederate

Figure 4. **First Cherokee Mounted Rifles Fording the Illinois River** *by Jim Wilson. Image courtesy of Cherokee Nation Businesses.*

government would pay $500,000 plus interest since 1835 for the Neutral Lands in Kansas.[7]

Ross later shared an easily understood metaphor with his full-blood followers to explain this pivotal turning point in tribal history. "We are in the situation of a man standing alone upon a low, naked spot of ground," he said, "with the water raising rapidly all around him. He sees danger but does not know what to do. If he remains where he is, his only alternative is to be swept away and perish. The tide carries him, in its mad course, a drifting log. It, perchance, comes within reach of him. By refusing it, he is a doomed man. By seizing hold of it he has a chance for his life. He can perish in the effort, and may be able to keep his head above water until rescued, or drift to where he can help himself."[8] Dedicated to unity in his tribe and seeing no alternatives for peace, Principal Chief Ross reluctantly led his people into the white man's war.

The Cherokee Nation, with rich resources, was coveted by both the North and South. There were horses and mules for cavalry, artillery units, and supply trains. There were large herds of cattle to feed troops and civilians. There were crops for food, grist mills to grind corn and wheat, salt works to preserve meat and season food, and lead deposits for bullets and artillery shells. Whoever controlled the Cherokee Nation had access to all of these critical resources needed to fight a war.

Heightening the importance of the Cherokee Nation was its strategic location between the Confederate states of Texas and Arkansas, the Union state Kansas, and the border state of Missouri. In addition to being a buffer that might protect those boundaries and keep the fighting away from homes and families, the army controlling the Cherokee Nation would dominate the region's two primary arteries of trade and travel, the Texas Road running north and south and the Arkansas River flowing east and west. At the junction of those two frontier cross-country routes was Fort Gibson, soon to become a hotly contested prize on the field of battle.

Most important to both sides in the struggle were Cherokee fighting men, tough frontiersmen born into a culture that honored warriors and raised in a land where the skills of hunting, riding, fighting, and outdoor life easily transitioned to life in a frontier regiment. By one estimate, the Five Civilized Tribes could provide more than twenty-five thousand soldiers, and the Cherokee Nation was the largest of the tribes.

As stipulated in the treaty with the Confederacy, the Cherokees were authorized to organize two regiments to fight under the Stars and Bars. The first to take the field was led by Stand Watie, the prosperous planter, attorney, and merchant who had already been commissioned a Confederate colonel on July 12, 1861. His regiment was called the Cherokee Mounted Volunteers, although it would quickly become known by the name of its commander. The other regiment, which had been organized earlier as a home guard under the command of John Drew, was called the Cherokee Mounted Rifles. Although both regiments shared a common desire to protect their homes and families, they reflected the old factionalism that had split the tribe since the 1830s.[9]

Watie's officer corps was a who's who of Cherokee mixed-bloods who were pro-slavery, economically tied to the South, and eager to fight the Yankees. One of the first to join the cause was Elias C. Boudinot, Watie's nephew, whose father had been one of the Ridge family members executed by the Ross Faction after removal. Boudinot, a Southern firebrand, had recently partnered with Watie to develop several farms near the Arkansas line, and he had already served the Southern cause as recording secretary of the Arkansas Secession Convention.[10]

Another Southern patriot in Watie's command was William Penn Adair, a thirty-one-year-old six-foot two-inch mixed-blood Cherokee who was a slave-owning planter, attorney, and member of the tribal senate from the Flint District. He was joined by his brother,

Figure 5. William Penn Adair. Image courtesy of the Oklahoma Historical Society.

Benjamin Franklin Adair, and his father, George W. Adair, who served as Watie's quartermaster. Like Watie's father and brother, the elder Adair had signed the Treaty of New Echota and earned the wrath of the antiremoval Ross Faction.[11]

The Southern sympathies of Watie's regiment continued down the ranks. Named a first lieutenant was Clement Vann Rogers, a twenty-two-year-old cousin of Rich Joe Vann and the son of Robert and Sallie Vann Rogers, who had built a five-room home in the Going Snake District near the Arkansas line. By the Civil War, the younger Rogers had already proven his frontier skills by driving a herd of longhorn cattle from his ranch near present-day Talala to St. Louis, Missouri, a trek that took four months. To honor one of his commanding officers, Rogers would eventually name his last child William Penn Adair Rogers. The world would know him as Will Rogers.[12]

Commanding the other Cherokee regiment was John Drew, a sixty-five-year-old merchant who dealt in cattle, grain, and slaves. When the war erupted, he lived near Webbers Falls, where he operated a salt works. Drew was a respected leader of the Old Settlers, who had moved west to Indian Territory before the Treaty of New Echota and had united with John Ross's faction of full-bloods in 1839. He also was Ross's nephew-in-law.[13]

Another Old Settler leader affiliated with the full-blood majority was Thomas Pegg, a fifty-three-year-old farmer who had represented the Saline District in the Cherokee Legislature, served as an associate Cherokee Supreme Court Justice, and joined Ross as a tribal delegate to Washington, DC. When the regiment was being organized and trained at Fort Gibson, Pegg was elected major.

The Ross family was scattered throughout Drew's regiment. The lieutenant colonel was William Potter Ross, a graduate of Princeton College and a former editor of the *Cherokee Advocate* who was being groomed to succeed his uncle in the world of Cherokee politics. He was married to his first cousin, Mollie Ross, the daughter of John Ross's brother Lewis Ross.[14]

The ranks of the regiment were filled

A Nation Divided 1861 - 1865

Figure 6. Third Indian Home Guard Crossing the Illinois River *by Jim Wilson. Image courtesy of Cherokee Nation Businesses.*

mostly with full-bloods willing to defend their homeland, although many had previously joined the antislavery Keetoowah Society advocated by the Baptist missionary Evan Jones. Lewis Downing, one of Evans's proteges, was named a chaplain in Drew's regiment. When they went into combat, the full-blood members of the Keetoowah Society wore crossed pins on their lapel or jacket to identify themselves.[15]

Watie's troops were the first to gain combat experience. In August 1861, even before John Ross had announced his support for an alliance with the South, Confederate Gen. Albert Pike took his Indian troops into southwestern Missouri where Union and Confederate forces were gathering for battle. With them were some of Watie's men. On August 10, in the heat of battle, the Cherokee warriors charged and captured a Union battery. Although Watie was not present, the Southern press instantly made him a war hero.[16]

Drew's regiment was first called to action in December when a large band of neutral Creeks, Seminoles, and Cherokees under the

Figure 7. Flag of the Cherokee Braves. Image from the National Park Service at Wilson's Creek Battlefield Museum.

command of Creek leader Opothleyahola tried to escape to Union Kansas with their families and stock. During the second battle of the campaign, most of Drew's full-blood troops refused to attack, then deserted the Confederate lines and joined the pro-Union Indians.

Watie's men, ordered to reinforce the Confederate army, arrived at the Big Bend of the Arkansas River in the Cherokee Outlet just as the battle of Chustenahlah was ending with Opothleyahola's retreat. Watie had pursued the fleeing families for twenty miles when scouts reported that a large force of the enemy had gathered in some low hills on his left flank. Watie split his force of three hundred men, with Major Boudinot in charge of the second wing, and attacked the fortified position. The two-hour battle ended with a Confederate victory and the capture of seventy-five prisoners and thirty pack horses. Watie's men followed the action by rounding up about nine hundred head of cattle and 250 horses left by the retreating families.[17]

Watie and Drew soon joined the Confederate command of General Pike, who had established his headquarters on fortified high ground on the south side of the Grand River within view of the abandoned Fort Gibson. Pike called the new post Fort Davis. Watie's men were sent on patrols throughout the Cherokee Nation, especially in the northern districts where they tried to stop fellow tribal members from joining the Union forces in Kansas.

In late February, Pike was ordered to join Confederate units in northwestern Arkansas where they were to stop a Federal invasion. On March 6, 1862, the two armies met a few miles outside the community of Bentonville at a place called Pea Ridge. Watie's and Drew's men were placed on the left flank when the battle began, about three hundred yards from the enemy lines. At a pivotal point of the action, Watie's dismounted soldiers charged the Union lines.

Joseph F. Murrow, a Baptist missionary with the Cherokee troops, described the action in a published letter. "I was in the battle throughout," he said. "Our Indians fought well, taking one battery of four guns, brass pieces, and held them until ordered off the field. We then burned the wheels and spiked the guns as well as we were able." After another Union battery started shelling them, Pike ordered his men to retreat to a nearby woods. By the next day, after continuing the battle for several hours, the Confederates retreated with the Cherokee units guarding the supply train until they were back in the Cherokee Nation.[18]

Vulnerable to attacks from the north, east, and west, Pike moved his headquarters south down the Texas Road to a site on the Blue River near old Fort Washita, which was easier to defend and easier to supply from bases in Texas. In a letter sent to Watie, he summarized his plans for the Cherokee Nation. "I will keep your Regiment and Colonel Drew's in your own Country," he wrote. "You will give information of the approach of the enemy, harass his flanks and rear, stampede his animals, destroy his small foraging parties, and at last if he still advances, gaining his front join me within my lines and aid in utterly defeating him there. I beg your men to bury all old animosities and remember only that all are now fighting for the honour, independence and safety of the Confederate States and the Cherokee People."[19] As Pike feared, Union leaders were already planning to invade the Cherokee Nation.

By spring 1862, Union officials had two reasons to march south out of Kansas into the Cherokee Nation. One, they had neutralized Confederate forces in northwest Arkansas after the battles of Pea Ridge and Prairie Grove, and if they could control the Cherokee Nation, they could secure all of the territory north of the Arkansas River and put pressure on the Confederate stronghold at Fort Smith. Just as importantly they wanted to return the pro-Union Indian refugees huddled in southern Kansas to their homes where they could join the fight and plant crops to sustain troops and allies.

On March 19, the first part of that strategy was set in motion when the US War Department approved two new regiments to be called the Indian Home Guard. The First Indian Home Guard included eight companies of Muscogees (Creeks) and Euchees and two companies of Seminoles. The Second Indian Home Guard was organized with several companies of Cherokees, Osages, Delawares, Quapaws, and Shawnees. Both regiments included runaway slaves and free blacks who had fled north out of the Indian

Figure 8. Rose Cottage, home of John Ross. Image courtesy of the Cherokee National Historical Society.

Territory with Opothleyahola. They served under the condition that they would primarily fight other Indians and that they would only be used in their own country to defend their homes and families. Although poorly armed and clothed, they started training under white officers at Fort Scott that spring.[20]

While their fellow Cherokees trained to fight them, Watie's men were making hit-and-run raids along the north border of the Cherokee Nation. On June 6, 1862, before the Federal invasion was launched, a force armed with artillery advanced and attacked Watie and his one thousand men camped at Cowskin Prairie, just south of the Kansas/Missouri line. Watie and his men escaped, but they lost more than five hundred head of cattle.[21]

Three weeks later on June 28, the Federal army with Cherokee soldiers from the Second Indian Home Guard left Baxter Springs, Kansas bound for the Cherokee Nation with their families following behind. While Watie and his mounted men harassed the scouts and kept track of the column's progress, a Union force split off and made a forced overnight march to attack a Missouri militia unit camped near present-day Locust Grove. The skirmish ended with the capture of the Confederate commander and one hundred of his men. Just as important, they captured a sixty-wagon supply train full of powder and supplies needed by the Confederate soldiers and civilian Cherokees.[22]

Many of the retreating soldiers covered the thirty miles to Tahlequah with word that the Union army was coming. Drew's regiment, instead of digging in to resist, simply melted away as most of the remaining full-blood members of the Keetoowah Society switched sides and rode north to join the invading force. Among them were John Ross's sons, James, Allen, Silas, and George. The Cherokees filled out the Second Indian Home Guard and became the first members of the Third Indian Home Guard, organized under the command of the abolitionist firebrand Col. William A. Phillips.[23]

With Confederate forces pulled back to Fort Davis across the Grand River from Fort Gibson, Union troops rode into Tahlequah unopposed and continued to Park Hill where Principal Chief John Ross was found at his Rose Cottage home. Ross faced a dilemma. He said he had no authority to nullify the treaty with the Confederacy because it had been approved by a popular vote of the Cherokee people. The Union commanders made the decision for him. They placed him under house arrest, gathered the records of the Cherokee Nation, and escorted him to Kansas where he was granted a pardon. Ross would spend the rest of the war in Philadelphia with his wife's family.[24]

At the same time, the Union officers who had pushed their fighting units deep into the Cherokee Nation had to make a decision whether they could maintain their position as far south as Fort Gibson. A scorching heat wave and drought had killed the grass and made life unbearable for many of the troops, especially those from the north. They had plenty of beef to eat, thanks to the still bountiful herds of domestic cattle in the Cherokee Nation, but there were no foodstuffs, and any effort to bring supplies from Fort Scott were vulnerable to border raiding parties. On July 18, 1862, the Union forces abandoned Fort Gibson and retreated to Fort Scott in Kansas.[25]

The Cherokee Nation quickly became a no man's land both militarily and politically with neither the North nor South able or willing to occupy the land with enough troops to control the borders and with no civilian government with the resources to maintain law and order. Ross was gone, his government dispersed, and although a group of southern Cherokees gathered in August 1862 to elect Stand Watie principal chief, it was largely meaningless other than formalizing his role as the Cherokee spokesman working with the Confederate government in Richmond. The Cherokee Nation quickly became a land ruled by raiding parties that either confiscated supplies they needed to survive or destroyed what was left behind to deny goods to the enemy. In the middle were the

Cherokee people. The wolf was at the door.

The suffering of Cherokee civilians closely followed the ebb and flow of political and military turning points during the first years of the war. When John Ross and the full blood majority initially united to approve the Confederate alliance with the pro-Southern faction led by Stand Watie, life continued much as it had with widely scattered farms and ranches, communities with stores, mills, schools, and churches, and most important, the rule of law with elected tribal officials, sheriffs, and a court system. By December 1861, the first cracks in this domestic tranquility began to appear.

When Opothleyahola's warriors and families reached Kansas after their running battles with Confederate forces, there were fifty-nine Cherokees among the forty-five hundred refugees. That number grew steadily by the following summer when the hastily organized first Federal invasion of the Cherokee Nation started with initial victories and the capture of Principal Chief John Ross but ended with a sudden retreat back to Kansas. In the wake of that lightening strike was the collapse of a working tribal government and the defection of many full-bloods to the Union ranks. Dredging up old feuds, the blood flowed as Cherokees fought Cherokees.

Hannah Worcester Hicks, the daughter of missionaries and the wife of full-blood Cherokee farmer Abijah Hicks, described the violence as it escalated. "Oh what a year to remember will this year ever be to me, and to us all," she wrote in 1862. "We thought we had some trouble last year, but how happy compared with this. On the 4th of July, my beloved husband was murdered, killed away from home, and I could not even see him…I begin to hear now that my poor husband was killed by Pins, but through a mistake…they intended to kill another man."[26]

"My house has been burned down," she wrote in another entry, "my horses taken, but I think nothing of that…today the soldiers went to the house where Mrs. Vann's things were and turned them up at a great rate. Took what they could, and promised to come back for more."

On November 17, 1862, after she had moved in with her mother, Hicks made another entry in her diary that captured the unrelenting reign of terror suffered by civilians.[27]

"Today," she wrote, "we have had experience in being robbed. As soon as it was light they came and began. They took many valuable things and overhauled every closet, trunk, box and drawer they could find. The most valuable things are gone for good and all… They took about three barrels of sugar, all my blankets, most of my quilts, sheets, pillow cases, towels, table cloths, my teaspoons, all but one, and oh, that large pretty white bed spread that Mrs. Ross had given me; so many little things that I most highly prized; ribbons, sewing silk, pins, needles, thread, buttons, boxes of letters, my mantilla, calicoes, woolen stuffs, white cloth that I was saving to make up, part of my underclothes and stockings."[28]

The suffering was shared by the roughly

two thousand pro-Union Cherokees living among the sprawling refugee camps in Kansas. In December 1862, after the victory at Prairie Grove secured tentative Union control of northwest Arkansas, military commanders and Indian agents moved many of the refugees from the Baxter Springs area to Neosho, Missouri, which was largely abandoned by pro-Southern families.

Wiley Britton, a Union officer, later described the advantages of the move. "There were four or five springs of pure water within the limits of the town," he wrote. "There was an abundance of hardwood timber for fuel, easily accessible…probably a dozen or more churches in town that would afford hospital facilities for the sick and feeble, and there were quite a few doctors who could be useful in attending the sick and afflicted. Some of the Indian families were brought over from Baxter Springs in Government wagons, and the same wagons could be used for hauling in forage for their Indian ponies and for the mounts of the Indian soldiers, besides hauling in corn and wheat to the mills in the vicinity to be ground into meal and flour for the Indian families." Britton described the successful blending of this mixed community from December 1862 to the early part of April 1863. "Their conduct was commendable in every respect," he wrote. "Their relations with the white families were friendly, and there was no charge of pilfering or unlawfully appropriating the property of their white neighbors or of causing annoyance by trespassing."[29]

In mid-February, despite ten inches of snow on the ground and temperatures dropping as low as four degrees below zero, the pro-Union Cherokee soldiers assigned to the Second and Third Indian Home Guard left their camps near Neosho and held a National Council on Cowskin Prairie, just inside the border of the Cherokee Nation. They repudiated the Watie government, declared tribal allegiance to the Union, and elected Maj. Thomas Pegg as acting principal chief, Lt. Col. Lewis Downing as president protempore of the upper house, and Spring Frog as speaker of the lower house. The Council also emancipated all slaves owned by the Cherokee, which was largely symbolic until military victory was achieved. In effect, there were two Cherokee governments in exile.[30]

More than anything, the Cherokee refugees wanted to go home. To make that possible, Federal forces had to reoccupy and control Fort Gibson, which would give them an advanced base for patrolling the Cherokee Nation and securing control of the Arkansas River above Fort Smith, which was still held by Confederate troops. They also had to move early in the spring so families could plant gardens and reclaim fields for wheat and corn. Colonel Phillips, the best friend the Cherokees had in the Union army, started gathering cornmeal and flour, seed corn, potatoes, vegetable seeds, and tools and harness needed to plow.

In early April 1863, preceded by the Indian Home Guard regiments, a wagon

Figure 9. General Douglas Cooper. Image courtesy of the Oklahoma Historical Society.

Figure 10. General James Blunt. Image courtesy of the Oklahoma Historical Society.

train one-mile long with about one thousand Cherokee civilians returned to the Cherokee Nation. Wiley Britton, a Union officer with the marching column, described the scene of reunion at Park Hill. "When information was received that the train of exiles was approaching near at hand, a battalion of Cherokees was drawn up in line and awaited them. There were many demonstrations of joy between the Indian soldiers and their families, having seen little of each other the last year…the restoring to their homes the families of exiles of a nation was almost as keen a satisfaction to the white soldiers as to the Indians." Phillips and the rest of his soldiers continued south and occupied Fort Gibson without opposition. Cherokee families, meanwhile, scattered to their farms where they repaired cabins, plowed fields, and planted crops.[31]

While his men strengthened the defenses at Fort Gibson and built a large brick oven to bake bread for soldiers and civilians, Colonel Phillips and his troops attacked communities that provided men and supplies to Confederate soldiers. Twice in April they raided Webbers Falls, the home of several prosperous, slave-owning families with extensive plantations and businesses such as mills, salt works, and stores.

Figure 11. The Battle of Honey Springs. Image courtesy of the Oklahoma Historical Society.

Ella Coodey, the sixteen-year-old daughter of a prominent Treaty Party leader and diplomat, described the destructive nature of the raids. "I was left alone with the little children when a detachment of negro soldiers from Colonel Phillips's division took possession of the house. They ripped open the feather beds…took all the groceries. Late that evening another detachment of Union soldiers came with Colonel Phillips himself in charge and set fire to the house and burned it to the ground." Within a few days, she recalled, the troops burned every building in the village.[32]

Confederate leaders, including Col. Stand Watie, knew they had to drive the Union forces out of Fort Gibson and back to Kansas if they hoped to keep and protect their families and friends in the Cherokee Nation. While Watie led daring raids trying to cut off supplies to the fort, Confederate Gen. Douglas Cooper gathered men and supplies twenty-four miles south of Fort Gibson at a little community on the Texas Road called Honey Springs. His force consisted of approximately six thousand troops, including part of Watie's Cherokee regiment, and four pieces of artillery. All he needed before the attack were additional troops marching from Arkansas.

While Cooper waited, the always aggressive Union Gen. James G. Blunt learned about the Confederate plans and moved to attack before the reinforcements coming from Arkansas arrived. His troops at Fort Gibson, including all three regiments of the Indian Home Guard, drove away Confederate pickets on the south side of the Arkansas River, crossed the river on rafts, and completed a night march to arrive at the steeply banked Elk Creek a mile north of Honey Springs. Cooper, with Watie's Cherokees protecting a ford on his flank, placed his troops in the timber with the creek to their backs.

The fighting began with an artillery barrage. The Federals held a decisive edge with twelve guns, including several twelve-pounders. Hand-to-hand combat began an hour later with both sides at first holding their own until a unit of Texas fighting men jumped from their protected positions and with a Rebel yell charged the Union lines. The Yankees held their lines, shouldered their rifles, and fired on order. The Confederate colors went down, but a brave soldier picked them up and started to charge again. Twenty seconds later another volley was unleashed. As bodies hit the ground, the charge stalled, then turned into a retreat. The Union victory ended with Cooper's men scrambling east to meet the column marching out of Arkansas. Union control of Fort Gibson would never be threatened again.[33] The tide of war had changed.

The Union victory at Honey Springs, combined with the mass resettlement of pro-Union Cherokees that spring and summer of 1863, gradually convinced many pro-Southern families to leave the Cherokee Nation until the war was over. Some moved as far south as Texas, where local officials collected a tax on Cherokee immigrants. Most moved to the Choctaw and Chickasaw nations to be near the protection of Confederate forces. These Cherokee refugees were sustained by a combination of goods brought with them when they fled their homeland, rations issued by Confederate forces operating out of North Texas, and an inconsistent flow of food and supplies sent by soldiers in the field. In one letter written by Col. Thomas F. Anderson to Stand Watie's wife in North Texas, he captured the spirit of Cherokee generosity and even a sense of humor that survived the barbarities of war.

"The Colonel started on a scout yesterday," he wrote on October 27, 1863, "with a crowd of Cherokee, Creeks, Chickasaws and white vagabonds and border ruffians and with reasonable luck will return after having burnt up Fort Gibson…The Cherokees were sent up here to keep the dogs off and since we came here, a few straggling Chickasaws and Creeks have got into our camp to get something to eat."

"You will receive by Mr. Matlock," he continued, "a bedstead, table, some chairs, 1 sack of coffee, some soap, candles, pepper, rice and desicated mixed vegetables. This latter article is intended to season soup with, though I believe that the article itself will make very good soup as the Boys say that they find it composed of hindlegs of bullfrogs, snails, screwworms, etc…There is also an ammunition box full

Figure 12. Elias C. Boudinot. Image courtesy of the Oklahoma Historical Society.

of delicacies & 1 Bot. vinegar sent by Major Thompson to his wife to be left in your care until you have an opportunity of sending this to her."[34]

By fall 1863, approximately three thousand Cherokee refugees were scattered along both sides of the Red River. In the Choctaw Nation the largest camps were near the community of Goodland, twenty miles west of Fort Towson. In the Chickasaw Nation, Cherokees built makeshift cabins along a forty-mile stretch of the Blue River from its mouth on the Red River to Tishomingo. Some provisions were distributed to the refugee families from a Confederate depot at Warren, Texas. Each Cherokee refugee was entitled to one and one-eighth pounds of flour or one and one-quarter pounds of corn meal, one and one-half pounds of beef, and a small amount of salt. Rarely did these meager rations get to where they were needed the most, and when they did, it was usually half rations.[35]

The Cherokee government-in-exile did not wait for military handouts. As early as May 30, 1863, a pro-Southern Cherokee Council meeting on Coody's Creek passed a law setting up a system to feed the destitute. Watie, serving in the dual capacity as military leader and civilian principal chief, appointed J. L. Martin commissioner of relief for Cherokee refugees. Confederate leaders in Texas cooperated by naming Martin an issuing agent for supplies distributed by the army.[36]

The funds to implement that plan were requested through Elias C. Boudinot, the Cherokee delegate to the Confederate Congress meeting in Richmond, Virginia. In November 1863, Boudinot secured a personal loan of $10,000, which he shipped to Watie, while he lobbied for more of their own tribal funds. In January 1864, President Jefferson Davis signed a bill appropriating $100,000 in Confederate money to the Cherokees. A courier delivered $45,000 to Martin in July and gave the remainder to the treasurer of the Cherokee Nation. Some of that money likely paid the expenses of five schools authorized by Council vote the previous July.[37]

Although often hungry and always short

of supplies, the pro-Southern Cherokees at least were largely safe from marauding bands of soldiers and outlaws who crisscrossed the Cherokee Nation with relative ease. By fall 1863, the Union agent to the Cherokees expressed his frustration with the lack of protection for the civilians who had made the trek from northern refugee camps back to their homes. "With 700 ragamuffins, Watie took everything he could ride, or drive, or carry off, and destroyed their crops, and prevented the tending of everything planted. Seed of all kinds and farming tools," he continued, "were furnished by the government, and all lost, nothing saved. What wheat was sown was not saved; there was nobody to save it but the military, and they were holding Fort Gibson…3,500 men, a strong fort, and six cannon, were all required to hold Fort Gibson and the territory as far as the cannon could reach."[38]

Annie Eliza Hendrix, a young Cherokee woman whose brother was serving as a Union soldier at Fort Gibson, described her memories of living with her family on a farm a few miles west of Tahlequah. "The Confederate soldiers never molested us personally," she recalled, "though they robbed our place of all cattle, hogs, chickens and everything we had to eat and everything else of value." Once a month, the family walked to Fort Gibson to draw rations and trade what little they could grow or gather. Annie survived to tell her story almost seventy years later.[39]

Survival aptly described the last year and a half of the war in the Cherokee Nation. Union forces, operating from the entrenched fortifications at Fort Gibson, were primarily concerned with feeding troops and civilians, whether it was protecting wagon trains bringing supplies or providing cover for harvesting hay and crops. Confederate forces, after losing control of Fort Gibson and Fort Smith, were largely confined to the Red River valley but regularly launched quick-strike raids to disrupt Union plans. Civilians on both sides survived as best they could.

The one exception to the Union's defensive strategy was a bold raid in February 1864 deep into the heart of the Choctaw and Chickasaw Nations. The architect of the plan was Colonel Phillips, commander of the Indian Brigade, who wanted to weaken support for Watie's raids and boost the morale of his own Cherokee allies. With one thousand troops, including several companies of the Second and Third Indian Home Guard, he led the strike force all the way to the Red River. They distributed copies of President Lincoln's amnesty proclamation, which offered federal recognition and protection for anyone pledging allegiance to the Union. Just as important, the troops were ordered to destroy the means of supporting war efforts, whether it was burning homes and barns or confiscating horses and cattle. The scorched earth tactic mirrored that of Gen. William T. Sherman's March to the Sea in the Deep South.[40]

Confederate leaders countered with their own plans for keeping the enemy off balance.

A Nation Divided 1861 - 1865

"ᎾᏍᏴᎾ ᏂᏚᏍᏛᎸ ᏧᏬᏍᎦ ᏗᏣᏢᎸ ᎾᎦᎢ ᎦᏍᏗᏝᏛ Ꭰ ᎠᎴᏢᎸ ᏍᎦᎯᏗᏞ Ꮃ ᏍᏣᏬᏍᎢ ᎠᏎᏃ Ꮎ ᎤᎠᏛ ᎢᏗᏟ ᎾᏍᎩ ᎤᎵᎢᏴ ᏂᏛᏆᎷᏛ ᏕᎥᏃ ᏴᎾᏂᏓᎦᏍᏗ ᎤᏍᏫᎢᎢ ᎾᏍᏓ ᎠᏞ ᏗᎯᏢᏇᎸ ᏗᏍᏗ ᏕᏍᎣᎢᎢ."

- ᎤᏫᎾᏯ ᏓᏞᏂ

"The condition of my uniform on that occasion was my shirt was without a back but the defect was covered by a friendly grey jacket with wood buttons."

- Richard L. Martin

In May 1864, Confederate President Jefferson Davis approved the promotion of Stand Watie to the rank of brigadier general, the only American Indian to achieve that rank during the war, with command over a reorganized First Indian Brigade. Included in his army were the First and Second Cherokee Regiments, the Cherokee Battalion, the First and Second Creek Regiments, the First Osage, and the First Seminole. His men did not have to wait long to get back in the saddle.[41]

Watie understood that the war had turned into a battle of attrition. Both sides needed fighting men and the means to feed, arm, clothe, and transport them, so the objective turned from killing men and holding ground to capturing or destroying the means for making war. For Watie that meant preventing wagon trains from getting to Fort Gibson down the Texas Road from Fort Scott or intercepting river boats coming from Fort Smith up the Arkansas River. In June 1864, as the waters of the Arkansas rose enough to allow a boat to clear the rocks at Webber Falls, he had his chance. The *J. R. Williams*, a steam-powered riverboat, was dispatched with commissary stores, quartermaster supplies, and sutlers' goods bound for Fort Gibson.

For his ambush, Watie chose a bend of the river at a place called Pleasant Bluff, about five miles below the mouth of the Canadian River where a riverboat had little room for evasive action. He placed three cannon on the bluffs overlooking the river about one hundred yards apart. His men were positioned in the brush ready to fire their rifles. Luckily for Watie, Union commanders had not sent a cavalry unit overland with the boat to look for such a trap. The only fighting force to protect the boat were twenty-six soldiers onboard.

When the boat came around the bend,

Figure 13. Daughters of the Confederate Honored Dead dedicating a memorial in front of the capitol building, c. 1900. Image courtesy of the Cherokee National Historical Society.

Watie's men held their fire until it was in front of the second cannon. Watie gave the signal and the battle began. Several cannon shots hit the vessel, driving it onto a sand bar, while the riflemen raked the top decks and drove the Union troops off the boat and into a defensive line on the sand bar. Meanwhile, the ship's crew deserted and joined the Confederate attackers. The Union commander, outnumbered in an exposed position and facing artillery fire, retreated downriver toward Fort Smith.

Watie's men swarmed the undefended boat. They found 150 barrels of flour, sixteen thousand pounds of bacon, and a wide assortment of goods ranging from uniforms and shoes to pots and pans. The Creek and Seminole units grabbed what they could carry and started home with their booty, much to Watie's disappointment, but he did not have wagons to haul everything anyway. He loaded what he could, burned the rest, and retreated south before a Union force of seven hundred men arrived the next day. On June 27 at Limestone Prairie in the Cherokee Nation, he called a Council meeting for his southern Cherokees. Every man reenlisted for the duration of the war.[42]

Three months later, after a series of daring raids, Watie learned that a large wagon train was coming down the Texas Road filled with supplies needed at Fort Gibson. With two thousand men and six pieces of artillery, he and Brig. Gen. Richard Gano set an ambush at the Cabin Creek crossing near present-day Vinita where Union commanders had built a small stockade for defense with large ricks of hay scattered for additional protection. Guarding the wagon train were 260 soldiers, including several companies of the Cherokee's Third Indian Home Guard.

About midnight the Confederates attacked the train and small fort. The teamsters fled immediately, but the Union soldiers initially held their lines against several charges. Eventually, Watie's and Gano's men moved their cannon within one hundred yards of the Union line where they had the enemy in a crossfire. The Union forces, outgunned and outnumbered, retreated, leaving behind a wagon train valued at $1.5 million. The booty included 740 mules and 130 wagons in good enough shape to carry the captured goods back to Confederate lines.[43]

Richard L. Martin, a soldier in Company D, Second Cherokee Mounted Rifles, described the immediate impact of the victory. "I didn't suppose we would have undertaken this enterprise had it not been for the fact we was destitute of clothing. The condition of my uniform on that occasion was my shirt was without a back but the defect was covered by a friendly grey jacket with wood buttons. My pants from the pockets down were only represented by the lining. My shoes was almost soulless with a good slice of the upper gone. On our side of the dead line (the Arkansas River) a division of goods took place, and then had Uncle Sam come upon us he would have claimed us for his soldiers as everyone of us was arrayed in bright blue uniforms." That winter, encamped at Boggy Depot, Watie and his men enjoyed creature comforts that had long been only a memory.[44]

While waiting for spring grass to support their mounts on the march, Watie and his officers found another way to supply their men and support refugees. They smuggled several bales of cotton through Texas into Mexico and used the money to buy supplies. By May, while making plans to mount a new offensive north of the Arkansas River, news arrived that Confederate Gen. Robert E. Lee had surrendered to Union Gen. Ulysses S. Grant on April 9. Two

ᎠᏫᏯᎵ 6

weeks later Gen. Kirby Smith surrendered all Confederate forces in the West. On June 23, 1865, Stand Watie became the last Confederate general to surrender. For the Cherokees, the war was over.[45] It was time to heal.

ᎠᏯᏙᎵ 7
ᏚᏃᏍᎨᏍᎨᎬ ᎤᏔᏍᎰᏍᏗ ᎠᏎᏍᎩ
1865-1887
Chapter 7: Reconstructing From Ashes

Figure 1. Cherokee Orphan Asylum faculty with Superintendent Walter Adair Duncan c. 1875. Image Courtesy Oklahoma Historical Society.

After four years of death, destruction, and sacrifice, the war was finally over. It was time for the Cherokee people to turn their backs on simple survival and face a future filled with uncertainties.

The losses seemed unreal. More than four thousand Cherokees, young and old, men and women, had died during the war, either from battle wounds, disease, or starvation. Most had been driven far from their homes, living with military units in the field or tethered to refugee camps scattered from Kansas and Missouri to Texas and the Choctaw Nation. Almost a third of all Cherokee women were widows. More than twelve hundred Cherokee children were orphans. Approximately three hundred thousand head of livestock had been lost. Homes, ranging from humble log cabins to grand mansions, had been looted and burned. Only one plantation in the entire nation survived, George Murrell's Hunters Home in Park Hill.

Col. William P. Ross, the nephew of Principal Chief John Ross, described the sad conditions of his country near the end of the war. "Everything has been much changed by the destroying hand of war," he said. "Nearly all farms are growing up in bushes and briars, houses abandoned or burnt…livestock of all kinds had become very scarce…We have not a horse, cow or hog left that I know of…there is a great increase in the number of wild animals. The wolves howl dismally over the land, and the panther's scream is often heard."[1]

The depth of destruction reflected the deadly combination of internal divisions and external forces that had made the Cherokee Nation a crossroads of war in the Indian Territory. The tribal community had been split with roughly half siding with the South and half fighting for the North. Neither faction could control the countryside, a no man's land of raids, intimidation, and retaliatory killing. Adding to the chaos were outlaws and paramilitary raiders from Missouri and Arkansas who used the pretext of war to loot, rob, and kill. Cherokee agent Justin Harlan, who shared many of the hardships afflicting the Cherokees, attributed much of the property loss to white predators. "Probably a majority of the Cherokee cattle south and all north of Grand River are gone," he wrote. "I think it is safe to say that more than four-fifths have been taken by white men."[2] For Cherokee survivors scattered to the four winds, it once again was time to start over.

For most Cherokees, reconstructing from ashes meant rebuilding homes, clearing fields, putting in crops, and feeding the family. For a few, the challenge was reconstructing a nation and charting a path to the future, especially the relationship between the Cherokee Nation and the United States. That process began

"Everything has been much changed by the destroying hand of war."

–Col. William P. Ross

when Union officials told the conquered tribes to gather in Fort Smith, Arkansas, to start negotiations.

The Cherokees were at a distinct disadvantage facing their longstanding adversaries. In July 1862, the US Congress had suspended all treaties with tribes that signed treaties of alliance with the Confederacy. Although under duress and with no alternatives, Chief John Ross had signed such a treaty, but both he and his full-blood majority had quickly repudiated it and worked with Union officials for much of the war. That made no difference, said those same Union officials. The Cherokees, although loyal allies who had lost so much fighting for the Union, were to be treated like those tribes that had sided with the South to the bitter end. The Union held all the cards and could make the rules.

Compounding their weakness going into negotiations were divisions in the Cherokee community. On one side were those led by John Ross who had fought for the North, including most full-bloods who had been victims of Southern fighters, had supported the abolition of slavery, and had clung most tenaciously to traditional values and national unity. On the other side were those led by Stand Watie who had fought for the South, including most mixed-bloods who had been victims of Northern fighters, had defended slavery, and were willing to consider options for integrating the Cherokee Nation into the non-Indian frontier, even if it meant allotment and the end of communal ownership of land. Fundamentally, the full-bloods sought the survival of cultural and social traditions, while the mixed-bloods demanded protection of private property and a clear path to creating wealth.[3]

The US delegation setting the stage for peace negotiations in Fort Smith offered a third and much more revolutionary agenda advanced by Kansas politicians Senator James Lane and newly appointed Secretary of the Interior James Harlan, who represented their frontier constituents and wanted access to the resources in the Indian nations. Their goals included land for American farmers, land to subsidize railroads, and a quick march to territorial government and statehood. To them, the Cherokee Nation should be abolished, and the Cherokee people should be swept into the melting pot of the expanding American nation. Their spokesman was Dennis Cooley, who recognized the weakness of a divided Cherokee Nation.[4]

With the tribal delegates gathered in Fort Smith on September 17, 1965, Cooley laid out the broad demands from his commission. All of the tribes, including the Cherokees, would have to abolish slavery and grant full citizenship to their former African American slaves; sell land to tribes with reservations in Kansas; grant rights-of-way to two railroads, one east to west and one north to south; and form an intertribal government with quasi-territorial status under federal control. Recognizing that the tribal delegations did not have the authority to ratify treaties, Cooley instructed them go home, consult with their citizens, and gather in Washington, DC, for final negotiations.⁵

The next month, the pro-Union Cherokees, numbering about nine thousand to ten thousand citizens, reaffirmed John Ross as their chief with the authority to fight back and negotiate a treaty. The National Council members approved a list of instructions. They wanted reparations for property lost during the war because the federal government did not protect them as stipulated in treaties. They wanted all trust funds reinstated and pensions paid to veterans, widows, and orphans. Most importantly, they wanted Ross and his delegation to fight the concept of a territorial government and keep the Cherokee Nation intact.

Meanwhile, the pro-Southern Cherokees, numbering from five thousand to six thousand citizens, elected Stand Watie as their chief with a different set of instructions. He was to advocate a separation of the Cherokee Nation into two divisions, one for the Ross Faction and one for the Watie Faction, with a proportional sharing of tribal funds. The rival National Council agreed to largely accept the demands laid out by Cooley in Fort Smith.

Seeing his opportunity to put pressure on the Ross delegation, Cooley negotiated first with the Watie Faction. They finalized a treaty in June 1866, including the division of the nation, large grants of land to railroads, a path to a territorial government, and citizenship for former slaves. The treaty was forwarded to President Andrew Johnson but was never submitted to the Senate. With that document as leverage, Cooley entered negotiations with Ross and his delegates, who pushed back and won concessions on some of the harshest policies suggested in Fort Smith. A month later on July 19, 1866, an agreement was announced.

The treaty stipulated one nation, one trust fund, but semiautonomous governance for the Southern Cherokees in the Canadian District south of the Arkansas River. Two railroads would be allowed to build through the nation, but right-of-way would be limited to one hundred feet on each side of the tracks. The Cherokees would attend an intertribal council, but any form of a limited territorial government would have to be approved by the National Council. Other provisions included citizenship for former slaves, amnesty for all acts committed during the war, repeal of the Confiscation Acts, the sale of the Cherokee Strip and the Neutral Lands, and the sale of land to other tribes. The US Senate ratified the treaty on July 27, 1866. Four days later, John Ross died, having served the Cherokee people one last time.⁶

Despite the new treaty with the United States and restoration of annuity payments, the healing process was delayed by the smoldering hatred and suspicion that had long divided the Ross and Watie Factions. The embers of those old passions were stirred once again on October 19, 1866, when the National Council filled the unexpired term of principal chief with William

Reconstructing From Ashes 1865 - 1867

Figure 2. Cherokee Nation 1866 delegation to Washington, DC. L to R: John Rollin Ridge, Saladin Watie, Richard Field, E. C. Boudinot, W. P. Adair. Photo by A. Gardner, Washington, DC. Image courtesy of the Cherokee National Historical Society Archives.

Potter Ross, John's nephew and protege. Many Cherokees saw Ross's election as a one-sided victory for the full-blood, pro-Union faction of the tribe. Stand Watie and more than two thousand Southern Cherokees refused to come home.[7]

William Potter Ross, like his more famous uncle, had deep roots in the factional wars within the Cherokee Nation. He was born in 1820 near Lookout Mountain, Tennessee, the son of a Scotsman who had married John Ross's sister Eliza. When the family came west in 1839, William was away at school. With a degree from Princeton, he taught school, became the first editor of the *Cherokee Advocate*, and served the nation as a merchant, attorney, and public official, holding various offices such as clerk of the senate and senator from the Tahlequah District for five terms.[8]

When the Cherokee Nation signed the treaty of alliance with the South, the younger Ross enlisted in the First Cherokee Regiment of Mounted Rifles and served as Lieutenant Colonel under the command of John Drew.

After Union troops captured his uncle in winter 1862, William received a "parole of honor" and opened a sutler's store at Fort Gibson serving the needs of the Cherokees fighting for the North in the Third Regiment Home Guard. A Confederate raiding party burned the store. At the end of the war, Chief John Ross named William a member of the Cherokee delegation to Fort Smith and Washington, DC, where he and the other delegates frustrated the Southern Cherokees' plans for a separate nation.[9]

William apparently did not share his uncle's diplomatic skills. Soon after his election, perhaps because he insisted on excluding the Southern Cherokees from the new government, he lost the support of Evan and John B. Jones, the father and son team of Baptist preachers who had helped rally full-blood support for a rejuvenated pro-Union, antislavery Keetoowah Society before the Civil War. Both of the Joneses threw their support to a compromise candidate who seemed more willing to reunite the nation. Their candidate was Lewis Downing.[10]

Downing, whose Cherokee name was ᎷᏲ ᏧᏩᏃᎠᏍᎩ (Luyi Tsuwanoasgi), was born in East Tennessee in 1823. He came west over the Trail of Tears with a party led by the Reverend Jesse Bushyhead and the Baptist missionary Evan Jones. By the age of twenty-one, he was an ordained minister selected to replace Bushyhead as pastor of the Flint Baptist Church in what is now Adair County. He was elected to the Cherokee Senate, led the pro-Union Ross Faction during the latter years of the Civil

Figure 3. Chief William P. Ross at the end of his term as principal chief of the Cherokee Nation, c. 1875. Image courtesy of the Oklahoma Historical Society.

War, and served as Lieutenant Colonel in the Indian Home Guard under the command of the abolitionist firebrand, Col. William A. Phillips.[11]

In fall 1867, as the election of principal chief approached, Downing sought to bring the Southern Cherokees back into the community and government. He was joined by Evan and John Jones, who had the trust of many full-bloods. Together, they reached out to some of the Southern leaders, perhaps while they were in Washington, DC, representing the competing factions in the treaty negotiations, and launched a new political force that soon would be called the Downing Party. On August 5, 1867, a combination of full-blood and Southern faction support provided the votes for Lewis Downing to become the new principal chief of the Cherokee Nation.[12]

In his first address to the National Council, Downing expressed his desire for peace and harmony. "The very great importance of the entire unity of our Nation cannot have escaped your attention," he said. "Our laws should be uniform, the jurisdiction of Courts should be the same over every part of the our Nation and over every individual citizen…[W]e should be one in our laws, one in our institutions, one in feeling and one in destiny. I therefore recommend that the Council adopt immediate measures for bringing about the removal of all such distinctions." Within months even Stand Watie moved back to the Cherokee Nation and started rebuilding his farm at Breebs Town on the Canadian River.[13]

Downing quickly followed his words with action. When he appointed his first delegation to Washington, DC, he appointed four members of the old pro-Union conservative faction, including himself, and four from the Southern faction, including Elias C. Boudinot and William Penn Adair, two of the most vocal advocates for the mixed-blood agenda. Their unity paid dividends when they negotiated a new treaty in spring 1868 that recognized tribal sovereignty, confirmed the federal obligation for removing intruders, and included critical financial provisions for selling the Neutral Lands and the Cherokee Strip at a fair price. At a more

Figure 4. Lewis Downing, principal chief of the Cherokee Nation. Image courtesy of the Oklahoma Historical Society.

personal level, they won provisions reimbursing Cherokees for property lost to either Union or Confederate forces and paying annuities withheld during the war.[14]

Cherokee agent William Davis, recognizing the unity of the Cherokee delegation, commented on the potential economic impact of the treaty. "The financial affairs of the nation," he wrote, "are of the greatest importance…the success of the merchant, mechanic, professional man and farmer all depends upon the promptness with which the national obligations are met…the blessings of peace have rested upon us and

> "ᎠᏎ ᏗᏌᏯᏔᏅᏗ ᏍᏂᎬᎾ ᎴᎵᏍᏗ, ᎤᎾ ᏭᏍ ᎢᏳᏒ ᎠᎶᎾᏗ, ᎤᎾ ᏭᏍ ᎢᏓᏓᏎᏗᎨᎢ ᎠᏙ ᎤᎾ ᏭᏍ ᎤᏗᏗᏗᎵᎢ."
> —ᎵᏍ ᏗᎶᎠᏗ
>
> "We should be one in our laws, one in our institutions, one in feeling and one in destiny."
>
> –Lewis Downing

genuine friendship and kindness have been manifested by all parties." Despite those high hopes, the US Senate refused to ratify the treaty, an early indication that the mood of the US Congress was turning against treating the tribes as sovereign nations.[15]

Until that day of reckoning arrived, the Cherokee people had to rebuild a sustainable economy, raise their families, and brace themselves for the winds of change howling across their land.

In 1866 economic recovery in the Cherokee Nation depended on agriculture. Most of the full-blood Cherokees returned to small plots of land in the eastern reaches of the nation, especially along the headwaters of creeks and rivers where they found resources similar to what they and their families had known in the southern Appalachian Mountains. There were natural springs flowing from the limestone hills, timber for cabins and fuel, scattered prairies for cattle and horses, and thin soil along the creek and river bottoms that could be plowed with crude tools. A full ninety percent of all Cherokee families lived east of the Grand River and relied on a combination of subsistence farming, hunting, and gathering.[16]

Improvements on Cherokee subsistence farms usually included a log cabin, a corn crib, and split-rail fencing around an average of sixteen acres of crops, ten of which would have been planted to corn. Most farms also had a garden with beans, squash, potatoes, fruit trees, and a variety of vegetables. The most common livestock included horses, chickens, and hogs, which roamed free in the woods feeding on natural forage. Cattle, if raised at all in the Ozark upland valleys, generally were considered a source of cash and could survive on the open range and be driven to distant markets. Fortunately for Cherokee farmers, the harvests of 1868 through 1870 were generally good.[17]

As before the war, cash crops and herds of cattle intended for distant markets were raised primarily by mixed-blood Cherokees who settled either along the broad bottom lands of the Canadian, Arkansas, and Grand Rivers or moved out onto the prairie plains west of the Grand. A good example of a market farmer before and

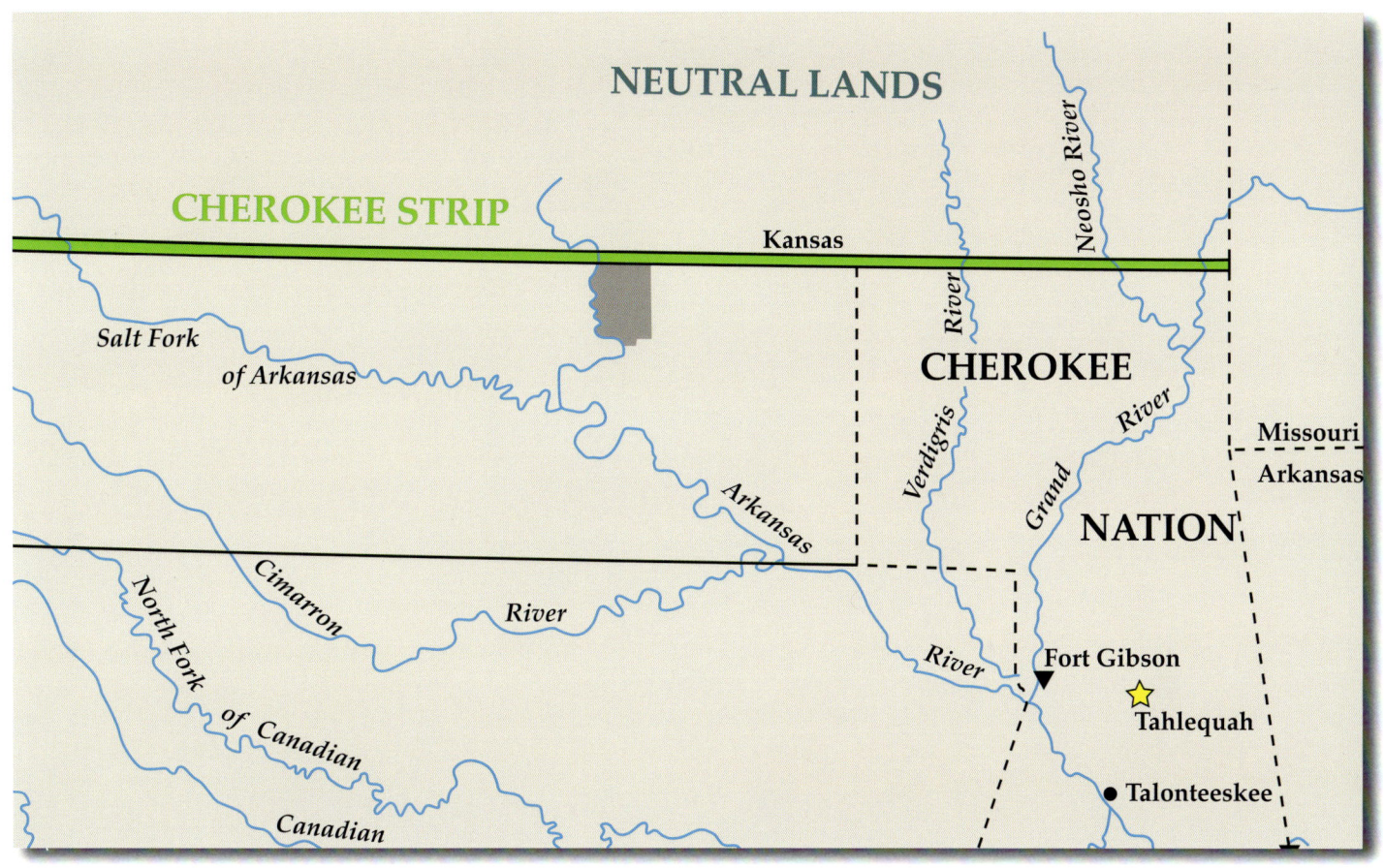

Figure 5. Cherokee Strip and the Netural Lands.

after the war is Thomas Jefferson Parks, a mixed-blood Cherokee who had carved out a farm on Beatties Prairie in the Delaware District, only six miles from the market town of Southwest City, Missouri.[18]

By the eve of the Civil War, the Parks family had made enough money to own four slaves and operate two stores, one at his log cabin home and one at Coodys Bluff. Both were looted and burned during the war. Parks joined Stand Watie's regiment and fought in some of the early engagements. He took a leave of absence and, accompanied by some of his troops, moved his wife and children to the Choctaw Nation where he rented a farm and put in a crop. After the Confederate victory at Cabin Creek in 1864, Parks's share of the booty included two wagons and two sets of mules, which he quickly took to the farm along the Red River. At the end of the war, he rebuilt the wagon to disguise its origins, used lye to burn the "US" brands off the mules, and moved the family back to the Cherokee Nation, where he put in a crop near Fort Gibson.

When the Parks family returned to Beatties Prairie, the only remaining evidence of their old farm was the stones used for front steps. He rebuilt a cabin, planted crops, and bought a few head of cattle. To earn extra cash, one of the kids took eggs eight miles into Southwest City and sold them for five cents a dozen. They hauled poles to town and cut it into

Figure 6. Log cabin representative of improvements made during post-war Cherokee Nation economic recovery. Image courtesy of the Oklahoma Historical Society.

firewood. They won a contract to furnish meat to the Orphan Asylum located near Tahlequah. Little by little, they rebuilt their farm and added to the economic recovery.[19]

The Mayes family experienced a similar story of economic ruin and recovery. In 1857 Wash and Charlotte Bushyhead Mayes moved from their first farm in the Going Snake District to Pryor Creek west of the Grand River. They brought in white tenants to put in a crop, raised horses and cattle for sale to pioneers in Missouri and Kansas, and butchered hogs that had fattened on persimmons, nuts, acorns, and roots in the creek bottoms. After the war started, Kansas Jayhawkers took all the stock and burned the house. The Mayes family fled to North Texas, then moved into the Choctaw Nation, where they rented a farm and put in a crop.

For two years, they raised corn, which sold for a dollar a bushel, and operated a ferry boat across the Red River. They charged fifty cents for a wagon and twenty-five cents for a person on horseback. In 1867 they sold the ferry boat for $100, used their income from corn to buy one hundred head of cattle and two teams and wagons, and moved back to the Cherokee Nation. They bought a home on the banks of the Grand River, about ten miles from Fort

Gibson, put in a crop, then moved back to Pryor Creek, where they built a new home and raised horses and cattle that could be sold to people in Missouri and Kansas.

Wash's son, George, continued the recovery after a good harvest in 1871. "That summer," he later wrote, "I went into the woods and split a lot of rails and started improving a small place for myself, and that fall I hewed the logs and hauled them to my farm with ox teams and built a good log house. I made clapboard shingles, puncheon floors, wooden doors with wooden hinges, and a sandstone chimney. The house was near a good spring of water."

In spring 1872, the younger Mayes married and started raising a family on the new farm. "I raised fine blooded horses and cattle," he wrote. "I matched these horses and sold them for $300 a span. As my cattle grew and fattened I shipped them to market. I kept improving and taking in more land until I had 1,500 acres." The Mayes family, with their farms as a foundation for seeking other economic opportunities, would be active in Cherokee life well into the twentieth century.[20]

Clem Rogers, the father of Will Rogers, provided yet another good example of economic recovery after the war. Like his neighbors, he lost everything he had accumulated through his early ranching, including a home, barn, fences, slaves, and cattle. In 1866 he rented a farm in the Arkansas River valley near Fort Gibson from Alabama Schrimsher Adair, his sister-in-law, and put in a crop of corn. With a hired hand tending to the crop, Clem worked as a teamster hauling goods for a merchant. Two years later, with a little savings and his former boss as a partner, he bought a herd of cattle and moved back to his old range on the prairie plains west of the Grand River. His ranch formed a V-shape, with the Caney River of one side and the Verdigris River on the other, converging a few miles east of present-day Claremore.

Clem's business plan consisted of buying longhorn cattle in Texas, usually for four or five dollars a head, fattening them on the rich bluestem grass of his ranch, and driving them to markets in Missouri where they were worth forty to fifty dollars a head. With free access to land and no taxes to pay, the only expenses other than the cost of cattle were the cowboys he hired to ride the range and help during roundup. By 1875 his cattle were roaming more than sixty-thousand acres of the Cherokee Nation.[21]

While Cherokee farmers and ranchers were reconstructing a way of life, the National Council allocated tribal resources to an agricultural fair that encouraged "scientific farming" and greater production to boost the economy of the Cherokee Nation. The concept was not new. In 1845 the Agricultural Society of the Cherokee Nation had hosted a one-day free fair to encourage the planting of cash crops and the improved breeding of cattle and horse herds. In 1871 the fair was resurrected and staged near Muskogee under the sponsorship of the Indian International Fair Association, led by the two Cherokees Joshua Ross, secretary, and J. A.

Foreman, president.

Within a few years the five-day fair offered $1,000 for competition premiums, a trade show, a public sale of livestock, and a daily schedule of social and entertainment events. The agricultural theme was clear in flyers distributed throughout the region. "We hope every energetic family will be represented with specimens of work, products, or animals," wrote the sponsors. "Our friends from the States are invited to bring their fine stock, manufactures, and farm implements, including threshing machines, portable engines, cotton gins, and wagons." The stock and farm activities were supplemented with horse racing, a convention of the Temperance Society, and a reunion of soldiers from the Northern and Southern Indian brigades who had recently fought each other during the Civil War. Reflecting the mixed-blood dominance of the fair, the entertainment included "full blood friends from the plains tribes…singing in their native tongues."[22]

As the National Council and Chief Downing anticipated, wealth generated by farming and ranching flowed into the local economy to support businesses that ranged from grist mills and saw mills to blacksmith shops and general stores. A good example of investment, growth, and service to the community was Beck/Hildebrand Mill on Flint Creek.

Stephen Hildebrand grew up in a large Cherokee family in Tennessee, where his German-born father and Cherokee mother operated a water-powered saw mill. After moving west on the Trail of Tears, Stephen married Polly Beck, a Cherokee whose uncle had built a water-powered grist mill on Flint Creek in 1845. Stephen and Polly improved the operation by expanding the water chase from four by four foot to eight by eight foot through solid limestone. The increased flow of water turned a twenty-foot diameter wheel that generated the power to grind corn and wheat. According to Cherokee law, the Hildebrands kept one-eighth of meal ground as their fee. The mill could grind twelve to twenty bushels of grain per hour.

After the Civil War, the profit center of the mill shifted to cutting timber. Flint Creek was a broad valley surrounded by thick stands of pine and hard wood needed by farmers and ranchers for homes, barns, and fencing. Under Cherokee law, the Hildebrands could cut all the trees needed for their operation as long as it was not inside the boundaries of a farm claimed by another Cherokee citizen. In 1892 when the mill was destroyed during a flood, the Becks rebuilt it and started selling lumber to merchants in Siloam Springs, Arkansas. The Beck family operated the mill until the 1960s.[23]

More common were general stores that popped up at crossroad communities wherever there was a concentration of enough farm and ranch families to create a demand. Some were small operations located in a room of a log cabin home, while a few were traditional stores built in emerging towns such as Tahlequah, Fort Gibson, and Webbers Falls. Most were owned by mixed-blood Cherokees from ten families–the Rosses,

Ridges, Mayes, Hicks, Thompsons, Vanns, Coodys, Lynches, Bryans, and Hildebrands.

After the Civil War, approximately one-third of the leading merchants were white men born in the North but married to Cherokee women. John S. Scott served as a good example. Born in Ohio, his family moved to the Kansas frontier in 1857. He opened a small store in Humboldt, Kansas, in 1860, but it was burned by Confederate soldiers from the Indian Territory. He joined the Union army, was captured by Confederates, and was imprisoned in Fort Smith, where he opened a small store during the war. In 1871 following a short return to Kansas, Scott moved to Fort Gibson, opened a store, and married Margaret Coody, a member of a prominent Cherokee merchant family. He was still in business in the 1890s.[24]

Another intermarried Cherokee merchant was Joseph Heinrichs, a native of Germany who moved to Fort Smith, Arkansas, in 1867. He started a shoe-making business, which he moved to Tahlequah in 1871. To supplement his shoe manufacturing, Heinrichs traded for furs and hides, then added groceries in 1879. In 1874 he married Lucy Kilpatrick, a Cherokee member of the large Hildebrand clan that had started in the milling business before the Civil War.[25]

About one-fifth of the merchants operating stores in the Cherokee Nation after the war were native-born Cherokees, including Maj. DeWitt C. Lipe, who was born west of Tahlequah in 1840 and attended Cherokee common schools and Cane Hill Academy in Arkansas. In 1861,

Figure 7. Golda's Mill. Image courtesy of the Oklahoma Historical Society.

on the eve of the war, he married Victoria Hicks, the daughter of Elijah Hicks, a prominent Cherokee merchant. Lipe served as an apprentice in his father-in-law's store in Tahlequah before he opened a branch store in Fort Gibson in 1870. One of his employees was Clem Rogers, who drove a team and wagon moving goods throughout the nation for two years before they went into the cattle business.[26]

Merchants such as Lipe, Heinrichs, and Scott made money by importing manufactured goods purchased at wholesale prices and sold at retail prices to farmers, ranchers, and the skilled workers serving them, such as attorneys, teachers, and public officials. Profit margins were low, reflecting limited demand, the cost of transporting goods long distances, and the scarcity of hard currency on the frontier, so the potential of retail sales alone growing the economy was limited. Many Cherokees saw manufacturing as the next step in the economic recovery, but there were few opportunities available on a frontier with limited capital and the unwillingness of outsiders to invest, especially before the coming of the railroads. One Cherokee who decided to break out of that economic straightjacket was the controversial but enterprising Elias C. Boudinot.

Boudinot saw an opportunity in the Reconstruction Treaty of 1866 that exempted Cherokee products from federal excise taxes, an economic benefit that had not been tested because the Cherokees had little of value to export to surrounding states. Distilling alcoholic beverages, that converted high volume, low-value corn into a transportable, high-value commodity was not possible because the Indian nations were theoretically alcohol free. Cotton was grown in volumes too small to warrant the investment in spinning and weaving operations. There was only one commodity that had the potential for export, and that commodity was tobacco.

The soil and climate of the Cherokee Nation was marginal for the growth of tobacco, producing a low-quality leaf that was suitable only for cut-plug chewing tobacco. Despite that limitation, Boudinot decided to take a risk because the numbers looked good. He calculated that it would cost him approximately forty-three cents a pound to buy, process, and ship a pound of flavored chewing tobacco. In surrounding states, a pound of plug sold for seventy-five cents, which for his state-side competitors included the federal excise tax. As a Cherokee citizen producing the plug in the Cherokee Nation, he would not have to pay the tax.

In 1868, with his business plan complete, he convinced his famous uncle, Stand Watie, to loan him $2,500 and his name to capitalize the Watie and Boudinot Tobacco Company. He borrowed the rest from a businessman in Arkansas, built several buildings at Wet Prairie, located near the Arkansas border, and ordered equipment to cut, flavor, and pack the tobacco. By fall 1869, he was making a profit large enough to attract the attention of other Cherokees who started building their own tobacco factories. Unfortunately for Boudinot, he also attracted the attention of tobacco companies in Arkansas and Missouri that paid taxes on their products. They filed a suit in federal court. On December 20, 1869, federal marshals raided the factory and seized forty-five hundred pounds of tobacco, sugar, grape juice, and hydraulic machinery used to produce the plug tobacco.

The suit and seizure cited an obscure federal law quietly passed in 1868 that imposed an excise tax on liquor, tobacco, snuff, and cigars imported into the United States. Boudinot, now joined by the Cherokee National Council, argued that the Treaty of 1866 explicitly granted to the Cherokees an exemption from such taxes. Their

Reconstructing From Ashes 1865 - 1867

Figure 8. Elias C. Boudinot. Image courtesy of the Oklahoma Historical Society.

Indian agent, a representative of the federal government, had already ruled as such. The US courts disagreed. In a ground-breaking ruling, the courts said that new laws passed by Congress could supersede provisions of existing treaties. Boudinot was the victim of confiscation, but the Cherokee Nation was now challenged by a federal government that claimed the right to unilaterally undermine treaties through congressional action.[27] Sovereignty of the Cherokee Nation was under siege.

While the struggle for national survival was entering this new stage of confrontation, the citizens of the Cherokee Nation fought back by working together through their government to create opportunity and provide a social safety net with education, public institutions, and the rule of law. Each of those services came with expenses, and without a national tax base on either land or income, the Cherokees had to rely on an innovative combination of annuities, land sales, and fees.

Annuity payments were based on the forced sale of Cherokee lands before removal to the West. The federal government held the proceeds in a trust fund and issued payments twice a year based on earned interest. In 1866, as one provision of the Reconstruction Treaty, the federal government released $150,000 in annuity payments that had been frozen during the war.

Typically, the Cherokee Nation would incur debt to provide services, usually issuing scrip that would be reimbursed whenever annuity payments might arrive. The value of the scrip varied on any given day, usually at a twenty to forty percent discount depending on how long it might have to be held before reimbursement, which meant that pay to teachers, judges, lawmen, jurors, government employees, and contractors could range from a deep discount to full value depending on their ability to wait for payment. In effect, national scrip served as a variable-rate currency in the Cherokee economy.[28]

The other major source of national revenue came from the sale of land. Under the provisions of the Reconstruction Treaty, the federal government was authorized to sell the Neutral Lands and Cherokee Strip for a fair price and place the proceeds in the trust fund. The Cherokee Nation also agreed to sell land and offer citizenship to tribes that the federal government wanted to remove from Kansas and other territories. The Delawares, with 985 tribal citizens, were the first to buy into the Cherokee Nation with $157,600 paid for land and $121,843 paid for their prorated share of costs for access to educational, social, and legal services.

The Shawnees, with seven hundred citizens, paid $50,000 for land and an annual fee of $5,000 for access to services. The largest sale of land went to the Osages, who exchanged their reservation in Kansas for 640,000 acres in the Cherokee Outlet west of the nintey-sixth parallel along the upper Arkansas River. The price paid to the Cherokees was ninety cents an acre. One deal that did not get approval from the Cherokee Nation was a plan to absorb the Navajo Nation. The southwestern tribe wanted 900,000 acres east of the Osages, which the Cherokees refused to give up.[29]

A much smaller source of national revenue came from fees imposed on a variety of permits and privileges. The government granted franchises to citizens to develop and monetize communally owned resources, such as salt, coal, and timber. Another source of fees were franchises to operate ferries over rivers, which in turn improved internal transportation and encouraged the flow of goods and services. More difficult to manage were permits to Cherokee citizens who wanted to import noncitizen labor, typically to work on farms. Mixed-blood citizens such as Elias C. Boudinot and Clem Rogers built huge ranches on communally owned land with permit laborers who rode the range, cut hay, and cultivated fields of corn and other grains. Although the labor permit laws generated a small stream of revenue and helped a few mixed-blood citizens expand their operations, the growing number of noncitizen white residents would soon create serious problems for the Cherokee Nation.

With growing income from annuities, land sales, and fees, the Cherokee Nation reestablished services that had been disrupted by the Civil War. First among its priorities was education. As before the war, the nation funded common schools, generally through the eighth grade, and high schools called seminaries, one for boys and one for girls. The National Council created a National Board of Education, consisting of three members appointed by the principal chief and subject to approval by the senate. Directly under the board was the superintendent of education, who was elected by a joint ballot of the National Council members.[30]

The number of schools grew every year to thirty-two in 1867, forty-two in 1869, and sixty-four by 1870. Within a decade of the Civil War's end, the Cherokee Nation was supporting more than one hundred common schools with an average enrollment of four thousand children a year and daily attendance

Reconstructing From Ashes 1865 - 1867

Figure 9. Paying the Indians for the Cherokee Strip–Scenes Around the Government Paymaster's Quarters *by Frederic Remington. Image courtesy of the Oklahoma Historical Society.*

hovering around twenty-five hundred. Local communities provided a school building, while the nation provided the teacher, textbooks, and the forms to report results. Each school district, with two five-month sessions a year, had a three-member board of education appointed by the superintendent. Teachers, hired by the local board, were paid a minimum of fifteen dollars a month plus one dollar for every student over fifteen in number with a maximum of fifty dollars a month.[31]

Many of the teachers assigned to the common schools were graduates of the two seminaries built and reopened by the National Council in 1872. The Male Seminary was located about two miles southwest of Tahlequah. The Female Seminary was a short distance north and east of Park Hill. Both were housed in identical brick buildings measuring 185 by 109 feet with full basements, two stories, and partial third floors. Basements were used for store rooms, furnaces, laundries, and work space. The first floors had recitation rooms, an auditorium, a library, a science laboratory, a textbook room, a

Figure 10. Light horsemen guarding the Cherokee Outlet payment at Fort Gibson. Image courtesy of the Oklahoma Historical Society.

dining hall, a kitchen, a parlor, and guest rooms. The second and third floors had living quarters for teachers, matrons, and students. Including baths, closets, and storage, each building had eighty rooms.[32]

From the beginning, both seminaries served about 125 students a year. Tuition was five dollars a month, which included room, board, laundry, textbooks, and medical care. Students from families that could not afford the tuition were given jobs in lieu of payment. Their course of study included arithmetic, geometry, geography, botany, history, Latin, Greek, psychology, philosophy, and the Bible. The teachers, recruited from eastern colleges such as Princeton, Dartmouth, Yale, and Mount Holyoke, were expected to not only teach the classics, but to also "direct students in a course of rigid morality as well as in intellectual pursuits."[33]

With a growing treasury, the National Council created and supported other institutions to serve Cherokee citizens. A school for freedmen, called a "colored high school" at the time, provided a segregated education to the sons and daughters of their former slaves, now considered citizens through a provision of the Reconstruction Treaty. The school was located about seven miles west of Tahlequah and included enough room to serve fifty students who received appointments from the principal

Reconstructing From Ashes 1865 - 1867

Figure 11. Cherokee Male Seminary, Tahlequah, OK. Image courtesy of the Oklahoma Historical Society.

chief. The curriculum was similar to that offered at the Male and Female Seminaries, but the quality of teachers rarely matched that given to the full-blood and mixed-blood Cherokees.[34]

In 1872 the National Council created two institutions to serve those Cherokees who could not help themselves. One was the Orphan Asylum, located on the old Lewis Ross place about forty miles from Tahlequah near the town of Salina. It was funded by dedicating $100,000 received from the sale of land to the Osages, with $20,000 used to construct the building and $80,000 invested to provide operating funds from the interest. The centralized asylum replaced an inadequate foster family system that had been poorly funded at the close of the Civil War when there were more than twelve hundred orphans in the Cherokee Nation.[35]

The National Council dedicated $100,000 from the sale of the Cherokee Strip in Kansas to a home for the insane, deaf, dumb, blind, and indigent. Located about six miles from Tahlequah, the 40-foot-by-148-foot brick asylum was completed in 1876 and opened the following year with twenty-two patients, fourteen of whom were male and eight were female. In his first report, the superintendent described his wards by categories: one with general debility, two with rheumatism, eleven with blindness, four "cripples," three "idiots," and one with consumption. Prior to the opening of the asylum, the Cherokee Nation supported its

Figure 12. Cherokee Female Seminary. Image courtesy of the Oklahoma Historical Society.

disabled citizens with direct pensions. The new centralized system included medical care.[36]

Similar investments were made in general government and the courts. In 1870 as revenues recovered, the National Council funded the construction of a two-story Capitol Building on the town square in Tahlequah, providing offices for a growing list of tribal officials that included the principal chief, assistant chief, members of the senate and council, supreme court members, high sheriff, treasurer, auditor, attorney general, and superintendent of education. In 1874 the National Council invested $6,000 in a jail near the Capitol.[37]

The need for a jail reflected a growing court system that required its own officers and employees paid by the National Council. Each of the nine districts had a sheriff, solicitor, judge, and variable number of Light Horsemen. Additional expenses included sitting grand juries, trial juries, and interpreters. English was considered the official court language, but testimony was taken in whichever language was most familiar to a witness. An interpreter, sworn to neither "over state nor under state the slightest particular," was made available so all jurors heard the evidence before rulings.[38]

One of the largest ongoing expenses assumed by the National Council outside of education and the courts was sending the annual delegations to Washington, DC, to represent the interests of the Cherokee Nation. Most

Reconstructing From Ashes 1865 - 1867

Figure 13. Cherokee Orphan Asylum kindergarten students, c. 1887. Image courtesy of the Cherokee National Historical Society.

delegations, appointed by the principal chief, included four to six people, each of whom received eight to ten dollars a day for per diem expenses. They typically arrived in Washington, DC, in January when congressional sessions began, and returned home in July as the session came to an end. Throughout the 1870s, the annual cost of the delegations averaged $30,000 a year. Lawyers and lobbyists assisting the delegation usually added about $7,000 to $8,000 a year to the cost. Although a major expense, the delegations to Washington, DC, were critical to the survival of the Cherokee Nation.[39]

Once again, the Cherokee people found themselves engulfed in a war, fought not with guns and armies, but with words and lawyers.

The new battleground was the US Congress. After 1866 four to five bills were filed every year to either abolish the Indian nations, open the land to non-Indian settlement, or start down the path of territorial status and eventual statehood. At first the battle cry for change came from surrounding states, primarily Kansas, Missouri, and Arkansas, where farmers and merchants cast a covetous eye on the resources of the Cherokee Nation. As long as the effort was regional, Cherokee delegations had little trouble defeating those efforts. That started changing in the early 1870s after the railroads built through the Indian nations.

Provisions in the Reconstruction Treaties of 1866 granted rights-of-way to two railroads,

Figure 14. Cherokee Capitol Building. Image courtesy of the Oklahoma Historical Society.

one running north and south, the other running east and west. Included in the language of the treaties was a conditional offer of large tracts of land for grants to the railroad companies to pay for the initial costs of construction. Triggering the grants would be a transition from tribally owned to publicly owned land that would require the abolition of tribal status and the creation of a territorial government under the US Constitution.

With the potential of a multimillion dollar land grab, the Missouri, Kansas, and Texas Railway, also known as the KATY, was the first to cross into the Cherokee Nation. The steel rails reached the town of Vinita in 1872 and Muskogee in 1874. The Atlantic and Pacific Railroad, later known as the Frisco, entered the Cherokee Nation on the Missouri border in 1871 and reached Vinita in 1872. Within a decade, the line would be extended to Claremore. The money to build both lines came from investors who bought bonds, tentatively backed by the value of the land to be granted after the Indian nations were dismantled through a territorial bill.

One member of Congress recognized the railroads' growing threat to Cherokee sovereignty. "Now those soulless corporations," he said, "hover, like greedy cormorants, over this territory and incite Congress to remove all restraints and allow them to sweep down and swallow 23 million acres of land…and why must

Reconstructing From Ashes 1865 - 1867

Figure 15. Cherokee Nation Jail. Image courtesy of the Oklahoma Historical Society.

we do this? In order that corporations may be enriched and railroad stocks advanced on Wall Street." The railroads, however, even with the lobbying support of Wall Street, could not win the fight to abolish the Indian nations as long as the majority of Americans respected the legal sanctity of treaties signed with the tribes. To most people, the rule of law had to be respected, and sovereignty was guaranteed by lawful treaties. Or so the Cherokees believed.[40]

Although the major cracks in the wall of Cherokee sovereignty would be delayed until the late 1880s, the war for American public opinion, expressed through their representatives in the US Congress, started changing after the coming of the railroads and the tidal wave of non-Indian intruders who followed the steel rails. This growing external threat to the Cherokee Nation was best illustrated through one highly publicized event that convinced many Americans that Cherokee independence could not survive as a nation within a nation. That event was the gunfight at Going Snake District Courthouse in 1872.

The trap was set by overlapping legal jurisdictions. By treaty and federal law, the

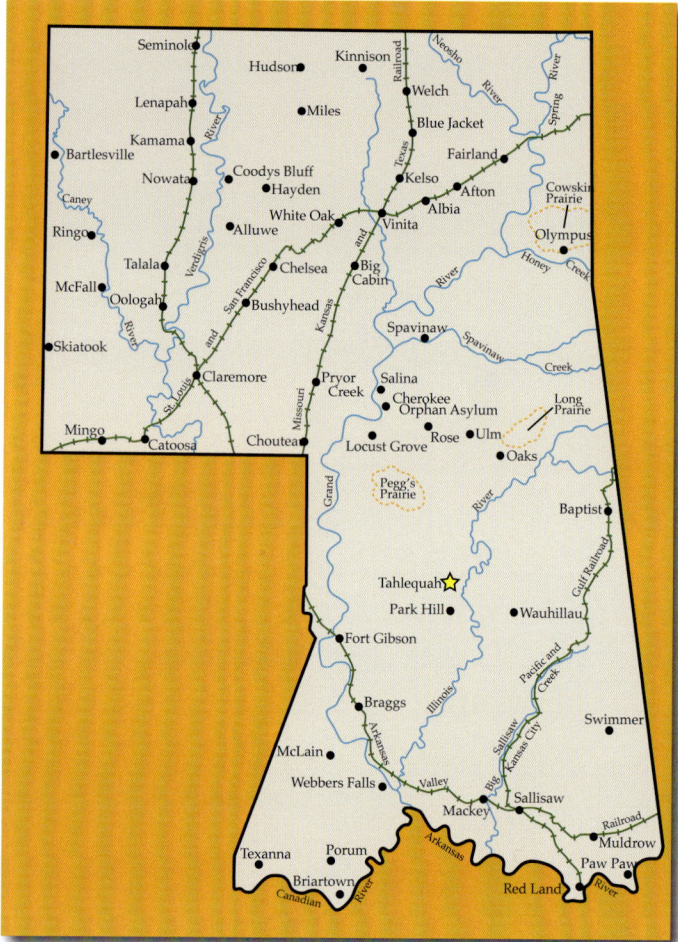

Figure 16. Map of railroads and towns in Cherokee Nation.

Cherokee court system had jurisdiction over civil or criminal cases involving Indians. When a non-Indian was involved, the federal court at Fort Smith, Arkansas, took jurisdiction. This had not been a major problem when there were few white people in the Cherokee Nation, but that was quickly changing after the arrival of the railroads, which in turn increased the chances for conflict.

The white man at the center of this controversy was James Kesterson, who had moved to the Cherokee Nation and married the sister of Zeke Proctor, a well-respected Cherokee leader and lawman. By Cherokee law and custom, the marriage made Kesterson a Cherokee citizen subject to Cherokee law. Trouble started when Kesterson abandoned Zeke's sister and moved in with another Cherokee woman named Polly Beck, a widow who owned a grist and saw mill on Flint Creek.

After securing the safety of his sister and her family, Zeke rode to the mill and confronted Kesterson. When Zeke drew his gun, Polly Beck threw herself between the two men and was shot and killed. Kesterson escaped to Fort Smith, where he filed charges that he had been the victim of an attempted murder. The federal judge issued a warrant for Proctor's arrest. Meanwhile, Proctor turned himself in to Cherokee authorities, and the trial was set for the courthouse in Going Snake District. On the day of the trial, the courthouse was packed with jurors, court officials, and members of Proctor's family when the US marshal from Fort Smith arrived on the scene with a posse of Polly Beck's vengeful family members. When the Becks barged into the courthouse, Proctor's brother confronted them. Guns were drawn and a shootout erupted. By the time the smoke cleared, nine people were dead, including Proctor's Cherokee attorney and eight members of the federal posse. In retaliation the federal judge in Fort Smith issued arrest warrants for the Cherokees involved, including the presiding judge. Zeke Proctor fled to the hills and was never arrested.

While the Cherokee judge and lawmen languished in prison, federal officials conducted several investigations and ruled that the US

Figure 17. Zeke Proctor. Image courtesy of the Oklahoma Historical Society.

District Court had started the trouble. The Cherokee officials were released, and Zeke Proctor was never arrested or tried in federal court. Although a partial victory for Cherokee law, the incident created outrage in the white communities of Arkansas and in the press across America. In the court of public opinion, the Cherokees were guilty for having their own independent system of justice. Subsequent cases of jurisdictional conflict, combined with a rising tide of white outlaws hiding in the Cherokee Nation, convinced many Americans that the days of tribal independence were numbered.[41]

The growing external threat to Cherokee sovereignty was matched by internal divisions within the tribe that would gradually diminish the will to fight for independence. Again, the economic impact of the railroads, matched by a flood of non-Indian intruders, widened the gulf between the traditional full-blood majority, content with communal ownership of land and subsistence farming culture, and the minority mixed-bloods, who saw the railroads as a welcome economic tool to grow domestic demand for their goods and services and lower transportation costs to and from distant markets. Gradually, Cherokee society was shifting from a sense of unity grounded on the survival of social and cultural traditions to class warfare based on economic status.

James Bell, the younger brother of Sarah Watie, Stand Watie's widow, clearly expressed the changing attitudes of the mixed-blood minority toward the full-blood majority as new economic frontiers opened with the coming of the railroads. In a letter opposing an increase in the cost of permits to import white laborers, Bell used terms such as "enlightened men of standing," "our best citizens," "progressive leaders," and the "enterprising class" to describe his fellow mixed-bloods. When talking about the full-bloods who controlled the National Council, he used terms such as the "hog and hominy class," "ignorant and backward class," "blanket Indians," and those who "cling blindly to the ancient system of communal land ownership." To Bell and his allies such as E.C. Boudinot and William Penn Adair, the solution to their jurisdictional problems, including the sanctity of property rights, was to allot the land to individual Cherokees, abolish the Cherokee courts, and submit to a territorial government and eventual statehood.[42]

    Facing mounting threats from outside their nation and growing discontent from within, the Cherokee people prepared for a different kind of war.

ᎠᏎᏉᎠᎢ 8
ᎤᏐᎩ ᎡᎵ ᏗᏆᏍᎠᏰ ᎤᏐᎢ ᎠᎦᎵ ᎤᏐᏉᎵ ᎤᏐᎤᏝᏢ 1876-1907

Chapter 8: Assault on Nationhood

Figure 1. Construction on the Ozark and Cherokee Railroad. Image courtesy of the Oklahoma Historical Society.

Just as their nation was recovering from the tempest of Civil War, the Cherokee people sailed into a perfect storm of economic, social, and political turbulence that threatened their way of life. They would fight back, and they would even make progress consistent with traditional values, but it would be a prolonged battle to keep their ship of state from sinking under the weight of those who wanted to blend the Cherokee people into the mainstream of the

Figure 2. Homestead with log cabin. Image courtesy of the Oklahoma Historical Society.

American frontier.

On one side were external threats, especially the farmers, merchants, and town boosters in Kansas, Missouri, and Arkansas who coveted access to the land, timber, coal, and anything else of value within the Cherokee Nation. The longer they were kept at bay, the louder they became with their attacks on the very foundations of tribal sovereignty. By the 1870s, that chorus was joined by the corporate voices of the railroads. Although fewer in number, their access to the halls of power in Washington DC made the railroad lobby a powerful adversary. Ironically, the battle in the arena of public opinion would shift only after the opponents of tribal sovereignty were joined by self-righteous reformers who assumed they knew what was best for the Cherokees.

Weakening the Cherokees in this all-out war were internal threats to unity. Old wounds, inflicted by removal and deepened by the Civil War, were passed from one generation to the next, stoking the embers of revenge, hatred, and distrust. These cracks in the wall of tribal unity were widened by the growing gulf between the prosperous mixed-bloods embracing land-based free enterprise and full-bloods clinging to their ancient traditions of communal land ownership and culture of sharing. Year by year, decade by decade, the two worlds would grow farther apart, a tectonic shift that would weaken the Cherokees just as they needed all hands on the ramparts of national defense. Although divided, the Cherokees did not give up without a fight.

Other than removal and the Civil War, the most momentous turning point in Cherokee history was the coming of the railroads. Before the steel rails pierced the isolation of the Cherokee Nation, there were few rungs on the ladder of economic opportunity for the ambitious to climb, whether it was a mixed-blood Cherokee or a non-Indian outsider. It was an agricultural economy with little cash in circulation, few crops that could be exported profitably, and a maze of tribal and federal restrictions that discouraged free enterprise. Merchants sold a limited range of products, usually on credit and in low quantities, while tradesmen needed in farming communities were likely to be paid in chickens and hogs. There might be slight differences in the lifestyles of mixed-blood merchants and full-blood farmers, but it was blurred by the almost universal dependence on a localized agricultural economy as the metronome of daily life.

The dependence on agriculture was reflected in Cherokee Nation towns. Before the railroads arrived, most crossroads communities were simple villages with services needed by farmers, such as grist mills, blacksmith shops, and general merchandise stores. The only two towns that could claim to have a main street were Tahlequah and Fort Gibson, both dependent on government resources as centers of authority and institutional largesse. With economic opportunity limited inside the Cherokee Nation, the biggest towns serving Cherokees were across state lines in places called Fort Smith, Bentonville, Fayetteville, and Baxter Springs.

A majority of Cherokees, especially the full-bloods, treasured this economic isolation and opposed allowing railroads to enter their nation. Elders remembered the repercussions of emerging economic opportunities in their ancient homeland in the Southeast, primarily in cotton and gold, and they associated those opportunities with forced removal and the pain of leaving their homes at the tip of a bayonet. To them, the railroads and the forces of free enterprise would threaten their communal way of life, and even more menacingly, attract a tidal wave of white Americans who once again would demand change from within.

Not all Cherokees opposed the railroads, especially the mixed-blood families who had straddled the two worlds of subsistence farming and commercial enterprise for three generations. To them, the railroads would lower the cost of importing manufactured goods, create a portal for exporting cattle, timber, and hay to outside markets, and create opportunities for economic development. Like their full-blood neighbors, most mixed-bloods at first wanted to defend sovereignty and secure the borders of the Cherokee Nation, but they wanted the ability to use that protected status as an economic advantage in the competitive world of frontier free enterprise. A good example of one man who initially wanted both opportunity and protection was Elias Cornelius Boudinot.

Boudinot was a charismatic, brilliant, and ambitious Cherokee who was considered a sage by some and a scoundrel by others, including virtually all full-bloods and a majority of mixed-bloods. His great uncle was Major Ridge, the traditional tribal leader who was murdered for signing the treaty that removed the Cherokee Nation from the Southeast to the West. His father was a highly educated mixed-blood leader who was the first editor of the *Cherokee Phoenix*. His uncle and mentor was Stand Watie, arch foe of John Ross and brilliant Confederate commander who helped send Boudinot to Richmond as one of the delegates from the Five Civilized Tribes. To both contemporaries and historians since, Boudinot's enigmatic story is comparable to the legacy of Alexander Hamilton on the national stage, a mixture of enviable talent and bold flashes of self-serving energy that created either binding friendships or bitter feuds. Not surprisingly, Boudinot saw the railroads the same way Hamilton had seen canals and other internal improvements in his era.

"I stand in no fear or dread of the railroad," said Boudinot in a speech dedicating the arrival of the first steel rails on June 4, 1870. "It will make my people richer and happier. I feel that my people are bound closer together and to the government by these iron bands." Boudinot did more than give speeches to support railroad expansion. In 1868, after his tribe had been forced to allow two railroads to cross through the Cherokee Nation, he proposed a bill to Congress that would create the Central Indian Railroad, owned and managed by Indians. Of course, he would be president of the company, but the investors would be the Five Civilized Tribes, and the directors would be the leaders of the five governments. With opposition from the railroad lobby, the bill failed to pass out of Congress.[1]

Boudinot found another opportunity by assisting the Union Pacific Railway Southern Branch, later known as the KATY, short for the Missouri, Kansas & Texas Railway Company. The KATY was in a race with a competing rail

"Dh ᏂᏙᏚ Ꮅ ᏚᏂᏯᏚᎦ ᎠᏊ ᎾᏬᎩ ᏂᎦᎾ∼ᏃᎪ ᏋᏣᎺᏓᏓᏆᎢ."

–ᏚᎳᏭᎣ∼

"I stand in no fear or dread of the railroad."

—Elias C. Boudinot

Figure 3. Elks Day in Vinita, Indian Territory. Image courtesy of the Oklahoma Historical Society.

line to reach the Cherokee Nation border, with the winner earning the right to build south to Texas. Boudinot offered his assistance in exchange for information where the KATY would enter the Cherokee Nation. With that advantage, he and his uncle Stand Watie claimed a ranch just south of the Kansas line. By enclosing sixteen thousand acres fed with water from Russell Creek, Boudinot planned to create a great cattle center with pasture, haying operations, feed lots, and loading pens where ranchers from the Cherokee Nation and Texas could fatten their cattle before shipping them by rail to markets in Kansas City, St. Louis, or Chicago. The same Cherokee laws that allowed him and his uncle the right to claim land gave Boudinot the right to import white permit workers to run the operation.[2]

While the victorious KATY crews laid track south through the Cherokee Nation, the Atlantic & Pacific Railroad started laying track from Missouri to the west-southwest. When Boudinot learned where the two lines were to intersect, again with inside information from his KATY allies, he and his mixed-blood partners enclosed two square miles of land and called the new town Vinita, in honor of Vinnie Ream, a famous sculptress and friend of Boudinot. Unfortunately for the frontier entrepreneur, Atlantic & Pacific officials changed their route and intersected the KATY line three miles north where the Cherokee Nation reserved the right to sell lots. Boudinot, admitting defeat, pulled up stakes and bought lots in the new town where he built the first hotel.[3]

The economic impact of the two railroads grew steadily year by year, visible not only in the growth of towns but also in the shift of population from the Ozark foothills east of the Grand River to the prairie plains to the west. Although the population growth would eventually be fueled by white permit workers and intruders attracted to the opportunities created by rail connections, the initial stages of development carried the distinct imprint of mixed-blood Cherokees. That evolution was most easily illustrated through the story of Vinita, the emerging economic center of the Cherokee Nation.

The land platted around the two railroad depots at Vinita was owned by the Cherokee people in common. Lots were sold by the tribal government, typically at a price ranging from fifty to seventy-five dollars, but the only legal buyers were Cherokee citizens, and their rights of ownership extended only to use, not fee title to the land. The Cherokee origins of the town were reflected in the physical layout of the plat. The avenues were named for districts of the nation: Delaware, Canadian, Illinois, Flint, and Sequoyah. The streets were named for prominent mixed-blood families: Vann, Scraper, Thompson, Bell, Adair, and Ross.[4]

The nucleus of the town was east of the KATY depot along Front Street. The first commercial enterprise was a general store owned by Johnson Thompson, a prominent mixed-blood Cherokee, followed closely by Boudinot's Railroad Hotel, built suspiciously close to the depot on land claimed by the railroad. Within five years, the commercial district included a blacksmith shop, livery and stables, warehouse, grist mill, cotton gin, and offices for doctor William T. Adair and attorney James M. Bell, both of whom were prominent mixed-blood Cherokees. By 1876 the town even had a newspaper, the *Vinita Progress*, which quickly became a voice for economic opportunity and town growth.[5]

The frontier town grew steadily through the 1880s. Cherokee merchants opened grocery stores, hardware stores, butcher shops, billiard halls, and even a marble works. In 1882, to serve the growing non-Indian population attracted to the town, the Worchester Academy opened with a tuition of five dollars per term. A nine-year-old son of a nearby rancher would soon enroll at the school. His name was Will Rogers. By 1886, when the population topped one thousand, the town had four churches, a school operated by the Cherokee Nation, and several newspapers, including the *Vinita Chieftain*, edited by a young mixed-blood Cherokee named Robert L. Owen, who later would become the first elected US Senator from the State of Oklahoma.[6]

Harry Arlington, a young newspaperman who arrived in Vinita by rail in 1884, described his first impressions. "Such lovely country," he

in this town…monarchs of all they survey. I am stopping at a boarding house owned by an Indian named Stephen Blue Jacket, $3.50 a week."[7]

Arlington also noticed a growing presence of white men, just as the tide of immigration was beginning to grow. "All of the white men in the business here are married to Indian women, which they have to do before they can carry on a business in their own name…a white man is a perfect blank here unless he marries into an Indian family." What the young man did not understand at the time was the lower class of white men and women who may not have owned property, but who worked for mixed-blood Cherokees on the permit system. Boudinot, who built the first hotel and established a truck farm on the edge of town, operated both with permitted white managers who considered themselves partners.[8]

The growth of Vinita, where the two railroads created access to the regional and national economy, was matched by a population shift from the Ozark foothills east of the Grand River to the prairie plains to the west. The driving force was simple supply and demand. The demand was coming from cities such as Kansas City, St. Louis, and Chicago, where growing populations needed meat to eat. The supply came from the prairie plains where Cherokee ranchers expanded their herds, fattened them on rich and abundant grasslands, and found an efficient means of transportation by rail.

Figure 4. Col. William Penn Adair. Photo by M. B. Brady & Co., Washington, DC. Image courtesy of the Oklahoma Historical Society.

wrote, "broad expansive prairies extending as far as the eye can see and seeming to kiss the skies in the far distance. But little farming is carried on here and that on a very small and ancient scale." The young man also noticed the distinct character of a mixed-race community. "I have seen more Indians in the two short hours of my stay here than in all my life before, some full-bloods and most three-fourth and half bloods, but civilized. They are THE people here. They carry on the principal part of the business

Figure 5. Dwight Mission, Cherokee Nation I. T. c. 1896. Image courtesy of the Oklahoma Historical Society.

Adding to the economic bonanza on the prairie plains were two technological innovations that encouraged the development of mixed agriculture. One was efficient and affordable water well drilling that overcame the traditional Cherokee dependence on springs and mountain streams typical of the Ozark valleys where most of the full-bloods still lived. The other was barbed wire that allowed mixed-blood Cherokees to enclose and control rangelands at a reasonable cost when competition for pasturage on the prairie was increasing. In 1872 Principal Chief William P. Ross had written that the prairie plains were "too remote from timber and water to make it useful to the Indians for agricultural purposes." By 1882 that was no longer the case.[9]

The lure of rich pastureland and railroad connections is reflected in changing settlement patterns that further separated the mixed-bloods from the full-bloods. In 1866 less than ten percent of Cherokees had lived west of the Grand River. By 1880 that percentage topped thirty percent, and by 1890 it exceeded fifty percent, and that did not include whites and blacks who were in the nation either legally or illegally. By 1890 the most populated district in the Cherokee Nation was Cooweescoowee, with 5,621 citizens located west of the Grand River.[10]

Indian Agent Robert L. Owen, a mixed-blood Cherokee, recognized the growing geographical gap between the mixed-bloods and

Assault on Nationhood 1876 - 1907

Figure 6. US Senator Robert L. Owen. Photo by Clinedest, Washington, DC. Image courtesy of the Oklahoma Historical Society.

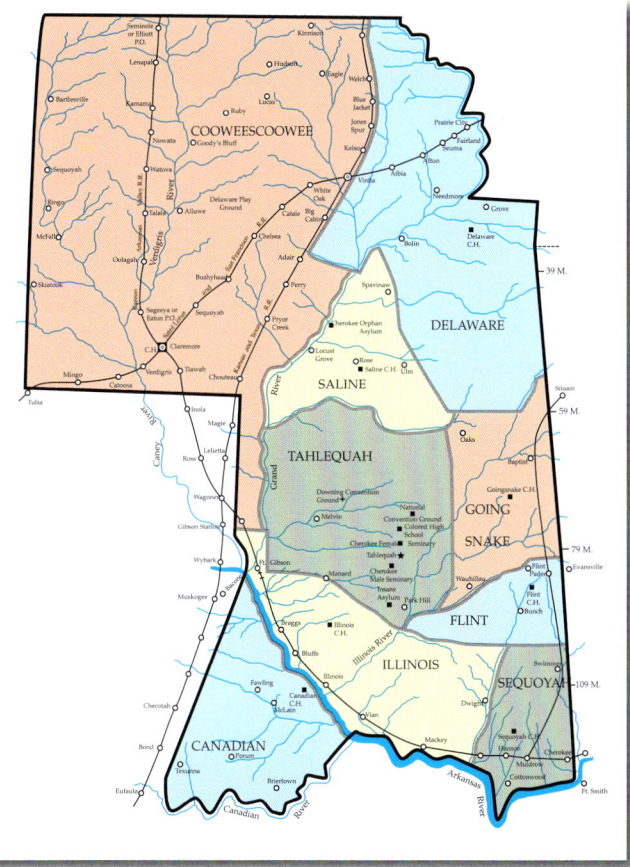

Figure 7. Map of Cherokee Nation c. 1890.

full-bloods. "Look at a Missouri town of 1,000 inhabitants and you see Vinita," he reported. "The town is composed almost entirely of half-breeds and citizens adopted by marriage… Passing over the country southeast, we pass farm after farm of considerable size, from 50 to 400 or 500 acres…There are suitable stables, cribs, meat houses, stock pens, hay-ricks…there are many orchards and occasionally a vineyard. The water is obtained mostly from wells, although there are some springs."[11]

By contrast he described the Ozark hill region as it had been for several generations. "We cross Grand River and get among the full-blood people," he wrote. "They are living on the streams in the hilly country…their fields are small, from 5 to 150 acres…the full-blood gets his water from a spring…He raises potatoes, beans, and other vegetables, enough corn for his own meal and hominy, enough to feed his horses and fatten his hogs…(they) live in a very humble manner, being content with their daily food, and equally satisfied when their own cribs have been emptied, to borrow of their neighbors."[12]

The railroads, offering a portal to the American dream of land-based economic opportunity, not only deepened the divide between mixed-blood and full-blood Cherokees,

Figure 8. Christy School with Cherokee students. Image courtesy of the Cherokee National Historical Society.

but also attracted a wave of white intruders who would soon add their political voice to the rallying cry for dismantling the Cherokee Nation.

The shifting tides of economic development and social change were reflected in the government of the Cherokee Nation. While support for internal improvements such as schools and public safety remained consistent regardless of who was in power, the relationship between the Cherokee people and the outside world became a battleground in the rough and tumble world of Cherokee politics.

Lewis Downing, who had been a true peacemaker in bringing the pro-Union and pro-Confederate Cherokee communities together after the war, died in office in 1875 just as the forces of economic and social change were gaining strength. Adding fuel to the fire was a prolonged drought, successive crop failures, and a national financial crisis in 1873 that shook the foundations of community cooperation. In a

Assault on Nationhood 1876 - 1907

and the mixed-blood minority that controlled a disproportionate amount of communally-owned land and commerce. Just as the demand for change reached a zenith, one man stepped onto the stage of history with a mixture of populist rhetoric and sincere belief in the traditional Cherokee values concerning social harmony, sharing, and cooperation. The man was Oochalata (ᎤᎧᎳᏓ), also known by his Anglo name of Charles Thompson.

Oochalata was the son of a full-blood father and a white mother who had been raised as a Cherokee. He came west with his family on the Trail of Tears and grew up along the headwaters of Brush Creek in what is now Delaware County. He became a disciple of the Reverend Evan Jones, joined the Keetoowah Society in 1859, and served in the Third Indian Home Guard during the Civil War under Lt. Col. Lewis Downing. After the war, he moved to a farm on Spavinaw Creek, operated a country trading post, and was elected as a senator to the National Council in 1867. He took the name of the man he succeeded in office, Charles Thompson.[14]

Figure 9. Charles Thompson. Image courtesy of the Oklahoma Historical Society.

letter to the Indian agent in Muskogee, William Penn Adair described the suffering. "It makes my heart ache to hear the pitiful stories of our full-blood Cherokees," he wrote, "many of whom are now sick and dying. It is no fault of their own that they are destitute. They all put in their crops and worked them, but the drought and grasshoppers ruined them. For God's sake, do all you can for our people as soon as possible."[13]

Desperately hungry and losing hope, the full-blood majority turned its wrath on the closest scapegoats–the railroads, white intruders,

Oochalata, fluent in both Cherokee and English, was a gifted orator who decided to run for the principal chief's office in 1875. In speeches defining the importance of the election, he portrayed complex problems in simple, moral terms. To him, the problems facing the Cherokees pitted the people against special interests, the common folk against the railroads, bankers, and speculators. In one speech, he

Figure 10. Cherokee senators at Tahlequah, I. T. Image courtesy of the Oklahoma Historical Society.

attacked the railroads. "They have mortgaged entire lines of their roads and have already issued and sold, chiefly to foreigners and New Yorkers, about $16,300,000 in bonds on the lands belonging to our people…in other words, these railroad companies have sold the finest portion of our country and are endeavoring to make these sales valid by throwing our lands into a territory of the U.S. and robbing us."[15]

The populist candidate also condemned the mixed-blood families engaged in large scale farming, ranching, and commerce. "The effort of some of our citizens to get possession of large tracts of land and timber and to hold an unlimited number of claims should be stringently prohibited," he said. The permit law, he claimed, allowed white men to enter the nation and work some of the best land, which was destroying the Cherokee Nation. To Oochalata and many of his followers, the root of the problem was comingling with the white majority. To him, separatism was the only answer.[16]

Just as the arrival of the railroads in 1871 had been a turning point in Cherokee economic history, the election of 1875 was a turning point in the tribe's political history. Previous victors running for the principal chief's office had preached unity as strength, division as weakness. This time, with both external and

Figure 11. Stilwell Hotel, Stilwell, I.T. Image courtesy of the Oklahoma Historical Society.

internal pressures pushing and pulling society in multiple directions, Oochalata and his opponent campaigned as us against them, mixed-bloods versus full-bloods, in a rigged system that had to be reformed. The full-bloods, still in the majority in 1875, put Oochalata in office by only a few votes and gave him a majority of eleven seats in the National Council.[17]

One of the first challenges Oochalata tackled was the mounting expense of keeping Cherokee delegations in Washington DC during congressional sessions. Although he had railed on the campaign trail about the "waste and fraud" of previous delegations, once in office, he found that the only way to fight the territorial bills seeking to dismantle the Cherokee Nation was to send delegates and hire costly consultants who knew how to navigate the hallways of power.

Another easy campaign target was the large and growing population of intermarried white men who claimed citizenship through their marriage to Cherokee women. Oochalata, with his narrow majority in the National Council, pushed for a bill in 1877 that prohibited intermarried white men from receiving or owning property in the Cherokee Nation. They could vote, but they could not share in per capita payments or claim property if their wives died. There was little the National Council could do to

"ᎾᏍᎩᏃ ᎤᏃᎳᏗᏍᏗ ᎠᏂ ᎠᏯᎵ ᎤᏪᏢᎦ, ᎾᏍᎩ ᏴᎾ Ꮎ ᎤᎾᎵᏍᏓᏍᎥᎠ, ᏞᏍᏓ ᏱᎵ ᏧᎾᏟᎠᏍᏙᎾ ᏧᏂᏴᏓᏍᎠ ᎢᏣᏍᏱᎲᏃ ᎾᏍᎩ ᎠᏂᏁᏙᎲᎦ ᏧᎾᎾᏍᏞᏂᎦ ᏱᎵᏙ ᏧᎳᎠᏙᎠ ᎤᎦᎳᏙᏍᎠ ᏓᏯᎠᏍᎬ ᎤᏂᏆᏴᎵᏙᎤ."

—ᎠᏂᏁᏙᎲᎦ ᏧᎾᎾᏍᏞᏂᎦ ᏣᏂ ᏡᏯᎦᏣᎩ

"The peace of the country, the protection of the people, cannot be secured unless the Agent can enforce his orders against intruders."

–Agent John B. Jones

strike back at the railroads, the target of so much political venom, but they could do something about the mixed-bloods' alleged abuse of the permit system.[18]

In 1879 the National Council with Oochalata's support passed a new worker permit law that raised the fee to twenty-five dollars a month and limited the system to only "school teachers, ministers of the Gospel, missionaries, and mechanics who could run cotton gins and grist mills." The bill included another feature that struck at what the full-blood majority saw as theft of communally owned resources. Any Cherokee found guilty of "removing timber, salt, coal, wood, lumber, or minerals of any kind" without a permit was subject to arrest and fine.[19]

Not content to prevent only future illegal use of national resources, the National Council included another provision that attempted to deal with existing intruders, a problem that had long been a point of contention with federal officials. According to the bill, the Cherokee Nation would decide who was intruding and send a list to the Indian agent. If the federal government did nothing, the bill authorized district sheriffs to remove the intruders by force if necessary. After years of tolerating federal disregard for treaty stipulations that required them to remove intruders, the Cherokee Nation was ready to force the issue to a final showdown.[20]

The deck was stacked in favor of the federal government. By treaties, tribal law, and federal law, removing non-Indian intruders was the responsibility of the federal government. Cherokee officials could make lists of intruders and seek their removal, but they could neither arrest them nor bodily remove them without being subject to charges of assault in the federal court at Fort Smith. The ultimate decision rested with the US Indian agent, military officers, and officials in Washington, DC.

Figure 12. Cherokee Advocate *Printing Office, c. 1900. Image courtesy of the Oklahoma Historical Society.*

Indian agent John B. Jones tried to follow the law in the early 1870s. "This a matter of great importance," he wrote his superiors. "The peace of the country, the protection of the people, cannot be secured unless the Agent can enforce his orders against intruders… These intruders are quite defiant and cannot be removed without military force." When the agent sought assistance from the military at Fort Gibson, one officer used lack of manpower as his excuse for inaction, while another said he would provide troops only if the agent led the mission in case there was violence. The officer knew that American public opinion did not support the removal of white intruders, and he did not want his career affected by any negative publicity.[21]

Federal officials' refusal to remove intruders was a direct attack on tribal sovereignty. As early as 1870, the Cherokee National Council had empowered census takers to examine the black freedmen's rolls and determine who was a citizen as defined by law and who was an intruder. The commission ruled that 1,545 of the applicants were legal Cherokee citizens but rejected seven hundred as intruders. The Bureau of Indian Affairs, in defiance of treaty stipulations, rejected the findings and refused to remove the intruders.[22]

Four years later, in a major power grab, the US agent to the tribe unilaterally issued

Figure 13. Exterior of the Cherokee Advocate *Printing Office, c. 1900. Photo by Jennie Ross Cobb. Image courtesy of the Oklahoma Historical Society.*

certificates similar to a visa to applicants who claimed to be Cherokee citizens. The Commissioner of Indian Affairs not only approved this illegal confiscation of powers granted to the Cherokee Nation but also ordered the National Council to establish a formal system to consider citizenship claims with one caveat–any decision by tribal officials had to be approved by the secretary of the interior. In effect, the government of the United States was telling the Cherokee Nation that they no longer had control over their own identity and, by inference, no control over their destiny.[23]

The inability to remove intruders, combined with the economic boom following the coming of the railroads, was tantamount to opening the flood gates and releasing pressure that had started as a trickle and would soon become a torrent. As late as 1880, after the National Council conducted its own census, there were 15,150 full-blood or mixed-blood Cherokees and 4,585 adopted citizens, including freedmen, other Indians, and intermarried whites. The number of noncitizens was only 5,352, which included permit holders as well as intruders. By 1890, when the United States government conducted another census, the number of noncitizen whites in the Cherokee Nation had risen dramatically to a staggering 29,166, making the 22,015 Cherokees and adopted citizens a minority in their own land. In Vinita that demographic turning point was reflected in the number of students enrolled when the first public school opened in 1899: 318 white children, 271 Cherokee children, and 101 black children.[24]

The corrosive impact of intruders and railroads and the widening gulf between full-blood and mixed-blood citizens would soon pale in comparison to the tidal wave coming toward the Cherokee Nation. It was the federal government's final assault on tribal sovereignty.

The battle lines in this extended war for national survival centered on the question of land ownership. The Cherokees rightfully saw communal ownership of the land as fundamental not just to constitutional governance but also to traditional values, community cohesiveness, and sense of identity. The federal government, with increasing forcefulness, applied constant pressure to break up the tribal lands and allot parcels to individual Indians. Without a land base to govern, federal officials argued, there would be no need for a tribal government, which in turn would open the door to statehood and US citizenship for all Indians.

Cherokees, especially the full-bloods, always cited treaties and the rule of law as their first line of defense. Had not the United States, in good faith, sold the land to the Cherokees in a legal transaction? The logical answer was yes, the treaties had been enforceable legal documents negotiated by presidential appointees and approved by the US Senate. But the political answer was no, treaties could and would be violated whenever and wherever the federal government decided it was convenient to do so.

The evolution of that corrosive policy had started in 1871 when Congress passed a law that forbade future treaties and thereafter refused to recognize Indian tribes as independent nations. That same year the US Supreme Court ruled that an act of Congress could invalidate existing treaties "as if the treaty were not an element to be considered." Eight years later, referring specifically to the Cherokees, the US attorney general ruled that the federal government was not obligated to respect or regard Cherokee law before taking action. The law of the land, whether federal or state, would be preeminent. As one historian noted, this was the "final nail in the concept of Cherokee sovereignty and self determination. The fight for sovereignty was over."[25]

The second line of defense for the Cherokees was the court of public opinion, which hopefully would be reflected in the votes of congressmen. For decades, the greatest respect for tribal survival had been centered in the New England and mid-Atlantic states, especially among the Quakers, where reformers supported mission work to the tribes, lobbied elected officials, and influenced public opinion through lectures and newspapers. By the 1880s the reformers' support was eroding under the influence of naked materialism and rampant nationalism.

Albert Smiley, a Quaker philanthropist, expressed this sea change in a letter to the secretary of the interior in 1880. "The greatest good for the Indian would be the speedy enactment of the pending (territorial) bills… providing for lands in severalty…and ultimate citizenship." Another Quaker reformer expressed his attitude in more colorful language. "Let the Indian lay aside his picturesque blankets and moccasins," he wrote, "and seek his chances of fortune or loss on the stern battlefield of life with the Aryan races."[26]

In 1883 a small but influential band of eastern reformers met at Lake Mohonk in New York State to discuss what they called "the Indian problem." Senator Henry L. Dawes from Massachusetts, one of their own, combined abstract humanitarian theory with a rare glimpse of the Cherokees during a recent trip to the West. "The head chief told us that there was not a family in that whole nation that had not a home of its own," he said. "There was not a pauper in the nation and the nation did not owe a dollar. It built its own capitol, in which we had this examination, and it built its schools and its hospitals. Yet the defect of the system was apparent."

"They have got as far as they can go," Dawes claimed, "because they own their land in common…there is no enterprise to make your home any better than that of your neighbors. There is no selfishness, which is at the bottom of civilization. Till this people will consent to give up their lands, and divide them among their citizens so that each can own the land he cultivates, they will not make much more progress." The same forces that had created the Gilded Age of corporate excess and elevated survival of the fittest to a new social gospel were overwhelming what little respect still remained for tribal independence and the fulfillment of treaty obligations. It was open season on the Indian way of life.[27]

This accelerating assault on tribal sovereignty found voices within the Cherokee Nation. One of the earliest and most persistent advocates for change from within was Elias C. Boudinot. In a speech delivered in Vinita as early as 1871, he had proposed allotment with 160 acres for every Cherokee, selling the surplus lands, splitting the proceeds, and granting US citizenship to all Indians. To Boudinot, who considered himself a realist, the dye was cast and the federal government would do as it pleased. "The Indian must," he wrote, "become civilized and learn to live by the sweat of his brow or he will be exterminated." Spencer Stephens, another mixed-blood Cherokee, published a pamphlet in 1887 with the title, *The Indian Question Discussed*. "It is necessary for the better condition

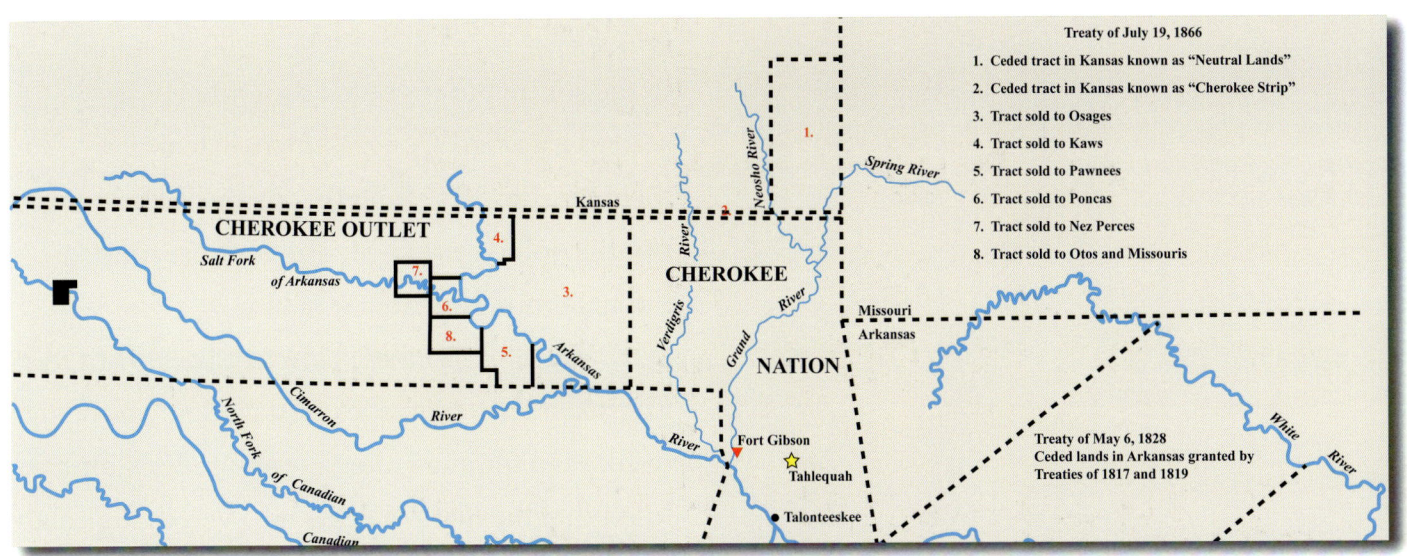

Figure 14. Map showing land cessions as a result of the Treaty of 1866.

of the Indian," he wrote, "to set aside as soon as possible the spirit of communism which is part and parcel of their tribal life, habits, faith, and traditions. Among the Cherokees, it is only individuality that provokes security… consequently we cannot accumulate."[28]

With growing faith in the healing powers of private land ownership, Congress acted in 1887 with passage of the General Allotment Act. Under its terms, tribal lands would be divided into privately owned parcels, 160 acres to every family, 80 acres to unmarried adults, and 40 acres to children. Of course, any surplus lands left over would be purchased by the federal government and thrown open to homesteaders. Although the Cherokees and the other Five Civilized Tribes were exempt from the law, most observers of the evolving Indian policy realized that would not last long.

While the Cherokees won a temporary reprieve from allotment, federal officials escalated their backdoor assault on tribal sovereignty. The issue this time was the Cherokee Outlet, a six million-acre block of land west of the Arkansas River that had been sold to the Cherokee Nation at the time of removal. Although it still belonged to the Cherokees, the Treaty of 1866 stipulated that other tribes, under federal pressure, could purchase parcels to relocate from Kansas and Nebraska. By 1883 the Outlet was separated from the Cherokee Nation by several reservations, most notably the Osages.

Some Cherokee leaders were anxious to sell the Outlet and divide the proceeds among tribal members on a per capita basis, but others saw it as a source of recurring income. Since the late 1860s, Texas ranchers had been pushing herds of longhorn cattle through the Outlet on their way to railheads in Kansas. As the cattle moved slowly north, they fattened on the rich grass of the Outlet. In 1883, to control access to that grass, a group of cattlemen met in Caldwell, Kansas, and organized the Cherokee Strip Live Stock Association. They, in turn, approached the Cherokee Nation about leasing the entire Outlet. Principal Chief Dennis Bushyhead negotiated a

Figure 15. Joel B. Mayes served as chief from 1887-1891. Image courtesy of the Oklahoma Historical Society.

five-year lease at $100,000 a year for five years. Payments were to be made in cash twice a year.[29]

Opponents of tribal sovereignty quickly protested. A group of mixed-blood Cherokees, led by Elias C. Boudinot, claimed that he and other tribal members had not been given a chance to bid on the lease. They shared their conspiracy theory of bribes and collusion at a congressional hearing in Washington, DC. Joining that chorus of protest were a frontier mob called the Boomers, who claimed that any lands not assigned to Indian tribes should be opened to non-Indian settlement. Their immediate target was the Unassigned Lands to the south, but they saw the Outlet as a secondary prize. Congressmen, listening to their constituents along the distressed farming frontier, joined the fight. The commissioner of Indian affairs was not far behind.

In 1888, as a new five-year lease with the Cherokee Strip Livestock Association was being negotiated for even more money, federal officials ruled that the lease was illegal, even though they admitted the Cherokees still owned the land. Congress quickly followed with an act creating a commission to negotiate a purchase from the Cherokee Nation. To strengthen their negotiating position, federal officials ordered all cattle removed from the Outlet. The offer was $1.25 an acre, and until that was accepted, the Cherokees were denied use or income.[30]

While that drama was unfolding, the noose tightened around the neck of tribal sovereignty. Congress, without tribal agreements this time, authorized another wave of railroad construction through the Indian Territory. In 1887 the Atchison, Topeka, and Santa Fe Railway completed two lines through the Cherokee Outlet, one north and south through the future towns of Perry, Guthrie, and Oklahoma City, and another farther west that went through the future town of Woodward. Then came the Rock Island, east to west and north to south. Each steel rail was a dagger in the heart of Cherokee national survival.

The point of no return was reached on April 22, 1889, when the federal government

Figure 16. The Dawes Commission. Image courtesy of the Oklahoma Historical Society.

opened the central section of Indian Territory to non-Indian settlement by land run. More than fifty thousand pioneers raced for land that day, claiming either 160-acre homesteads in the country or lots in towns born grown. In August 1890, Congress created Oklahoma Territory, a beachhead from which other lands were claimed from tribes such as the Sac and Fox, the Pottawatomie, and the Cheyenne and Arapaho. As implementation of the General Allotment Act gained momentum, attention returned to the Five Civilized Tribes.

On March 3, 1893, Congress created a three-person commission to "negotiate" with the Cherokee and the other Five Civilized Tribes for allotment of lands in severalty. The chairman of the commission was the old reformer turned revisionist, Senator Henry Dawes, who now saw private land ownership as the only hope for saving the Indians from themselves. He and his commissioners took their holy crusade to the Indian Territory, where they met stiff resistance from all five of the tribes, including the Cherokees. They returned to Washington, DC, recommended that Congress force allotment on the tribes, and offered testimony that painted

Figure 17. Redbird Smith. Image courtesy of the Oklahoma Historical Society.

the worst possible picture of life in the Indian nations.

Attempts at negotiation continued, but all the cards were in the hands of the Dawes Commission. While the Cherokees refused to even meet, much less negotiate, Congress landed a one-two punch. In 1895 authority was granted to survey the Cherokee Nation, followed the next year with authorization and funds to prepare a census of Cherokees eligible for allotments. With or without the participation of the Cherokees, the Dawes Commission was moving ahead.

The Cherokees pushed back. In one congressional hearing, after listening to what they considered lies printed in territorial newspapers, tribal delegates refuted the testimony and summarized their closing remarks in a letter to Principal Chief Samuel Mayes. "In the scheme of the Dawes Commission," they predicted, "it would become easy for capitalists and monied men of less degree to soon become the owners of millions. But what about the other side? What about our people, who are, now, the legal owners and sovereigns of these lands? Why, the question is easy of answer. Crushed to earth under the hoofs of business greed, they would soon become a homeless throng, more scoffed at and abused than a Coxey's army. No territorial or state legislation can protect the Indian in his rights. Business has no moral consciousness; when a statute comes in its way, it will invoke the aid of a higher law and grasp the Indian's property anyhow."[31]

While tribal leaders fought the Dawes Commission on the twin battlefields of politics and public opinion, a growing segment of the full-blood Cherokee population responded with a spiritual revival that defined Cherokee patriotism and survival in ethnic and cultural terms. They called themselves the Keetoowahs, a name that had been and would repeatedly be used in the future for various causes, both political and corporate. In this case, the Keetoowah movement was based on ancient traditions and the sacred fire that could be traced to the mound builders. By the 1880s, the sacred

Figure 18. Keetoowah Nighthawks. Image courtesy of the Oklahoma Historical Society.

fire had been restored in the isolated hills of the Illinois District in a place called Redbird Holler.[32]

The leader of the spiritual movement was Redbird Smith, who had been tutored in the ancient ways by Creek Sam, a well-known holy man. Smith sought renewal of Cherokee identity through the three symbols of White Path, Sacred Fire, and Wampum. White Path was the way a virtuous man or woman should live their lives, pure of mind and body, peace and righteousness, with protection from God. The Sacred Fire was the living manifestation of God, carrying prayers to heaven and sharing spiritual messages from place to place on earth. The seven Wampum belts, once lost but now recovered, symbolized binding agreements between people and their God. The symbols on the belts, if properly understood, would reveal what the Cherokees had lost.[33]

From the 1880s to the 1900s, Redbird Smith and the elders of the Keetoowah Society shared their message of hope with a growing segment of Cherokee people who met at a number of ceremonial grounds. Smith moved his own ceremonial ground to Blackgum Mountain after railroad tracks were built through his former community. At the center of the stomp grounds was a deep hole consecrated by ashes

Figure 19. Full-blood Cherokees who came to enroll at the Dawes Commission. Image courtesy of the Oklahoma Historical Society.

from the original sacred fire and lit anew with flint and steel. Thirty yards west of the fire was a pole for a stickball grounds. Around the stomp grounds were seven arbors, one for each of the seven clans of the Cherokee. At the height of the Keetoowah revival, there would be twenty-two ceremonial grounds scattered through the hills.[34]

True believers in the Keetoowah Society did not recognize the reality of the Dawes Commission and refused to participate. To members, being Cherokee was a spiritual matter between a person and God, a belief system, not a physical relationship based on material possessions, political affiliations, or definitions created by white people. In 1896, when the Dawes Commission started compiling the final rolls, approximately five thousand to six thousand full-blood Keetoowahs refused to take part.

The political leaders of the Cherokee Nation had no such choice. In 1898, with the Cherokees the only tribe not engaged in negotiating for allotment, Congress passed the Curtis Act, which effectively ended the era of tribal self-government. There would be no tribal law, no tribal courts, and federal control of schools and other institutions. The only task remaining for the principal chief and the National Council was to sign off on the final terms of allotment. Still, the Cherokee leaders fought for the best possible deal for their people.

They wanted tax-exempt status for all allottees for thirty-five years. They wanted guarantees that Cherokees with half-blood or greater blood quantum could not be cheated out of their land for an extended time. Most surprising, the mixed-blood leaders in this final series of negotiations wanted full-bloods to have the right to choose allotments in one contiguous area where the land would be held in a corporation for their joint use under communal title. Federal officials, with the hammer of the Curtis Act in their hands, refused the latter privilege but granted some of the restrictions on alienation of land.[35]

The Cherokee Nation finally capitulated in 1902, the last of the Five Civilized Tribes to do so, and signed an allotment agreement. By dividing the total acreage of the Cherokee Nation, 4,420,068 acres, by the number of Cherokee citizens, 41,824, each Cherokee could claim an average of 105 acres, but the actual number of acres allotted to each person would vary for several reasons. Children would get fewer acres than adults, while each black freedman would receive only forty acres. Complicating the final numbers even more was the ability to claim allotments based on value, not total acreage.

The Dawes Commission evaluated the price of land based on ability to produce wealth. The worst land, in their opinion, was rocky mountain country that could not be plowed. The best land, again in the opinion of white outsiders, was the rich prairie plains to the west where farmers could plow under the sod and grow cash crops. Each of the nineteen classifications carried a different value. Cherokees could claim what the Dawes commissioners ironically called "homesteads," the land where they lived at the time of enrollment, then select so-called "surplus" land in other others. The average "credit" that each Cherokee adult received for their land selection was $325.60.[36]

Although not included in the valuation process, another complicating factor in what land would be selected was mineral rights. Under the allotment agreement, Cherokee leaders rejected federal efforts to keep mineral rights as communally owned property. Instead, mineral rights were to be allotted with surface ownership. Federal officials would approve leasing of mineral rights, usually three to five dollars an acre, and distribute lease money and royalty checks to individual surface owners. From 1902 to 1907, federal officials approved 4,366 oil and gas leases in Indian Territory covering 363,000 acres in two fields, most of which were in the Cherokee Nation. A deep field extended from the Kansas line on the north to the western edge of the Cherokee Nation, south

Figure 20. Henry Meigs, pioneer settler of Park Hill. Image courtesy of the Oklahoma Historical Society.

to Bartlesville, and on to Tulsa in the Creek Nation. A shallow field was discovered near Chelsea and Coody's Bluff and extended up the Verdigris River to Kansas.[37]

Another evaluation of land not calculated in the allotment process was the potential of town lots. Federal officials, under provisions of the Curtis Act, started platting towns and selling lots in 1899 with proceeds held for the tribe. Towns such as Claremore, Wagoner, Sallisaw, and Stillwell were formally recognized with private ownership of land no longer restricted to Cherokee citizens. The sale of town lots would eventually generate $773,302 in revenue for the tribal trust fund.[38]

Meanwhile, the Dawes Commission was compiling what it called the Final Rolls of who was a Cherokee citizen entitled to an allotment. Starting with the 1896 census assembled by the Cherokee Nation, field agents scattered across the countryside and interviewed individuals to determine family lineage and claims to citizenship. The enrollment process was complicated by two opposing trends. On one side, field agents were inundated by white people who claimed either Indian blood or relationships through marriage and by blacks who claimed they had long been denied legal status as freedmen deserving citizenship. On the flip side, field agents found that many full-blood Cherokees who still did not believe in the legality of allotment were "conveniently" away from home at the time of enrollment. Redbird Smith, leader of the Keetoowah movement, described his own resistance in testimony to a congressional panel.[39]

"When the Dawes Commission was here for the purpose of making the enrollment for final settlement by the allotment of the land," he said, "I was at home enjoying myself in peace when I was arrested and taken to prison. I and several other Indians were arrested and taken together to the Muskogee jail for standing up for our rights–my old treaty with the United States Government–as I have always stood for it without violating any part of it, nor have

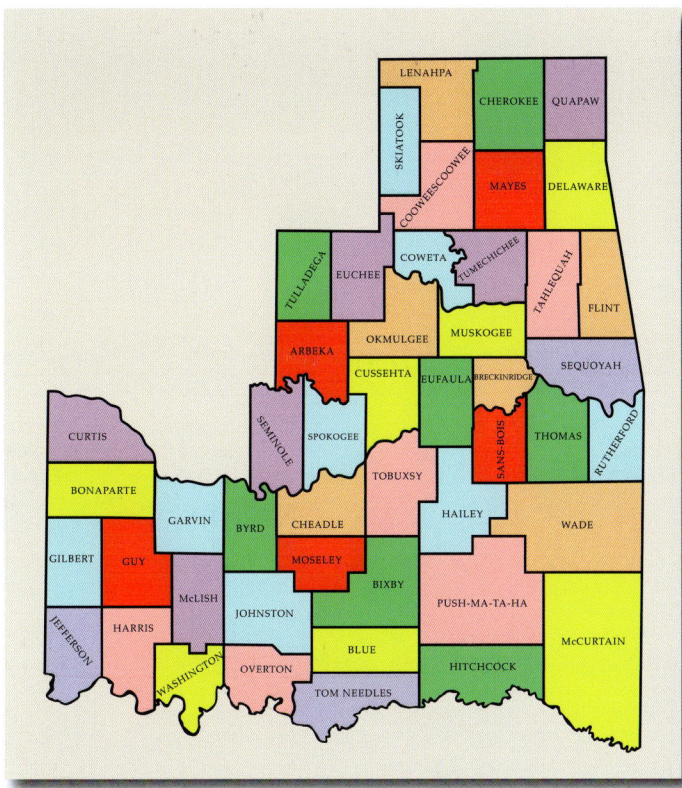

Figure 21. Proposed State of Sequoyah.

I violated any law." After one senator asked him what happened next, he answered, "On Saturday evening they put me in jail and they kept me all night in jail and on Sunday morning they let me out, and then they took me to the commissioner's office and made me enroll against my will." At the time of statehood in 1907, almost two thousand full-blood Cherokees had still not claimed their allotments.[40]

Many claims made by whites and blacks for a place on the final rolls were settled in court. In 1906 the US Supreme Court ruled that Cherokee citizenship laws must be recognized as legal documents. Whites who had married Cherokees after 1877 had no claim on citizenship or property based on a law passed by the Cherokee Council at the time. Furthermore, whites who had married other whites considered intermarried citizens before 1877 were denied citizenship. Of the 3,627 whites who claimed to be intermarried before 1877, only 286 were included on the rolls. Another victory for the Cherokees was a ruling that citizens who had moved out of the nation after 1839 and who had not been readmitted to citizenship by the National Council were no longer citizens. When the final rolls were completed, the Dawes Commission determined that Cherokee citizenship was shared by 8,703 full-bloods, 27,916 mixed-bloods, 286 intermarried whites, and 4,919 freedmen.[41]

As the allotment process neared its gloomy end, the Cherokees still did not give up all hope. In July 1905, Cherokee Chief William Rogers joined other tribal leaders to call for a constitutional convention to create a new state separate from Oklahoma Territory. Local conventions in the federal recording districts of the Cherokee, Choctaw, Creek, and Seminole nations met on August 7 and elected seven delegates and seven alternates for the proposed convention. The delegates met in Muskogee on August 21 and chose a committee of fifty to draft a constitution. Of the fifty, forty were tribal citizens.

The delegates returned on September 5 and adopted a constitution creating the State of Sequoyah. It was submitted to a vote of the people on November 7, 1905, and was overwhelmingly approved. It was sent to Congress where it was ignored. The prospect of two new western states, both populist and both dominated by Democrats, had little appeal to a Congress comfortably controlled by Republicans and probusiness boosters from the East Coast. The only benefit of the entire exercise for the Cherokees was the network of friends made during the Sequoyah Convention. The single state convention authorized by Congress as well as the first slate of state officials elected to office starting on November 16, 2007, would be dominated by the men who shaped the State of Sequoyah constitution.[42]

  Less official but more meaningful in the long run was another ceremonial gathering of Cherokees who still wanted to control their own destiny. It was the Keetoowah Society, composed mainly of full-bloods who did not recognize allotment and the State of Oklahoma. In a series of meetings at their stomp grounds in 1906 and 1907, the Keetoowahs changed their organization from a committee to a Seven Clan Council, one member from each clan. They also changed the title of their leader from chairman to chief.

  To many Cherokees, both full-blood and mixed-blood, the United States might have the power to abolish their constitutional government and force them to take individual allotments of land, but no one could take away their identity. The Cherokee Nation would survive.

ᎠᏫᏙᏛᎢ 9
ᎤᏣᎰᎷᏅᏜᏩᏅ ᎾᏏᎢ ᎠᏍᏧᏉᎯ
ᎾᏜᎩ ᎤᏂᏍᎽᏧᎡᎩ 1907-1935

Chapter 9: Adrift in a Sea of Survival

Figure 1. Cherokee National Male Seminary, prior to burning, c. 1910. Image courtesy of the Cherokee National Historical Society.

Cherokees' reaction to statehood varied by their understanding of a new order of government and their expectations of economic well-being. Statehood became a personal issue and topic of conversation as opposed to a philosophical principle of government.

To the Keetoowah Society, statehood was despised as the feared destructive agent of their ancient culture and identity. The mixed-blood and intermarried Cherokees

Figure 2. Northeastern Normal School. Image courtesy of the Cherokee National Historical Society.

were more apt to view the new order as an opportunity to improve their way of life both economically and socially. The Cherokees who had experimented with the white man's way of life via opportunities that opened up due to the various federal actions greeted statehood with anticipation of improving their lot.

The land-hungry white residents both within and without the Indian Territory were especially optimistic about the future of Oklahoma. Most Cherokees had some degree of uncertainty, from the bitter rejection of the Keetoowahs to the realization of the more assimilated Cherokees that their nation was gone.

Considering the magnitude of change, the transition occurred without public protest. Certain changes were immediate and highly visible. Cherokee Nation physical holdings were transferred to the new State of Oklahoma. This included the Capitol Building, Supreme Court Building, National Jail, the district court houses, the Orphan Asylum, and all school buildings. The state did work out an agreement later for the Department of Interior to operate some of the schools until the state could hire teachers and supply teaching materials.

The Indian Appropriation Act of 1908 authorized the Department of Interior to sell tribal land and buildings. Most of the physical holdings of the tribe were purchased at appraised value by the State of Oklahoma.

Adrift in a Sea of Survival 1907 - 1936

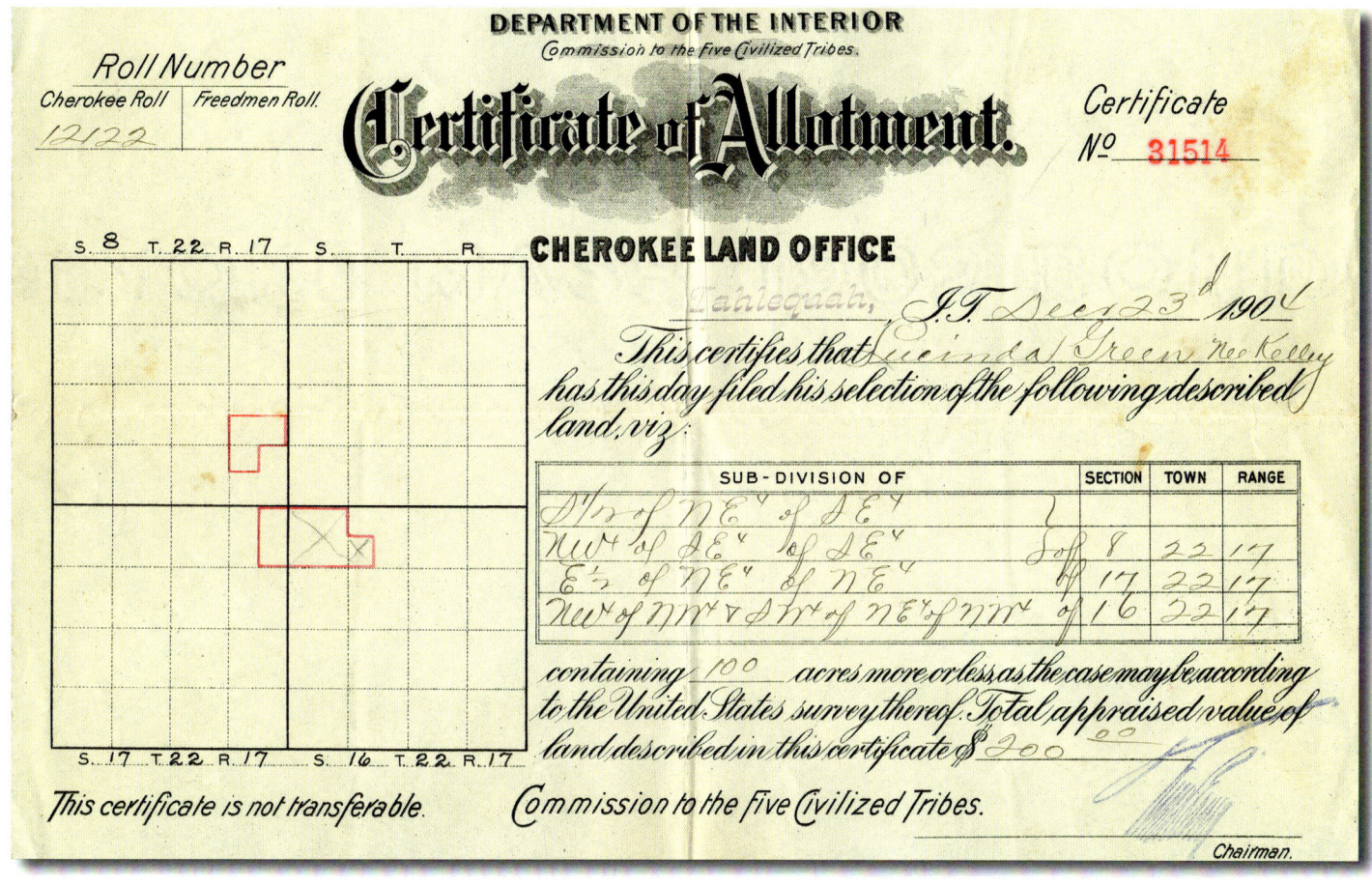

Figure 3. Cherokee Land Office allotment slip. Image courtesy Cherokee National Historical Society.

The Female Seminary was acquired by the state to serve as the site for a two-year state normal school that opened in 1909. The Capitol Building, Supreme Court Building, and National Jail were acquired by the newly formed Cherokee County for use by the county government.

The disposal of Sequoyah Orphan School was delayed until all school functions were ceased by the holdover Cherokee Nation. In 1910 the federal government, through the Department of the Interior, assumed ownership of the school property and changed its function to a boarding school. By the time of Oklahoma statehood in 1907, the "Indian Question" had lost its significance in Congress.

Historian Angie Debo provided a clear analysis of dangers posed for Indians by the political parties of the new state of Oklahoma. Both the Democratic and Republican platforms did not bode well for Indians. The Democratic platform for the first legislative session included removal of restrictions from allotted lands; termination of all federal bureaus along with the immediate settlement of all tribal affairs; the immediate distribution of all tribal funds; removal of restrictions on sale and lease of lands, except homesteads of full-bloods; and protection of the mentally incompetent, of whatever race should be the jurisdiction of state courts and not the federal government. The Republican platform likewise cast covetous eyes on Indian land and resources with similar goals. Foremost was removal of all restrictions upon alienation of lands belonging to Indians. The party leaders also recommended "enactment of such laws by Congress as will give to each member of the Indian tribes in this state all rights and privileges of other American citizens, including the right to control, sell, lease, mortgage, or devise the lands allotted to him, the same as white persons under similar conditions: except that the homestead of full bloods shall be inalienable, as now provided by law, and we request our members in Congress to urge such immediate legislation."[1]

Debo pointed out that many people were of the opinion that these platforms did not go far enough. She included an excerpt from the *Muskogee Phoenix* newspaper that expressed dissatisfaction. Tams Bixby, former chair of the Dawes Commission, held controlling interest in the *Muskogee Phoenix*. Mr. Bixby, an influential Republican, wrote, "The plea that the full-blood will be reduced to beggary by the removal of restrictions is not valid. Society is under no obligation to feed him who will not work. The Indian who has sold his land and spent the money ought to stand just where any other citizen of the state stands—there will be work for him to do even if he be a profligate, and if he will not do it, organized society cannot be made, by any conceivable argument, to be his pension giver."[2]

Office holders in state government were for the greater part Democratic. When the legislature convened, Robert L. Owen, former Cherokee Nation and federal official, was chosen

Figure 4. Robert L. Owen. Image courtesy of the Oklahoma Historical Society.

as US senator along with Thomas P. Gore from Lawton. The Enabling Act had created federal congressional districts for five representatives. The territorial representatives filled these positions. The former Indian Territory was served by Chickasaw citizen Charles D. Carter and James S. Davenport. The former Oklahoma Territory representatives were Bird McGuire, the only Republican representative, Elmer Fulton of Oklahoma City, and Scott Ferris of Lawton. The entire Oklahoma delegation to the US Congress was solidly committed to removal of restrictions on Indian land.[3]

Adrift in a Sea of Survival 1907 - 1936

The transition from federal government to state government held little promise for improvement of the Cherokees' lot in life. The majority of Oklahoma political office holders at county and state levels were supported by companies and individuals who were interested in making money through land and mineral speculation involving Indian and freedmen land allotments.

Historian Daniel Littlefield has written about the racial hatred exhibited during Oklahoma's constitutional convention in November 1906 and the first legislative session in 1907. According to Littlefield, convention Democrats campaigned for seats in the convention based on separate schools, separate railroad coaches, separate depots, prohibition of mixed marriages, and opposition to election of African Americans to public office. They also favored a Jim Crow provision in the constitution. The Jim Crow provision was not included in the constitution but was deferred to the first legislative session due to fears of a veto by President Theodore Roosevelt. This was a heavy blow to the black population of Oklahoma. A Jim Crow bill was introduced in both houses on December 2, 1907, and became effective on February 16, 1908. "Jim Crow" was the title of a popular black minstrel song. The application of this name to segregation of blacks came to mean traditional discrimination and segregation against blacks in all situations. The black population of the state was further disenfranchised in 1910 when Oklahoma adopted further general discrimination measures. One reason for such harsh measures toward the black citizens was to allow land speculators to divest them of allotted land that blacks had received through the Dawes Commission. Blacks were accustomed to disputes with the Cherokee government over land issues and education. Schools were segregated under Cherokee law. Blacks participated in Cherokee governmental functions including voting, serving in office, influencing governmental issues, and access to Cherokee courts.[4]

In 1907 a final roll of Cherokee citizenship was approved by the Department of the Interior. The count was 8,703 full-bloods, 27,916 mixed-bloods, 286 intermarried whites, and 4,919 freedmen, totaling 41,824. After statehood 5,605

"ᎾᏍᎩᏃ ᎠᏂ ᎡᎦᎯ ᎤᏓᏴᎵ ᎤᏩᏩᎳᎢ ᎾᏍᎩ ᏒᎦᎦᎩ ᎠᎵᏗ ᏆᏳᎲᏍᏩᎠᏱ."

—ᎾᎵ ᏝᏣᏴ

"We spoiled the best territory in the world to make a state."

–Will Rogers

children were added as result of a 1912 Supreme Court decision.[5]

Cherokee historian Rennard Strickland summarized Oklahoma's early government with the following statement: "To understand Oklahoma government one must remember that it was conceived when land speculators, Indians, cowboys, dirt farmers, and coal miners came together to settle on the laws that would control their own use of the resources of the new state."[6]

Strickland also quotes Will Rogers on Oklahoma statehood: "We spoiled the best territory in the world to make a state" and "Indians were so cruel they were all killed by civilized white men for encroaching on white domain."[7]

Edward Everett Dale, whom Strickland labeled the dean of Oklahoma's white historians, provided a sad quote from a Cherokee woman who remembered statehood: "This Cherokee woman," he wrote, "married to a white man, refused to attend the statehood ceremonies with her husband."

He returned and said to her: "Well, Mary, we no longer live in the Cherokee Nation. All of us are now citizens of the state of Oklahoma." Tears came to her eyes thirty years later as she recalled that day. "It broke my heart. I went to bed and cried all night long. It seemed more than I could bear that the Cherokee Nation, my country and my people's country was no More."[8]

The Cherokees faced a majority culture that viewed Indians as inherently inferior and responsible for their own failures. The writers of the multi-volume *The History of Nations* provided a twentieth-century perspective of the Indian in America that continued to label Indians as lower status beings in America. Henry Cabot Lodge, the editor of the series, devoted a chapter to discuss aboriginal America. For the damage and destruction of tribal groups, the coming of the white man was identified as the chief reason. The white man was not criticized, however, for their downfall. In comparing Indians to whites, Lodge viewed Indians in the following statements:

"For this destruction the coming of the white man is chiefly responsible. Neither in war nor in peace has the Indian been able to stand against or beside him. Sentamentalists have inveighed against the whites for this; but history teaches that inferior people must yield to a superior civilization in one way or another. They must take on civilization or pass out…In most cases the Indian kept faith when dealt with fairly, even when being gradually pushed backward from his hunting grounds. But at best he was a dirty savage, dwelling in squalor and filth and content therewith. In consequence, epidemic diseases have often decimated the tribes."[9]

The writings listed above were published in 1913. The conditions outlined did not typify the Cherokees at that time. Many writers as well as the general public were blind to the fact that tribal members in America enjoyed social and economic status in accordance with location and opportunity.

The fact that the Cherokees, who appeared to be most successful by white or US government measures, were functioning as members of the dominant or white society was used to encourage assimilation. The federal government through its interaction with the Cherokee via the Office of Indian Affairs rewarded the adoption of white ways. Many government programs had assimilation as the ultimate goal. The naming by the federal government of the Five Civilized Tribes was a reward for copying the ways of the white man.

The Dawes Commission, the Curtis Act, and Oklahoma statehood were designed to hasten acceptance of assimilation and thereby relinquishment of tribal land holdings to accommodate white settlement and expansion of America. The process would have been far less controversial if the Indians had been participants rather than protestors. These final acts to complete the process of assimilation were preceded by acts to pacify Indians who were being evicted from their traditional lands.

The mass eviction years from the 1820s to the 1840s led to a large number of sick and starving Indians in America. Publicity concerning the desperate plight of Indians caused Congress to reassess the government's role in dealing with the "Indian question." After the American Civil War, Congress urged the president to provide emergency relief to needy tribes. This focused attention caused Congress to embark on a vigorous program of assimilation with legislation and federal funds supplied to the Office of Indian Affairs for provision of Indian schools, health care, and general emergency assistance. Most assistance programs were designed to hasten assimilation.[10]

The assimilation era produced the off-reservation boarding schools which became a trend in the 1880s and peaked in enrollment during the 1920s. The boarding schools were viewed as a means of assimilation by removing the children from influences of the home, Indian community, tribe, and culture, thus hastening assimilation. By 1887 fourteen thousand Indian students were enrolled in 227 schools across America. The Office of Indian Affairs operated 163 of the schools. Private agencies and church-related groups operated sixty-four schools.[11]

Cherokee students were not sent to boarding schools in numbers equal to the other four major tribes in Indian Territory. This was due to the legislative and budgetary support by the Cherokee Nation for a national system of schools including the male and female seminaries and neighborhood schools.

Family disruptions, including death of parents, lack of family income to support children at home, and in some instances a desire of parents to provide a head start for assimilation, were the main reasons for sending Cherokee children to boarding schools. After 1920 the participation in boarding school enrollment increased. Cherokee elementary students went to Seneca Indian School, located near Wyandotte, Oklahoma. Older students enrolled at Chilocco Indian Agricultural School. By 1925 Cherokee students represented the largest tribal group at Chilocco. Other schools attended by Cherokees included Haskell Indian School in Lawrence, Kansas, and Sequoyah Indian School in Tahlequah, Oklahoma. Seneca and Sequoyah did not become Office of Indian Affairs boarding schools until after Oklahoma statehood.[12]

In addition to educational advancement, the influence of several towns within the Cherokee Nation contributed to the adoption of white lifestyles and commerce. Three towns with vibrant commercial districts and progressive leaders were Claremore, Tahlequah, and Vinita. At the time of statehood all three towns had active commercial clubs (forerunners of chambers of commerce), active political involvement, progressive business interests, and active church and social groups. Town leadership for all three supported land allotment and statehood for Oklahoma. Access was supplied by major railroad service to Claremore and Vinita. Tahlequah did not acquire rail service until 1902. All three of the towns had units of major national civic, service, and social organizations. Their attraction to the better elements of assimilated society did not lead to rejection of Cherokee ways or culture. The majority of Cherokees seem to have chosen to embrace the white man's marketplace, his government, and his society while maintaining the Cherokees' personal Indianness.

The early years of Oklahoma statehood posed many problems and adjustments for Cherokee citizens no matter their status on economic or social scales. Perhaps the most difficult adjustment was the realization that they could not turn to former Cherokee governmental services for assistance or guidance.

In 1905 W. C. Rogers, the elected chief from the Downing Party, was preparing to close-out the government of the Cherokee Nation. Chief Rogers refused to issue a call for election to the National Council. His reasoning was that the business of the tribe was over. Under the urging of the Keetoowah Society, the Council conducted an election without a call from the chief, and members of the Council opposed to Rogers were elected. While Chief Rogers was in Washington, DC, the recently elected members impeached him and chose Frank J. Boudinot as chief. Secretary Ethan A. Hitchcock of the Department of Interior recognized Rogers as chief and ended Boudinot's claim.[13] Chief Rogers remained in office as titular chief until his death in 1917.

After Chief Rogers's death, Congress authorized presidential appointment of chiefs for the Cherokees. Appointees served the same role as Chief Rogers. Most were appointed for one day only, with functions limited to signing of documents. Some of the Cherokee Nation office holders were not opposed to statehood. Most office holders were quite well-off financially and saw the new era as holding opportunities for their advancement both financially and socially. The towns of Tahlequah, Vinita, and Claremore offered a way of life superior to places of their size in neighboring states. For this segment of the Cherokee population, the future looked bright.

Adrift in a Sea of Survival 1907 - 1936

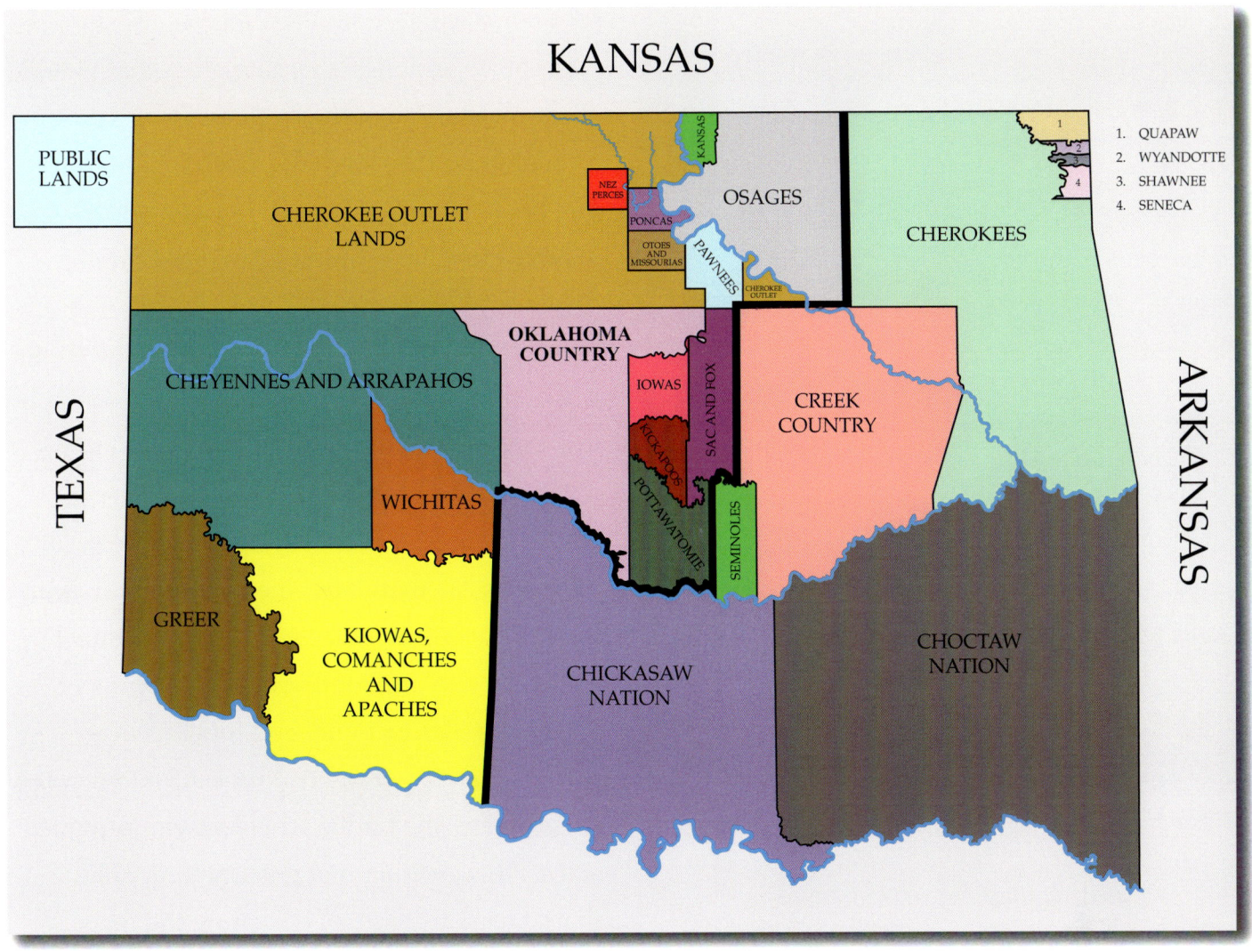

Figure 5. Combined map of Indian and Oklahoma Territories.

The full-blood families in the secluded hills of the districts similar to Flint and Delaware had a totally opposite view of the future without a Cherokee government. This caused the schism between the full-bloods and mixed-bloods to grow wider and was, to a large degree, a factor causing the government of the Cherokee Nation to remain dormant for more than sixty years.

Many in the mixed-blood elite of the tribe considered statehood as an opportunity to enhance financial well-being and as an opportunity to vie for leadership roles in the new state's political arena. A large number of this group had completed their formal education in the Cherokee seminaries or at prestigious schools in the East. For many, particularly those engaged in business and law, the Dawes Commission process had resulted in a quick path to riches. Their status set them apart as examples of success to federal officials who desired assimilation for the Cherokees. To the traditional Cherokees, those who favored assimilation were set apart as traitors to Cherokee identity and tradition.

The full-blood traditional groups considered allotment of land and statehood

Figure 6. Chief W. C. Rogers. Image courtesy of the Oklahoma Historical Society.

as a serious threat to Cherokees as a tribe. The Keetoowah groups sought unification in opposition to the new order. Their protests over land allotment continued for years beyond statehood. Debo describes their passive resistance by refusing land allotments and removing to the hill regions of present northeastern Oklahoma. By 1912 nearly two thousand had refused to accept allotment. As late as 1915, many were still returning correspondence from the agency in Muskogee.[14]

The vast majority of Cherokees were strangely silent during the transition to governmental extinction. Organized public protests did not occur. The Keetoowah Society, Inc. voiced opposition to federal officials and sent representatives to Washington, DC, in attempts to establish alternate plans that would allow recognition of the Keetoowah as a group located separately from the Cherokee Nation. The Keetoowah Society, Inc. was not successful in any of its efforts for recognition as the successor government.

Perhaps one of the reasons for a business as usual attitude shown by the Cherokee people was the continuation of the Cherokee Nation public school system. The Cherokee citizens valued their educational system. Provisions of the Curtis Act mandated the continuation, even expansion, of the educational system. Since it was the only unit of Cherokee government that was fully functional and touched more citizens than any former Cherokee Nation unit of government, the public school system provided at least the semblance of government. The shared responsibility of operating the schools by the Department of the Interior and Cherokee officials proved to be a positive endeavor.

The dual administration of the schools (rural schools by Cherokee Nation and town schools by Department of Interior), coupled with cooperative efforts in maintaining quality of instructional staff, progressed in a somewhat amicable fashion during the federal imposition of a transitional period from 1898 to 1907. The justification for complete takeover of the education system by the Department of the Interior was couched in terms derogatory to the Cherokee Nation's administration of the schools. Federal officials cited lack of quality

Adrift in a Sea of Survival 1907 - 1936

Figure 7. Wauhila Home Guards, 1918. Image courtesy of the Cherokee National Historical Society.

in instruction and, most severe of all, of the appropriateness of the curriculum.

　　The attack on the curriculum brought up former references to federal intent for Cherokee males to pursue agricultural interests and females to be schooled in domestic arts. The Cherokee schools, under the operation by federal authorities, faced the reintroduction of federal mandates for drastic changes in the overall philosophy of education for Indians. The following excerpt was from the 1889 annual report authored by federal appointee superintendent John Benedict and was included as part of his annual report to Washington, DC: "Indian Territory is essentially an agricultural and stock-raising community. By one or the other of these pursuits must the great majority of the people earn their livelihood in the future.

Yet tending toward the pursuits they must hereafter follow is unheard of in their schools. It is unquestionable that the breaking up of Indian Territory and its resolution into the remainder of the country is only a matter of time, and then these boys and girls must receive a portion of the public domain for their separate use. The course of study pursued at the various schools is in the line of training for a collegiate course looking to a professional life. Girls, instead of being taught the domestic arts, are given a course of Latin and mathematics, while such simple arts as sewing, cooking, and other branches of domestic economy are studiously neglected. The dignity of work receives no attention at their hands. Although each of the boarding schools has a farm surrounding it, no attention is paid to teaching the boys to become better farmers or

Figure 8. Hickory Ridge School, in the Canadian District, c. 1907. Image courtesy of the Cherokee National Historical Society.

stock-raisers, either with an educative value or as a matter of reducing expenses at the schools. In other words these schools are not in line with the best thought so far as education matters are concerned."[15]

Other reports from the Department of Interior voiced concerns about the lack of agricultural and industrial training and went so far as to assert that the schools had been much better off under missionary control. This allegation was especially offensive to Cherokees since the Cherokee Nation Public Schools had never been under missionary control.

The general provisions of the 1898 Curtis Act directed the secretary of the interior to appoint a superintendent of schools for the Indian Territory and four supervisors of schools. One supervisor was to be assigned for onsite supervision for the Cherokee, Choctaw, Creek, and Chickasaw Nations.[16]

John Benedict was named superintendent with an office in Muskogee. Benjamin Coppock was appointed US school supervisor for the Cherokee Nation on May 1, 1899. Superintendent Benedict expressed as his first concern the lack of educational opportunity for white children. Other conditions Benedict frequently voiced as concerns were regular attendance, lack of training for teachers, and lack of examinations for teachers. Benedict also offered a possible solution to the lack of education for whites. He proposed to allow dual enrollment in areas where both races resided. In contrast to negative rhetoric by both sides of the school

Figure 9. Spring house on the site of the old Cherokee Orphan Asylum in Salina. Image courtesy of the Oklahoma Historical Society.

issue, the assumption of control of the schools by the Department of Interior was carried out, for the most part, in a spirit of harmonious cooperation.[17]

The three-member board of education continued Cherokee input, with the principal chief appointing two of its members. Collaboration allowed many changes that had been recommended by former boards, but had not been acted upon by the Cherokee Nation Council. Major changes included lengthening the time and expanding content of required summer normal school sessions for certifying teachers and adopting of rules and regulations pertaining to directors and teachers.

The major increase in student enrollment resulted from changes in enrollment eligibility and additional funding. The 1902 regulations provided for enrollment of white children who resided in tax-supported incorporated towns, and in 1906 Congress appropriated $150,000 for maintenance of existing schools, construction of new schools, and provision for attendance by noncitizens.[18]

Both seminaries operated at capacity during the Department of Interior's domination in the prestatehood era. Both institutions maintained a strong liberal arts education

Figure 10. Cherokee Council 1890. Image courtesy of the Cherokee National Historical Society.

appropriate for transfer to universities in the states, particularly in the East. A change in political philosophy resulted in full-blood domination of Cherokee politics in the late 1800s. Most of the new council members were members of the Keetoowah Society. The new order called for a greater full-blood representation in the seminaries. Their efforts resulted in establishing a primary unit and an indigent unit at each seminary.[19]

Both of these alterations required additional curricula to accommodate students who were unable to pay the seminary fees or were unable to pass entry exams. In addition to meeting the new requirements for admitting students, the seminaries continued their demanding classical education preparatory departments.

During the transition from 1898 to 1907, the seminaries and the Negro High School experienced growth in enrollment. For the seminaries, the 1907 enrollment totaled 180 girls and 138 boys. The Orphan Asylum near Salina operated at capacity, usually at approximately 170 students. During the 1902-03 school year, the instructional emphasis at the orphanage was changed to industrial training. On November 17, 1903, the school was destroyed by fire. A replacement facility was constructed on a new site located approximately six miles south of Tahlequah on the site of the present Sequoyah High School. In 1907 seventy-three pupils were moved into the new facility. In 1914 the property was transferred to the US Department of Interior for $5,000. In 1925 the name of the facility was changed to Sequoyah Orphan Training School.

As the need for a facility to care for orphans lessened, the Department of Interior changed the function to a Bureau of Indian Affairs Boarding School. With this action, the US Department of Interior won its battle for manual training versus classical education for Cherokee youth.[20]

The Cherokee Nation School System was in a phase-out mode from 1907 through 1910. The inclusion of the Cherokee Nation in Oklahoma for educational purposes was not possible for the 1907-8 school year due to lack of state funds. Because of the Dawes property restrictions, some of the former Indian Territory land was not taxable. Additionally, Oklahoma Territory had received grants for school land. Indian Territory did not receive school land grants. The end result was that the Department of Interior, which had full control of Cherokee Nation schools at statehood, assumed the obligation to continue operations using both tribal and federal funds to manage the schools until Oklahoma could meet its obligation. The seminaries continued to function on a borrowed time. The last year of operation for the Female Seminary was 1905-6. The Indian Appropriation Act of 1908 authorized the Department of Interior to sell the buildings of tribes. The building and campus of forty acres comprising the site of the Cherokee Nation Female Seminary were bought by the State of Oklahoma for $45,000 to be used as the site of the proposed Northeastern State Normal School.[21]

The sale of the Female Seminary Building resulted in a coed high school at the Male

Figure 11. Cherokee seminary students shearing sheep. Image courtesy of the Cherokee National Historical Society.

Seminary site for the 1909-10 school year. The arrangement was short-lived, however, due to the destruction of the Male Seminary Building by fire on March 20, 1910. An illustrated souvenir catalog highlighting the Cherokee Nation education system and its accomplishments from 1850 to 1906 was published following the close of the final year (1905-6) for the Cherokee National Female Seminary. Mrs. R. L. Fite, a seminarian from Muskogee, contributed a history of the Female Seminary for the publication. Her closing statement, though sad, provides an element of pride plus a subtle

Figure 12. Cherokee Male and Female Seminary graduates assembled in front of the Cherokee Capitol, c. 1900. Image courtesy Cherokee National Historical Society.

challenge for future generations: "The past and present we know, but what of the future? We ask no higher reward than it be worthy of the name it bears and that its identity be not lost in the coming years, but may the thread that is broken now be woven in a brighter and fresher web. May its volume of usefulness be increased and enriched as it flows down into the remote future and may every Cherokee woman hand down to her posterity the fact that this institution was the creation of their forefathers and the pride of their hearts. The sun has set forever on the Cherokee National Female Seminary."[22]

The Male Seminary location would be acquired by the reorganized Cherokee Nation many decades later, and the facilities would eventually be used for a physical fitness center for the Cherokee Nation. At the time of the closing of the Male Seminary, the Cherokee people were without a governmental structure and were citizens of a new state. Never had the need been greater for leadership among the Cherokee.

The seminary system's former students, both men and women, filled vital roles during the statehood and beyond era. The area of politics, law, and education were well served by former students of the seminaries. The alumna of the Female Seminary filled critical positions in the new state's educational system including Northeastern State Normal School. One of the Male Seminary's most illustrious graduates, William Wirt Hastings, class of 1884, served with distinction as US Representative from Oklahoma's Second Congressional District from 1915 to 1921 and from 1923 to 1935. Representative Hastings was responsible for legislation that created the W. W. Hastings Hospital in Tahlequah, Oklahoma.

Male Seminary graduate Emmet Starr was responsible for major publications dealing with Cherokee history. His *History of the Cherokee Nation* is used today for establishing historical dates and for genealogical research.[23] Natalie Panther summarizes the leadership initiatives of the Male Seminary graduates in this manner: "they turned their education into a tool for serving Cherokees and protecting tribal sovereignty."[24]

The largest population group residing in and immediately adjoining the Cherokee Nation prior to and during early days of statehood was composed of white land seekers. Much of the Cherokee land remained open or unoccupied. The unoccupied land posed a major enticement to the horde of landless persons seeking a fresh start.

Many of the intruders came from farm regions in Europe. When their industrial jobs played out in the Northeast, they fled to areas where land for homesteading was available. Since many of the European immigrants had farm experience in their former homelands, the US westward expansion and possible ownership of land were very attractive to them. This also accounted for the large number of white farmers residing in the Cherokee Nation prior to statehood. Resident status was obtained by various means: (1) marriage to a Cherokee that permitted application for citizenship in the Cherokee Nation; (2) leasing farm land from Cherokee citizens; (3) working for large Cherokee farming/grazing coops; or (4) squatting on unoccupied land by fencing, building residences, and planting crops. The latter was a common practice due to inaction by the federal government to live up to its agreement to remove intruders from Cherokee property. As early as 1890, the persons residing in the Cherokee Nation listed in (1) through (4) above outnumbered the Cherokee citizens. Thus, the Cherokees were a minority within their own nation and consequently a minority within their portion of the new state of Oklahoma.[25]

The occupation of former Cherokee Nation land by non-Indian settlers did not stop with the conclusion of the Dawes Commission allotments and statehood for Oklahoma. Swift action by the US Congress in 1908 for the removal of restrictions for certain classes of Dawes allottees opened up 12,002,997 acres of allottees' land in Indian Territory for possible sale. The act of 1908 removed restrictions from most minors who were direct allottees including lands which minors inherited from deceased allottees. The availability of land for sale along with the recently enacted Oklahoma probate court provisions for approving sales of land owned by minors opened the way for corrupt guardians and county judges to sell minors' lands.[26]

In addition to minors, whites, freedmen, and mixed-bloods of less than one-half Indian blood were released from all restrictions; mixed-bloods of one-half or more and less than three-fourth Indian blood were free to sell their surplus lands (acreages in addition to homesteads); and Indians of three-fourths or more Indian blood remained restricted in all categories of holdings.

The large number of land seekers found a new way to acquire homesteads. In league with land speculators, corrupt guardians, and county probate judges, land was plentiful.[27] This new wave of corrupt practices was one more step in degradation of the Cherokee. For many Cherokees, the lack of governmental services by the Cherokee Nation during the period from implementation of the Curtis Act to Oklahoma statehood had caused general feelings of mistrust in white sponsored government. The implementation of state government and its anti-Indian sentiment increased their feeling of loss.

Historian William McLoughlin summarized the elusive quest for sovereignty as a social and psychological dilemma of the Cherokees which lay in the inability of white Americans to accept the fact that the United States was, had always been, and would always be a multiracial and multicultural nation. At the time of the planned downfall of the Cherokee Nation, most US citizens were adamant in their belief that the USA was white man's country. Their beliefs and desires as translated to their elected governmental officials resulted in reducing the status of Indians to second class citizenship under the guise of improving their lives.[28]

The feelings of the disenfranchised Cherokees, after having lost their sense of self, are difficult to imagine. They were a people without a country. McLoughlin explored some of the reasons that allowed such inhumane acts of the federal government to degrade Cherokee people under the guise of helping them. McLoughlin pointed out the steps taken by the federal government to weaken the Cherokee, such as allowing hordes of intruders to invade them; denying Indian nations determination of who were their own citizens; catering to the demands of frontier non-Indian citizens and external business interests; and allowing and abetting both groups in their quest for Cherokee land and resources. Then, as a final act after Cherokee country was destabilized, Congress declared the Indians incapable of self-governance. McLoughlin quoted Charles Royce, a historian of the Cherokee who wrote, "They felt they were, as a nation, being slowly but surely compressed within the constricting coils of the giant anaconda of civilization; yet they held to the vain hope that a spirit of justice and mercy would be born of their hopeless condition."[29]

It is difficult to determine the number of intruders who were assigned to allotments during the Dawes Commission proceedings. The cost to the Cherokee Nation for its attempts to enforce federal law in protecting their assets due to failure of federal authorities to intervene is also an unknown number. Agricultural leases, freedmen's land, and the land of minors with guardians were controlled by land grafters who filed for ownership when lands became alienable. In 1924 the Board of Indian Commissioners reported that among the Five Civilized Tribes ninety percent of the Indian land allottees no longer owned their allotments.[30]

The allotment legacy was labeled by Angie Debo as "an orgy of plunder and exploitation probably un-paralled in American history."[32] Intruders were able to influence legislation to provide support for removal of restrictions on allotted land, and to ease the regulations on land transactions with minors. The numerical advantage for intruders was particularly significant at ballot boxes as the new state addressed Cherokee issues that were formerly federal issues.[31]

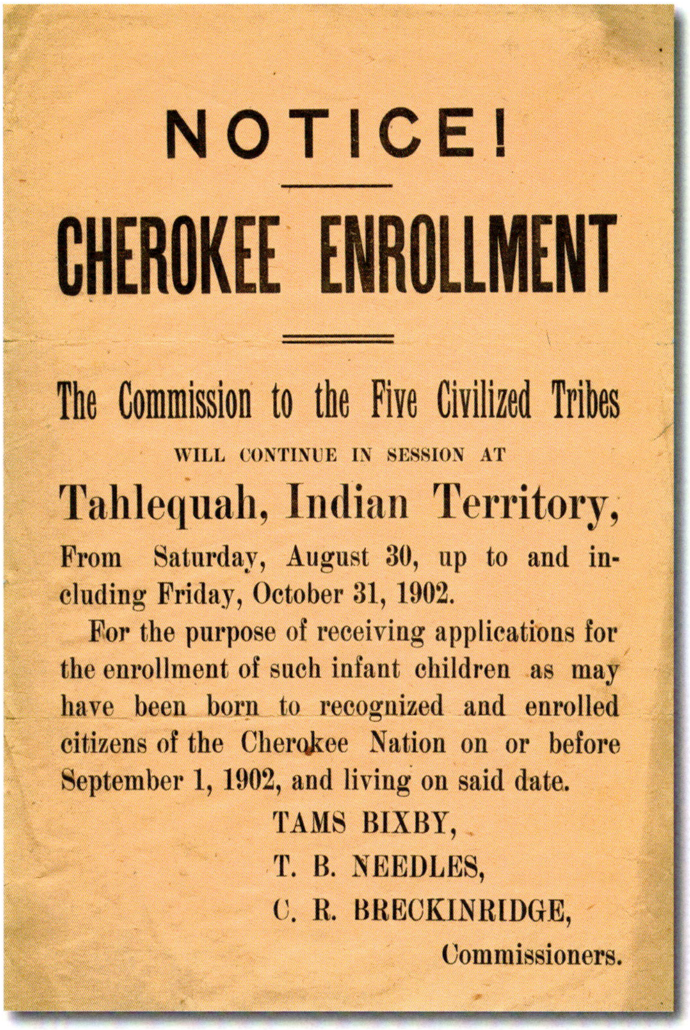
NOTICE!

CHEROKEE ENROLLMENT

The Commission to the Five Civilized Tribes

WILL CONTINUE IN SESSION AT

Tahlequah, Indian Territory,

From Saturday, August 30, up to and including Friday, October 31, 1902.

For the purpose of receiving applications for the enrollment of such infant children as may have been born to recognized and enrolled citizens of the Cherokee Nation on or before September 1, 1902, and living on said date.

TAMS BIXBY,
T. B. NEEDLES,
C. R. BRECKINRIDGE,
Commissioners.

Figure 13. Notice of Cherokee land allotment. Image courtesy of the Cherokee National Historical Society.

Despite the lack of federal and state recognition for a government, the Cherokees clung to their identity as a community. The largest formal political organization of Cherokees during the early years of statehood was the Keetoowah Society, Inc. This unit of Keetoowahs was formed in 1905 under the leadership of Richard Wolfe and the Keetoowah Society attorney, Frank Boudinot. The society's intent was to establish a political unit through incorporation that would be in place to succeed the Cherokee Nation in the event that the federal government proceeded with abolishment of the Cherokee Nation government.[32]

After Oklahoma statehood the Keetoowah Society members publicly claimed they assumed political leadership for all Cherokees. The Keetoowah Nighthawks viewed this move as entirely different from their goals, and it further divided the two groups. The realignment

Figure 14. Interior of the Tahlequah Land Office used by the Dawes Commission for allotment c. 1900. Image courtesy of the Cherokee National Historical Society.

through incorporation resulted in two distinct groups of Keetoowah. The primary groups were the Nighthawks under the leadership of Redbird Smith and the Keetoowah Society, Inc.

This book's authors asked John Ross, Jr., former Chief of the United Keetoowah Band of Cherokee Indians in Oklahoma, to provide written summaries of basic information concerning historical and current aspects of the Keetoowah organizations. Chief Ross served as chief of the United Keetoowah Band of Cherokee Indians in Oklahoma for two terms, 1991 to 1998.

He is currently a translation specialist for the Cherokee Nation Education Services Language Department. Ross's comments and statements follow.

"The word 'Keetoowah' has been closely interwoven into the fabric of Cherokee history. It was the name of the Principal Town, a seat of authority before the removal to Indian Territory. It also was the name applied to one of the two remaining dialects still spoken among the Eastern Band of Cherokees in North Carolina. It seems to have been the name by which centuries ago the Cherokee called themselves.

After allotment and statehood the traditional Cherokees did not abandon the idea of land held in common. The Keetoowahs favored the establishment of settlements as a way to become self-sufficient. Redbird Smith established a bank, started a cattle business, and bought land for the Keetoowah Nighthawks to reestablish the old way of life where land was owned commonly.

The importance of a land base to the Cherokee people cannot be overstated. It provided not only a home but also a livelihood. Cherokees did not believe in the private ownership of land. Any land controlled by the tribe belonged to the people; each member had the same right to use it as did every other member. This concept of land ownership was a guiding principle of the Indian life and culture; land could not be privately owned, which meant that the members of the community had to work together to plant, harvest, or gather what they could from the land. On the other hand, white people tended to glorify private ownership of land and individual wealth.

The two groups attracted new members with their missions. The Nighthawks concentrated on spiritualism and traditional ways with little attention to political affairs. Their leader, Redbird Smith, concentrated on rejuvenating traditional spiritual aspects of the Keetoowah. He sought land away from the former Cherokee Nation to resettle his followers when early attempts to obtain adjoining

Figure 15. Keetoowah Nighthawks. Image courtesy of the Oklahoma Historical Society.

allotments for Nighthawks through the Dawes allotment process was not allowed. Redbird's plan for a large block of land to be held communally was not approved by the Office of Indian Affairs.

Redbird's second plan was to review a previous unfulfilled attempt to relocate with his followers to Mexico. There had been discussion for movement to Mexico since before statehood. After statehood discussion resumed and in January, 1908, a group with membership from the Cherokee and other Five Civilized Tribes departed for Mexico on a fact-finding mission.

Their visit to the Colonia and Tampico in the State of Tamaulipas resulted in glowing accounts of farming conditions, wild game, and a climate to allow year round crops. The plan did not materialize due to lack of capital for relocation. The Department of Interior failed to approve the removal of restrictions on their allotments. The idea or wish to relocate reemerged through the 1920s, but action was not initiated. The provision for communal blocks of land was included in the 1934 Indian Reorganization Act but attracted little interest among Cherokees. No projects were completed.

From the beginning, the Keetoowah Society limited membership only to full-bloods. It was estimated that seven out of every ten Cherokee men belonged to the Keetoowah Society. This comprised almost everyone who was not a southern sympathizer. This organization had no connection to the historical Keetoowah of North Carolina. However, they did believe they were descendants of the ancient Keetoowah, and they were the only ones who were preserving the ancient Cherokee culture.

There is a misconception about the Keetoowah and the Pins. It is believed that the Keetoowahs were the same as the "Pin Indians." This is not the case. The crossed pins they wore during the Civil War designated them as the Pins. Not all the Keetoowah belonged to the Pins. However, the Pins were probably all Keetoowah.

Redbird Smith was the moving force of the original Keetoowah Nighthawks, the traditional Cherokee organization. Redbird was born near Fort Smith on July 19, 1850. He learned at a young age the ancient customs and practices of the Cherokees. He went around the Cherokee Nation talking to the elders in different communities in the districts to learn from them. However, the Cherokees had lost their stomp dance songs and rituals due to the missionaries forbidding the practice. Redbird Smith had to go to the Creek Nation to learn the stomp dance songs. The stomp dance songs and rituals are an influence from the Creeks.

On January 31, 1899, a general election was conducted to accept the allotment. The Cherokee people voted to accept the allotment, the Keetoowah Society voted against it, they lost by 2,015 votes.

Redbird Smith took the position that it was extremely unfair for the United States Government as trustee to force the Cherokee people to totally change their way of life. He advised his people (about 5,000) that he had confidence in the authority of the United States Government to uphold its treaty stipulations and that sooner or later the government would see the injustice and would take active measures to correct the situation. In 1900 Redbird Smith split from the Keetoowah Society and formed the group called Keetoowah Nighthawks, and they became very active against the termination of the Cherokee Nation. They were referred to as the "Original Keetoowahs." Redbird Smith traveled to Washington D.C. several times. The Keetoowah Nighthawks were trying to get the

Cherokee government back. Redbird believed that the federal government was powerless to abolish the Cherokee Nation government without the consent of the people and that the federal government would eventually decide in favor of the Cherokee people.

The conservative Cherokee were protecting their culture, land, and welfare before statehood. After Oklahoma statehood the Keetoowah Society publicly claimed they took political leadership of all Cherokees. The Keetoowah Council petitioned the Territorial Court in Tahlequah on September 20, 1905, for articles of incorporation. The incorporation was granted and they became the Keetoowah Society, Inc. The Keetoowah Nighthawks viewed this move entirely different from their goals which further divided the two groups.

Redbird's fire at Blackgum Mountain became the main fire for the Nighthawks. Redbird traveled at night secretly all over the Cherokee Nation teaching the people in the communities their sacred ceremonies. They had approximately twenty-two fires in the Cherokee Nation. An atmosphere of rivalry existed among the groups. Most of the groups claimed to have original roots to antiquity. Each group, however, appeared to have a distinct role and a dedicated following. As years passed and living conditions improved, the need for multiple groups of Keetoowah Society for addressing pressing societal needs slackened. Community and family-based groups continued to meet and to maintain ceremonial fires. The Nighthawk Keetoowahs continued to focus on spiritual, traditional matters and the successor to the Keetoowah Society, Incorporated became the federally recognized United Keetoowah Band of Indians in Oklahoma and continued to focus on the political aspects of survival as an Indian tribe."[33]

The authors wish to thank John Ross, Jr., for sharing this narrative history.

Just as they preserved tradional ceremonies, many Cherokees continued their warrior traditions. The participation by Cherokees during World War I was significant. The factor that made the massive and rapid buildup of soldiers was the large number of volunteers. Diane Camurat's research supports the premise that at least fifty percent of all Indians serving in World War I were volunteers.[34]

The number of Cherokee volunteers is an elusive target. At the time of their induction, Cherokees were citizens of the United States and Oklahoma. Therefore, there was not a practical reason for the Selective Service System or the War Department to record tribal membership. A second reason for the absence of a Cherokee record for World War I is the Cherokee did not serve in segregated units. Cherokees were assigned throughout the American Expeditionary Force and became American soldiers.

The early voluntary involvement of Cherokees in US military units included a contingent of approximately six hundred

Figure 16. Cherokee Code Talker *by Roy Boney, Jr. Image courtesy of the artist.*

seasoned Cherokee and Choctaw members of the Oklahoma National Guard. Each received assignment to the 142nd Infantry of the Thirty-sixth Texas-Oklahoma National Guard Division.[35]

Another local example of volunteerism by Cherokees was found in the *Muskogee Phoenix* newspaper dated April 14, 1917. The newspaper reported that fourteen recruits from Adair County, former Flint District of the Cherokee Nation, had processed through Muskogee on April 13, 1917, enroute to Fort Logan, Colorado for training as part of Company F, Oklahoma National Guard. Seven of the fourteen were Cherokee.

The literature chronicling American Indian involvement in World War I is replete with code talking or the use of tribal languages to confuse the enemy. Choctaw and Navajo language usage are often mentioned. Specific details of Cherokee usage is limited. Code talking was a secret tactic to relay messages. Therefore, widespread information was not revealed about the new and effective tactics. The Cherokee may have been among the first, along with the Choctaw, to utilize native speakers to transmit messages while in battle zones in France during World War I. The Cherokee troops were members of the American Thirtieth Infantry Division under temporary attachment to a British Command in September, 1918.[36]

When Germany surrendered on November 11, 1918, the returning Cherokee soldiers were welcomed into their home communities. Their greatly expanded world view had a definite positive impact on their families and their communities. Their service appeared to influence a new attitude toward the US government as evidenced by statements included in a letter from Nighthawk Keetoowah Sam Smith to Levi Gritts:

"It is gratifying to note, that with all the effusive commendations and extravagant expressions of appreciation on the part of the American people, for the creditable manner in which our people acquitted themselves in the

War with Germany, the Indians have not become imbued with the idea of self-importance. In their own estimation they did no more than any loyal citizen should have done. It was a spontaneous response to a Great Government, who by virtue of being entangled in a World crisis, called upon its whole people to a united effort."[37]

During the latter part of the nineteenth century, the federal government had established policies with the desired result of transforming Indian life to closely compare with the lifestyles of white America. By the mid-1920s, it had become evident that the policies had failed in improving the status of Indians.

In 1926 the federal government requested the Institute for Governmental Research (known today as Brookings Institution) to perform an extensive review of economic and social conditions among Indians and Indian communities. The report, *The Problem of Indian Administration*, was edited by Lewis Merriam, a graduate of Harvard University with a law degree from George Washington University and a PhD from the Brookings Institute.

Merriam assembled a research team that represented appropriate disciplines and experiences for a comprehensive study. The on-site fieldwork indicated major shortcomings resulting from federal legislation and administrative policies of the Department of Interior. Many large-scale government initiatives received scathing reviews. The Dawes land allotment legislation was an example. The final paragraph on findings and recommendations appearing on page fifty-one of the report is reproduced here to illustrate the magnitude of the need for action:

"The belief is that it is a sound policy of national economy to make generous expenditures in the next few decades with the object of winding up the national administration of Indian affairs. The people of the United States have the opportunity, if they will, to write the closing chapters of the history of the relationship of the national government and the Indians. The early chapters contain little of which the country may be proud. It would be something of a national atonement of the Indians if the closing chapters should disclose the national government supplying the Indians with an Indian service which would be a model for all governments concerned with the development and advancement of a retarded race."[38]

The *Merriam Report* provided some alarming data documenting poverty, suffering, desease, malnutrition, short life expectancy (forty-four years), and insufficient per capita annual income ($100).[39] In addition to providing data supporting the miserable existence of the nation's Indians, the report identified the two principal causes as the Bureau of Indian Affairs, which was inadequately meeting the needs of Indians in education and health, and the fact that Indians were being ignored and excluded from management of their own affairs.[40]

After circulation of the *Merriam Report*, a change in philosophy and resulting government action in Indian affairs became evident. A new

Figure 17. Two Cherokees in uniform during World World I, c. 1917. Image courtesy of the Cherokee National Historical Society.

Indian affairs in 1933 was not a routine political appointment. John Collier was not an Indian. He was, however, an experienced social reformer with a plan for rectifying the mistakes made in previous legislation and policies harmful to Indians.

Rennard Strickland, the prolific writer of Indian history, summed up the Indians' plight during the Great Depression in one sentence. "The Great Depression brought to the rest of the nation economic conditions that many Oklahoma Indians had known since statehood."[41] The Great Depression was more severe and was longer in duration in America than in any other industrialized nation of the world. The failure of the American stock market awareness of the mismanagement of Indian affairs caused increased attention and activity by Congress resulting in legislation for the Wheeler Howard Act of 1934 and the Oklahoma Indian Welfare Act of 1936. New personnel in charge of the Department of Interior and inclusion of Indians and Indian needs in President Franklin D. Roosevelt's New Deal provided a new focus on reform measures. President Roosevelt's appointment of John Collier as commissioner of

"ᎤᏃᏆ ᎤᏃᎴᏗᎢ ᎾᏍᎩ ᎤᏃᏔᎠᏣ ᎠᏂᎠ ᏉᎠᏛ ᎤᎾᏛᏂᏛᎩ."

—ᎸH Smith

"In their own estimation they did no more than any loyal citizen should have done."

—Sam Smith

Figure 18. Brown's Business College at Northeastern Teachers' College. An early example of vocational training for Cherokees. Image courtesy of the Cherokee National Historical Society.

in 1929 ended a decade of urban prosperity. As a result, America's political and economic thought drastically changed. The governmental presence in American life increased greatly as the government rushed to provide assistance to a suffering population.[42]

Will Rogers, Oklahoma's favorite son, provided Depression Era assistance by hosting fundraising meetings in Oklahoma to provide immediate assistance for the poorest of the poor. According to folklore, Will stipulated that a portion of funds raised would be designated for use by isolated full-blood communities in the Cherokee Nation.

William Penn Adair Rogers was born in Indian Territory on November 4, 1879, on the Rogers Ranch between Oologah and Claremore. He was the son of Clement Vann Rogers and Mary Schrimsher Rogers. Will's mark upon the world included every major adult venture that caught his fancy. One of his sons, Jim Rogers, summed up his "Pop's" life as "a mixed-blood Cherokee cowboy, actor, comedian, columnist, radio personality, and humorist who was taken

Figure 19. Tom Buffington (center) c. 1920. He served as chief in 1891 and then from 1899-1903. Image courtesy of the Oklahoma Historical Society.

into the hearts of the American people as no other private citizen has been." His political sayings from the 1920s and 1930s continue to ring true to the American public with continued relevance in today's newspapers.

    Readers in the Cherokee Nation have the benefit of "Will Rogers Says" quotes from the *Tulsa World* on a daily basis. Will's statue in the US Capitol joins Sequoyah as Oklahoma's representatives in the National Statuary Hall. Will's life and brilliant career were cut short by an airplane crash in August, 1935. Two public facilities that provide a living memorial to Will's life and times are the Will Rogers Memorial Museum in Claremore, Oklahoma, and the Will Rogers Dog Iron Ranch, in Oologah, Oklahoma, his birthplace home.[43]

    Social service relief programs were limited during the Great Depression. This left unemployed poor persons without sources of relief. The full-blood rural enclaves of Cherokees were particularly hit hard by lack of necessary resources for living. The full-blood Cherokees were attached to the home place and seldom traveled beyond their immediate area of birth. Kinship and privacy defined their rural hill-folk enclaves. New Deal program delivery was limited in its extension to the rural isolated hills occupied by Cherokee full-bloods.[44]

The Great Depression was especially harmful to full-blood Cherokees. Most had been divested of their allotted land except for their homesteads. The Bureau of Indian Affairs had lost contact with the majority of Cherokees before the Depression era commenced.[45] The Great Depression may have had a greater negative impact on some rural Cherokee citizens than the myriad setbacks to their welfare suffered since removal from the East over the Trail of Tears. Strickland made note of hearings on reported famine among Oklahoma Indians held by the US Senate. He also provided comments from well recognized Cherokees pertaining to the severity of conditions among Cherokee communities.

Ross Daniels testified, "They are in bad condition. A lot of them do not have bread or grease. They are in the worst sort of condition. I believe they have died from the effects of improper nourishment." S. W. Peak reported, "I have not found any family that was faring anyways like they ought to." Jackson Wolfe predicted that "we are going to be turned out like hogs. We have not much land anymore. It is pretty nearly all gone. The way it is going now we will be blowed up; that is all. We won't have any home or any place."[46]

Cherokees did not participate to a significant degree in the Okie migration to California, which was popularized in the *Grapes of Wrath* by John Steinbeck, even though the novel's debarkation point for California was located within the Cherokee Nation–the Sequoyah District of the former Cherokee Nation and Sequoyah County, Oklahoma.

The graft-driven legal theft of allotted land continued through the Great Depression era. The willingness to sell for any price was heightened by the need for ready cash. In addition to loss of land through sales, land subject to county taxation was, in many instances, taken through tax liens.

The largest movement by the federal government to provide Great Depression economic relief and the beginning of reforms in policy for Indian tribes came about through President Franklin D. Roosevelt's New Deal programs. Multiple programs directed toward easing the desperate plight of Depression era Indians were a result of focused programs designed by John Collier, commissioner of Indian affairs, and President Roosevelt's New Deal program. The combination of efforts provided some immediate relief. The long-range application of programs became known as the Indian New Deal.

Collier's appointment as commissioner of Indian affairs caused a radical change in the Department of Interior's policies and procedures for dealing with Indians. Collier's proposed changes were sweeping in reversing federal policy going back to the Dawes Act of 1887.

Many of his proposals were too change-oriented for congressional approval. Collier served as commissioner of Indian affairs from 1933 to 1945. His influence on federal Indian policy had long-range effects. Oklahoma Indians were excluded from some of his early New Deal programs. Landmark legislation that came about during his tenure as commissioner influenced later efforts in promoting tribal self-governance and in regaining tribal land holdings.

The New Deal programs had a general positive effect on the Cherokee populations. There was a sharp contrast in benefits to mixed-bloods and full- blood Cherokees. Some of the programs included construction jobs. Lack of transportation and relocation funds prevented the isolated Cherokees from participating. Of the ten basic New Deal programs, two were especially practical and attracted participation in Cherokee country, the Works Progress Administration (WPA) and the Civilian Conservation Corps (CCC).[47]

The CCC provided employment programs for building public parks and recreation areas. Young adult males comprised the target recruit groups. The men were housed in temporary camps. The camps were organized in military style and were operated by the US Army. The CCC recruits were paid a small monthly stipend of approximately thirty dollars. Twenty to twenty-five dollars of the monthly pay was sent to the recruits' homes. This small infusion usually went toward the purchase of basic foodstuff for the recruits' families.

Figure 20. Will Rogers. Image courtesy of the Oklahoma Historical Society.

Recruits were housed and fed on-site and received medical attention. Major sites located within the original boundaries of the Cherokee Nation were in park areas and potential park areas throughout northeast Oklahoma. The CCC camps were natural transition units for the military at the outbreak of World War II.

WPA jobs were initially outside the work experiences for many Cherokee males. The WPA programs provided labor and materials

Figure 21. Go Back Christie and his son Harold Amos, chairmakers at their saw mill, 1937. Image courtesy of the Oklahoma Historical Society.

for municipal buildings, schools, and public tourist facilities. Large public building projects provided work opportunities for both skilled workmen and for beginning laborers. Part-time work and communal connections of reciprocity and exchange, along with knowledge of the land's resources, allowed the isolated full-bloods to survive.

The focus on relieving the hardships that tribes experienced during the Great Depression and President Roosevelt's New Deal efforts provided a new environment that led to rethinking government policies for Indian affairs. Roosevelt's Secretary of the Interior Harold Ickes, Indian Commissioner John Collier, and Associate Solicitor Felix Cohen were reformers. They cooperated in effecting changes that were drastic departures to the assimilation mode championed by Congress.

John Collier lobbied Congress for legislation that would strengthen tribal governments, stop allotments, restore lands to communal tribal holdings, provide organizational process, allocate funds for tribal involvement in economy building, grant preference in hiring for Indians in Indian Affairs jobs, and aid tribes in developing and maintaining cultural components. The legislation that was developed to enable Collier's desired changes was known as the Wheeler-Howard Act of 1934, or by its more popular title, the Indian Reorganization Act. The majority of the content of the bill was created by Collier.[48]

Prior to passage, the bill attracted supporters and detractors. Interior Secretary Ickes supported John Collier in seeking approval. Opposition came from multiple fronts. Senator Burton Wheeler, one of the bill's authors, grew to dislike the bill since he supported the government plan for long-range assimilation of Indians. Oklahoma Senator Elmer Thomas, who was allied with Oklahoma businessmen and lawyers involved with Indian land deals, was opposed to the bill. Some opposition existed in all five of the Civilized Tribes. Assimilated Cherokees were not in favor of the bill due to its concentration on tribalism. The Keetoowah, Inc., group was in favor of the bill and presented a resolution representing six thousand Cherokees to John Collier upon the occasion of his speech in support of the bill at Muskogee, Oklahoma, in March 1934.[49] By the time the bill reached the decision stage in Congress, many of its original components had been deleted. The deletions and revisions rendered most of its provisions inapplicable to the Five Civilized Tribes.

Although the Indian Reorganization Act of 1934 had minimal immediate impact on the Cherokee tribe, the discussions resulting from the bill's introduction helped to prepare tribal members for future legislation supported throughout John Collier's terms as director of Indian affairs (1933-1945). In 1936 legislation was introduced with provisions specific to Oklahoma tribes, the Oklahoma Indian Welfare Act.

ᎠᏯᏙᎴᏗ 10
ᎤᏛᏍᏆᏍᎬ ᎦᏍᎩ ᏔᎴ ᎠᏗᎵᎯᏍᏗᎢ
1936-1996

Chapter 10: A Glimmer of Hope for Rebuilding

Figure 1. Cherokee family butchering a hog, c. 1922. Image Courtesy Oklahoma Historical Society.

The latter half of the 1930s ushered in a period of awakening and a renewed sense of community among Oklahoma Cherokees. They had survived the erosion of their land base and resulting decrease in economic capabilities. Federal policies since Oklahoma statehood were intent on the transformation of Indians to assimilated members of American society. In this new status, the desired characteristics were English-speaking Christian farmers. Under this federal definition, the Cherokees were destitute by 1936, the mid-point of the Great Depression.[1]

Although the 1934 Indian Reorganization Act did not result in major improvement in Cherokee life, the act and other New Deal initiatives caused a change in the course of federal Indian policy. In the provisions of the Indian Reorganization Act of 1934, reinforced by broader opportunities revealed during the planning stage for the Oklahoma Indian Welfare Act of 1936, there was the hint that tribes might be empowered to function in governing their citizens and advancing their economic and social development.[2]

The plight of American Indians and the failure of past federal policy in meeting their needs were broadcast nationally by the new Commissioner of Indian Affairs, John Collier, via his Indian New Deal efforts in a bi-weekly magazine titled *Indians at Work*. The magazine portrayed Indians in positive roles and provided summaries of New Deal programs with economic opportunities and positive impact on Indian tribes. The broad array of social and economic reforms promoted by John Collier revealed that he was intent on changing legislative thought about Indians, from cultural repression and assimilation to support of tribes with tribal decision makers.[3]

The last major New Deal legislative initiative was the Oklahoma Indian Welfare Act of 1936, also known as the Thomas-Rogers Act. The act carried out Collier's plan to rebuild tribal societies, return land to tribes, aid tribal government, and promote native culture. Work began on the bill's content in early 1934. When

Figure 2. Cherokee Woman Using a Spinning Wheel. Image Courtesy the Oklahoma Historical Society

introduced the act contained forty-eight pages, including rewritten versions of some of the sections of the 1934 Indian Reorganization Act. The original Thomas-Rogers Act drew heavy opposition from whites interested in continuing their lucrative land dealings and drew heavy opposition from Cherokees who were satisfied with Cherokee non-government status quo. The Osages, neighbors to the Cherokees, were opposed to removing probate control of Indian land and property from Oklahoma courts.

Due to strong opposition to the bill in its original form, the Oklahoma congressional delegation caused a revised version of the bill to be introduced. The alternate version concentrated on acquisition of land by individual Indians and tribes, enabling tribes to adopt constitutions, acquire land, and obtain credit. Osage County was excluded from the bill. Issues involving probate and inheritance were left to state courts. The Oklahoma Indian Welfare Act was passed by the U.S. Congress on June 26, 1936.[4]

The Cherokee Nation did not attempt to reorganize under the bill. Rather, the Cherokees continued to show an interest in self-government through informal meetings and contacts with Congress through influential Cherokee citizens. As early as 1924, a small group of Cherokee business and professional persons participated in informal meetings to discuss Cherokee affairs. Their discussions at times resulted in action by contacting governmental officials. The Cherokees had two citizens who were long-serving members of Congress, Robert L. Owen, U.S. Senator from Oklahoma, and W. W. Hastings, Representative of the Second District of Oklahoma. In 1924 the pre-constitutional Cherokee government group employed Senator Owen and Representative Hastings to represent them in filing a claim for damages against the federal government. The claim was later dismissed. Both elected officials had standing and rapport with the Cherokee citizenry. This was especially true for the mixed-blood elite. Both Owen and Hastings had been in favor of allotment of Cherokee land and were in favor of Oklahoma statehood.[5]

Another historic meeting of the unofficial Cherokee group was held at Fairfield in the Goingsnake District in Adair County on August 8, 1938. Three hundred Cherokees attended. An issue of representation arose which resulted in dismissal of the agenda. The meeting was recessed after selection of a committee to work for a system of unified Cherokee leadership. Committee recommendations for unified leadership resulted in J.B. Milam's selection as "permanent chair." Robert L. Owen and Houston Teehee were selected as speakers. Lawyers were selected to pursue claims against the federal government. Those legal representatives were Robert L. Owen, Houston Teehee, Frank S. Boudinot, and Earl Boyd Pierce.[6] These same individuals would play major roles in a Bureau of Indian Affairs sanctioned convention of Cherokees a decade later. The selection of J.B. Milam as the permanent chair of the Cherokee organization to represent tribal citizens was interpreted by many as his designation as chief. Franklin D. Roosevelt appointed Milam Chief of the Cherokees on April 16, 1941 for a four-year appointment followed by reappointments in 1943 and 1947 for four-year terms.[7] Even without a constitution, the Cherokees once again had a traditonal government.

The federal office responsible for the nation's relationship with Indian tribes had been known by various names since its founding in 1775 as a committee on Indian Affairs headed by Benjamin Franklin. In 1824 Secretary of War John C. Calhoun administratively named the service as Bureau of Indian Affairs. In 1849 the office was transferred to the newly formed US Department of Interior where it was known variously as the Indian Office, Indian Bureau, Indian Department, and Indian Service. Finally, on September 17, 1947, the US Department of Interior adopted the name Bureau of Indian Affairs for the agency.[8]

The status of Cherokee citizens following the midpoint of the Great Depression was still bleak. The majority of the New Deal programs were implemented first in the more populated areas while the majority of unemployed Cherokees resided in rural areas. Other factors inhibiting rural Cherokees from participating in work programs and economic incentive programs were lack of transportation and lack of training in basic construction trades. Although every Oklahoma county located within the former Cherokee Nation jurisdiction received construction projects through the Works Progress Administration (WPA), few Cherokees received jobs in construction.[9]

The largest WPA project in the Cherokee area was the Pensacola Dam, also known as the Grand River Dam. The impounded area created Grand Lake of the Cherokees in Mayes County, Oklahoma. The impounded area resulted in the loss of 1,285 acres of Cherokee lands. The New Deal Public Works Administration provided $20 million in loans and grants for construction, and a combination of state funds and Grand River Dam Authority bond sales provided an additional $7 million. The project started in 1938 and was completed in 1941. The work force included about three thousand WPA workers who received an average pay of $16 per week.[10]

Despite relief efforts to soften the harshest impacts of the Great Depression, the Cherokees were still preoccupied with survival. Even when New Deal work programs provided opportunity to work, most of the jobs were short-lived. This created a cycle of constant job seeking to keep funds coming in for maintaining households. The new direction in Indian Affairs engendered by John Collier and Harold Ickes in their association and leadership with the Indian New Deal did not have a major impact in Cherokee country. The Cherokee citizenry had all the government they could tolerate. In years past, new action by the federal government had resulted in hardship and loss to the Cherokee. Almost a generation in time had elapsed since the federal government takeover of Cherokee life, but the Cherokees remembered and told stories about their once proud nation.

The Oklahoma Indian Welfare Act empowered Indians to adopt constitutions and to organize under corporate charters. The Act also provided for federal purchase of land which would be placed in trust for tribal entities and loan provisions to Indians for economic development projects.[11]

The provisions and opportunities provided by the Oklahoma Indian Welfare Act were appropriate counter measures to the confusion and hardship caused by the Dawes Commission. At the time of the Dawes Commission, a full-blood group under the

Figure 3. Grand River Dam. Image Courtesy Oklahoma Historical Society.

leadership of Redbird Smith had sought to separate some land for communal living. Their efforts were rejected by the commission.[12]

By 1936 the Cherokees had adapted to a new order. The depression era hardships caused a significant number of Cherokees to seek employment and a new life away from the Cherokee Nation. A US Department of Commerce report examined the 1930 US Census and concluded that of the total 40,904 population of Cherokees in Oklahoma, 7,651 Cherokees resided in counties of Oklahoma outside the original jurisdiction of Cherokee land.[13]

During the discussions concerning both the Indian Reorganization Act and Oklahoma Indian Welfare Act, former Cherokee Nation citizens showed little interest in reorganizing as a new tribe. The Keetoowah groups showed interest and made attempts to organize under the provisions of the Oklahoma Indian Welfare Act. Their efforts were extended over several years. The federal purchase of land for use by Indians received some attention. Projects were initiated in southern Adair County and in the Kenwood area of Delaware County. Both projects were of short duration.

New Deal social and economic reform efforts affecting Cherokees were not limited to the Oklahoma Indian Welfare Act. John Collier and his allies in Congress created a number of programs that dealt with specific issues in Indian country. One of the most important was the

Figure 4. Cherokee students participating in a Cherokee social dance at an event hosted by Cherokee Nation's Johnson O'Malley Program. Image courtesy of Cherokee Nation Johnson O'Malley Program.

Johnson-O'Malley Act of 1934. Goals included funding to improve education and medical assistance, to address social welfare issues, to move Indian children from federal schools and place them in neighborhood schools closer to home, and to provide funds to local school districts enrolling Indian students. By 2016 the Cherokee Nation would serve as sponsor for the Johnson-O'Malley program in the Cherokee Nation. That year the Cherokee Nation distributed $1,757,165 to serve 34,804 Indian students.[14]

Another significant program affecting Cherokees in the future was the Indian Arts and Crafts Act of 1935. Goals included multicultural perspective for economic recovery programs, expansion of the market for products of Indian art and craftsmanhip, and creation of the Indian Arts and Craft Board empowered to investigate counterfeit Indian goods. Provisions of the act would be amended in 1990 and 2000. The increased activity in marketing Indian arts and crafts led to the need to amend the original act. The Indian Arts and Crafts Act of 1990 (P.L.

101-644) added truth-in-advertising regulations to prohibit misrepresentation in marketing of Indian-produced products in the United States. The law covered all Indian and Indian-style traditional and contemporary arts and crafts produced after 1935. The Indian Arts and Crafts Board created by the 1935 Indian Arts and Crafts Act would be responsible for the implementation of the 1990 act. The increase in marketing of Indian art and craft items, especially through e-commerce led to amendment of the Act again in 2010. Tribes and Indian artists voiced concerns about the continued misappropriation of Indian images, symbols, and designs by non-Indian companies and individuals. The 2010 amendment strengthened the law enforcement provisions and clarified the responsibility of federal, state, and tribal officials for enforcing the Act.[15]

Economic benefits gained by Cherokees through arts and crafts during the Great Depression years were minimal. The Bureau of Indian Affairs provided assistance to a few local cooperatives and provided instruction in reviving Cherokee traditional art forms that were in danger of being lost. John Ketcher and Bill Ames, Office of Indian Affairs employees, led the arts and crafts revival among the Cherokees. Under their direction the Cherokee Weavers Cooperative was formed in the Briggs community located east of Tahlequah. The cooperative was successful. As the weavers aged, without young trainees to take their place, the Cherokee Weavers became inactive. The Cherokee Nation would eventually offer loom weaving classes under the direction of Dorothy Ice. Ms. Ice was one of the original weavers and has been honored as a "Cherokee National Treasure" for preserving traditional arts of the Cherokee. In later years, John Ketcher, the originator of the weaving project, served the Cherokee Nation with distinction as Speaker of the Council and Deputy Principal Chief.[16]

John Collier's attempts to include provisions for establishing tribal court systems in the 1936 Oklahoma Indian Welfare Act were unsuccessful. He redirected his efforts by implementing programs to preserve the records of tribal dealings with the federal government. The results of his efforts enabled tribes to present data in Indian Court of Claims cases to assist in documenting the validity of their requests for redress of previous inequities.

The New Deal Public Works Program compiled historic government documents on Indian policies and placed the documents in the National Archives. Felix Cohen, a solicitor in the Office of Indian Affairs, collected federal laws and policy documents which applied to tribes. His work was published in 1941 as the *Handbook of Federal Indian Law*. Cohen's handbook was edited and updated by Rennard Strickland in 1982.[17]

For the Cherokee people, the reforms of the New Deal were more promise than reality. Before the programs could make a significant difference in daily lives, the federal government's attention turned from social

Figure 5. Cherokee Loom Weaving. Image courtesy of the Cherokee National Historical Society.

reform to fighting for a way of life. World War II changed everything. The Cherokee response to World War II was an expanded version of their commitment to World War I. Voluntary enlistments far exceeded the draft for service men. In addition to Cherokee males serving, Cherokee women served in the Army Nurse Corps, WACS, and WAVES. While the enlistments and draftee assignments were principally for the U.S. Army in WW I, the new recruits for WW II chose a variety of service units including Army, Navy, and Marine Corps. Cherokees experienced action in both the Pacific and European theaters. The Forty-fifth Infantry Division, the Thunderbirds, had a high concentration of Indians in the 157th, 179th, and 180th regiments from Oklahoma, Colorado, New Mexico, and Arizona. The Thunderbird Division was one of the first racially diversified divisions since the Civil War. One company within the 180th Regiment was made up totally of Indians from Chilocco Indian School.[18]

Jack C. Montgomery, a Cherokee reared in Sequoyah County, Oklahoma, was platoon leader in Company I of the 180th Regiment of the Forty-fifth Infantry Division of the Oklahoma National Guard. His company was an entirely Indian company consisting of students from Bacone College in Muskogee, Oklahoma. First Lieutenant Montgomery saw action from North Africa through Italy before he was wounded on February 22, 1944, near

A Glimmer of Hope for Rebuilding 1936 - 1996

Figure 6. Cherokee National Treasure Cecil Dick a pioneer of twentieth century flat style painting. Image courtesy of the Cherokee National Historical Society Archives.

Padiglione, Italy. Prior to receiving serious wounds from mortar fragments, Montgomery was involved in solo heroic actions to aid his platoon members who were surrounded by German troops. Acting alone he killed eleven of the enemy, captured thirty-two, and wounded an unknown number. For his actions he was awarded the Congressional Medal of Honor by President Franklin D. Roosevelt.[19]

The Cherokee Nation Veterans' Center has records of a second Cherokee citizen who was awarded the Congressional Medal of Honor for service in World War II. Pfc. John Noah Reese, Jr. graduated from Central High School in Tulsa, Oklahoma in 1941 and joined the Army from Pryor, Oklahoma in 1942. Pfc. Reese was a member of Company B, 148th Infantry Regiment, 37th Infantry Division. While engaged in an attack on a railroad station in the Philipines Reese and his partner Private Cleto Rodriguez launched a daring attack on more than three hundred enemy soldiers who were blocking the American advance. Their action materially aided the advance of the American troops. Pfc. Reese was killed in the endeavor. His body was returned and buried at the Fort Gibson National Cemetery.[20]

Another Cherokee of note serving in World War II was Admiral Joseph J. Clark. Admiral Clark was born in Chelsea, Cherokee Nation in 1893. He graduated from the United States Naval Academy in 1918, the first American Indian to graduate from Annapolis, and he became the highest-ranking officer of indigenous lineage in the history of the United States.[21] Admiral Clark saw action in World War I, World War II, and Korea. Clark became Vice-Admiral and Commander of the 7th Fleet during the Korean War and ended his career as a full admiral.[22]

World War II had a significant impact on Cherokee citizens. New opportunities for choices in life styles and careers emerged. On the reverse side, new opportunities disrupted old patterns and lifestyles of the Cherokee community environment. Many of the returning Cherokee warriors chose to settle into the mainstream of the postwar economy, adopting a non-Indian

Figure 7. Jack C. Montgomery. Image courtesy of the Cherokee National Historical Society.

way of life. A significant number, however, after proving they could adapt well to white America, returned to Cherokee communities. The war experiences prepared them for new roles in community and tribal leadership. World War II Cherokee veterans were at the forefront of Cherokee political activities during the unprecedented development of the tribe during the last half of the Twentieth Century.[23]

On a larger scale, the specter of further land loss emerged as a result of the war. Many Indian nations were forced to give up parts of their land for the war effort. Nationally this included approximately 876,000 acres. In the year of 1941 and 1942, eighty-four new military training camps were approved in America to meet the needs of the war effort. One of the new camps was scheduled for the Greenleaf Area near Braggs, Oklahoma. The acreage comprising the camp included Cherokee Nation holdings and land allotted to individual Cherokee citizens by the Dawes Commission.

A portion of Camp Gruber was appropriated from existing land under federal stewardship after its acquisition for possible park and recreation purposes. This portion of the camp's land consisted of approximately 27,300 acres. The total acreage at end of camp construction was between 60,000 and 70,000 acres. Most of the additional acres were acquired through condemnation, including approximately 22,000 acres owned by the Cherokee Nation and by Cherokee citizens allotted land by the Dawes Commission. The owners were allowed only a maximum of forty-five days to vacate their farms. Their crops were in their fields but not ready for harvesting. A small relocation payment was offered, but all evictees had not received the payment by time of their forced departure. Newly appointed Principal Chief Milam announced that he would work toward a fair compensation for the lost Cherokee land. Official action was pending at the time of his death.[24]

The topic of reparation for damages continued to resurface. Chief W.W. Keeler made

A Glimmer of Hope for Rebuilding 1936 - 1996

Figure 8. Joseph J. Clark. Image courtesy of the Oklahoma Historical Society.

Cherokees from their homeland for service in the military and for civilians to take jobs were major disruptions to tribal life. In the words of one writer, "They learned to adapt to their various World War II roles and in the process, they went from being American Indians to Indian Americans."[26] Contact with the world outside of Indian Country contributed to changes in Indian culture. John Collier, the long serving U.S. Indian Commissioner stated, "The war caused the greatest disruption of Native life since the beginning of the reservation era."[27]

The waning years of the Great Depression, the war years, and the post-war era of prosperity set the stage for the Cherokees to begin the process of reestablishing a formal government. The disparate groups who attempted to light the fire of regaining tribal identity came together during the 1940s to regain a sense of tribal self that had become dormant during the difficult time of clashing between tribal traditions and imposed social improvement.[28] A new day of constitutional government was dawning.

By 1940 two groups of Keetoowahs were still active, the Keetoowah Society Inc. and the Nighthawk Keetoowahs. The central governing tenet of each group remained intact from the allotment era. The Keetoowah Society Inc. stressed political involvement and unity among Keetoowah groups. The Nighthawk Keetoowahs stressed allegiance to ancient Cherokee teachings and traditional religious practices. The Keetoowah Society Inc. persisted with efforts to gain federal recognition for their group, a

reference to the possibility of seeking redress for the appropriated Camp Gruber Cherokee lands in an address to the Cherokee Nation Elected Community Representatives at a regular meeting of the group in Tahlequah on June 2, 1973. An official action did not emerge.[25]

One of the greatest impacts of World War II on the Cherokee people was the opportunity to find employment in the defense industry plants located in cities such as Tulsa, Pryor, Oklahoma City, and Wichita, Kansas. The departure of

"ᏂᏍᎦᏬᏙᎢᏙEZ ᎾᏍᏴ ᏞᏞᎠ ᏉᎪᎠ ᎤᏂᏃᎠᏞᏁᎢ Ꮎ ᎠᏴᎾᏬ ᎡᏑᎢ ᎾᏍᏴ ᎫᏞᏊᏂᏬE ᎠᎳᏬᏞᎠ ᏋᎶᏬᏔᎤ ᏓᏂᏏᏉᏬᏔᎤ."

— ᏣᎵᏂ ᎤᎾᏞᏍᏍᎠ ᏴᎾᏬᏍᎠᏞᏂᏜᎵᎤᏎᎷ Ꮳh Collier

"The war caused the greatest disruption of Native life since the beginning of the reservaton era."

— U.S. Indian Commissioner John Collier

path they followed after passage of the 1936 Oklahoma Indian Welfare Act. Their application was denied in 1937.[29]

During the next two years the Keetoowah Society Inc. explored various avenues of utilizing their 1905 charter of incorporation, which was approved by the US District Court in Tahlequah in 1905, as evidence of earlier legal organization. On June 9, 1939, various Keetoowah factions came together to form the United Keetoowah Cherokee Indians. An elected committee wrote a constitution and adopted the pre-statehood Cherokee National Council apportionment districts and polling sites. The framework of government was utilized in 1940 to elect a full contingent of officers for the United Keetoowah Cherokee Indians. The Keetoowah denied membership to freedmen and intermarried whites. The Superintendent of Indian Affairs ruled that the Cherokee Tribe continued to own all remaining land and tribal assets, and those assets would be omitted from the new organization. Under that distinction, intermarried whites and freedmen would lose no rights if excluded from the new Keetoowah organization. The first election of the United Keetoowah Cherokee Indians resulted in the defeat of the sitting chief, Levi Gritts, who withdrew from the organization and took some of the members with him.[30]

The Keetoowah factions did not make major efforts toward federal recognition during the World War II years. Levi Gritts, the defeated chief who left the United Keetoowah Cherokee Indians, continued his efforts to gain federal recognition for the Keetoowah Society Inc. by correspondence with US elected officials including Representative William Stigler from Oklahoma and by traveling to Washington, DC, to meet with other members of Congress.[31]

Representative Stigler prepared a bill (H.R. 341) which was passed by Congress on April 21, 1946, and signed by President Truman on August 10, 1946. The legislation, however, did not contain language to settle the issue. The bill

A Glimmer of Hope for Rebuilding 1936 - 1996

Figure 9. Keetoowah Nighthawk Society displaying wampum belts c. 1917. Image courtesy of the Oklahoma Historical Society.

appeared as follows: "Be it enacted by the Senate and House of Representatives of the United States of America in Congress Assembled, That the Keetoowah Indians of the Cherokee Nation of Oklahoma shall be recognized as a band of Indians residing in Oklahoma within section 3 of the Act of June 26, 1936 (49Stat. 1967)."[32]

This was not what the Keetoowah Society Inc. group desired. Recognition as a band within the Cherokee Nation of Oklahoma did not bestow the independence or successive government desired by the group. Furthermore, the language did not specify a specific group of Keetoowah Indians for recognition. At the time the language was written there were contenders for exclusive designation of Keetoowah groups within the original jurisdiction of the Cherokee Nation, the Nighthawk Keetoowah, the United Keetoowah Cherokee Indians, and the Seven Clans Society under the leadership of Eli Pumpkin. There were other smaller Keetoowah factions with efforts concentrated on communities and welfare of their members who were not interested in unified Keetoowah efforts for federal recognition.[33]

While the Keetoowah issue was drawing attention, Chief Milam convened the first Office of Indian Affairs-sanctioned Cherokee government assembly in the twentieth century. The convention was authorized by the Commissioner of Indian Affairs for the appointment of a standing executive committee to draw up a contract with attorneys for prosecution of claims against the federal government and to represent the tribe with the principal chief in negotiations with the government. The *Muskogee Daily Phoenix* printed a detailed account of the July 30, 1948 Convention in the *Phoenix* on July 31, 1948. One of the opening paragraphs of the account outlines the historic significance of the meeting:

"A convention of approximately 700 Cherokees, hurdling a factional road block, formed a tribal organization here Friday to prosecute approximately $50,000,000 in claims before the Indian Claims Commission and to promote the general welfare of the tribe.

"The convention authorized J.B. Milam of Claremore, Principal Chief of the Cherokee Nation, to appoint a standing executive committee to draw up a contract with attorneys for prosecution of the aging claims against the government and to represent the tribe, with the chief in all negotiations with the government."[34]

The convention reestablished limited tribal government under the direction of the principal chief and the executive committee with representative districts identical to the Cherokee Nation districts of pre-Oklahoma statehood with the exception of out-of-jurisdiction representation by the newly formed executive committee as listed in Table 1.[35]

The first action of the executive committee was the selection of attorneys to litigate claims for Cherokee compensation for past wrongs by the federal government. Attorneys approved to pursue claims before the Indian Claims Commission were Woodson Norvell of Washington, DC, George L. Norvell of Tulsa, Houston B. Teehee of Tahlequah, Dennis W. Bushyhead of Claremore, and Earl Boyd Pierce of Muskogee.

The power to appoint tribal attorneys reached back to 1855 when Congress established a Court of Claims to hear suits brought by individuals, including Indians, against the federal government. During the Civil War, members of Congress who were angered because some tribes supported the Confederacy barred tribes from presenting claims to the Court of Claims. In 1946 Congress established the Indian Claims Commission to hear cases concerning the illegal taking of tribal lands and other wrongs by the United States. The commission was established with a termination date of 1952. The 1946 to 1952 window was designed to clear tribal claims and to support the federal governments' shift away from Indian affairs.[36]

The *Muskogee Daily Phoenix* estimated the attendance at the convention to be seven hundred. Attendees were encouraged to register by providing name, residence, and Dawes roll number. The official attendance sheet contains 497 entries with Dawes roll numbers. Those too young to possess a roll number used the number from a relative. Cherokee citizens residing in close proximity to Cherokee County comprised the largest representation for the convention. Registrants from Cherokee County numbered 211. The second highest number of registered

Executive Committee Members named at the July 30, 1948 Convention

District	Member	Residence
Cooweescoowee	Judge N.B. Nelson	Claremore
Delaware	Ben Smith	Kenwood
Tahlequah	Eldee Starr	Tahlequah
Flint	J.B. Sixkiller	Stilwell
Goingsnake	Hill Stansill	Westville
Sequoyah	William Peak	Vian
Illinois	Dan Coody	Muskogee
Canadian	Judge O.H.P. Brewer	Muskogee
Saline	Amanda Morgan	Tip
At-Large	W.W. Keeler	Dewey
At-Large	C.C. Victory	Tulsa

Table 1. July 30, 1948 Cherokee Convention.

attendees were from Adair County with 199. Eighty–six post offices were listed including seven Oklahoma sites external to the original Cherokee jurisdiction and three from other states.[37]

Early in the convention and immediately preceding the first agenda item subject to a vote, Levi Gritts, representing a Keetoowah faction, interrupted the meeting to present an objection. Gritts desired a standing committee of nine members elected from Cherokees assembled to govern the agenda for the day. Gritts was opposed to Chief Milam as an appointee to the principal chief's office. Gritts was also opposed to any involvement in the proceedings by Earl Boyd Pierce, who had been employed by the Keetoowah Society, Inc. prior to his employment with the Cherokee Nation. After a delay, the meeting recommenced and followed the agenda which had been approved prior to the date of the meeting.

The main order of business called for unity among the various groups in recognition of an entity to interact with the federal government. The resolution stressed that the assembled delegates represented Eastern or Immigrant Cherokees who came on the Trail of Tears, Western Old Settler Cherokees who arrived prior to the Trail of Tears with many coming to present area after being forced from Arkansas, the United Keetoowah Band, the Seven Clans Cherokee Society, and the Texas Cherokees. Gritts protested several procedural issues, but did not gain a following. The convention adopted resolutions and took action on all agenda items.[38]

The broad representation of communities at the convention and the regional publicity by newspapers spread the word that the Cherokee government had come back to life. The meeting schedule for the Executive Committee during Chief Milam's tenure was a called arrangement by the chief. A regular meeting every two months was later implemented by Chief W.W. Keeler, with called meetings for emergency issues. The committee continued to function as the informal legislative body of government until the installation of an appointed Council in 1975.

Chief Milam adapted well to the new expanded role of Cherokee government. He was well versed in the Oklahoma political scene and had extensive experience in business affairs. Background information on the life and times of Chief Milam revealed a broad array of preparation and experience from which he drew to support his efforts in reforming the Cherokee Nation.

Chief Milam is especially remembered for insisting that the 1948 Convention of Cherokees proceed according to the agenda in the face of strenuous opposition from a representation of the United Keetoowah Band of Cherokee Indians. Chief Milam was a member of the United Keetoowah Band. A couple of weeks after the 1948 Convention, the United Keetoowah Band took formal action to expel J.B. Milam from membership. This was a setback for efforts to gain tribal unity.

Howard Meredith, one of Milam's biographers, described Milam's unique ability to forge ahead with goals for Cherokee advancement. "Milam was able to maintain more freedom than many Cherokee people because of his education and training. Milam managed to work through the system despite its many ambiguities which were used all too often to strip away Cherokee people's rights and privileges in addition to their allotments."

Chief Milam's fourth appointment as Principal Chief was cut short by his death on August 13, 1948. His work, however, would be continued by others. Following the death of Chief Milam, President Truman appointed William Wayne Keeler to replace him. Keeler had entered the world of Cherokee politics in 1948 when Chief Milam named him to serve on the Executive Committee as vice chair. His leadership in the vice chair role influenced his fellow committee members to recommend him as the successor to Chief Milam.

President Harry S. Truman named Keeler principal chief on December 8, 1949. For the next quarter century Keeler worked to reestablish the Cherokee government which had been dormant for fifty years. In the process of rebuilding the Cherokee Nation, the tribe regained limited sovereignty and became a major participant in the overall economy of northeastern Oklahoma.

Keeler's levels of involvement in the corporate world and the Indian political world did not leave him without critics. His immediate decisions in the Cherokee political world caused many Cherokee detractors to question the motives and integrity of a white man (Keeler was one-sixth Cherokee). In the corporate world and on the national scene, Keeler and Phillips Petroleum Company were charged with the

Figure 10. J.B. Milam. Image courtesy of the Cherokee National Historical Society.

J. B. Milam
(1884 - 1949)

Bartley Milam's mother, Sarah Ellen Couch, was born in Texas. Sarah Ellen's mother went to Texas in 1863 to escape the unrest of the Civil War. Milam's father, William Guion Milam, came to Texas from Alabama. He married Sarah Ellen Couch in 1881. The young couple resided in Texas until 1887. J. B. Milam was born near Italy, Texas on March 10 1884. In 1887, the Milam family moved to Sarah's family acreage near Chelsea, Indian Territory.

Milam's formal education included two years at the Cherokee National Male Seminary and two years at the Metropolitan Business College in Dallas, Texas. After college, he returned to Chelsea and was employed in his father's businesses. In 1904, J. B. Milam and Elizabeth Peach McSpadden were married. Elizabeth graduated from the Cherokee National Seminary. In 1905, J.B.'s future business partner in the oil business, Woodly Phillips, married Elizabeth's sister, Maude.

The Milam family bought controlling interest in the Bank of Chelsea in 1908. This new venture sparked an interest in banking that resulted in J.B.'s ownership of interests in several banks. Oil was another successful business venture for Milam. Oil was struck on Milam land. By 1930 the Phillips and Milam Oil Company owned more than 1,000 active wells. Milam's acumen in oil and financial business dealings gained the respect of business and political leaders in Oklahoma as well as the Nation at large.

Chief Milam was also well schooled in Cherokee culture, history and politics. His priorities as chief focused on reconstructing the Cherokee government, pursuing claims through the Indian Claims Commission, rebuilding the tribal land base, and preserving the cultural and historical assets of the tribe. He started the preservation process by purchasing the site of the original building housing the National Cherokee Female Seminary and by establishing the Cherokee National Historical Society.[39]

illegal supply of election funds to President Nixon. Keeler was charged with making an illegal contribution to Nixon's 1972 presidential campaign. He pleaded guilty to a misdemeanor charge and was fined. In 1973 Keeler reached mandatory retirement age at Phillips and at age seventy-five reached the end of his elective term as Principal Chief of the Cherokee Nation. His retirement years were spent in Bartlesville where he died in 1987 at the age of seventy-nine.

Keeler's emergence as principal chief of the Cherokee Nation caused excitement in Cherokee communities. His stature in the corporate world did not go unnoticed. The expectation level for better things to come from a leader with a proven record was heightened by the past accomplishments made by Chief Milam. The rudiments of a government, although in its infancy, had been established by Milam. Keeler moved quickly to ensure the Executive Committee that they would continue as the major policy group of the tribe. His next move was to spend time in Tahlequah and other county-seat towns to become known and to become knowing about Cherokee citizens. This practice resulted in strong support by full-blood traditionalists as well as the mixed-blood assimilated Cherokees. He traded the boardroom setting and approach from Phillips to a shaded-bench setting on courthouse lawns to deliver his message and to listen to the people.

The first ten years of his service did not include major initiatives except for filing claims with the Indian Claims Commission. Time was devoted to establishing a sense of being among the Cherokees. The majority of the adult population was born after the Cherokee Nation was abolished. The events of allotment, statehood, and the abolishment of constitutional government, much like the Trail of Tears, were too bitter to remember. As a result, stories of the Cherokees' golden years in the last quarter of the 1800s did not occupy a significant place in oral history.

Another factor hampering Cherokee awareness was a total lack of the symbols of government. Former governmental buildings had lost their identity as Cherokee. When Chief Keeler presided at his informal meetings with Cherokees, the meetings in Tahlequah were advertised to take place at the Cherokee County Courthouse, not the Cherokee Nation Capitol Building.

There was no office site for the Cherokee Nation until after 1960 when a small shop site on South Muskogee Avenue in Tahlequah was opened. This humble site was not staffed for several years and served only as a meeting and mail drop site. A formal office with conference space, personnel, and office equipment did not come about until December 1968.[40]

Chief Keeler's persistent message as he traveled the hills, homes, and towns of Cherokee country was to recount the events of the 1948 Cherokee Convention held in Tahlequah. Two actions of the Convention were the product of Chief Milam's determination to reestablish the government of the Cherokee Nation. The major

Figure 11. W. W. Keeler. Image courtesy of the Cherokee National Historical Society

W. W. Keeler
(1908-1987)

Keeler was born April 5, 1908 in Dalhart, Texas. His family was involved in the cattle business in the Cooweescoowee District of the Cherokee Nation. His father contracted to feed a herd of cattle during the winter of 1908 and to deliver the herd by rail to Dalhart, Texas in the spring. Mrs. Keeler accompanied him on the rail trip. This accounts for Keeler's Texas birthplace instead of his hometown of Bartlesville, Oklahoma. While in high school he worked part-time for Phillips Petroleum Company.

He continued his part-time work with Phillips while enrolled at the University of Kansas where he planned to major in chemical engineering with financial assistance from a Harry E. Sinclair scholarship. The cancellation of the scholarship funds during the Teapot Dome Scandal caused Keeler to reassess his higher education goals. He dropped out of his college venture and went to work full-time in a Phillips refinery in Kansas City where he met Ruby Lucille Hamilton.

After their marriage in 1933 Keeler was transferred to Phillips refineries in Texas where he gained knowledge in multiple phases of the refining process. This earned him a transfer home to Bartlesville, Oklahoma, where he became technical assistant to the vice president of refining in 1943. The World War II years brought further recognition. He served on several refining technical committees of the Petroleum Administration for War and served as chair of the Military Petroleum Advisory Board. By the end of the war he was manager of Phillips Refining Department, and in 1947 he was promoted to vice president of refining. In 1951 he was appointed vice president of the executive department and member of Phillips Board of Directors. His rapid rise through the ranks of Phillips included executive vice-president in 1956 and to chair of the executive committee in 1962. In 1967 Keeler became president and chief executive officer of Phillips Petroleum Company.[41]

accomplishments toward Milam's objective were the establishment of an executive committee to assist and guide the Principal Chief and the employment of a cadre of attorneys to seek monetary redress for past wrongs by the federal government during their relentless taking of Cherokee land. Successful suits filed by the attorneys named at the Convention did not reach fruition until after Chief Milam's death. His foresight provided the funds necessary for the new Cherokee Nation.

Chief Keeler's second endeavor was to unify the Cherokees through encouraging community activities especially in the more remote areas of the fourteen-county Cherokee jurisdictional area. Keeler soon realized that the Cherokee populace was divided into two groups. One group was primarily full-blood and committed to a traditional lifestyle. The majority of this group was associated with some faction of the Keetoowah Society and as such was disappointed that the federal government failed to recognize their group as the successor to the former Cherokee Nation. During the years without a government, the more spiritual Keetoowahs split with the political Keetoowahs. However, both groups named chiefs during the years of exile who were purportedly chief of all Cherokees. The other distinct Cherokee group consisted of Cherokees who were for the most part mixed-blood, intermarried, and advocates for assimilating with white society. This segment of the population had favored allotment of Cherokee land and statehood for Indian Territory. The thoughts of these two groups were of long standing from 1808 at the time of Jefferson, to forced removal in the 1830s to American Civil War, to allotment of land, to dissolution of government, to fifty years without Cherokee government.

For most Indians, the two decades after World War II were years of watching and waiting for damaging legislation from the U.S. Congress. Relocation was the first major legislation to strike a blow, even though the Cherokee did not participate in great numbers. The next dooms-day rhetoric dealt with termination. The Cherokee Nation was in danger of losing government benefits according to a preliminary write-up for a Congressional bill. The Cherokees were vulnerable for inclusion in a list of tribes for termination. The major criterion for federal designation in selection of tribes for termination was the degree of assimilation with white business, government, and society. The other four tribes in Oklahoma designated by the federal government as "civilized" were also in danger of termination.

The Five Civilized Tribes had met together in a combined yet informal council during the era of the Dawes Commission, the Sequoyah Convention, and statehood for mutual protection and combined support to thwart federal action. Following statehood formal meetings of all five tribes were discontinued. During the fall of 1949, the tribes' leaders participated in meetings to form an organization to seek equitable adjustments of tribal affairs and to promote their common welfare. The group approved a constitution on February 3, 1950. After congressional recognition of the Inter-Tribal Council of the Five Civilized Tribes, the council's first major accomplishment was to influence Congress to withdraw House Concurrent Resolution Number 108, the tribal termination policy. The policy provisions were slated for application to the Choctaw Nation. Under pressure from the Inter-Tribal Council, Congress withdrew the Choctaw Termination Act of 1971.[42]

The united approach by the Five Civilized Tribes served them well. In addition to the unified approach in lobbying the US Congress, each of the Five Tribes maintained their own direct contacts to both state and national lawmakers. The Council would continue to meet to the present day on a quarterly basis with host responsibilities on a rotation basis.

The Cherokee Nation maintained a close relationship with Representative Ed Edmondson of the Second U.S. Congressional District. Congressman Edmondson was elected in 1952. By the time of the Cherokee rebuilding of government, he had gained considerable seniority on key committees. He remained friendly toward Cherokee endeavors throughout his twenty-year tenure in Congress. On March 9, 1971, he introduced eight bills to assist Indians. The Cherokee Nation, for the most part, had a positive relationship with elected officials during the years of rebuilding.[43]

The decade of the 1960s saw a rush to provide employment for Cherokees. The principal hampering factor to Cherokee Nation involvement and direction toward industrial development for job growth was lack of available capital for start-up and developmental costs. Many of the companies willing to relocate to the Cherokee Nation or to start new companies were strapped for cash and hesitant to engage an untrained workforce. The Cherokee Nation sought to remedy the situation by implementing a workforce training program through federal grant funds. Prospective employees were paid a subsistence wage while participating in a variety of skill training for construction and manufacturing jobs. Funds to address building and start-up costs became available in 1961, with a decision on the Outlet land case before the Indian Claims Commission. The Cherokees were awarded $14.7 million dollars following ten years of legal work. In 1962 Congress directed per capita payment to be made from the funds to all persons or their legal heirs who were enrolled by the Dawes Commission. The BIA was assigned the task of making per capita payments at the expense of the Cherokee Nation. More than eighty thousand individuals received payments. Congress also provided that funds not allocated per capita be spent by the principal chief under approval by the secretary of the interior. This provision provided ready capital for economic development and start-up costs for a fledgling human services department.[44]

Immediate employment of Cherokees was made possible through the efforts of the

Figure 12. Cover of the History of the Inter Tribal Council of the Five ivilized Tribes *booklet. Image courtesy of Northeastern State University's Special Collections.*

Keeler administration in providing improved housing for Cherokees through Housing and Urban Development grant funds. The housing effort quickly became a major service program and a major source of employment for Cherokees. As the program continued to expand beyond the levels of sufficient management and accountability as an internal Cherokee program, the function was contracted to external firms with certain responsibilities retained by the Cherokee Nation. After a few years of this arrangement, the Cherokee Nation chose to discontinue the home building program in wake of allegations of mismanagement and failure to account for funds.

Several companies external to the Cherokee Nation opened manufacturing plants in the newly formed industrial complex south of Tahlequah, Oklahoma, near the present site of the Cherokee Nation Complex. None of the early externally operated companies survived. Most of the new companies made the decision to locate in the Cherokee Nation due to low lease arrangements in Cherokee facilities and access to a ready labor supply with salary assistance from federal sources. Tribally owned businesses, however, were more successful, though having minor impact on the overall employment rate in the Cherokee Nation.

The early businesses that survived after start-up in the 1960s and 1970s included the Cherokee Heritage Center owned and operated by the Cherokee National Historical Society. Although not an entity of the Cherokee Nation, Cherokee funds have subsidized the operation since initial construction. Principal economic benefits included seasonal employment of Cherokees in its portrayal of an ancient Cherokee village. Chief Keeler was a supporter of the facility through the use of his private funds and funds from the Cherokee Foundation. Another enterprise that survived the start-up efforts was Cherokee Nation Industries in Stilwell, Oklahoma, established in 1969 to

Figure 13. Ray's Grocery Store in downtown Tahlequah, 1960 Image courtesy of the Cherokee National Historical Society.

serve as the economic and workforce arm for the Cherokee Nation. The company experienced a steady growth pattern in aerospace and defense contracting. In later years when Cherokee Nation Businesses was named a separate wholly owned entity of the Cherokee Nation, Cherokee Nation Industries was named the manufacturing and distribution division of Cherokee Nation Businesses.[45]

Chief Keeler's persistent urging of Cherokee community organizations and community representatives to maintain lines of communications was a success. By 1968 several communities had established schedules of meeting times and tentative agenda topics. The appearance of Chief Keeler at the Maryetta Community meeting on March 11, 1968, to address more than five hundred Cherokees showed the influence and ability of the Elected Community Representatives to bring large groups together to discuss Cherokee business.

Keeler's call for grass roots representation resulted in ventures to organize a fourteen-county organization with representation from each community. After a few monthly meetings the group took steps to establish their organizational framework and to elect officers. Eighteen of the community-based

Figure 14. The Ancient Village at the Cherokee Heritage Center. Image courtesy of the Cherokee National Historical Society.

organizations had representatives present to participate in organizing the Elected Community Representatives. The charter officers were Chair Hiner Doublehead, Co-chair Jackson McLain, and Secretary John Davis. The group grew in community units and in levels of responsibility as Chief Keeler broadened their responsibilities to include input on personnel selection and tribal expenditures.

Federal legislation enacted on October 22, 1970, as Public Law 91-495 authorized the Five Civilized Tribes of Oklahoma to select their principal officers.[46] The Cherokee Nation scheduled an election on August 14, 1971 to name a principal chief. Six candidates filed for the office: Sidney Brown from California, Sam Hider from Jay, Ross Hutchins from Tulsa, Ralph Keen from Tulsa, William Wayne Keeler from Bartlesville, and Noah Still from Muskogee. Three of the contenders had previous associations with the Cherokee Nation. William Wayne Keeler had served as appointed principal chief for twenty-two years. Sam Hider had served as Keeler's vice-chief appointee, and Ralph Keen had served as tribal business manager. The total votes cast were 10,086 of 15,000 registered Cherokees. Keeler received 7,595 votes, or seventy-five percent of the total votes cast.⁴⁷

Keeler's landslide election proved his campaign critics wrong in their predictions that the Cherokees would not elect a person for chief who was only one-sixth Cherokee and that the voters would prefer Sam Hider, a full-blood fluent in the Cherokee language. Keeler's election as chief and expansion of tribal services set the stage for recognition of rebirth of the Cherokee Nation. The Chief's inaugural address included a consistent theme of new days ahead:

"…Today we see the beginning of the realization of everything that was only a dream during the lifetime of most of us here today.

Cherokee Nation was never dead; only asleep. Today it stirs and begins to awaken. Today our children see the dream that you and I have had for so many bleak years.

We are again entrusted with the management of our own affairs. We are now free to elect our own leaders. We are free to train our people for jobs; to improve the educational opportunities of our children; to provide adequate medical care for all who need it; to record and promote our noble heritage…"⁴⁸

The remainder of the decade of the 1970s was an unprecedented period of growth for the Cherokee Nation. Funds realized through the Court of Claims provided opportunities for transforming ideas into action for strengthening government and for providing social services to Cherokee citizens delivered by Cherokee Citizens.

Indian affairs on the national level served to influence tribes on a local basis. This included Indian activism and the emergence of an improved attitude and philosophy of the US Congress toward Indian tribes. President Nixon's special message to Congress setting forth legislation to move away from relocation and termination and to move toward promotion of self-governance for tribes was encouraging news for Cherokee leaders.

Chief Keeler's announcement early in 1975 that he would not be a candidate for chief in the 1975 election cycle caused much discussion and speculation concerning leadership of the tribe. The June 1975 election became a highly controversial topic in May with an announcement by Keeler that filing for council seats and for deputy principal chief would be postponed indefinitely due to lack of an approved constitution. A proposed constitution had been submitted to the secretary of the interior, but an approval for referendum had not been received. Therefore, the final step in approval by the Cherokee people was blocked. Approval for referendum by Commissioner Morris Thompson was made on September 5, 1975. Therefore, election for council members and deputy principal chief was delayed until 1979.⁴⁹

The race for chief was scheduled for August 2, 1975, with the following contenders: Sam Drywater, Tahlequah; James Gordon, Stilwell; Sam Hider, Jay; J.D. Johnson, Wagoner; Ralph Powell, Grove; Charles Sanders, Stilwell; David Shell, Stilwell; Ross Swimmer, Tahlequah;

"ᏣᏫ ᎠᏂᎨᎵ Ꮃ ᏆᏇᎪᏼ ᎤᎶᏫᏨ ᏏᎮ4Ꭲ; ᏕᏣᏫᏙ. ᎠᎦ ᏔᏍ ᎠᏈᏓᏆᏬᏍᏴ ᎠᏊ ᎠᏓᏊᎯ ᎠᏛᎡᎢ. ᎠᎦ ᏔᏍ ᏗᎲᏂᏣ ᏚᏣᏓᏔᏢi ᎠᎲᎠᏣᎢ ᎾᏍᏴ ᎠᏛᎤᏋᏢᎢ Ꮎ ᏂᎠ ᎠᏊ ᎠᏯ ᎩᏃᎠᏣᏨᎡ ᎾᏍᏴᎾ ᎠᎾᏝ ᎤᎅᎠ4Ꭿ ᎢᏧᏍᎯᏆᏝ ᎩᎩᏂᏣᎤ."

- ᎤᎡᎾᏨᎯ ᎾᎵ Keeler

"Cherokee Nation was never dead; only asleep. Today it stirs and begins to awaken. Today our children see the dream that you and I have had for so many bleak years."

- Chief W.W. Keeler

Butler Welch, Claremore; and George Wickliffe, Kenwood.⁵⁰ See Table 2 for detailed results.

The winner was Ross Swimmer. Five of the unsuccessful candidates filed protests and pleas for recount with the Cherokee Election Committee. Ross Swimmer's plurality of twenty-eight percent of all votes cast was a protest rallying point. The election committee rules, however, did not provide provisions for a run-off contest. The election committee ordered a recount that did not affect the election outcome.

A native Oklahoman, Swimmer graduated from Putnam City High School and attended the University of Oklahoma where he received the Bachelor of Arts and Juris Doctor degrees. Swimmer practiced law in Oklahoma City prior to his employment as general counsel for the Cherokee Nation. In addition to his 1975 election, he was also reelected in 1979 with sixty-seven percent of votes cast. In 1984 he was appointed by President Reagan to serve as assistant secretary of Indian affairs. In 2001 President George W. Bush appointed Swimmer to be director of Indian trust transition. He currently resides in Tulsa where his wife, Margaret, is a partner with the Hall Estill law firm. Swimmer remains involved with several business ventures in banking and consulting on Indian enterprises.[51]

After being elected Swimmer moved forward appointing Advisory Council Members and deputy chief to serve until final approval of the proposed Cherokee constitution. R. Perry Wheeler of Sallisaw was appointed deputy principal chief. Appointed council members were Rachel Lawrence, Jimmy Chumwalooky, Betty Potter, Will Rider, W.W. Keeler, Kenneth Wright, Bob McSpadden, Lucille Maish, Mary Sellers, Glen Henson, Don Mabrey, Marie Wadley, Robert Swimmer, and Moses Frye.[52]

Early in September following the 1975 election, Chief Swimmer met with the elected

Candidates	Total County	Adair	Cherokee	Craig	Delaware	Mayes	McIntosh	Muskogee	Nowata	Ottawa	Rogers	Sequoyah	Tulsa	Wagoner	Washington	Absentee	Totals
Ross Swimmer	1,309	125	254	69	52	80	15	132	36	31	126	102	139	15	133	944	2,253
George Wickliffe	144	16	9	3	41	40	0	0	2	0	26	3	3	0	1	29	173
Sam Hider	775	237	92	27	187	94	1	13	4	12	21	30	37	8	12	123	898
David Shell	88	33	42	1	2	5	0	0	0	0	0	3	1	1	0	15	103
James Gordon	1,357	406	164	12	361	106	1	36	4	5	19	162	59	5	17	265	1,622
Sam Drywater, Jr.	86	4	21	1	4	21	0	5	2	1	4	0	19	0	4	34	120
J.D. Johnson	145	36	22	1	28	6	0	3	2	0	5	23	5	8	6	334	479
Charles Sanders	29	7	2	2	1	0	0	4	0	0	2	5	4	2	0	19	48
Butler Welch	1,107	58	209	64	207	124	2	20	20	15	68	83	167	9	61	868	1,975
Ralph Powell	344	10	16	42	76	11	2	17	10	89	15	5	33	3	15	105	449
	5,384	932	831	222	959	487	21	230	80	153	286	416	467	51	249	2,736	8,120

Table 2. Results of the 1975 Cherokee Nation Election for Principal Chief.

community representatives. He stated that he did not plan to disband the group but that the legislative function of the tribe would be carried out by the appointed Council until final approval of the constitution and election of a representative Council by Cherokee citizens. Swimmer further explained the concept and function of the Council, "I believe each Cherokee has a share of the Cherokee Nation. The council will act much like a board of directors of a large company to conduct the business of the tribe for these shareholders."

In December of 1975, Chief Swimmer and financial officers of the tribe engaged the services of the accounting firm of Peak, Marwick, Mitchell Co. to examine the tribes financial accounting practices. The report by the firm recommended a process of striking a balance of assets and liabilities for a starting point in fiscal accountability. This recommendation was adopted to enable an annual audit and to provide guidance in meeting outstanding debts incurred by the housing authority and the motel.⁵³

The early years of the Swimmer leadership were devoted to managing the growth of the tribe. The election of a Council to replace the appointed Council did not happen in accordance with the announced schedule. The proposed constitution was approved for referendum by Commissioner of Indian Affairs Morris Thompson on September 5, 1975. It was approved by the citizenry on June 26, 1976.⁵⁴

The appointed Council had been seated for more than six months when the constitution was finally approved. Since the Council was organized by department committees according to the major functions of the tribe, it was deemed appropriate to continue with the seated group and to provide for Council election in the 1979 regular election cycle.

Swimmer was reelected in 1979. The election was historic as the first election for Council members and deputy chief in the new era of Cherokee government. Swimmer was reelected with sixty seven percent of all votes cast. Perry Wheeler was elected vice chief.

Thirty-five persons filed for a seat on the Council. The constitution did not provide for representation by district until the 1991 election. All seats on the Council were designated as at-large. This required candidates to campaign in the entire jurisdictional area of the Cherokee Nation plus at-large areas. Eight members of Chief Swimmer's appointed Council members were elected and seven new members won seats.

Figure 15. Ross O. Swimmer. Image courtesy of the Cherokee National Historical Society.

Holdover members were Sam Ed Bush, Gary Chapman, Don Crittenden, Leo Fishinghawk, Rachel Lawrence, Robert McSpadden, Goodlow Proctor, and Robert Swimmer. New members were Amon Baker, Dr. Robert Collins, J.B. Dreadfulwater, Stan Hummingbird, Patsy Morton, Betty Smith and Clarence Sunday.⁵⁵

Swimmer was reelected to serve a third term in 1983. Near midway in his third term, September 1985, President Reagan nominated him to head the Bureau of Indian Affairs. He was confirmed by the US Senate on December 4, 1985, after serving ten years as chief.⁵⁶

Wilma Mankiller had been elected deputy chief as Swimmer's running mate in the 1983 election and served in that position for approximately two years. After Swimmer's federal appointment she was sworn in as principal chief. In 1987 she was elected as chief in her own campaign. In 1991 she was reelected with eighty three percent of the vote. She served until 1995.

Wilma was an outspoken advocate for independence from federal control in tribal operations. On the local level she focused on involving Cherokee citizens in community development. On the national level she promoted open federal-tribal relations. Her efforts in both local, national and international affairs gained acclaim and recognition. She and the Cherokee Nation received numerous awards during her tenure as chief, including the Medal of Freedom presented to Chief Mankiller by President Bill Clinton.

Chief Mankiller did not seek reelection for a third full term due to health issues. She retired to her ancestral Dawes Commission allotment. She remained active, however, in Native American causes. Northeastern State University named her their first Sequoyah Scholar in 2009. Chief Mankiller died on April 6, 2010.⁵⁷

Swimmer and his successor Wilma Mankiller were, perhaps, the first Cherokee chiefs to enjoy leading the people without threats from federal authorities. The specter of

Figure 16. Wilma Mankiller. Image courtesy of Gina Olaya and Cherokee Nation.

relocation and termination had faded away to be replaced with a new movement in congress to involve tribal members in preparation for lessening of Bureau of Indian Affairs control over tribes. The new direction provided for tribes to contract for services and to administer programs of educational assistance, agricultural assistance, and social welfare. The new movement was introduced in the US Senate as S. 1017 on February 26, 1973, and signed into law by President Gerald R. Ford on January 4, 1975, as PL 93-638.

"The Self-Determination Mission was clearly stated, "To promote and advocate maximum Indian participation in the programs and services conducted by the Federal Government for Indians; and to encourage and support the development of tribal capacity to better manage the opportunities and responsibilities of self-determination."[58]

In 1991 an Office of Self-Governance was created in the office of the Secretary of the Interior to accomplish primary functions of implementing and carrying out the self-governance initiatives. Foremost were consolidating P.L. 93-638 contracts and grants into single annual funding agreements, providing for tribal initiatives in determining funding priorities, and permitting tribes to consolidate and modify programs according to local needs and local decisions.

Seven tribal compacts of self-governance were negotiated for the initial demonstration operational year of FY 1991. These seven tribes were referred to as the First Tier Compact Tribes. The self-governance tribes conducted a one-year to two-year planning process prior to implementing their self-governance programs. The Cherokee Nation was included in the group along with the Absentee Shawnee-Oklahoma, Hoopa Valley Tribe-California, Jamestown S'Klallam-Washington, Lummi Indian Nation- Washington, Mille Lac Chippewa Indians-Minnesota and Quinault Indian Nation-Washington.

An Independent Assessment Team, consisting of representatives from the American Indian Law and Policy Center of the University of Oklahoma and the Center for Tribal Studies at Northeastern State University, Tahlequah, Oklahoma, was charged with assessing the advantages and disadvantages of participation by tribes in the Self-Governance Demonstration Project. The Assessment Team's findings, based on a review of tribal documents and on-site review with each tribe, were complimentary toward all involved with the new era of Indian and federal government relationship. The authors of the report credited part of the success as an evolutionary historical circle which had returned tribal governments and tribal decision-making to tribal members—to those most accountable to Indian people.[59]

Chief Mankiller was an advocate for self-governance. The Cherokee Nation was chosen to participate in the pilot group of tribes in implementing the program. After more than a century of assault on tribal sovereignty, the Cherokees were poised for a new Golden Age of Cherokee History.

ᎠᏯᏙᎸᎢ 11
ᎤᏩᏒ ᏧᎦᎧᏺᏂᏏᏍᏗ - ᏣᎳᎩᏱ ᏚᏍᏛᏂᏏᏍᏗ

Chapter 11: Self Determination – the Cherokee Way

Figure 1. Cherokee Nation W. W. Keeler Tribal Complex. Photo by Stephanie Remer.

The authors decided to conclude this history of the Cherokee Nation as the recurring stories of challenges and opportunities entered the 1970s. There are several reasons for that decision.

One, the 1970s served as a new dawn for the Cherokee people in terms of self rule and self determination. With a new constitution and the leadership of W.W. Keeler, Ross Swimmer, and Wilma Mankiller, the Cherokee people not only set a new course for their own government, but also launched a new era of cultural preservation,

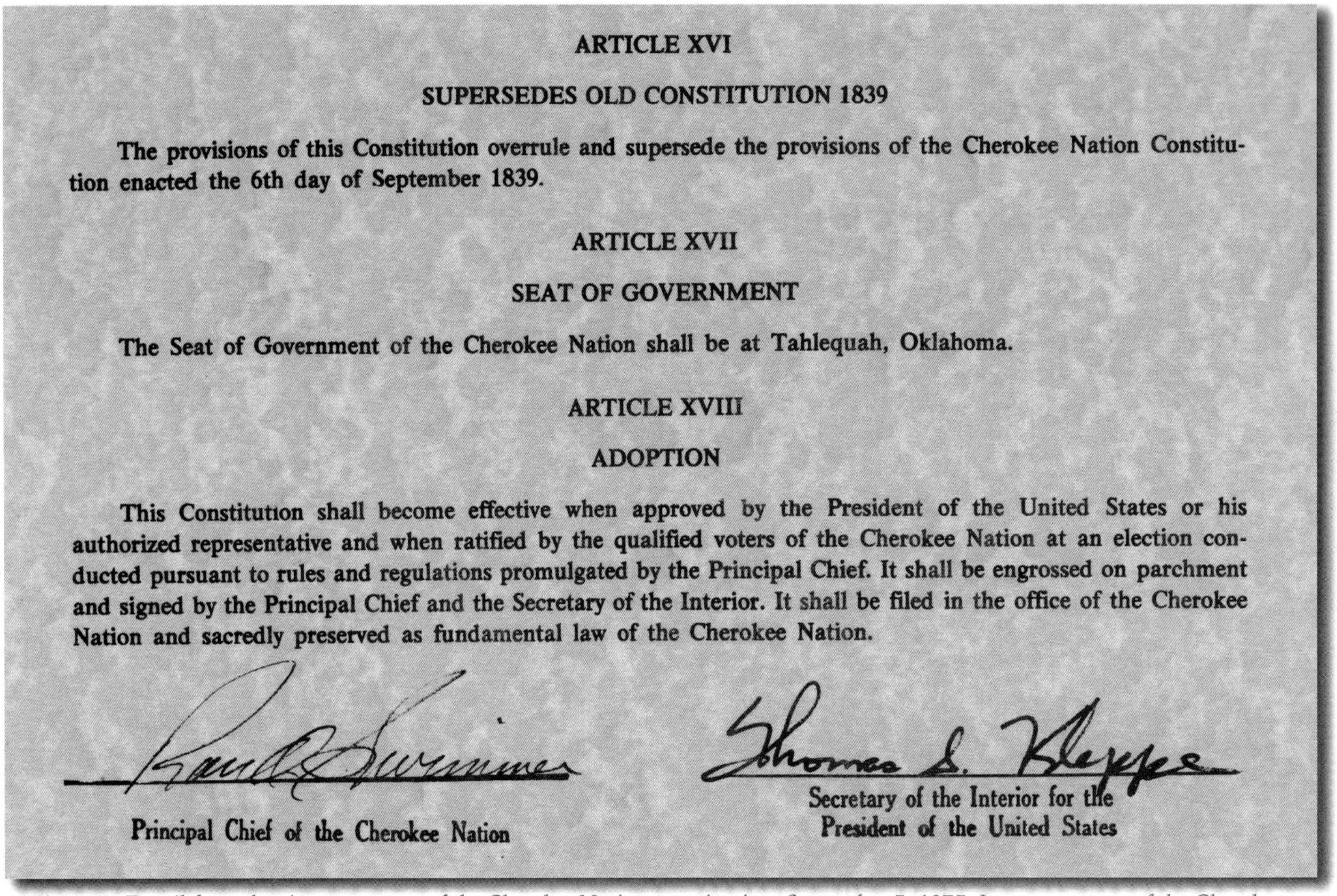

ARTICLE XVI

SUPERSEDES OLD CONSTITUTION 1839

The provisions of this Constitution overrule and supersede the provisions of the Cherokee Nation Constitution enacted the 6th day of September 1839.

ARTICLE XVII

SEAT OF GOVERNMENT

The Seat of Government of the Cherokee Nation shall be at Tahlequah, Oklahoma.

ARTICLE XVIII

ADOPTION

This Constitution shall become effective when approved by the President of the United States or his authorized representative and when ratified by the qualified voters of the Cherokee Nation at an election conducted pursuant to rules and regulations promulgated by the Principal Chief. It shall be engrossed on parchment and signed by the Principal Chief and the Secretary of the Interior. It shall be filed in the office of the Cherokee Nation and sacredly preserved as fundamental law of the Cherokee Nation.

_____
Principal Chief of the Cherokee Nation

_____
Secretary of the Interior for the
President of the United States

Figure 2. Detail from the signature page of the Cherokee Nation constitution, September 5, 1975. Image courtesy of the Cherokee National Historical Society.

expression, and most importantly, their own identity.

Second, as historians, we need more time to gain perspective on what has happened since the 1970s. Without the luxury of time, we will not fully realize the importance of certain people, events, and trends until the small pieces of the larger mosaic fit together to show us high points, low points, and turning points. With time, the picture will come into focus.

Instead, we want to add this postscript to the story with a snapshot of the Cherokee Nation in 2017. Future historians will have to fill in the gaps, once again tracing the footprints that take the story back in terms of political, social, and economic history.

The heart and soul of the Cherokee Nation are the Cherokee people. Today, there are more than 360,000 Cherokee citizens. Roughly half are scattered across fourteen counties in northeastern Oklahoma, the traditional homeland of the Cherokees after they were removed to the West, with the others residing throughout Oklahoma, the nation, and in more than twenty countries around the world. They come from all walks of life, some living traditional lives deep in the hills of Cherokee country and others adapting to new ways and new places. Two things bind them together. One is their history and heritage, a common story that grounds them in their ancient homelands and ties them to the traditions of their own families. The other binding force is their government.

In some ways, the Cherokees never lost their government despite the Curtis Act, allotment, and Oklahoma statehood. If we are bound by Western European definitions, then yes, maybe there was no tribal government with federal recognition and paid employees from 1907 to the 1960s. But Cherokees have never been bound by Western European definitions. To traditional Cherokees, their government has always been based on tribal identity and a sense of community. In the mid-1770s that tribal cohesion helped them survive the first waves of European and American assault. In the twentieth century that tribal cohesion helped them survive allotment, exploitation, the Great Depression, and federal policy dedicated to tribal destruction.

The resurrection of traditional western-style government for the Cherokee people began in the 1960s as many Americans embraced new-found respect for civil rights, whether it was voting rights for young people old enough to fight for their country or equal protection under the law for African-Americans, women, the elderly, the disabled, and the poor. The civil rights movement, in one of its many manifestations, poured new fuel on the old question of tribal sovereignty. Should Indian people have their own governments within the federal system?

From 1961 forward, every president of the United States advocated the end of tribal termination policies and sought new ways to restore self government for tribes. In 1969, in a speech delivered to the nation, President Richard Nixon joined the chorus and asked for new legislation that would end decades of treating Indian people like conquered victims and return them to citizens of sovereign tribal nations. Six years later, in 1975, Congress passed the Self Determination and Education Act that gave tribal governments the right of contracting with the Bureau of Indian Affairs to use federal funds based on tribal priorities and traditions. For the Cherokee people, it meant they could work together to set priorities and deliver services to their own people, the Cherokee way.

A roadmap to the Cherokee way was created in 1976 when the citizens of the tribe approved a new constitution. Reflecting the structure of the nineteenth century Cherokee government, it had three branches: legislative, judicial, and executive. The legislative branch consisted of a Tribal Council with fifteen members elected to four-year terms. All council members' positions were at-large. In 1991 fifteen districts were created within the tribe's fourteen county jurisdiction. In 2003 council districts were remapped creating council seats within the fourteen county jurisdiction and two at large seats. The primary duties of the Tribal Council were to establish laws protecting and serving Cherokee people and allocating the resources needed to achieve those goals.

The judicial branch consisted of a Judicial Appeals Tribunal with three members. Members of the judiciary were appointed by the Principal

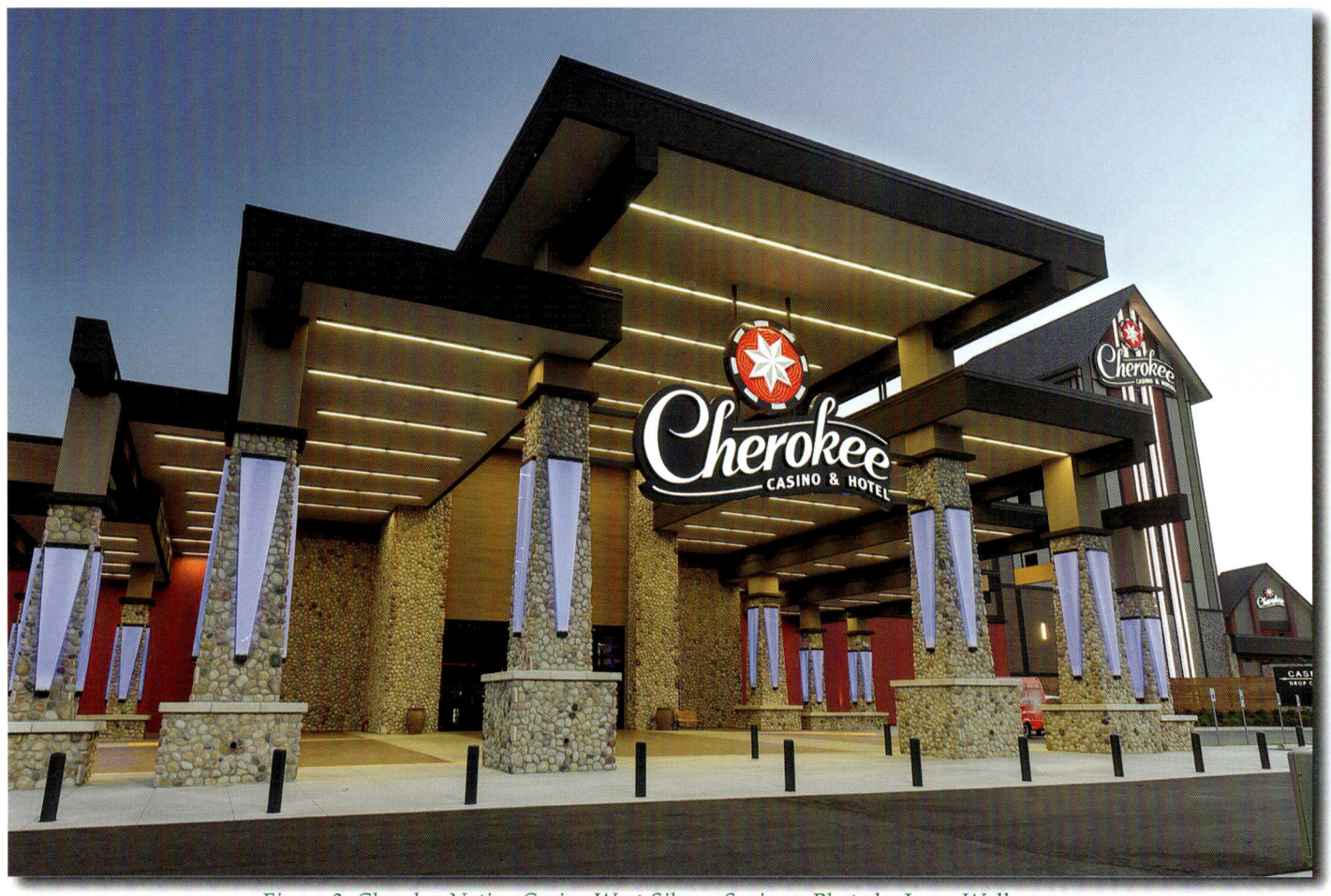

Figure 3. Cherokee Nation Casino West Siloam Springs. Photo by Jason Wallace.

Chief and confirmed by the Tribal Council. The primary function of the judiciary was to interpret the law to achieve the highest levels of public safety and social order. In the 1999 constitution, voted on in 2003 and ratified in 2007, the Judicial Appeals Tribunal was renamed the Supreme Court. The Supreme Court is composed of five members appointed by the Principal Chief and confirmed by Tribal Council. Each member serves a four year term.

The executive branch, consisting of a Principal Chief, Deputy Principal Chief, and cabinet officers nominated by the Principal Chief and confirmed by the Tribal Council, was given the task of executing Cherokee laws, establishing policies for general welfare, and delegating authority to tribal employees to serve the Cherokee people. In 2017 the six cabinet positions were Secretary of State, Treasurer, Marshal, Attorney General, Secretary of Natural Resources, and Chief of Staff.

Self rule and solid, constitutionally based leadership were essential to restoring the service capacity of the Cherokee Nation, but self determination and delivery of those services at the grassroots level could only be achieved with access to greater resources. And without a land base to generate property, sales, or income taxes, the Cherokee Nation had to find other streams of revenue. In the 1990s, as mentioned in chapter 10 of this book, part of the solution was direct tribal control of resources allocated by the fed-

Figure 4. Redbirth Smith Health Center, Sallisaw, Oklahoma. Photo by Stephanie Remer.

eral government to Indian people. In addition to increased services, this self-directed allocation of federal resources fostered improved internal capacity and the growth of a professional bureaucracy separated from the revolving door of elections.

While this gradual transition was empowering the Cherokees to take care of Cherokee people, a turning point in the ability of the new government to serve its citizens was achieved in 1988 when the Cherokee Nation entered into the first compact with the State of Oklahoma to legalize gaming. Gaming was more than entertainment and jobs. It meant tribal revenue, a substitute for taxes that could be used to foster a better quality of life for Cherokee people. By 2017 the Cherokees operated ten casinos that helped generate an economic impact of more than $2 billion a year. The combination of self-directed federal funds, increased internal capacity, and self-generated revenue achieved the promise of true self determination.

The results of self determination can best be viewed in the field of health care. Since the early 1990s the federal government has offered opportunities to tribes for joint ventures, whereby the tribes help fund facilities and equipment and the federal government covers most of the operational costs. Selection is based on the needs of tribal citizens and the ability of tribal governments to fund and support the construction and operational efforts. Only thirty joint ventures have been approved in the entire nation, and the Cherokees have won three of them.

The most recent is the 490,000-square foot expansion of the W.W. Hastings Hospital in Tahlequah, which will be the largest tribal medical center in the United States when it is completed in 2019. The Cherokee Nation is investing about $200 million in construction and $75 million in equipment and information technologies. In a recent news report, Principal Chief Bill John Baker explained the need for this kind of investment. "For many years Native people, including Cherokees, have faced the worst health disparities in our country," he said. "Through planning, focus, and partnerships, we have an opportunity to change that history and truly make the health of our people a priority." In addition to the W.W. Hastings Hospital, the Cherokee Nation in 2017 raised pay for doctors, built two new clinics, and committed additional funds for care at non-Cherokee hospitals.

Cherokee efforts to improve health and happiness among tribal members have gone well beyond hospitals and access to doctors. On the preventive side, the tribal government in 2017 provided USDA food assistance to 62,505 households, served more than 20,000 meals at senior nutrition sites, and sponsored a farm to market program that recently evolved from a tailgate service to a regularly scheduled delivery of fresh vegetables and fruits deep in the food deserts of Cherokee Country. On the recovery side, the Cherokee Nation in 2017 filed a lawsuit against opioid distributors and large chain drugstores claiming they had flooded the Cherokee Nation with enough prescription opioid painkillers to provide every man, woman, and child with 153 doses.

In 2015 Principal Chief Bill John Baker appointed the tribe's first cabinet Secretary of Natural Resources to do even more about a healthy environment. One of Principal Chief Baker's priorities was to reduce the carbon footprint of tribal programs. In 2017 the tribe purchased its first electric vehicles and installed solar energy charging stations at tribal headquarters. On the supply side, the tribe leased 4,000 acres for a wind farm that not only will provide clean energy but also generate approximately $1 million a year to the tribe in earned revenue.

Healthy lives start with healthy places to live. In 2016 the Cherokee Nation provided a wide range of housing services that helped 187 Cherokee families become first-time home owners, helped another 1,800 families with rental assistance, and provided $1,000 per semester to 135 students for housing while they were enrolled in college. To help protect housing and reduce the costs of private home insurance, the Cherokee Nation in 2016 granted more than $700,000 to 184 rural police and fire departments and completed eleven water and sanitation projects.

The Cherokee people have always considered education as a high priority. In the nineteenth century, one of the first accomplishments of the tribe once it arrived in the West was an education system that included country schools and seminaries for older students. In 2016 the

Figure 5. The Place Where They Play–the Sequoyah High School Gym. Photo by Stephanie Remer.

Cherokee Nation honored that long held tradition with support for seven Early Head Start facilities, twelve Head Start facilities, creative teaching grants to teachers, and direct grants to more than 4,000 students to attend college. That same year, the Cherokee Nation distributed $4.7 million in aid to more than 100 school districts in fourteen counties. Unlike some grants, the Cherokee Nation funds came with no strings attached. The money was to enhance the educational experience for all students.

Cherokee Nation has taken a proactive approach to language revitalization. It has language programs that reach all ages from babies to the elderly, including the Cherokee Immersion Charter School, free language classes in the fourteen county jurisdictional area, and free online language classes for those who cannot attend in person. The online classes reach far beyond the fourteen counties, including international participation. The language program also has adult immersion learning for Cherokee Nation staff and citizens. The tribe has a language staff consisting of professional translators, teachers, and language technologists. The Cherokee syllabary has transitioned into the digital age with its inclusion in software platforms from the world's most prominent technology companies such as Apple, Google, and Microsoft. Language revitalization efforts also include a partnership with the United Keetoowah Band of Cherokee Indians and the Eastern Band of Cherokee Indians

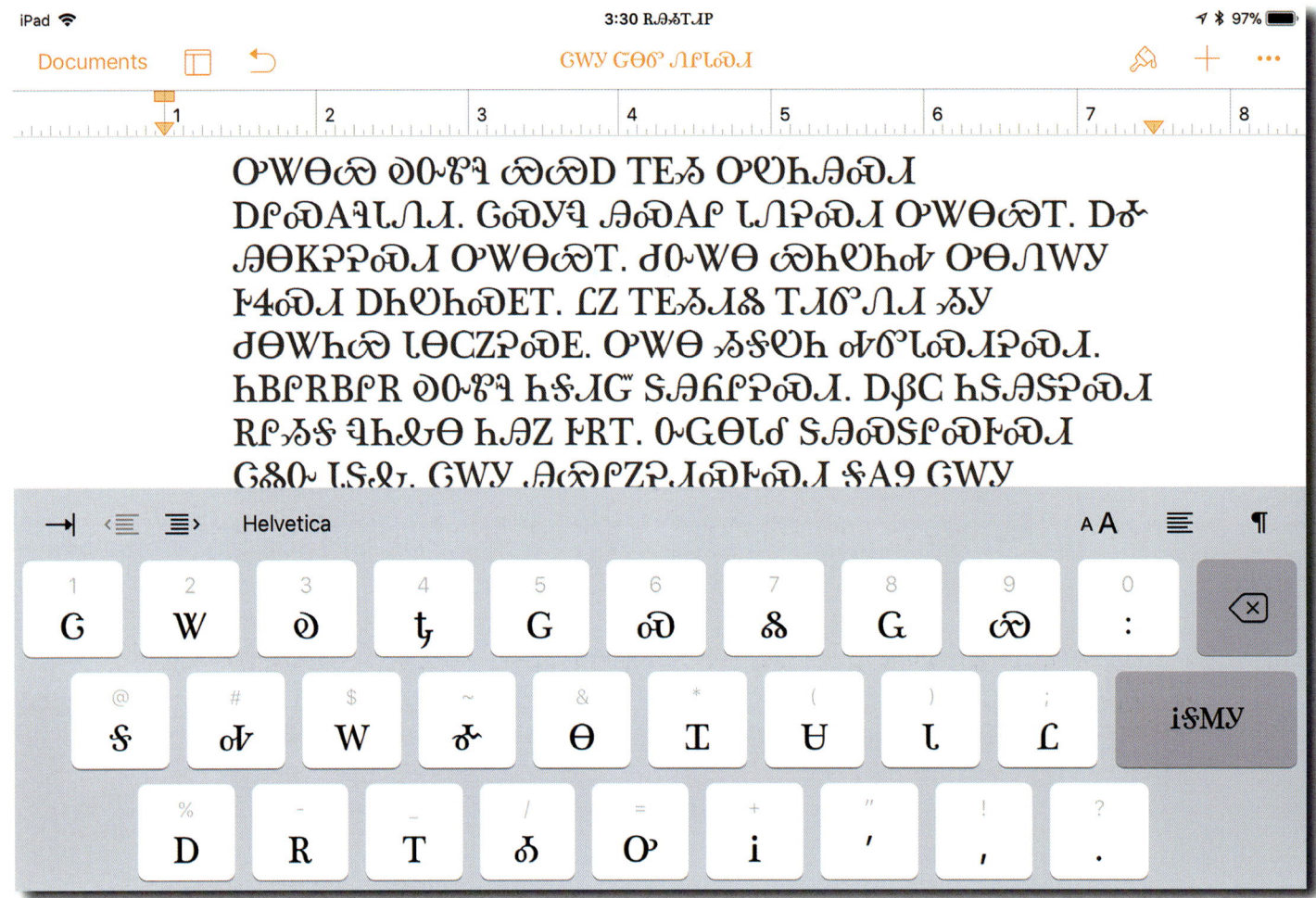

Figure 6. Cherokee langauge keyboard being used on an iPad. Image courtesy of the Cherokee Nation.

through the Cherokee Language Consortium.

The evolution of the Cherokee Nation as a champion of its citizens' quality of life is reflected in external affairs as well as internal improvements. In 2015, after many years of unrewarded contention, Principal Chief Bill John Baker signed an agreement with the Oklahoma State Wildlife Department that granted all Cherokee Nation citizens who are Oklahoma residents the right to hunt and fish anywhere within the state. In return, by granting more than 100,000 new fishing and hunting licences, the State of Oklahoma received an additional $4 million in federal funds for wildlife conservation efforts.

A similar diplomatic victory with mutual benefits was achieved in 2016 when the Cherokee Nation purchased the Sequoyah Home Park from the Oklahoma Historical Society, a state agency that had invested several million into preserving the historic site since 1936. Principal Chief Bill John Baker and several hundred Cherokee elders gathered with Dr. Bob Blackburn of the Oklahoma Historical Society to transfer title in a moving ceremonial event that recognized not only the right of the Cherokee Nation to own and operate the sacred ground of Sequoyah's home, but also recognized the ability of the tribe to run it in a professional way, the Cherokee Way.

The Cherokee Nation has come a long

Figure 7. Sequoyuah Cabin Museum. Photo by Stephanie Remer.

way since the 1960s when W.W. Keeler dreamed of a reenergized tribal government worthy of its sovereignty and dedicated to improving the lives of its citizens. If the last fifty years are any indication of what is to come, the future of the Cherokee Nation is bright with promise.

Endnotes

ᎩᏬᎻᏍᎡ ᏚᏬᎹᎢ
Endnotes

Chapter 1

1. James Mooney, "Myths of the Cherokee," *19th Annual Report of the Bureau of American Ethnology*. (Washington, DC: Government Printing Office, 1900), 14.
2. Ibid., 16-17.
3. T. M. N. Lewis and Madeline Kneberg, *Hiwassee Island: An Archaeological Account of Four Tennessee Indian Peoples* (Knoxville: University of Tennessee Press, 1946), 11-12.
4. Floyd G. Lounsbury, "Iroquois-Cherokee Linguistic Relations," *Symposium on Cherokee and Iroquois Culture, Bureau of American Ethnology, Bulletin No. 180* (Washington, DC: Government Printing Office, 1961), 11.
5. "Document of 1691," *Collections of the South Carolina Historical Society*, 1 (1857): 126; as cited in Mooney, "Myths," 31.
6. Alexander Hewatt, *An Historical Account of the Rise and Progress of the Colonies of South Carolina and Georgia.* (London: Donaldson, 1779), I: 216.
7. Mary Rothrock, "Carolina Traders among the Overhill Cherokees, 1690-1760," *East Tennessee Historical Society Publication*s 1 (1929): 3-18.
8. Verner Crane, "The French on the Tennessee," *Mississippi Valley Historical Review*, III 9-13, n.
9. Samuel Cole Williams, *Early Travels in the Tennessee Country, 1540–1800.* (Johnson City, TN: The Watauga Press, 1928), 94.
10. Mooney, "Myths," 32-33.
11. Crane, "French on the Tennessee," 182.
12. Hewatt, *Historical Account*, 258.
13. Charles C. Royce, "The Cherokee Nation of Indians: A Narrative of Their Official Relations with the Colonial and Federal Governments." Chicago, Smithsonian Institution Press: (1975 Reprint of pages 121-378, *Fifth Annual Report of the Bureau of American Ethnology for the Years 1883-1884* (Washington, DC: Government Printing Office, 1887; Chicago, Smithsonian Institution Press, 1975), 256. Citation refers to Smithsonian Edition.
14. George Chicken, "Journal to the Cherokees, 1725," in *Travels In the American Colonies by Newton D. Mereness*, (New York: Macmillan, 1916), 97-172.
15. David H. Corkran, *The Cherokee Frontier: Conflict and Survival, 1740-62* (Norman: University of Oklahoma Press, 1962), 16.
16. Ibid.

17. Ibid., 39
18. Ibid. 142-62
19. *South Carolina Gazette*, January 12, 1760 as cited in Corkran, *Cherokee Frontier*, 189.
20. British Public Record Office, Kew, C.O. 5/59 Fol. 101, Original Correspondence, Secretary of State, Military Dispatches: 1760. July 2, 1760. Montgomery's description of his second march into the Cherokee country.
21. British Public Record Office, Kew, C.O. 5/61 Fol. 379, Original Correspondence, Secretary of State, Military Dispatches: 1761 Copy of Colonel James Grant's journal of the march against the Cherokees, 12. see also Corkran, *Cherokee Frontier*, 254; Duane H. King, "The Powder Horn Commemorating the Grant Expedition Against the Cherokees," *Journal of Cherokee Studies* 1 (Summer 1976): 23-40.
22. Duane H. King, ed., *The Memoirs of Lt. Henry Timberlake: The Story of a Soldier, Adventurer, and Emissary to the Cherokees, 1756-1765*. (Cherokee, NC: Museum of the Cherokee Indian Press, distributed by the University of North Carolina Press, 2007).
23. The battle of Echowee Pass (near present-day Franklin, NC) occurred June 27, 1760, and the capitulation of the garrison of Fort Loudoun (near present-day Vonore, TN) was on August 8, 1760. About two dozen members of the garrison were killed by Cherokees at Cane Creek on August 10, 1760. British Public Record Office, Kew, C.O. 5/59 Fol. 101, Original Correspondence, Secretary of State, Military Dispatches: 1760. July 2, 1760. Montgomery's description of his second march into the Cherokee country.
24. *The Gazetteer* and *London Daily Advertiser,* July 9, 1762.
25. *The Monthly Chronicle* July 8, 1762.
26. *The Public Advertiser*, July 10, 1762.
27. This description was recorded by Elizabeth Percy, the duchess of Northumberland, Queen Charlotte's lady of the bedchamber, who along with the queen, escorted the Cherokees from the presence chamber during their visit to Saint James Palace on July 8, 1762. See James Greig, ed., *The Diaries of a Duchess: Extracts from the Diaries of the First Duchess of Northumberland* (London: Hodder and Stoughton, 1926), 47, diary entry for August 8, 1762. For an overview of this extraordinary woman's life, see Harriet Blodgett, "Percy, Elizabeth, [*née* Lady Elizabeth Seymour], duchess of Northumberland and Baroness Percy (1716–1776), courtier and diarist'," in *Oxford Dictionary of National Biography* (Oxford: Oxford University Press, 2004) online edition.
28. 0176.1015 *Cunne Shote (Stalking Turkey)* by Francis Parsons, 1762, oil on canvas, half-length portrait (35.125" h x 27.75"w) framed size (46.375" h x 39" w x 3" d). Purchased by Thomas

Endnotes

Gilcrease Foundation, July 30, 1946, from James P. Labey Ancient and Modern Paintings, 108 West 57th Street, New York, NY, for $4,500. In files of Witt Library, Courtauld Institute, London, is a large photograph of this marked "Bromhead, Cutts & Co., London, 1924"; Witt Library Index queried by William C. Sturtevant on April 23, 1996 indicates this was an art dealer and publisher in London in existence from at least 1920 until 1924.

29. 0176.1017 *Scyagust Ukah* by Sir Joshua Reynolds, 1762, oil on canvas, half-length portrait (48" h x 35.5" w) framed size (55" h x 43.125" w x 2.65" d). Purchased by the Thomas Gilcrease Foundation, January 6, 1959, from M. Knoedler & Co., Inc. 14 East 57th Street, New York, NY.

30. On my first visit to the Gilcrease Museum in the summer of 1972, I saw the portraits of two eighteenth century Cherokee leaders, *Cunne Shote* by Francis Parsons and *Ostenaco* by Sir Joshua Reynolds. I was struck by the attention to detail in the portraits particularly the medallions above the military gorget worn by Cunne Shote. The medallions were so accurately portrayed that I knew, with sufficient research, they could be identified. In 1980 Laurence Brown published *A Catalogue of British Historical Medals, 1760-1960, Volume I.* Ringwood, Hampshire, UK: Seaby Publications Ltd., 1980). On page 5 was a wedding medallion of George III and princess Charlotte, an exact match for the medal worn over the proximal end of the left collarbone in the portrait of Cunne Shote. The second medal worn over the right collarbone was not pictured. However, the description of medal number 4 on page 4, proclaiming George III as king on October 26, 1760 seemed to match the image in the portrait.

31. Algernon Graves and William Vine Cronin, *A History of the Works of Sir Joshua Reynolds*, P.R.A. (London: IV 1533, H. Graves and Co. 1889).

32. Grieg, 1926:47.

33. *St. James Chronicle,* July 3, 1762, and *Lloyd's Evening Post,* #777, 17:5-7 July 1762.

34. *The Royal Magazine*, (London), July, 1762.

35. The Third, Fourth, and Fiftth Cherokee signatures on the peace treaty signed at the Long Island of the Holston on November 20, 1761, are Autassety (Ostenaco), Skiagunsta, and Cunnesaughte, most likely the three members of the Cherokee delegation to London.

36. It is not known if the painting was commissioned. It is also possible that Reynolds painted the Cherokees for his own edification or recognition of the historical value in documenting their visit.

37. *The British Chronicle,* June 30- July 2, 1762; see also Carolyn Foreman, *Indians Abroad, 1492-1938* (Norman: University of Oklahoma Press, 1943), 70.

38. Volume 4, medal number 4.

39. Ibid., 1, medal number 1, and ibid., 4 medal number 3.

40. Ibid., 1 medal number 2.
41. Ibid., 18-19 medal numbers 21-24.
42. "Yesterday, the Cherokees were at St. James to take their leave of His Majesty." *London Chronicle,* August 7, 1762, and *Lloyd's Evening Post*, August 6-9, 1762.
43. *London Magazine*, August 8, 1762.
44. *St. James Chronicle*, August 5-7, 1762.
45. *The London Gazette Extraordinary*, August 12, 1762.
46. *Lloyd's Evening Post*, August 11-13, 1762.
47. Ibid., August 13-16, 1762.
48. This was Elizabeth Davies, who originated the role of Margery in Thomas Arne's *Love in a Village.* She married composer Jonathan Battishill on December 19, 1765. She moved to Ireland with actor Anthony Webster in 1776 and died in Cork, Ireland, in October 1777.
49. Edward Edwards *Anecdotes of Painters, Who Have Resided or Been Born in England* (London: Luke Hansford and Sons, 1808), 286. Edwards states: "The artist for some time studied in the Academy at St. Martin's-lane, but with no great success, and he became a picture-dealer and cleaner, a good resource for the invalids in painting. He lived and kept a shop for some years in Albermarle-street, afterwards removed into Picadilly, where he died sometime in the year 1804."
50. John Chaloner Smith. *British Mezzotinto Portraits.*…"being a descriptive catalogue…arranged according to the engravers," (London Henry Sotheran, 1883), 854. "Cunne Shote, the Indian Chief. A great Warrior of the Cherokee Nation. Was in England in 1762. Sold at the Golden Head, in Queen Square, Ormond Street. Pr. 2s 6d." Beneath image he noted: "F. Parsons pinxt. Js. McArdell fecit." H. 13 7/8", Sub. 12 1/8", W 9 7/8".
51. Thomas Jefferys, *A Collection of Dresses*…(London: Thomas Jefferys, 1757). "Habit of Cunne Shote a Cherokee Chief. Cunne Shote Chef des Chiroquois. 207" Full length. 24.7 x 20.3 cm." On page 27 it is said to be "from a metzotinto print scraped by MacArdell, from a painting of Mr. Parsons."
52. Jefferys, "Cunne Shote. / Chef des Chiroquois / d'apres Parson / Paris chez Duflos rue St. Victor A.P.D.R." Colored engraving. Full length. 11" x 8 5/8".
53. William C. Sturtevant, "Visual Representations of the Cherokee Kings in London, 1762," *The Memoirs of Lt. Henry Timberlake: The Story of a Soldier, Adventurer, and Emissary to the Cherokees, 1756-1765.* (Cherokee: Museum of the Cherokee Indian Press), 85-92.
54. *Court Magazine*, 1, XI, (August 1762), facing p. 491; see also *Royal Magazine* (July 1762), facing p. 16; and *British Magazine*, 3 (July, 1762), facing p. 378.

Endnotes

55. Here they are identified as the Stalking Turkey, the Pouting Pidgeon, and the Mankiller.
56. It was "sold in Marys Buildings Covent Garden, according to Act, by G. Bickham," Full lengths. Image 8 ½" x 11 ¼".
57. "Lieutenant James Gorrell's Journal," *Collections of the Historical Society of Wisconsin* (1855): 33,38, as cited in *John Adams*, 1999, p. 32.
58. Johnson to Gage, 2-20-1766. Johnson Papers, Volume 12, page 23.
59. Gage to Johnson, 3-3-1766. Johnson Papers, Volume 12 page 34.
60. King, ed. *The Memoirs of Lt .Henry Timberlake: The Story of a Soldier, Adventurer, and Emissary to the Cherokees, 1756-1765*, xxxvi, and 125.

Chapter 2

1. J. G. M. Ramsey, *Annals of Tennessee* (Charleston, SC: Walker and James Steam Power Press, 1853), 117-118; John Haywood, *Natural and Aboriginal History of Tennessee* (Kingsport, TN: F. M. Hill Books, 1823), 105.
2. Samuel Cole Williams "Henderson and Company's Purchase within the limits of Tennessee," *Tennessee Historical Magazine* 5 (1919-1920): 5-7.
3. Samuel Wilson, deposition in the *Calendar of Virginia State Papers I*, 283.
4. Henry Stuart to John Stuart, 25 August 1776, William L. Sanders, ed., *Colonial Records of North Carolina*, (Raleigh: P. M. Hale State Printer, 1886), 10:764.
5. Williams, "Henderson and Company's Purchase," *Within the Limits of Tennessee*, 5-27.
6. Ibid., 24.
7. Henry Stuart to John Stuart, *Colonial Records of North Carolina*, 765-66.
8. Philip Hamer, Alexander Cameron to John Stuart, 7 May 1776, *The East Tennessee Historical Society Publication*, 3, 110-11; Library of Congress, Manuscripts of British Public Record Office, Colonial Office Papers, Class 5, 77, 273.
9. Henry Stuart to John Stuart, *Colonial Records of North Carolina*, 764.
10. Philip Hamer, Alexander Cameron to John Stuart, 7 May, 1776, *The East Tennessee Historical Publication*, 3, 110-11.
11. Ibid., 111.
12. Henry Stuart to John Stuart, 25 August 1776, *Colonial Records of North Carolina*, 771-72.
13. Ibid., 773.
14. Ibid., 774.
15. Ibid., 777.
16. Ibid., 778-79.
17. J. P. Brown, *Old Frontiers* (Kingsport, TN: Southern Publishers, Inc., 1938), 147; R. S. Cotterill, *The Southern Indians* (Norman: University of Oklahoma Press, 1954), 40.
18. Henry Stuart to John Stuart, *Colonial Records of North Carolina*, 781.
19. Ibid., 781.
20. James O'Donnell, *Southern Indians in the American Revolution* (Knoxville: University of Tennessee Press, 1973), 38.
21. Henry Stuart to John Stuart, *Colonial Records of North Carolina*, 781.
22. Ibid., 782.
23. Grace Steele Woodward, *The Cherokees* (Norman: University of Oklahoma Press, 1963), 94.
24. Henry Stuart to John Stuart, *Colonial Records of North Carolina*, 784.

Endnotes

25. Ramsey, *Annals of Tennessee*, 148-50.
26. Ibid., 158.
27. George Christian to Lyman Draper, 4 December, 1842, Draper Manuscripts, 14 DD111, Wisconsin Historical Society.
28. Duane H. King, "The Cherokees and the Frontier of 1776," in *Unto These Hills,* souvenir program for the 1976 season, 6-10.
29. Ramsey, *Annals of Tennessee*, 159; Samuel Cole Williams, *Tennessee During the Revolutionary War* (Nashville: The Tennessee Historical Commission, 1984), 43.
30. Ramsey, *Annals of Tennessee*, 157-59.
31. Brown, *Old Frontiers*, 159.
32. J. G. Hamilton, ed., "Revolutionary Diary of William Lenoir," *Journal of Southern History* 6 (May 1940): 247-59.
33. Brown, *Old Frontiers*, 154-156.
34. James Mooney, *Myths of the Cherokees*, Nineteenth Annual Report of the Bureau of American Ethnology (Washington, DC: Government Printing Office, 1900), I, 53.
35. Oliver Taylor, *Historic Sullivan* (Bristol, TN: King Printing Company, 909), 68.
36. Duane H. King, "Long Island of the Holston: Cherokee Sacred Ground," *Journal of Cherokee Studies* I (Fall 1976): 120-21.
37. Taylor, *Historic Sullivan*, 68-69.
38. Ibid., 70.
39. Samuel Cole Williams, "William Tatum, Wataugan," *Tennessee Historical Magazine* 7 (July 1921): 176-78, reprinted in *Journal of Cherokee Studies,* 1 (Fall 1976): 128-29.
40. Taylor, *Historic Sullivan*, 70.
41. James W. Hagy and Stanley J. Folmsbee, "The Lost Archives of the Cherokee Nation, Part III, 1777," *East Tennessee Historical Society Publications* 11 (1973): 95.
42. Ibid., 97.
43. Samuel Cole Williams, "Nathaniel Gist: Father of Sequoyah," *East Tennessee Historical Society Publications* 4 (1933): 51-53.
44. Samuel Cole Williams, *Tennessee During the Revolutionary War* (Knoxville: University of Tennessee Press, 1974), 48-60; J.G. Hamilton, ed., "Revolutionary Diary of William Lenoir," 247-59.
45. Williams, *Tennessee During the Revolutionary War*, 91-99.
46. Samuel Cole Williams, ed., *Early Travels in the Tennessee Country, 1540-1800* (Johnson City, TN: Watauga Press 1928), 256.

47. John Rogers, et al. US Congress, House, Committee on Indian Affairs, *Memorial of John Rogers, Principal Chief and James Carey and Thomas L. Rodgers, Chiefs and Head Men, Being Members of a Committee on Behalf of the Cherokee Old Settlers West of the Mississippi, for themselves and Their People*, 28th Cong., 1st sess., H. Doc. 235, 3; Charles C. Royce, *The Cherokee Nation of Indians: A Narrative of Their Official Relations with the Colonial and Federal Governments* (Chicago: Smithsonian Institution Press, 1975), reprint of pages 121-378 in the *Fifth Annual Report of the Bureau of American Ethnology* for the years 1883-1884 (Washington, DC: Government Printing Office, 1887), 76.

48. William L. Anderson and James A. Lewis, *A Guide to Cherokee Documents in Foreign Archives* (Metuchen, NJ and London: The Scarecrow Press, 1983), 600, 602.

49. Lawrence Kinnaird, *Spain in the Mississippi Valley, 1765-1794* (Washington DC: U.S. Government Printing Office, 1949), translations of materials from the Spanish Archives in the Bancroft Library, Annual Report of the American Historical Association for the Year 1945), 2: 254-55; Perez to Mira, 31 May 1788, *Spain in the Mississippi Valley*, 2:255.

50. Samuel S. Forman, Narrative of a Journey Down the Ohio and Mississippi in 1789-90," (Reprint, Bowie, MD: Heritage Books, 1990), 49-50; Arthur P. Whitaker, "Spain and the Cherokee Indians, 1783-1798," *North Carolina Historical Review* 4 (1927): 252-69;

51. Williams, ed., *Early Travels*, 256.

52. Woodward, *The Cherokees*, 109.

53. Louis Houck, ed., *The Spanish Regime in Missouri* (Chicago: R. R. Donnelley and Sons, 1909), 2: 83.

54. "Indian Chronicle," *Boston Gazette and Weekly Republican Journal*, July 28: 1. Boston.

55. Joseph Brown, "Captivity Narrative," *Southwestern Monthly Magazine* (1852): 11-16, 72-78; Royce, *The Cherokee Nation of Indians*, 43.

56. *American State Papers: Indian Affairs*, I: 543; Robertson 1899: 84-88.

57. Clarence Edwin Carter, *The Territorial Papers of the United States*, 26 vols. (Washington DC: Government Printing Office, 1934-62).

58. Mooney, *Myths of the Cherokees*, 78, 79.

Endnotes

Chapter 3

1. John P. Brown, "Eastern Cherokee Chiefs," *Chronicles of Oklahoma* 16, 1. (March 1938).
2. William G. McLoughlin, *Cherokee Renascence in the New Republic* (Princeton: Princeton University Press, 1986), xvii
3. McLoughlin, *Cherokee Renascence,* 299.
4. *The Territorial Papers of the United States*, comp. Clarence Edwin Carter (Washington: Government Printing Office, 1934-1962) 13: 228-29.
5. Charles C. Royce, *The Cherokee Nation of Indians: A Narrative of Their Official Relations with the Colonial and Federal Governments* (Chicago: Smithsonian Institution Press, 1975), 74; reprint of pages 121-378 in the *Fifth Annual Report of the Bureau of American Ethnology for the years 1883-1884* (Washington, DC: Government Printing Office, 1887).
6. Royce, *The Cherokee Nation of Indians*, 75.
7. Reuben Gold Thwaites, *Original Journals of the Lewis and Clark Expedition*m (Milwaukee: State Historical Society of Wisconsin, 1905; reprint, New York: Arno Press, 1969), 6: 112, citation refers to Arno edition.
8. McLoughlin, *Cherokee Renascence*, 145-69; Dianna Everett, *The Texas Cherokees: A People Between Two Fires, 1819-1840 (*Norman: University of Oklahoma Press, 1990), 10.
9. Royce, *The Cherokee Nation of Indians*, 75-76.
10. Carl I. Wheat, *Mapping the Transmississippi West* (San Francisco: Institute of Historical Cartography, 1957); Gary Moulton, *Atlas of the Lewis and Clark Expedition* (Lincoln: University of Nebraska Press, 1983).
11. Konnetue to Meigs, June 11, 1811; Konnetue, St. Francis to Return J. Meigs, Highwassee Garrision June 17, 1811.
12. Kannetoo to Meigs, March 14, 1813; Konnetue, Post of Ozark to R.J. Meigs, Highwassee Garrision March 14, 1813.
13. Meigs to Dearbourn, April 6, 1811. Meigs, Return J. Highwassee Garrison to Henry Dearbourn April 6, 1811, (Secretary of War, 1811, Washington, DC).
14. Anonymous, "1812 The Earthquake," *Aurora General Advertiser* (February 22):2-3. Philadelphia.
15. Thomas L. McKenny and James Hall, *History of the Indian Tribes of North America with Biographical Sketches and Anecdotes of the Principal Chiefs,* 3 (Philadelphia: Claxton Press, 1857), I: 64-65.
16. Louis Bringier, "Notices of the Geology, Mineralogy, Topography, Productions, and Aboriginal Inhabitants of the Regions Around the Mississippi and Its Confluent Waters," *American Journal of Science and Arts* 3, (1828): 39-41.

17. Talontiskee to R.J. Meigs March 14, 1813; Toluntiskee, Post of Ozark, Arkansas, to R.J. Meigs March 14, 1813.
18. Gary Moulton, ed. *The Papers of Chief John Ross, 1807-1839* (Norman: University of Oklahoma Press, 1985), 1: 10-11.
19. Ibid., 10-12.
20. "Treaty of Fort Jackson," 9 August 1814, 4826.2, John Ross Papers, Gilcrease Institute.
21. Pathkiller to Cherokee Delegation, 10 January 1816, 4026.18a; William C. Crawford to Return J. Meigs, 2 March 1816, 4026.22; John Lowry to James Madison, 19 February 1816, 4026.19a; Conversation between John Lowry and James Madison, 22 February 1816, 4026.17, John Ross Papers, Thomas Gilcrease Institute, Tulsa, Oklahoma.
22. Copy of Remarks of Andrew Jackson, no date, 4026.1978.1, John Ross Papers, Thomas Gilcrease Institute.
23. The 1797 date of origin seems to have emerged in the 1950s when fundraising efforts were underway to save the historic structure. See Gary E. Moulton, *John Ross Cherokee Chief* (Athens: University of Georgia Press, 1978), 6.
24. John Ross to Return J. Meigs, April 11, 1817, Record Group 75, M 208, Roll 7, National Archives; Moulton, *The Papers of Chief John Ross* (Norman: The University of Oklahoma Press, 1985), 1: 30.
25. John Ross to Calvin Jones, December 8, 1818, Miscellaneous Collections, Tennessee State Historical Society, Tennessee State Library and Archives, Nashville, as published in Moulton, *The Papers of Chief John Ross*, 1: 30.
26. Georgina G. DeWeese, W. Jeff Bishop, Henri D. Grissino-Mayer, Brian Parrish, and S. Michael Edwards, "Dendrochronological Dating of the The Chief John Ross House, Rossville, Georgia." *Southeastern Archaeology* 31 (Winter 2012): 221-30.
27. Modern builders of log cabins agree that trees should be felled in early winter. The cooler temperatures make for slower drying time that reduces log checking, crackin, and splitting. It's also easier to haul logs over hard or frozen ground. Logs for construction are seasoned by stacking off the ground with stickers or smaller logs in between the courses for maximum air flow around the logs and allowed to air dry for one to two years before use.
28. The last letter from John Ross with the Rossville address was to Hugh Montgomery dated February 23 or 27, 1827, Record Group 75, M 208, Roll 10, dated February 23 and Record Group 75, M 234, Roll 72, 373-374, dated February 27, National Archives; On August 1, 1827, Ross wrote to James Barbour from his new home at the Head of Coosa, Record Group 75, M 234, Roll 72, 251-3, National Archives; See also Moulton, *The Papers of Chief John Ross*, 129-130.

Endnotes

29. Royce, *The Cherokee Nation of Indians*, 88.
30. Ibid., 76.
31. Ibid., 90.
32. Ibid., 94.
33. Ibid., 115-117.
34. Resolution of National Committee and Council, 31 October 1831, John Ross Papers, Gilcrease Institute, 4026.99; *The Constitution and Laws of the Cherokee Nation* (Washington, DC: Gales and Seaton, 1840), 6-15, 22-25, 33. See also Duane King, "Sequoyah or George Guess (Gist)," *Dictionary of Georgia Biography,* ed. Kenneth Coleman and Stephen Gurr (Athens: University of Georgia Press, 1983), 2: 878-80.
35. Ghigooie was born about 1730; William Shorey was born about 1720 and died on board the frigate *L'Epreue* on June 4, 1762, according to the ship's log kept by Capt. Peter Blake. A microfilm copy can be found in the Museum of the Cherokee Indian Archives, Cherokee, North Carolina.
36. The Shoreys' oldest daughter was Annie Shorey, who was born about 1746 and died on May 28, 1825. Annie married John McDonald (ca 1747-ca 1824), who emigrated from Scotland to Charleston, South Carolina in 1766. In 1770 he was appointed assistant superintendent for Indian affairs. Their daughter Mary Molly McDonald was born on November 1, 1770, and died in 1808.
37. See John P. Brown, *Old Frontiers: The Story of the Cherokee Indians from the Earliest Times to the Date of Their Removal to the West, 1838* (Kingsport, TN: Southern Publishers, 1938), 163.
38. Moulton, *John Ross: Cherokee Chief*, 5-6.
39. Samuel Cole Williams, "Christian Missions to the Overhill Cherokees," *Chronicles of Oklahoma*, 12 (March 1934), 66.
40. Emmet Starr, *History of the Cherokee Indians and Their Legends and Folklore* (Oklahoma City: The Warden Company, 1921), 410.
41. Royce, *The Cherokee Nation of Indians*, 120.
42. Ibid., 121-22.
43. Letter from J. H. Eaton to Colonel Ward, 2 August 1830, 4026.77; Letter from John E. Wool to Cherokee People, 19 September 1836, 4026.345, John Ross Papers, Thomas Gilcrease Institute.
44. Francis Paul Prucha, *The Great Father: The United States Government and the American Indians* (Lincoln: University of Nebraska Press, 1984), 1: 206.
45. Note from Kooweeskoowee, no date, 4026.3047, John Ross Papers, Thomas Gilcrease Institute.
46. Letter from W.W. [William Wirt] to Geo. R. Gilmer, Governor of Georgia. Concerning legal

representation of Cherokees, 4 June 4 1830, 4026.71; William Wirt to John Ross, 4 June 1830, 4026.72, as cited in Mouton, *The Papers of Cherokee Chief John Ross,* 1: 189-190.

47. John Ross to William Wirt June 8, 1832, Wirt Papers, Maryland Historical Society, Baltimore, as cited in Moulton, *The Papers of Cherokee Chief John Ross,* 244-6.

48. Samuel Rhea Gammon, Jr., *The Presidential Campaign of 1832* (Baltimore: The Johns Hopkins Press, 1922).

49. James Atkins Schackford, *David Crockett: The Man and Legend* (Westport, Connecticut: Greenwood Press, 1981), 116-117; see also Donna Akers "Native Nations in an Age of Western Expansion, 1820-80," in *American Indians American Presidents: A History,* ed. Clifford Trafzer (Washington, DC: Smithsonian Institution Press, 2009), 76.

50. John Ross to David Crockett, 13 January 1831, Ross Papers, Newberry Library, as cited in Gary Moulton, *The Papers of Chief John Ross*, 1: 210-212.

Endnotes

Chapter 4

1. Jack Weatherford, *Indian Givers: How the Indians of the Americas Transformed the World* (New York: Ballantine Books, 1988), 70-71.
2. Ibid., 63-73.
3. Ibid., 42-45.
4. Ulrich B. Phillips, *Georgia and State Rights* (Antioch, Ohio, 1968), 29-35.
5. *Ratification of the Agreement Between the United States and Georgia, by the Legislature of the Latter* (Washington City, 1802), 5-8.
6. Carl J. Vipperman, "Forcibly If We Must: The Georgia Case for Cherokee Removal," *Journal of Cherokee Studies* (Spring 1978): 103-110.
7. Richard Peters, *The Case of the Cherokee Nation against the State of Georgia* (Philadelphia: John Grigg, 1831), 265-66.
8. Wilson Lumkin, *The Removal of the Cherokee Indians from Georgia, 1827-1841* (New York, 1971), 39-40.
9. *Worcester v. Georgia*, 6 Peters 515.
10. Lewis Cass, Secretary of War, to John Ellis Wool, June 20, 1836, *American State Papers*, No. 744, 549.
11. M. M. Payne to Roger Jones, June 17, 1836, S. Doc. 120, at 3; John Ellis Wool to Alexander Macomb, Commanding US Army, October 12, 1836, S. Doc. 120, at 47.
12. War Department Special Orders, June 20, 1836, 37.
13. John E. Wool to Lewis Cass July 22 and July 25, 1836. National Archives.
14. John E. Wool to Alexander Macomb, August 1, 1836, S. Doc.120, at 23-24.
15. John E. Wool to R. Jones, August 8, 1836, S. Doc.120, at 25.
16. John E. Wool letter, November 6, 1836. *American State Papers.*
17. C.A. Harris to John E. Wool, 1836.
18. This resulted in the landmark decision *Worcester v. Georgia* in 1832.
19. Elizur Butler to David Greene, June 1, 1838.
20. Brig. Gen. Charles Floyd, commander of the Georgia Militia reported the numbers of Indians disembarking on June 9.
21. The actual encampment was upstream of Ross's Landing near Citico Creek. Henry W. Two copies of Wiltse's manuscript are on file in the Chattanooga Public Library under TNR, 976.882.
22. A. E. Blunt to David Greene, secretary to the American Board of Commissioners for Foreign Missions (Boston), Candy's Creek Station, May 28, 1838. Houghton Library,

Cambridge, Massachusetts.
23. Scott to Poinsett, June 18, 1838, National Archives, M-234, Roll 115.
24. Stephen Foreman to David Greene, May 31, 1838.
25. *The Niles Register*, August 18, 1838.
26. Papers of Winfield Scott, Record Group 75, National Archives.
27. Robert Hodsden, the physician for the Whiteley detachment reported an even higher number. He stated that either 73 or 74 of the 875 members of the detachment died in route. His journal, "Medical Report of Dr. Robert Hodsden," is the in the collection of the Five Civilized Tribes Museum in Muskogee, Oklahoma.
28. Ibid.
29. The highest estimate given by John Ross on the cost of removal was $13,000,000. See "Memorandum of Estimates Regarding the Removal of the Cherokee Nation." Samuel L. Southard Papers, Library, Princeton University, Princeton, New Jersey. For a detailed accounting of addtional claims submitted by John Ross, see US H.R. Rep. No. 288. "Removal of the Cherokees," 27th Congress, 3rd Session. (Washington: No Imprint, 1843).
30. (Starr, 1969: 104-5; McLoughlin, 1993: 3-4).

Endnotes

Chapter 5

1. Grant Foreman, "The Murder of Elias Boudinot," *Chronicles of Oklahoma* 12 (March, 1934): 19-24.
2. William Potter Ross (August 28, 1820-July 28, 1891) was born on the Ross ancestral farm, at the foot of Lookout Mountain near Chattanooga on the Tennessee River. His mother was a sister of Principal Chief John Ross, the benefactor who paid for his education.
3. John Mix Stanley, *William Potter Ross*, oil on canvas, 1843, Thomas Gilcrease Institute, Tulsa, Oklahoma.
4. William Potter Ross taught the Cherokee children of Fourteen Mile Creek in their log cabin school-house during the 1842-43 school year, but after hearing the wampum explained by Assistant Chief Major George Lowry to the chiefs and warriors of twenty-one nations and tribes at the Grand Council of Peace in 1843, he decided to devote his life to Cherokee public service.
5. Return Jonathan Meigs (April 3, 1812-August 6, 1850) was the oldest son of Timothy Meigs and Elizabeth (Holt). He was the son-in-law of Principal Chief John Ross, having married the oldest daughter Jane (Jennie) in 1838 at Cleveland, Tennessee, just before the forced removal.
6. The original letter from William P. Ross and Jane Ross Meigs to John Ross, November 5 and 7, 1845, is in the Gilcrease Museum and was published in Gary E. Moulton, ed., *The Papers of Chief John Ross*, (Norman: University of Oklahoma Press, 1985), 2: 271-274. Also see Patricia Lockwood, "The Legacy of Caleb Starr," *Chronicles of Oklahoma* 61 (Spring 1983), 302-3; Carolyn Thomas Foreman, "The Lighthorse in Indian Territory," *Chronicles of Oklahoma* 34 (1956): 21.
7. James Starr and nineteen other Treaty Party members signed the controversial Treaty of New Echota on December 29, 1835, ceding all remaining Cherokee lands east of the Mississippi in exchange for land in the Indian Territory. He emigrated with the B. B. Cannon detachment of 365 Cherokees, which left the Cherokee Agency on the Hiwassee River on August 14, 1837, and arrived at Mr. Bean's in the Indian Territory just across the Arkansas line on December 27, 1837.
8. The typical manner of painting in preparation for war was to paint the face half red and half black with a vertical dividing line down the length of the nose.
9. Mary Starr was born in May 1829, Cherokee Nation East, married Andrew Easky in 1850, and died in 1909, Adair County, Oklahoma.
10. The *Van Buren Arkansas Intellingencer* issue of November 15, 1845, included a letter of George Starr dated November 12, 1845, Evansville, describing the murder of his brother James Starr by police. The letter also indicates that James Starr's sons Buck Starr and Washington

Starr were wounded, that Sewell Rider was shot and killed, and Jos Starr, son of James Starr, was wounded. It reported that police attacked the nine year-old son of Jesse Mayfield, a nephew of the Starrs.

11. The gravesite was marked by an elongated triangular uninscribed block of limestone. James Starr's daughter Lucinda Malzerine "Lucy" Starr, born on October 19, 1838, Goingsnake District, Cherokee Nation, was seven years old and present at the funeral of James Starr. She identified the gravesite for her granddaughter, who was born in 1909, who identified it for David Hampton in 1972, who identified it for the author and others in 2012. Lucinda married George Washington Adair VI about 1859, Sequoyah District, Cherokee Nation, Indian Territory, and had three children with him Mattie, born 1860; Samuel T. born 1866; and Lula "Ah-No-Hee" born in 1869. She later married William T. Russell on August 25, 1872. She died on August 24, 1925, Stilwell, Adair County, Oklahoma.

12. Matthew Arbuckle (December 28, 1778-June 11, 1852) was born in Greenbrier County, Virginia, now West Virginia. He entered the US Army as an ensign in 1799, became a captain in 1806, a major in 1812, and was commissioned as colonel of the Seventh US Infantry Regiment in 1820. In 1830 he was brevetted brigadier general. He was in command of the military forces stationed in the eastern part of the present state of Oklahoma for nearly twenty years.

13. Cave Johnson Couts noted in his diary, "on the morning of 13 Nov[ember] I went out hunting and on my return in the evening found that the whole company had left for the line…Next day I overtook them and heir have had the most disagreeable and disgusting duty that any officer ever was placed in service." He had graduated from West Point in 1843 and arrived at Fort Gibson on August 17, 1845.

14. Cave Johnson Couts (November 11, 1821-June 10, 1874) was born in Springfield, Tennessee, the third of twelve children born to William and Nancy Johnson Couts. He attended schools in Springfield, Tennessee, and Hollowell Preparatory Academy in Alexandria, Virginia.

15. Letter of General Matthew Arbuckle to Acting Chief George Lowery, November 15, 1845, printed in the *Cherokee Advocate*.

16. George Lowery (or Agina Agili "Rising Fawn") was born about 1770 at the town of Taskeegee on the Little Tennessee River in present-day Monroe County, Tennessee. He was the son of a Scottish trader by the same name (b. 1740) and a Cherokee woman named Oolootsa (b. 1748), who was the daughter and granddaughter of Echota chiefs. He was a cousin of Sequoyah or George Gist (1776-1843), who was also born at Taskeegee and who later devised the Cherokee writing system.

17. Letter of George Lowery to Cherokee Agent James McKissick, November 26, 1845.

Endnotes

18. S. Doc. No. 298, 29th Cong., 1st Sess., pt. 3, no. 7-D, at 169 (1846).
19. Major Bonneville's explorations in the far west were widely publicized, and he, himself, had been immortalized in Washington Irving's third book on the American West entitled *The Adventures of Captain Bonneville*, published in 1837.
20. S. Doc. No. 298, 29th Congress First Session, April 13, 1846, at 199 (1846).
21. Journal of Cave J. Couts, CT 2541 (1-2), 6, Huntington Library, San Marino, California.
22. Ibid., 5.
23. Couts wrote in his diary, "We frequently attend dances around, and I enjoy myself at them exceedingly–have had several at our camp, and dance and play always until morning. The favorite play, is that which has the most kissing in it, and which all (no exception) are very fond of–they can kiss quicker, and smack louder than you can imagine–and very sweet at that."
24. The English translation is "Stand." A man referred to as "Big Stan" was a member of Tucquo's group during the murders of James Starr and Suel Rider on November 9, 1845.
25. William G. McLoughlin, *After the Trail of Tears: The Cherokee Struggle for Sovereignthy, 1839-1880* (Chapel Hill: University of North Carolina Press, 1993), 56.
26. Moulton, ed. *The Papers of Chief John Ross, 1807-1839*, 2: 712-13.
27. McLoughlin, *After the Trail of Tears*, 58.
28. Articles of a treaty made and concluded at Washington, DC, between the United States of America by commissioners Edmund Burke, William Armstrong, and Albion K. Parris, and John Ross, principal chief of the Cherokee Nation; David Vann; William S. Coody; Richard Taylor; T. H. Walker; Clement V. McNair; Stephen Foreman; John Drew; and Richard Fields, delegates duly appointed by the regularly constituted authorities of the Cherokee Nation; George W. Adair, John A. Bell, Stand Watie, Joseph M. Lynch, John Huss, and Brice Martin, a delegation appointed by and representing that portion of the Cherokee tribe of Indians and recognized as the Treaty Party; John Brown, Captain Dutch, John L. McCoy, Richard Drew, and Ellis Phillips, delegates appointed by and representing that portion of the Cherokee Tribe of Indians known and recognized as Western Cherokees, or Old Settlers. I like Ellis Phillips, delegates appointed by, and representing, that portion of the Cherokee Tribe of Indians known and recognized as Western Cherokees, or Old Settlers.
29. Article 2 reads: "All difficulties and differences heretofore existing between the several parties of the Cherokee Nation are hereby settled and adjusted, and shall, as far as possible, be forgotten and forever buried in oblivion."

30. Journal of Cave J. Couts, 6
31. McLoughlin, *After the Trail of Tears*, 92
32. Meigs to Dearbourn, January 22, 1810. Return J. Highwassee Garrison to Henry Dearbourn April 6, 1811, (Secretary of War, 1811, Washington, DC) BIA RCIAT.
33. Dianna Everett, *The Texas Cherokees: A People Between Two Fires, 1819-1840* (Norman: University of Oklahoma Press, 1990), 23.
34. Ibid., 51; Barker, 1928, 274.
35. Woldert, 1923, 193; Everett, *The Texas Cherokees*, 51.
36. Ibid., 71, 104-5.
37. Ibid., 108-9.
38. McLoughlin, *After the Trail of Tears*, 153.
39. Ibid., 345; Mooney, 1900, 15.
40. Dale, 1939, 108; McLoughlin, *After the Trail of Tears*, 158.
41. Ibid., 125
42. McLoughlin, *After the Trail of Tears*, 279, 125.

Endnotes

Chapter 6

1. "John R. Ridge to Stand Watie, July 2, 1849," in Edward E. Dale and Gaston Litton, eds, *Cherokee Cavaliers*, University of Oklahoma Press, 64-66.
2. T. L. Ballenger, "The Keetoowahs and Their Dances," *Chronicles of Oklahoma*, 61 (Summer 1983): 194-196.
3. Gary E. Moulton, *John Ross: Cherokee Chief* (Athens: The University of Georgia Press, 1978), 166-8.
4. Ibid., 168-69.
5. "William P. Adair and James M. Bell to Stand Watie, August 29, 1861," in Dale and Gaston, *Cherokee Cavaliers*, 108-110.
6. Moulton, *John Ross: Cherokee Chief*, 169-70.
7. Ibid., 172.
8. Ibid., 172-173.
9. Kenny Franks, *Stand Watie and the Agony of the Cherokee Nation* (Memphis: Memphis State University Press, 1979), 117-120.
10. Ibid., 121-122.
11. Cherrie Adair Moore, "William Penn Adair," *Chronicles of Oklahoma*, Vol. x, xx, 37-38.
12. Ben Yagoda, *Will Rogers: A Biography* (Norman: University of Oklahoma Press, 2000), xx-xx.
13. Mary Jane Warde, *When the Wolfe Came: The Civil War and the Indian Territory* (Fayetteville: University of Arkansas Press, 2013), 74-75.
14. John Bartlett Meserve, "Chief William Potter Ross," *Chronicles of Oklahoma*, 15 (March 1937): 25.
15. John Bartlett Meserve, "Chief Lewis Downing and Chief Charles Thompson," *Chronicles of Oklahoma*, 16 (September 1938): 317-320.
16. Franks, *Stand Watie and the Agony of the Cherokee Nation*, 118.
17. Warde, *When the Wolfe Came*, 83-84.
18. Ibid., 98-99.
19. Franks, *Stand Watie and the Agony of the Cherokee Nation*, 125-126.
20. Annie Heloise Abel, *The American Indian as a Participant in the Civil War* (Cleveland: Arthur Clarke, 1919), 108-122.
21. Whit Edwards, *The Prairie Was on Fire: Eyewitness Accounts of the Civil War in the Indian Territory*, (Oklahoma City: Oklahoma Historical Society, 2001), 17-18.
22. Ibid., 19-20.
23. Ibid., 21-22.
24. Moulton, *John Ross: Cherokee Chief*, 174-75.

25. Wiley Britton, *The Union Indian Brigade* (Kansas City, MO, Franklin Hudson Publications), 82-83.
26. Muriel Wright, "Notes on the Life of Mrs. Hannah Worchester Hicks Hitchcock and the Park Hill Press," *Chronicles of Oklahoma*, 19 (December 1941): 350-51.
27. Ibid., 350.
28. Ibid., 351.
29. Wiley Britton, "Some Reminiscences of the Cherokee People Returning to Their Homes the Exiles of a Nation," *Chronicles of Oklahoma*, 6 (June 1928): 174-75.
30. Moulton, *John Ross: Cherokee Chief*, 177-78.
31. Britton, *The Union Indian Brigade*, 84.
32. Carolyn Foreman, "The Coodey Family of Indian Territory," *Chronicles of Oklahoma*, 25 (Winter 1947): 323-41.
33. Edwards, *The Prairie Was on Fire*, 57-71.
34. Edward E. Dale, "Additional Letters of General Stand Watie," *Chronicles of Oklahoma*," 1 (October 1921): 135-36.
35. Warde, *When the Wolfe Came*, 192-94.
36. Franks, *Stand Watie and the Agony of the Cherokee Nation*, 144-45.
37. Ibid., 145.
38. Warde, *When the Wolfe Came*, 195-96.
39. Ibid., 196-97.
40. Edwards, *The Prairie Was on Fire*, 90-92.
41. Franks, *Stand Watie and the Agony of the Cherokee Nation*, 159-60.
42. "The Sinking of the J. R. Williams, *Chronicles of Oklahoma*, Vol. x xxx,
43. Franks, *Stand Watie and the Agony of the Cherokee Nation*, 170-72.
44. Edwards, *The Prairie Was on Fire*, 120.
45. Ibid., 132.

Endnotes

Chapter 7

1. William P. Ross to Willie Ross, December 27, 1864, Ross Papers, Gilcrease Institute.
2. Justin Harlin to W. G. Coffin, September 2, 1863, *Annual Report for the Office of Indian Affairs*, (Washington, DC: Government Printing Office, 1864), 179
3. William G. McLoughlin, *After the Trail of Tears: The Cherokee's Struggle for Sovereignty, 1839-1880* (Chapel Hill: University of North Carolina Press, 1993) 217.
4. Ibid., 217.
5. Ibid., 219.
6. Ibid., 224-27.
7. John Bartlett Meserve, "Chief William Potter Ross," *Chronicles of Oklahoma*, 15 (March, 1937): 21-28.
8. Ibid., 280.
9. Ibid., 280.
10. McLoughlin, *After the Trail of Tears*, 246.
11. John Bartlett Meserve, "Chief Lewis Downing and Chief Charles Thompson," *Chronicles of Oklahoma*, 16 (September, 1938): 315-319.
12. Ibid., 320-22.
13. Ibid., 322.
14. McLoughlin, *After the Trail of Tears*, 248-250.
15. Ibid., 251.
16. Leslie Hewes, "Cherokee Occupance in the Oklahoma Ozarks and Prairie Plains," *Chronicles of Oklahoma*, 22 (Fall, 1944): 327.
17. Ibid., 330.
18. T. L. Ballenger, "The Life and Times of Jeff Thompson Parks: Pioneer, Educator, Jurist," *Chronicles of Oklahoma*, 30 (Summer, 1952): 173-174.
19. Ibid., 174-180.
20. Harold Keith, "Memories of George W. Mayes," *Chronicles of Oklahoma*, 24 (Spring, 1946): 44-51.
21. Ben Yagoda, *Clem Rogers: Rancher, Businessman* (Norman: University of Oklahoma Press, 19xx).
22. V. A. Travis, "Life in the Cherokee Nation a Decade After the Civil War," *Chronicles of Oklahoma*, 4 (March, 1924): 29-30.
23. Bob Blackburn, *Crossroads of Commerce: A History of Free Enterprise in Oklahoma* (Oklahoma City: Oklahoma Historical Society, 2016), 18.
24. Duncan M. Aldrich, "General Stores in the Cherokee Nation," *Chronicles of Oklahoma*, 79 (Summer, 1979): 129-130.

25. Ibid., 130.
26. Ibid., 130.
27. McLaughlin, *After the Trail of Tears*, 265-268.
28. Aldrich, "General Stores in the Cherokee Nation," 123.
29. Charles G. Royce, *The Cherokee Nation of Indians* (Chicago: Alden, 1975) 242-47.
30. Travis, "Life in the Cherokee Nation," 22.
31. Ibid., 24-25.
32. Ibid., 23.
33. T. L. Ballenger, "The Cultural Relations Between Two Pioneer Communities," *Chronicles of Oklahoma*, 34 (Fall, 1956): 294.
34. Travis, "Life in the Cherokee Nation," 23-24.
35. Carl T. Steen, "The Home for the Insane, Deaf, Dumb, and Blind of the Cherokee Nation," *Chronicles of Oklahoma*, 21 (December, 1943): 403.
36. Ibid., 405-406.
37. Travis, "Life in the Cherokee Nation," 16-17.
38. Renard Strickland, *Fire and the Spirits: Cherokee Law from Clan to Court* (Norman: University of Oklahoma Press), 146-47.
39. McLoughlin, *After the Trail of Tears*, 262-263.
40. Morris Wardell, *A Political History of the Cherokee Nation* (Norman: University of Oklahoma Press, 1938), 260-61.
41. McLaughlin, *After the Trail of Tears*, 299-301.
42. Ibid., 313.

Chapter 8

1. James W. Parins, *Elias Cornelius Boudinot: A Life on the Cherokee Border* (Lincoln: University of Nebraska Press, 2006), 110.
2. Ibid., 116.
3. Ibid., 126.
4. O. B. Campbell, *Vinita, I. T.: The Story of a Frontier Town of the Cherokee Nation, 1871 to 1907* (Oklahoma City: Colorgraphics, 1969), 35-55.
5. Ibid., 35-55.
6. Ibid., 550.
7. Ibid., 41-42.
8. Ibid., 69-83.
9. Hewes, 327-328.
10. Ibid., 331-335.
11. *Annual Report of the Commissioner of Indian Affairs for the Secretary of the Interior for the Year 1886* (Washington, DC: Government Printing Office, 1886), 147-49.
12. Ibid., 149.
13. Grant Foreman, *A History of Oklahoma* (Norman: University of Oklahoma Press, 1942), 203.
14. John Bartlett Meserve, "Chief Charles Thompson," *Chronicles of Oklahoma*, 16 (Winter, 1938): 316-24.
15. William G. McLoughlin, *After the Trail of Tears: The Cherokee Struggle for Sovereignty, 1839-1880* (Chapel Hill: University of Northc Carolina Press, 1993), 340.
16. Ibid., 315.
17. Ibid., 315.
18. Ibid., 315.
19. *Cherokee Advocate* (Tahlequah, Indian Territory), Dec. 13, 1878.
20. Ibid.
21. McLaughlin, *After the Trail of Tears*, 285.
22. Ibid., 283-85.
23. Ibid., 348-52.
24. Russell Thornton, *The Cherokees: A Population History* (Lincoln: University of Nebraska Press, 1990), 106-107; Campbell, *Vinita, IT*, 83.
25. McLoughlin, *After the Trail of Tears*, 360.
26. Ibid., 369.
27. Angie Debo, *And Still the Waters Run: the Betrayal of the Five Civilized Tribes* (Princeton

University Press, 1940), 21-22.
28. Spencer Stephens, *The Indian Question Discussed*, 1887. A document in the Western History Collections, Norman, Oklahoma; Parins, 170-171.
29. William Savage, "Of Cattle and Corporations: The Rise, Progress and Termination of the Cherokee Strip Live Stock Association." *Chronicles of Oklahoma*, 71 (Spring, 1993): 138 -151.
30. Ibid., 156.
31. Debo, *And Still the Waters Run*, 27-30.
32. Hendrix, 42-44.
33. Ibid., 52-54.
34. Ibid., 60-65.
35. Debo, *And Still the Waters Run*, 34-35.
36. Ibid., 45-50.
37. Ibid., 87-88.
38. Ibid., 75-76.
39. Kent Carter, "Deciding Who Can Be Cherokee: Enrollment Records of the Dawes Commission," *Chronicles of Oklahoma*, 69 (Spring, 1991): 174-202.
40. Dawes Commission Report, 1902, 31-34.
41. Debo, *And Still the Waters Run*, 46-47.
42. Ibid., 161-164.

Chapter 9

1. Angie Debo, *And Still the Waters Run: The Betrayal of the Five Civilized Tribes*, 4th ed. (Princeton: Princeton University, 1991), 168-69.
2. Ibid., 169.
3. Ibid., 170.
4. Daniel F. Littlefield, Jr., *The Cherokee Freedmen: From Emancipation to American Citizenship*, (Westport, CT: Greenwood Press, 1978), 254-55.
5. Nancy Hope Sober, *The Intruders: The Illegal Residents of the Cherokee Nation 1866-1907*, (Marceline, MO: Walsworth Publishing Co., 1991), 124-25.
6. Rennard Strickland, *The Indians in Oklahoma*, (Norman: The University of Oklahoma Press, 1980), 53.
7. Ibid., 54.
8. Ibid., 72, 73.
9. Henry Cabot Lodge, ed., *The History of Nations*, 3rd ed., (New York: P. F. Collier & Son, 1913), 1: 3-18.
10. Sharon O'Brien, *American Indian Tribal Governments*, (Norman: University of Oklahoma Press, 1989), 263.
11. *Wikipedia*, "American Indian boarding schools," accessed February 26, 2017, https://en.wikipedia.org/wike/American_Indian_boarding_schools.
12. *Encyclopedia of Oklahoma History and Culture*, "Chilocco Indian Agricultural School," by K. Tsianina Lornawaima, accessed February 26, 2017, www.okhistory.org.
13. Morris L. Wardell, *A Political History of the Cherokee Nation*, (Norman: University of Oklahoma Press, 1938), 348-49.
14. Debo, *And Still the Waters Run*, 51-58.
15. Department of the Interior, *Annual Report from the Commissioner of the Five Civilized Tribes, June 30, 1899*, (Washington, DC: US Government Printing Office, 1899), 91-92.
16. Robert H. Skelton, *A History of the Educational System of the Cherokee Nation, 1801-1910*, (Ann Arbor: University Microfilms, 1970), 200-20.
17. Ibid., 207-210.
18. James D. McCullagh, *The Teachers of the Cherokee Nation Public Schools: 1870-1907*, (Tahlequah: Cherokee Heritage Press, 2010), 51-54.
19. Natalie Panther, *To Make Us Independent: The Education of Young Men at the Cherokee Male Seminary, 1851-1910*, (Ann Arbor: University Microfilms, 1970), 64-71.
20. Skelton, *History of Educational System*, 242-49.

21. Ibid., 139.
22. Mrs. R. L. Fite, *Cherokee National Female Seminary: An Illustrated Souvenir Catalog*, (Chilocco, OK: Indian Print Shop, 1906), 11, 23.
23. Panther, *The Education of Young Men*, 134-35.
24. Ibid., 139.
25. Debo, *And Still the Waters Run*, 10-13.
26. Kent Carter, *The Dawes Commission and the Allotment of the Five Civilized Tribes, 1893-1914*, (Orem: Ancestry.com 1999) 176-177.
27. Debo, *And Still the Waters Run*, 183-84.
28. William G. McLoughlin, *After the Trail of Tears: The Cherokee's Struggle for Sovereignty* (Chapel Hill: University of North Carolina, 1993), 367, 380.
29. Ibid., 368-369.
30. Sober, *The Intruders*, 133.
31. Debo, *And Still the Waters Run*, 89-91.
32. Georgia Rae Leeds, *The United Keetoowah Band of Cherokee Indians In Oklahoma* (New York: Peter Lang Publishing, Inc., 2000), 10.
33. John Ross, Jr., "Keetoowah Organizations," (Interview aligned with prepared narrative held with W. Neil Morton at Cherokee Nation on April 03, 2017, entirety of prepared narrative included in Chapter 9).
34. Diane Camurat, "The American Indian in the Great War," submitted to the Institute Charles V of the University of Paris VII, 1993, accessed November 18, 2016, https://net.lib.byu.edu/estu/wwi/comment/Cmrts/Cmrt6.html.
35. *Wikipedia*, "Cherokee Military History," accessed on December 12, 2016, https://en.wikipedia.org/wiki/Cherokee_military_history_.
36. *Wikipedia*, "Code Talkers," accessed December 13, 2016. https://en.wikipedia.org.wiki.Code_talker.
37. Emmet Starr, *History of the Cherokee Indians and Their Legends and Folklore*, (Oklahoma City: Warden Co., 1921), 485.
38. Lewis Merriam, ed., *The Problem of Indian Administration*, (Baltimore: The John Hopkins Press, 1928) online facsimile, accessed January 1, 2017, http://www.eric.ed.gov/PDFS/E0087573.pdf., 3-15.
39. *Literary Digest*, "A Bill of Rights for the Indians," (April 7, 1938), accessed online April 6, 2017, http://historymatters.gmu.edu/d/5059/.
40. O'Brien, *American Indian Tribal Governments*, 81.

41. Strickland, *The Indians in Oklahoma*, 72.
42. Digital History, "Overview of the Great Depression," accessed December 17, 2016, http://www.digitalhistory.uh.edu/era.cfm?eralID= 14Ssmital=1.
43. Joseph H. Carter, *Never Met a Man I Didn't Like – The Life and Writings of Will Rogers* (New York: Avon Books, 1991), vii-ix, 3-47.
44. Albert L. Wahrhaftig, "A Report on the Cherokee Indians in Oklahoma," *American Indian Economic Development*, ed. Sam Stanley (Paris: Mouton Publishers, 1948), 412-23.
45. Strickland, *The Indians in Oklahoma*, 73.
46. Ibid., 72.
47. Martin Kelly, "Top 10 New Deal Programs," accessed May 7, 2016, http://american-history.about.com/programs.htm.
48. O'Brien, *American Indian Tribal Governments*, 82.
49. James Gribble Hochtritt, Jr., "Rural Cherokees, Chickasaws, Choctaws, Creeks, and Seminoles in Oklahoma During the Great Depression, " (Ph.D. diss., University of Oklahoma, 2000), 158.

Chapter 10

1. *Encyclopedia.com*, "American Indians 1933-1941, The Great Depression," accessed November 01, 2016, http://www.encyclopedia.com/education/news-and-education-magazines/american-indians.
2. *Encyclopedia.com*, "American Indians 1933-1941." accessed November 01, 2016, http://www.encyclopedia.com/education/news-and-education-magazines/american-indians.
3. John Collier, "Indians at Work," Magazine of Social Interpretation, 23, no. 6 (June 1934), accessed May 01, 2017, http://newdeal.feri.org/survey/34261.htm,
4. Bryan F. Rader, "Oklahoma Indian Welfare Act," Encyclopedia of Oklahoma History and Culture, accessed October 30, 2016, www.okhistory.org.
5. Howard Meredith, *Bartley Milam Principal Chief of the Cherokee Nation* (Muskogee, OK: Indian University Press, 1985), 30-31.
6. Ibid., 37-40.
7. Stanley W. Hoig, *The Cherokees and Their Chiefs: In the Wake of Empire* (Fayetteville: University of Arkansas Press, 1998), 261.
8. Bureau of Indian Affairs, "Who We Are – BIA," accessed March 10, 2017, https://www.bia.gov/WhoWeAre/BIA.
9. James Gribble Hochtritt, "Rural Cherokees, Chickasaws, Choctaws, Creeks and Seminoles in Oklahoma During the Great Depression" (Ph.D. Dissertation, University of Oklahoma, 2000), 6-7.
10. "Grand River Dam Authority" by Glen Roberson, accessed March 27, 2017, *The Encyclopedia of Oklahoma History and Culture,* www.okhistory.org.
11. Rader, "Oklahoma Indian Welfare Act," Encyclopedia of Oklahoma History and Culture.
12. Debo, *And Still the Waters Run*, 58-60.
13. Oklahoma Department of Commerce," Population of Selected Counties in Oklahoma: 1930 Census, January 4, 1934," Cherokee National Historical Society Archives (Park Hill, OK), 1-2.
14. Cherokee Nation Education Services, "Johnson O'Malley Report FY 16," Cherokee Nation Education Services file, Cherokee Nation Headquarters (Tahlequah, OK), 1-3.
15. Congress.Gov, "Indian Arts and Crafts Amendments Act of 1910, HR.725, Public Law 111-211," accessed May 06, 2017, https://www.congress.gov/bill/11th-congress/house-bill/725.
16. Shawna Morton Cain and Pamela Jumper Thurman, eds., *Cherokee National Treasures*, (Tahlequah, Oklahoma, Cherokee Nation, 2017), 71, 135, 265, 266, 274.
17. Wikipedia, "Felix Solomon Cohen," accessed May 11, 2017, https://en.wikipedia.org/wiki/Felix_S_Cohen.

18. Christopher B. Bean and Jack C. Montgomery, "A Little Big Man, " *Chronicles of Oklahoma*, 82: no. 4, (Winter, 2004/05), 480.

19. Ibid., 486, 487.

20. Cherokee Nation Veterans' Center Archives, vertical file, "Congressional Medal of Honor." (Tahlequah, OK)

21. Utility Press, Inc., "Biography of Rear Admiral Joseph James "Jocko" Clark," accessed September 23, 2017, http://jacklummus.com/Files/Files_rear-admiral-joseph-james-jocko-clark.htm.

22. *MaritimeQuest.com*, "Admiral Joseph James Clark USN" by Michael W. Pocock, accessed March 25, 2017, http://www.maritimequest.com/warship_directory/us_navy_pages/frigates/pages/clark_ffg.

23. Thomas D. Morgan, "Native Americans in World War II," *Army History: The Professional Bulletin of Army History,* 35 (Fall 1995), accessed May 8, 2016, http://www.shsu.edu/his_ncp/NAWWII.html.

24. Lori N. Curtis, "Camp Gruber," *Cherokee Quarterly – A Journal of Cherokee History and Culture* (Tulsa: Territorial Book Foundation, 1999), 84-85.

25. *Cherokee Nation News*, "Minutes Cherokee Nation Elected Community Representative Meeting," June 2, 1973, (Tahlequah, Oklahoma).

26. Armed Forces History Museum, "The Role of Native Americans During World War II," accessed November 18, 2016, http://armedforcesmuseum.com/the-role-of-native-americans-during-world-war-ii/.

27. *Boundless.com.*, "American Indians and the War Effort," accessed November 1, 2016, https://www.boundless.com/u-s-history-textbook.

28. Hoig, *The Cherokees and their Chiefs,* 262.

29. Georgia Rae Leeds, *The United Keetoowah Band of Cherokee Indians in Oklahoma*, (New York: Peter Lang Publishing, Inc., 1996) 14, 15.

30. Ibid., 16.

31. Ibid., 20.

32. Ibid., 21.

33. Ibid., 23.

34. *Muskogee Daily Phoenix Newspaper*, "1948 Convention," July 31, 1948(Muskogee, OK) 2.

35. Cherokee National Historical Society Archives, "Minutes of 1948 Convention," (Park Hill, OK).

36. Harvard Project on American Indian Economic Development, "The State of the Native Nations," (New York, Oxford: Oxford University Press, 2008), 97.

37. Cherokee National Historical Society Archives, "Stenotype Record of 1948 Convention Proceedings," (Park Hill, OK).

38. Leeds, *The United Keetoowah Band of Cherokee Indians in Oklahoma*, 22, 23.
39. Philip Viles, Jr., "Jesse Bartley Milam, Principal Chief, 1941-1949," *Cherokee Quarterly – A Journal of Cherokee History and Culture* (Tulsa: Territorial Book Foundation, 1999), 82.
40. *Cherokee Nation News*, "Tribal Office Progress," November 26, 1968, (Tahlequah, Oklahoma), 4.
41. Brad Agnew, Kenneth T. Jackson, ed., *In Scribner Encyclopedia of American Lives*, Vol. 2, 1986-1990, (New York: Charles Scribern's Sons), 476-478.
42. Ingrid P. Westmoreland, "Inter-Tribal Council of the Five Civilized Tribes," *Encyclopedia of Oklahoma History and Culture,* (accessed May 8, 2015), www.okhistory.org.
43. *Cherokee Nation News*, "Edmondson Introduces Bills," March 9, 1971, (Tahlequah, OK).
44. *The Tulsa Tribune*, "Cherokees Get Belated Justice," April 16, 1975, 1B (Tulsa, OK).
45. *Cherokee Nation Businesses/Products and Services*, Cherokee Nation, accessed August 8, 2017, http://www.cherokeenationbusinesses.com/PagesproductionServices.aspx.
46. Oklahoma State University Library, *Indian Affairs: Laws and Treaties,* accessed May 4,2015, http://digital.library.okstate.edu/kappler/.
47. *Cherokee Nation News*, "W.W. Keeler Wins Election," August 17, 1971, (Tahlequah, OK).
48. W. W. Keeler, "Inaugural Address," Northeastern State University, Special Collections, (Tahlequah, OK).
49. The Pictoral Press, "Constitution Change Postpones Filing," May 8, 1975. (Tahlequah, OK).
50. *Cherokee Nation News*, "Election of Principle Chief," August 8, 1975.
51. Cherokee National Historical Society Archives, "Biographical File - Ross O. Swimmer," (Park Hill, OK).
52. *Cherokee Nation News*, "Swimmer Appoints Advisory Council," November 7, 1975. (Tahlequah, OK).
53. *Cherokee Nation News*, " New Council Discusses Financial Status of Tribe," December 12, 1975. (Tahlequah, OK).
54. Constitution of the Cherokee Nation, Referendum June 26, 1976, Cherokee National Historical Society Archives. (Park Hill, OK).
55. *Cherokee Advocate*, "Swimmer Wins," June 1979, (Tahlequah, OK).
56. *Cherokee Advocate*, "1985, Year in Review," January, 1986, (Tahlequah, OK).
57. Cherokee National Historical Society Archives, "Wilma Mankiller," (Park Hill, OK).
58. Congress.Gov, "Indian Self-Determination and Educational Reform Act, PL 93-638," Accessed August 19, 2017, https://www.congress.gov/bill/93rd-congress/senate-bill/1017.
59. Neil Morton and Rennard Strickland, *Trying a New Way: Assessment of First Tier Tribes Under Self-Governance*, Northeastern State University Archives (Tahlequah, OK), Ch. 1.

Selected Bibliography

ᎠᎦᏓ ᏗᎪᏪᎵ ᏗᎫᏪᎶᏛᏯ ᏎᏉᎳᎤᎧ
Selected Bibliography

Books

Abel, Annie Heloise. *The American Indian as a Participant in the Civil War.* Cleveland: Arthur Clarke, 1919.

Agnew, Brad and Jackson, Kenneth T., eds., 1990 *Scribner Encyclopedia of American Lives, Vol. 2, 1986-1990.* New York: Charles Scribner's Sons.

Akers, Donna. "Native Nations in an Age of Western Expansion, 1828–80," in *American Indians–American Presidents: A History*, ed. Clifford Trafzer. Washington, DC: Smithsonian Institution Press, 2009.

Anderson, William L. and James A. Lewis, *A Guide to Cherokee Documents in Foreign Archives*, Metuchen, NJ and London: The Scarecrow Press, 1983.

Blackburn, Bob. *Crossroads of Commerce: A History of Free Enterprise in Oklahoma.* Oklahoma City: Oklahoma Historical Society, 2016.

Britton, Wiley. *The Union Indian Brigade in the Civil War.* Kansas City: Franklin Hudson Publications, 1922.

Britton, Wiley. "Some Reminiscences of the Cherokee People Returning to their Homes the Exiles of a Nation." *The Chronicles of Oklahoma*, 6 (June, 1928).

Brown, J. P., *Old Frontiers.* Kingsport, TN: Southern Publishers, Inc., 1938.

Cain, Shawna Morton and Pamela Jumper Thurman, 2017 *Cherokee National Treasures.* Tahlequah, Oklahoma: Cherokee Nation.

Campbell, O.B. *Vinita, I.T.: The Story of a Frontier Town of the Cherokee Nation, 1871 to 1907.* Oklahoma City: Colorgraphics, 1969.

Carter, Clarence Edwin, *The Territorial Papers of the United States.* Washington, DC: US Government Printing Office, 1934.

Carter, Joseph, *Never Met a Man I Didn't Like – The Life and Writings of Will Rogers.* New York: Avon Books, 1991.

Carter, Kent, *The Dawes Commission and the Allotment of the Five Civilized Tribes, 1893-1914.* Orem: Ancestry.com., 1999.

Cohen, Felix S. and Wilkins, David E., eds., 2006 *On the Drafting of Tribal Constitutions.* Norman: University of Oklahoma Press.

Corkran, David H. *The Cherokee Frontier: Conflict and Survival, 1740–62.* Norman: University of Oklahoma Press, 1962.

Cotterill, R. S. *The Southern Indians*. Norman: University of Oklahoma Press, 1954.

Crane, Verna. "The French on the Tennessee." *Mississippi Valley Historical Review*, III 9–13.

Dale, Edward E. and Gaston Litton, eds. *Cherokee Cavaliers*. Norman: University of Oklahoma Press, 1939.

Debo, Angie, *And Still the Waters Run: The Betrayal of the Five Civilized Tribes*, 4th ed. Princeton: Princeton University, 1991.

Department of the Interior, "Annual Report from the Commissioner of the Five Civilized Tribes," Washington: U. S. Government Printing Office, 1899.

Edwards, Edward. *Anecdotes of Painters Who have Resided or Been Born in England*. London: Luke Hansford and Sons, 1808.

Edwards, Whit. *The Prairie Was on Fire: Eyewitness Accounts of the Civil War in the Indian Territory*. Oklahoma City: Oklahoma Historical Society, 2001.

Everett, Diana. *The Texas Cherokees: A People Between Two Frontiers, 1819–1848*. Norman: University of Oklahoma Press, 1990.

Fite, Mrs. R. L., *Cherokee National Female Seminary: An Illustrated Souvenir Catalog*. Chilocco, Oklahoma, Indian Print Shop, 1906.

Foreman, Carolyn Thomas. *Indians Abroad, 1492–1938*. Norman: University of Oklahoma Press, 1943.

Foreman, Grant. *A History of Oklahoma*. Norman: University of Oklahoma Press, 1942.

Foreman, Samuel S. *Narrative of a Journey Down the Ohio and Mississippi in 1789–90*. Bowie, MD: Heritage Books, 1790.

Franks, Kenny. *Stand Watie and the Agony of the Cherokee Nation*. Memphis: Memphis State University Press, 1979.

Gammon, Samuel Rhea, Jr. *The Presidential Campaign of 1832*. Baltimore: The Johns Hopkins Press, 1922.

Gravers, Alergnon and William Vine Cronin. *A History of the Works of Sir Joshua Reynolds, P. R. A.* London: IV 1533, H. Graves and Company, 1889.

Greig, James, ed. *The Diairies of a Duchess: Extracts from the Diaries of the First Duchess of Northumberland*. London: Hodder and Stoughton, 1926.

Harvard Project on American Indian Economic Development, 2008 *The State of the Native Nations*. New York: Oxford University Press.

Selected Bibliography

Hewatt, Alexander. *An Historical Account of the Rise and Progress of the Colonies of South Carolina and Georgia.* London: Donaldson, 1779.

Hoig, Stanley W., 1998 *The Cherokees and Their Chiefs: In the Wake of Empire.* Fayetteville: University of Arkansas Press.

Houck, Louis, ed. *The Spanish Regime in Missouri.* Chicago: R. R. Donnelly and Sons, 1909.

King, Duane H. *The Memoirs of Lt. Henry Timberlake: The Story of a Soldier, Adventurer, and Emissary to the Cherokees, 1756–1765.* Cherokee, NC: Museum of the Cherokee Indian Press: 2007.

Kinnaird, Lawrence. *Spain in the Mississippi Valley, 1765–1794.* Washington, DC: US Government Printing Office, 1949.

Leeds, Georgia Rae, 1996 *The United Keetoowah Band of Cherokee Indians in Oklahoma.* New York: Peter Lang Publishing, Inc.

Lewis, T. M. N. and Madeline Kneberg. *Hiwassee Island: An Archaeological Account of Four Tennessee Indian Peoples.* Knoxville: University of Tennessee Press, 1946.

Littlefield, Jr., Daniel F., *The Cherokee Freedmen: From Emancipation to American Citizenship.* Westport, CN, Greenwood Press. 1978.

McCullagh, James D. *The Teachers of the Cherokee Nation Public Schools: 1870-1907.* Tahlequah: Oklahoma, Cherokee Heritage Press, 2010.

McKenny, Thomas L. and James Hall. *History of the Indian Tribes of North America with Biographical Sketches and Anecdotes of the Principal Chiefs.* Philadelphia: Claxton Press, 1857.

McLoughlin, William G., *After the Trail of Tears: The Cherokee's Struggle for Sovereignty.* Chapel Hill: University of North Carolina. 1993.

—. *Cherokee Renascence in the New Republic.* Princeton: Princeton University Press, 1986.

Meredith, Howard, 1985 *Bartley Milam, Principal Chief of the Cherokee Nation.* Muskogee, OK: Indian University Press.

Moulton, Gary E. *Atlas of the Lewis and Clark Expedition.* Lincoln: University of Nebraska Press, 1983.

—. *John Ross: Cherokee Chief.* Athens: The University of Georgia Press, 1978.

—. *The Papers of Chief John Ross, 1807–1839.* Norman: University of Oklahoma Press, 1985.

O'Brien, Sharon, *American Indian Tribal Governments.* Norman: University of Oklahoma Press, 1989.

O'Donnell, James. *Southern Indians in the American Revolution.* Knoxville: University of Tennessee Press, 1973.

Parins, James. *Elias Cornelius Boudinot: A Life on the Cherokee Border*. Lincoln: University of Nebraska Press, 2006.

Peters, Richard. *The Case of the Cherokee Nation Against the State of Georgia*. Philadelphia: John Grigg, 1831.

Prucha, Francis Paul. *The Great Father: The United States Government and the American Indians*. Lincoln: University of Nebraska Press, 1984.

Ramsey, J. G. M. *Annals of Tennessee*. Charleston, SC: Walker and James Steam Power Press, 1853.

Royce, Charles G. *The Cherokee Nation of Indians*. Chicago: Alden, 1975.

Shackford, James Atkins. *David Crockett: The Man and Legend*. Westport, Connecticut: Greenwood Press, 1981.

Sober, Nancy Hope, *The Intruders: The Illegal Residents of the Cherokee Nation 1866-1907*. Marceline, MO: Walsworth Publishing Company, 1991.

Starr, Emmett, *History of the Cherokee Indians and Their Legends and Folklore*. Oklahoma City: Warden Company, 1921.

Strickland, Renard. *Fire and the Spirits: Cherokee Law from Clan to Court*. Norman: University of Oklahoma Press, 1976.

Strickland, Rennard, *The Indians in Oklahoma*. Norman: The University of Oklahoma Press, 1980.

Thornton, Russell. *The Cherokees: A Population History*. Lincoln: University of Nebraska Press, 1990.

Thwaites, Reuben Gold. *Original Journals of the Lewis and Clark Expedition*. New York: Orno Press, 1969.

Warde, Mary Jane. *When the Wolfe Came: The Civil War and the Indian Territory*. Fayetteville: University of Arkansas Press, 2013.

Wahrhaftig, Albert L., *American Indian Economic Development*, ed. Sam Stanley. Paris: Mouton Publishers, 1948.

Wardell, Morris L., *A Political History of the Cherokee Nation*. Norman: University of Oklahoma Press, 1938.

Weatherford, Jack, *Indian Givers: How the Indians of the Americas Transformed the World*. New York: Ballantine Books, 1988.

Williams, Samuel Cole. *Early Travels in the Tennessee Country, 1540–1800*. Johnson City, TN: Watauga Press, 1928.

Woodward, Grace Steele. *The Cherokees*. Norman: University of Oklahoma Press, 1963.

Selected Bibliography

Yagoda, Ben. *Will Rogers: A Biography*. Norman: University of Oklahoma Press, 2000.

Interview

Ross, Jr., John, "Keetoowah Organizations." Cherokee Nation, Tahlequah, Oklahoma.

Journals

Aldrich, Duncan M. "General Stores in the Cherokee Nation." *The Chronicles of Oklahoma*, 79 (Summer, 1979).

Ballenger, T.L. "The Cultural Relations Between Two Pioneer Communities." *The Chronicles of Oklahoma*, 34 (Fall, 1956).

——. "The Keetoowahs and Their Dances." *The Chronicles of Oklahoma*. 61 (Summer, 1983).

——. "The Life and Times of Jeff Thompson Parks: Pioneer, Educator, Jurist." *The Chronicles of Oklahoma*, 30 (Summer, 1952).

Bean, Christopher B. and Jack C. Montgomery, Winter 2004/05 "A Little Big Man." Oklahoma Historical Society – *The Chronicles of Oklahoma*, Volume LXXXII No. 4.

Carter, Kent. "Deciding Who Can Be Cherokee: Enrollment Records of the Dawes Commission." *The Chronicles of Oklahoma*, 69 (Spring, 1991).

Curtis, Lori N., Summer 1999 "Camp Gruber." *Cherokee Quarterly*. Territorial Book Foundation: Tulsa, Oklahoma.

Dale, Edward E. "Additional Letters of General Stand Watie." *The Chronicles of Oklahoma*, 1 (October, 1921).

DeWeese, Georgina, W. Jeff Bishop, Henri D. Grassino-Mayer, Brian Parrish, and S. Michael Edwards. "Dendrochronological Dating of the Chief John Ross House, Rossville, Georgia." *Southeastern Archaeology*, 31: Winter 2012.

Foreman, Carolyn Thomas. "The Coodey Family of Indian Territory." *The Chronicles of Oklahoma*, 25 (Winter, 1947).

——. "The Lighthorse in Indian Territory." *The Chronicles of Oklahoma*, 34 (1956).

Foreman, Grant. "The Murder of Elias Boudinot." *The Chronicles of Oklahoma*, 12 (March 1934).

Hewes, Leslie. "Cherokee Occupance in the Oklahoma Ozarks and Prairie Plains." *The Chronicles of Oklahoma*, 22 (Fall, 1944).

Keith, Harold. "Memories of George W. Mayes." *The Chronicles of Oklahoma*, 24 (Spring, 1946).

King, Duane H. "Long Island of the Holston: Cherokee Sacred Ground." *Journal of Cherokee Studies*: Fall 1976.

——. "The Powder Horn Commemorating the Grant Expedition Against the Cherokees." *Journal of Cherokee Studies,* Cherokee, NC: Museum of the Cherokee Indian Press: 1976.

——. "Sequoyah or George Guess (Gist)." *Dictionary of Georgia: Biography,* ed. Kenneth Coleman and Stephen Gurr. Athens: University of Georgia Press, 1983.

Lee, Keun Sang. "The Capture of the J.R. Williams." *The Chronicles of Oklahoma,* 60 (Spring, 1982).

Literary Digest, April 7, 1938 "A Bill of Rights for the Indians." Accessed April 6, 2017, http://historymatters.gmu.edu/d/5059/.

Lockwood, Patricia. "The Legacy of Caleb Starr." *The Chronicles of Oklahoma,* 61 (Spring 1983).

Lounsbury, Floyd G. "Iroquois–Cherokee Linguistic Relations." Symposium on Cherokee and Iroquois Culture, *Bureau of American Indian Ethnology, Bulletin No. 180.* Washington, DC: Government Printing Office, 1961.

Meserve, John Bartlett. "Chief Charles Thompson." *The Chronicles of Oklahoma,* 16 (Winter, 1938).

——. "Chief William Potter Ross." *The Chronicles of Oklahoma,* 15 (March, 1937).

——. "Chief Lewis Downing and Chief Charles Thompson." *The Chronicles of Oklahoma, 16 (September, 1938).*

Mooney, James. "Myths of the Cherokee." 19*th Annual Report of the Bureau of American Ethnology.* Washington, DC: Government Printing Office, 1900.

Moore, Cherrie Adair. "William Penn Adair." *The Chronicles of Oklahoma.* 29 (Spring, 1951).

Savage, William. "Of Cattle and Corporations: The Rise, Progress and Termination of the Cherokee Strip Live Stock Association." *The Chronicles of Oklahoma,* 71 (Spring, 1993).

Steen, Carl T. "The Home for the Insane, Deaf, Dumb, and Blind of the Cherokee Nation." *The Chronicles of Oklahoma*, 21 (December, 1943).

Travis, V.A. "Life in the Cherokee Nation a Decade after the Civil War." *The Chronicles of Oklahoma*, 4 (March, 1924).

Viles, Philip, Jr., 1999 "Jesse Bartley Milam, Principal Chief, 1941-1949." *Cherokee Quarterly – A Journal of Cherokee History and Culture.* Tulsa: Territorial Book Foundation.

Williams, Samuel Cole. "Christian Missions to the Overhill Cherokees." *Chronicles of Oklahoma,* 12 (March 1934).

Selected Bibliography

Wright, Muriel. "Notes on the Life of Mrs. Hannah Worchester Hicks Hitchcock and the Park Hill Press." *The Chronicles of Oklahoma*, 19 (December, 1941).

Newspapers and Periodicals

Cherokee Nation News, November 26, 1968 "Tribal Office Progress."

Cherokee Nation News, March 9, 1971 " Edmondson Introduces Bills."

Cherokee Nation News, August 17, 1971 "W. W. Keeler Wins Election."

Cherokee Nation News, June 2, 1973 "Minutes Cherokee Nation Elected Community Representative Meeting."

Cherokee Nation News, November 7, 1975 "Swimmer Appoints Advisory Council."

Cherokee Nation News, December 12, 1975 "New Council Discusses Financial Status of Tribe."

Muskogee Daily Phoenix Newspaper, July 31, 1948 "1948 Convention." Muskogee, Oklahoma.

The Pictorial Press, May 8, 1975 "Constitution Change Postpones Filing."

The Tulsa Tribune, April 16, 1975 "Cherokees Get Belated Justice, 1B."

Theses and Dissertations

Camurat, Diane, "The American Indian in the Great War." Master's Thesis, Charles V of the University of Paris VII, 1993.

2000 Hochtritt, James Gribble. "Rural Cherokees, Chickasaws, Choctaws, Creeks and Seminoles in Oklahoma During the Great Depression." University of Oklahoma.

Panther, Natalie, "To Make Us Independent: The Education of Young Men at the Cherokee Male Seminary, 1851-1910." Ph.D. Dissertation, Oklahoma State University. Ann Arbor: University Microfilms, 2013.

Skelton, Robert H., "A History of the Educational System of the Cherokee Nation, 1801-1910." EdD. Dissertation, University of Arkansas. Ann Arbor: University Microfilms, 1970.

Unpublished Reports

Morton, Neil and Strickland, Rennard, 1996 *Trying a New Way: Assessment of First Tier Tribes Under Self-Governance*. Tahlequah, Oklahoma.

Archival Collections

Cherokee Nation Communications, "Ross Swimmer," Bio Material.

Cherokee Nation Education Services, 2016 "Johnson O'Malley Report FY 16." Cherokee Nation Education Services file.

Cherokee Nation Veterans' Center Archives, *Congressional Medal of Honor,* vertical file.

Cherokee National Historical Society Archives, *Constitution of the Cherokee Nation*, Referendum June 26, 1976.

Cherokee National Historical Society Archives, *Minutes of 1948 Convention.*

Department of Commerce, 1934 "Population of Selected Counties in Oklahoma: 1930 Census, January 4, 1934." Cherokee National Historical Society Archives.

Gilcrease Institute and Helmerich Research Center

Northeastern State University, Special Collections, *W. W. Keeler Inaugural Address.*
The Oklahoma Historical Society

World Wide Web

Armed Forces History Museum, (accessed November 18, 2016) *The Role of Native Americans During World War II.* http://armedforcesmuseum.com/the-role-of-native-americans-during-world-war-ii/.

Boundless.com, (accessed November 1, 2016) *American Indians and the War Effort.* https://www.boundless.com/u-s-history-textbook.

Bureau of Indian Affairs, (accessed March 10, 2017) *Who We Are—BIA.* https://bia.gov.WhoWeAre/BIA.

Cherokee Nation, (accessed August 8, 2017) *Cherokee Nation Businesses/Products and Services,* http://www.cherokeenationbusinesses.com/PagesproductionServices.aspx.

Collier, John, (accessed May 01, 2017) *Indians at Work.* Survey Graphic, Magazine of Social Interpretation, Vol. 23, No. 6, June 1934. http://newdeal.feri.org/survey/34261.htm.

Congress.gov, (accessed August 19, 2017) *S. 1017-93rd Congress* (1973-1974), https://www.congress.gov/bill/93rd-congresssenate-bill/1017.

Congress.gov, (accessed May 06, 2017) *Indian Arts and Crafts Amendments Act of 1910, Public Law 111-211.* https://www.congress.gov/bill/11th-congress/house-bill/725.

Digital History, "Overview of the Great Depression." Accessed December 17, 2016, http://www.digitalhistory.uh.edu/era.cfm?eralID=14Smital=1.

Selected Bibliography

Encyclopedia.com, (accessed November 01, 2016) *American Indians – 1933-1941.* The Gale Group, 2002. http://www.encyclopedia.com/education/news-and-education-magazines/american-Indians.

Falkenberg, J.C., III, ed., (accessed November 1, 2016) *Native Americans In World War II.* http://www,ww2f,com/topic/13583-native-americans-in-world-war-ii.

Lomawaima, K. Tsianina, "Chilocco Indian Agricultural School," *The Encyclopedia of Oklahoma History and Culture*, accessed February 26, 2017, www.okhistory.org.

Martin, Kelly, "Top 10 New Deal Program." Accessed May 7, 2016, http://american-history.about.com/programs.htm.

Merriam, Lewis, ed. "The Problem of Indian Administration,"accessed January 1, 2017, Baltimore: The John Hopkins Press. http://www.eric.ed.gov/PDFS/E0087573.pdf.

Morgan, Thomas D., (accessed May 8, 2016) "Native Americans in World War II" (excerpted from *Army History: The Professional Bulletin of Army History*, No. 35, Fall 1995). http:www.shsu.edu/his_ncp/NAWWII.html.

Oklahoma State University Library, (accessed May 5, 2015) *Indian Affairs: Laws and Treaties,* http://digital.library.okstate.edu/kappler/.

Pocock, Michael W. and MaritimeQuest.com., (accessed March 25, 2017) *Admiral Joseph James Clark USN.* http://www.maritimequest.com/warship_directory/us_navy_pages/frigates/pages/clard_ffg.

Rader, Bryan F., (accessed October 30, 2016) "Oklahoma Indian Welfare Act." *Encyclopedia of Oklahoma History and Culture.* www.okhistory.org/publications/enc/entry,php?entry-OK059.

Roberson, Glen, (accessed March 27, 2017) "Grand River Dam Authority." *The Encyclopedia of Oklahoma History and Culture.* www.okhistory.org.

Utility Press, (accessed September 23, 2017) *Biography oof Rear Admiral Joseph James "Jocko" Clark*, http://jacklummus.com/Files/Files_rear-admiral-joseph-james-jocko-clark.htm.

Westmoreland, Ingrid P., (accessed May 8, 2015) "Inter-Tribal Council of the Five Civilized Tribes," *Encyclopedia of Oklahoma History and Culture, www.okhistory.org.*

Wikipedia, (accessed February 26, 2017) "American Indian boarding schools." https://en.wikipedia.org/wiki/American_Indian_boarding_schools.

Wikipedia, (accessed December 12, 2016) "Cherokee Military History." https://en.wikipedia.org/wiki/Cherokee_military_history.

Wikipedia, (accessed December 13,2016) "Code Talkers." https://en.wikipedia.org.wiki.Code_talker.

Index

Adair, William Penn 93, 117, 147
American Revolution frontier war 20-28
Attacullaculla 29
Baker, Bill John x-xii, xiv, xv, 230, 231, 232
Barnes, Zachary xv
Bell, James 135
Benge, Bob 34
Bixby, Tams 168
Black Fox 36
Blackburn, Bob xv
Bloody Fellow 34
Blossom, Neesie xvi
Blunt, James photo of 102
Boney, Roy Jr. xv
Boudinot, E.C. 93, 96, photo of 105, 117, 124-125, photo of 125, photo of 140, 140-142, 155, 156
Boudinot, Elias Sr. 73
Boudinot, Frank 183
The Bowl 37, 80-84
Bradford, Brenda xvi
Britton, Wiley 101, 102
Bryant, Tonya xvi
Bushyhead, Dennis 156
Cabin Creek battle 109
Camp Gruber 206
Charlestown traders 2-5, 6
Cherokee Advocate 74, photos of 151, 152
Cherokee Braves flag photo of 96
Cherokee Heritage Center 218
Cherokee Home Guard 90
Cherokee Mounted Rifles 93
Cherokee Mounted Volunteers 93
Cherokee Nation Industries 218-219
Cherokee Nation v. Georgia 48-49, 60, 61
Cherokee Outlet, leasing 155-156
Cherokee Phoenix 36, 42, 59
Cherokee, act of union in 1840 78
Cherokee, allotment of land 161-162
Cherokee, asylums 129
Cherokee, boarding schools 171-172
Cherokee, capitol building 130, photo of 132
Cherokee, census of 1880 153
Cherokee, census of 1890 153
Cherokee, constitution of 1828 43-45
Cherokee, constitution of 1839 73
Cherokee, constitution of 1976 229
Cherokee, constitutional government 36
Cherokee, delegates to Washington DC 130-132, 149-150
Cherokee, education 126-129
Cherokee, education services 231
Cherokee, election of 1971 220-221
Cherokee, election of 1975 221-222
Cherokee, election of 1979 224
Cherokee, executive branch 229
Cherokee, face paint 9-10
Cherokee, farms 118-120
Cherokee, final rolls 162-163, 169-170
Cherokee, first national offices 214
Cherokee, food assistance 230
Cherokee, gaming 230
Cherokee, health care 230
Cherokee, homelands 1-2, 4
Cherokee, housing services 231
Cherokee, hunting and fishing licenses 231
Cherokee, jail 130, photo of 133
Cherokee, judiciary 36, 229
Cherokee, land sale to other tribes 126
Cherokee, language 2-3
Cherokee, language language program 231
Cherokee, merchants 122-123
Cherokee, milling 122
Cherokee, mineral rights 162
Cherokee, National Council 36, 42, 229
Cherokee, natural resources 230
Cherokee, population 4
Cherokee, sale of buildings to state of Oklahoma 166-167
Cherokee, schools 36, 79, 174-181
Cherokee, sovereignty 133-136, 137-140, 153-164
Cherokee, standing executive committee 209-212
Cherokee, syllabary 44, 231
Cherokee, towns 15-16, 139-140, 172
Cherokee, tribal income 125-126
Cherokee, work permits 126, 148-150
Cherokee, World War I 187-188
Cherokee Weavers Cooperative 203
Christy School photo of 146

Index

Chunestudy, Callie, xvi
Civil War immigrants 104-105
Clark, Joseph "Jocko" 205, photo of 207
Collier, John 193-196, 198
Confederate Treaty 90-91, 93
Coody, Margaret 123
Cooper, Douglas photo of 102
Corn Tassel 28-29, 30-31
Cox, Diana xvi
Crawler, Dennis xv
Creek war 5, 39
Crockett, David 49
Cunne Shote 7-9, painting of 11, 13, 15
Curtis Act 161
Dawes Commission photo of 157, 158-159
Dawes, Henry L. 154
Debo, Angie 167-168
Doublehead 34, 37
Downing Party 116
Downing, Lewis 95, 101, 116-117, photo of 117, 147
Dragging Canoe 18-19, 20, 22-23, 26, 27, 33
Dreadful Water 4
Drew, John 93, 94, 96
Dwight Mission photo of 144
Edmondson, Ed 217
Edwards, Jeff xv
Edwards, Phillip xv
First Indian Home Guard 97
Fort Gibson 101-104, 106
Fort Smith Conference 113
General Allotment Act 155
Gist, George 32
Gist, Nathaniel 26, 31-32
Going Snake District Courthouse battle 133-134
Grand Council of Peace painting of 71, 73-74
Grand River Dam 200
Gritts, Bud 85
Gritts, Levi 208
Gwin, Pat xvi
Hastings, William Wirt 181, 199
Heinrichs, Joseph 123
Hendrix, Annie Eliza 106
Hicks, Hanna Worcester 100
Hicks, Victoria 123
Hider, Sam 220-221
Hildebrand/Beck's Mill 122-123

Honey Springs Battle 103-104
Horseshoe Bend Battle 39-40
Hoskin, Chuck Sr. xiv, xv
Hunt, Kayla xvi
Indian Arts and Crafts Act of 1935 202-203
Indian Claims Commission 210, 217
Indian International Fair 121-122
Indian New Deal 193-196
Indian Removal Act 48, 59
Inter-tribal Council of the Five Civilized Tribes 217
J.R. Williams riverboat 107
Jarvis, Molly xvi
Johnson-O'Malley Act of 1934 202
Jones, Evan 84, 116
Jones, John 84, 116, 151-152
Keeler, William Wayne xiv, 212-215, 219-221
Keetoowah Nighthawks photo of 159, 159-161, 174, 184-187, 207-208
Keetoowah Society 84-85, 88-89
Keetoowah Society Inc. 183-184, 207-208
Kiamee 37
Kilpatrick, Lucy 123
King George III 7-8
King, Duane xv
Lake Mohonk Conference 154
Light Horse 36
Lipe, DeWitt 123
Lowery, George painting of 77
Mankiller, Wilma xv, 225
Martin, Joseph 31
Martin, Richard L. 109
May, Jon xvi
Mayes, George 120-121
Mayes, Joel B. photo of 156
Mayes, Samuel 158-159
Mayes, Wash 120-121
McCarty, Jason xvi
McClain, Blain, xvi
Merriam Report 189-190
Milam, J.B. 199, 209-212, 213
Montgomery, Jack C. 204-205, photo of 206
Morton, Neil xv
Moytoy 4
Murrell Home 81
Murrow, Joseph 97
Muskogee 132

Northeastern Normal School photo of 166
Oconastota 6-7, 15, 17-18, 29
Oklahoma Indian Welfare Act of 1936 190, 198-200
Olaya, Gina xvi
Old Abram 26-28
Old Hop 5
Old Settlers in Arkansas 37-38, 41-42, 46-47, 71-72, 78-79
Oochalata (Charles Thompson) 147-150
Opothleyahola 96
Ostenaco 7-9, 11, 13, 15
Owen, Robert L. 143, photo of 145, 145, photo of 168, 168, 199
Panther, Natalie xvi
Park Hill 73
Parks, Thomas Jefferson 119-120
Pea Ridge Battle 97
Pegg, Thomas 94, 101
Phillips, William 106
Pigeon, Jennifer xvi
Pike, Albert photo of 89
Pins 84-86
Proctor, Zeke 134, photo of 135
Public Law 91-495 220
Public Law 93-6384 (Self Determination Act) 225-226, 229
Rackliff, Nancy xvi
Railroads, 131-133, 139-140
Raven 28-29
Reconstruction Treaty of 1866 114
Reese, John Noah Jr. 205
Remer, Stephanie xvi, 231, 233, 235
Ridge, John painting of 61, 73, 88
Ridge, Major painting of 62, 73
Rogers, Clement Vann 94, 121, 191-192, photo of 194
Rogers, Will 191-192, photo of 194
Rogers, William C. 164, 172, photo of 174
Rose Cottage painting of 98
Ross, John 38-41, home of 41, 42-46, 89, 91, 92, 99, 113-114
Ross, John Jr. xv, 184-187
Ross, Joshua 121
Ross, Quatie (Elizabeth) 46, 70
Ross, William P. photo of 74, 94, 112, 115-116
Scott, John S. 123

Scyagust Ukah 10-11, 12, painting of 13
Second Indian Home Guard 97, 98, 99, 101, 106
Sequoyah 42, 44
Sequoyah Home 231-232
Sixkiller, Anna xv
Sixkiller, Dennis xv
Slavery 85-86, 88-89
Smith, Red Bird photo of 158, 158-161, 163, 184-187
South Carolina frontier war 6-7
Spring Frog 101
Stalking Turkey 12
Starr family 75-76
Starr, Emmet 181
State of Sequoyah 164
Statehood and the Cherokees 167-168
Stephens, Spencer 155
Stillwell photo of 149
Stoddard, Ashley xvi
Strickland, Renard 170
Sugar, Verlita xvi
Swimmer, Ross xv, 222-225
Tahlequah 73
Texas Cherokees 80-84
Third Indian Home Guard painting of 95, 99, 101, 106
Thompson, Jerry xvi
Tohluntuskee 37
Trail of Tears 51-52, 63-70
Treaty at Long Island 29-30
Treaty of 1828 47-48
Treaty of 1846 79
Treaty of New Echota 51-52, 63, 78
Treaty of Sycamore Shoals 1
Treaty Party 62-63, 72, 78, 79
Turkey 33
United Keetoowah Cherokee Indians 208-209
Vann, James 35
Vann, Joseph 29
Vinita 132, 142-144
Vinita Chieftain 143
Vinita Progress 142
Virginia frontier war 6
Virginia traders 2-4
W.W. Hastings Hospital 230
Ward, Nancy 27, 28, 31
Washington, George 6

Index

Watie and Boudinot Tobacco Company 124-125
Watie, Stand 74-75, 93, 96, 98, 99, 104, 107-110
Watts, John 34
Wheeler, R. Perry 222-224
Wheeler-Howard Act of 1934 190
Wolfe, Richard 183
Worcester v. Georgia 48-49
Woyi 7-9, 11
Zwink, Tim xv

ᏚᏳᎪᏛᏉ ᎾᏍᎩ ᏑᎾᏛᏁᏆ ᏳᏗᏝᏒ ᎤᎾᏙᏢᎾᏁᎯ ᎨᏒ ᎠᎴ ᎤᎾᏝᏍᏕᏍᏙᏗ ᏣᎳᎩ
ᎾᏙᏝᎪᎯ ᎨᏒᎢ, ᎠᎴ ᎾᏍᏉ ᏧᎬᏩᎶᏗᏉ ᏂᎨᏒᎾ ᎪᎱᏍᏗ ᎤᏅᏙᏗ ᎢᎦᎢᏉ ᎦᏓ
Ꮟ, ᎠᎴ ᏂᎦᎥᏉ ᎪᏙᏙᏗ ᎨᏒ ᏂᎦᎥᏉ ᎪᎱᏍᏗ ᎬᏔᏂᏓᏍᏗ ᎨᏒᎢ ᎢᎬᏩᏓᎴᎩᏉ
ᎨᏒᎢ, ᎤᎬᏩᎵ ᎪᎵᏙᏗ ᎠᎴ ᎠᏍᏕᏍᏙᏗ ᎨᏒ ᎾᏍᎩ ᏕᎦᏍᏆᏍᏓᏁᏍᏗ. Ꭿ Ꭰ Ꮧ-
Ꮖ Ꮝ Ꮥ Ꮝ Ꮧ. ᎢᏳᏃ ᎠᏂᏴᏫᏯ ᎨᏒ ᏴᏫ ᏆᎾᏛᏅ ᎤᎾᏤᎵ ᎨᏒ ᎪᎱᏍᏗ ᏗᎬ-
ᏁᏆᎯ ᎠᎴ ᏗᏖᏆᏅᎯ ᏑᏆᎵᏍᏔᏅ ᎠᏎ ᏚᏳᎪᏛ ᎢᎦᎢ ᏧᎬᏩᎶᏗ ᎨᏒ ᏗᏗᏴᎡᏗ
ᏕᏒᏍᏗ. Ꭰ Ꮄ Ꭼ Ꮒ Ᏻ Ꮙ, ᎾᏍᎩ ᎤᏚᏓᏕᏫᏛ ᏗᎦᏚᏩᎢ ᏆᏩᏂᏌᏅ ᎣᏁᎢᏍᏔᏅᎯ

Ꮟ ᎠᏆ ᎦᎵᏉᎩ ᎢᏳᏆᏗᏅᏛ ᎢᏳᏟᎶᏛ ᎢᎩᏛ ᎠᏆ, ᎤᏬᏚᏍᏗ ᎯᎠ ᎤᏍᏆᎸ
ᎢᏗᏢ ᎾᎪᏬᏛ ᎣᏁᎢᏍᏔᏅᎯ ᏂᎩ, ᏧᎾᏟᏍᏗ ᏌᏉ ᎾᎬᏯᏆᏗ ᎢᏳᎵᏍᏙᏗ ᎦᏚ
ᏗᎢ, ᏟᎶᏃ ᏚᏟᏗᏝᏅ ᎾᏞ ᎦᏓ ᎠᏆ, ᏚᎵᏚᎾᏍᏛ ᎯᎠ ᏆᏍᏗᏝᏅ: ᎠᏓᎴᏂᏍᎩ
ᏯᏬ ᏆᏍᏛ ᏅᎩ ᏧᏅᏏᏬ ᏌᏉ ᎢᏗᏢ ᏅᎩ ᎢᏬᏔᏏᏗ ᎢᎦᏅᎯᏛ. ᎯᏍᎩᏁᏃ ᎠᏰᎵ
ᏬᏔᏏᏗ ᎢᎦᏘ, ᎾᏍᎩᏃ ᏅᏯ ᎦᏒᎬ ᎠᏏ ᏅᏩᏓᎴ ᏅᏯ ᎢᎠᏂᏒᎦ ᎤᎦᎾᏮ ᏫᏚᏳᎪᏛ
ᏓᏕᏒᏛ ᏌᏉ ᎢᎦᏅᏅᎯ ᎢᏴᏛ, ᏉᎢᏃ ᏅᏩᏓᎴ ᏅᏯ ᎢᎠᏂᏒᎦ ᎤᏕᎵᎬ ᏫᏚᏳᎪᏛ
ᏍᏉ ᎤᏓᏕᏒᏛ ᏌᏉ ᎢᎦᏅᏅᎯ ᎢᏴᏛ, ᎾᏞᎾ ᏗᎪᎥᎯ ᏂᎩ ᎤᏬᏘ ᏟᎶᏛ ᎬᏗᏛ
ᏕᎵᎬ ᎠᏍᏛ ᏚᏬᏓᏛ ᎢᏤ ᏍᎦᏚᎩ ᏆᎵᏍᏔᏅᎢ ᏚᏬᏓᏛ ᎡᏉᏂ ᎤᏬᏴ ᎤᏴᏢ ᎢᏗᏢ
ᏚᏳᎪᏛ ᎯᏍᎩᏦᏁ ᎢᏳᏟᎶᏛ ᎢᏴᏛ; ᎾᏞᏃ ᎤᎴᏅᏛ ᎤᎦᎾᏮ ᎢᏗᏢ ᏫᏚᏳᎪᏛ ᏫᏂ-
Ꮕ ᏉᎢᏦᏁ ᎢᏳᏟᎶᏛ ᏔᎳᏍᎪ ᏧᏁᎳ ᎢᎦᏅᏅ ᎤᏓᏕᏒᏛ ᎢᏬᏍᏗ ᏗᎨᏛ ᏌᏏ
ᎡᏉᏂ ᎤᏬᏴ ᎤᏴᏢ ᎤᏕᎵᎬᏃ ᎠᏰᎵ ᎢᏗᏢ ᎨᏒ ᎠᏲᏳᏟᏗ, ᎢᏴᏛ ᏒᎬ ᏂᎩ ᏐᏃᏍᏚ-
Ꮹ, ᏍᎩᎦᏚ ᎢᏬᏏᏔᏗᏍᏗ ᎢᎩᏛ ᏗᎬᏩᏫᏒᎯ, ᎤᎦᎾᏮ ᏫᏚᏳᎪᏛ ᏗᏫᏆᎬᏃ ᎠᏰᎵ
ᏓᏔᏍᎪ ᏌᏉ ᎾᏍᏓᏅᏅ ᎡᏣᎯ ᎠᏟᏫᎥ ᏦᎠᏍᎪ ᏌᏉ ᎢᏳᏟᎶᏛ ᎠᏓᏬᎯᏔᏛᎯ ᏗᏫ-
ᏆᎬ ᏫᏚᏳᎪᏛ, ᏅᎦᏍᎪ ᏦᎢ ᎢᏬᏍᎪᎯᏧᏈᏁ ᎦᏅᏅᎯ ᎤᏓᏕᏒᏛ ᎯᎠ ᎢᎬᏂ ᎪᏬᏔ